INTRODUCTION TO FINANCIAL ACCOUNTING

INTRODUCTION TO
FINANCIAL ACCOUNTING

PETER SCOTT

OXFORD
UNIVERSITY PRESS

OXFORD

UNIVERSITY PRESS

Great Clarendon Street, Oxford, OX2 6DP,
United Kingdom

Oxford University Press is a department of the University of Oxford.
It furthers the University's objective of excellence in research, scholarship,
and education by publishing worldwide. Oxford is a registered trade mark of
Oxford University Press in the UK and in certain other countries

Impression: 1

Published in the United States of America by Oxford University Press
198 Madison Avenue, New York, NY 10016, United States of America

British Library Cataloguing in Publication Data

Data available

Library of Congress Control Number: 2018954398

ISBN 978-0-19-878329-9

Printed in Great Britain by
Ashford Colour Press Ltd, Gosport, Hampshire

BRIEF TABLE OF CONTENTS

FULL TABLE OF CONTENTS

ACKNOWLEDGEMENTS

Thanks are due to many individuals. Firstly, to all of the staff at Oxford University Press who have been involved with this project: to Amber Stone-Galilee, Commissioning Editor, who first proposed this book in June 2015 and who provided help and encouragement throughout the writing process; to Nicola Hartley who was initially entrusted with the development process; Livy Watson, Development Editor, who then took up the development role and who has been a model of enthusiasm, patience and quiet encouragement throughout; and to Fiona Burbage who was responsible for turning my ideas and outlines into the online resource material. Secondly, a big thank you to the many reviewers who took the time to work through the draft chapters to put together positive and constructive comments that have informed the development of this book and its online workbook. Thirdly, thanks must go to the hundreds if not thousands of students who have, over many years, been the testing ground for the material presented here: their ability to grasp concepts, ideas and techniques served up in various different formats has helped guide me in the formulation of my ideas on the most effective approach to providing the solid foundations upon which later studies in accountancy are built. Fourthly, thanks go to all my former colleagues at De Montfort University for their constant interest, encouragement and enthusiasm for the project. Finally, the deepest debt of gratitude must go to my family, and above all to my wife, Christine, for their forbearance, patience and encouragement during the time it took to develop and write this book.

Peter Scott, June 2018

The author and publisher would like to sincerely thank all those people who gave their time and expertise to review draft chapters throughout the writing process. Your help was invaluable.

Thanks are also extended to those who wished to remain anonymous.

Dr Sandar Win, University of Bedfordshire
Dr Brian Gibbs, University of Bolton
Dr Octavian Ionescu, University of East Anglia
Dr Alaa Alhaj Ismail, Coventry University
David Gilding, University of Leeds
Dr Kelvin Leong, Wrexham Glyndŵr University
Dr Gizella Marton, University of Dundee
Dr Nick Rowbottom, University of Birmingham
Mostafa Abuzeid, University of Sheffield
Barry McCarthy, University College London
Dave Knight, Leeds Beckett University
Nicola Horner, University of the West of England
David Kyle, York St John University
Dr Emer Gallagher, Liverpool John Moores University
Samuel O Idowu, London Metropolitan University
Dr Anwar Halari, The Open University

Dr Pik Kun Liew, University of Essex
Dr Abdelhafid Benamraoui, University of Westminster
Dr Chandana Alawattage, University of Aberdeen
Stephanie Tiller, University of Worcester
Dr Oluseyi O Adesina, Canterbury Christ Church University
Dr Androniki Triantafylli, Queen Mary University of London
Michael Barker, Coventry University
Chris Soan, Newcastle University
Kevin Burrows, University of Plymouth
Acheampong Charles Afriyie, University of Gloucestershire
Dr Naser Makarem, University of Aberdeen
Dr Sayjda Talib, Lancaster University
Susan Lane, University of Bradford
Samuel Hinds, University of Surrey
Dr Akrum Helfaya, Keele University, UK & Damanhour University, Egypt

PREFACE

Accounting: building a solid foundation

Welcome to your study of financial accounting. This first year of your accounting studies is extremely important as the understanding you develop in the next few months and the techniques you learn will provide the foundation upon which both your future studies and your professional career will be built. Everything you study in this first year will continue to be relevant in the next two years of degree studies and throughout your time in the accounting profession. At this initial stage of your studies, the approach to the subject adopted in this package is completely practical: accounting is a 'doing' subject and the best way to learn how it works and what it does is to practice the various techniques and approaches as frequently as possible. You are provided with careful, step-by-step guidance showing you how to construct and evaluate various accounting statements and how to summarise and record accounting information. You are then given numerous further opportunities to apply what you have learnt with a view to enhancing your understanding and ability to produce and interpret accounting information. Only once you have mastered the techniques and practice of accounting can you move forward to look at the more theoretical aspects of the subject and question why things are done as they are.

The integrated online workbook: how this package works

This textbook is published with a free online workbook containing a large bank of examples and exercises that relate to, and are thoroughly integrated with, the material in each chapter. (For details on how to access this, please refer to the 'Guided tour of the online workbook'.)

The integration of these online resources with the textbook provides the supportive learning environment necessary to allow you to develop the specialist practical skills required in financial accounting. Clear signposts in the chapters offer you numerous opportunities to reinforce, revisit, and revise your understanding of the subject, prompting you to apply your knowledge as you work through each topic. Your understanding of the material will strengthen as approaches and techniques are frequently recapped, including the use of running examples throughout the book.

The textbook

You are initially introduced to two of the three key financial accounting statements (the statement of profit or loss and the statement of financial position) and shown how to construct these from first principles. You are then provided with an in-depth and detailed guide to double-entry bookkeeping to show you how the accounting records are built up over the course of the financial year and how these records are then summarised and presented in the statement of profit or loss and the statement of financial position. The third key accounting statement, the statement of cash flows, is then introduced and detailed guidance on how to prepare this statement is offered. Once the financial statements have been put together, accountants must then interpret these statements to show what information they provide about an entity's profitability and performance and its ability to survive into the future.

Users of financial statements require reassurance about the accuracy and integrity of the information they are presented with and, in addition, they want to be confident that companies are good corporate citizens who always do the right thing. Therefore, the final chapter provides an introduction to the corporate governance rules, corporate social responsibility reporting and sustainability, topics that you will go on to consider in much greater depth in both your degree and professional studies.

A note on terminology

Business is increasingly international in its focus. As a result, the accounting terminology adopted throughout this book is that of international accounting standards rather than that of UK standards. Where different terms for the same statements are in common usage, these are noted throughout the book as they arise and summarised in the terminology converter at the back of the book.

GUIDED TOUR OF THE BOOK

Identifying and defining

Learning outcomes

Clear, concise learning outcomes begin each chapter and help to contextualise the chapter's main objectives. This feature can help you plan your revision to ensure you identify and cover all the key concepts.

LEARNING OUTCOMES

Once you have read this chapter and worked through the questions and examples in both this chapter and the online workbook, you should be able to:

● Understand that profit does not equal cash

● Appreciate that without a steady cash inflow from operations an entity will not be able to survive

● Describe the make up of operating, investing and financing cash

Key terms and glossary

Key terms are highlighted where they first appear in the chapter and are also collated into a glossary at the end of the book. This provides an easy and practical way for you to revise and check your understanding of definitions.

applications of financial accounting to provide you with a very strong fo build your further degree and future professional studies. We shall consi accounting statements, the statement of financial position (balance sheet), the stat the statement of cash flows that you will encounter on a daily basis in your pro to underpin your understanding of financial accounting and its role in b we shall also be taking an in depth look at how double-entry bookkeep lyses information on the transactions that form the building blocks of thes

Statement of cash flows A summary of the cash inflows and outflows of an entity for a given period of time.

Statement of financial position A summary of the assets, liabilities and equity of an entity at a particular point in time.

Statement of profit or loss A statement of income and expenditure for a particular period of time. Also referred to as the income statement or the profit and loss account. The

Understanding accounting principles

Illustrations

Illustrations display accounting statements and documents and serve to set out the numbers discussed in the text in an easily readable format. This enables you to follow the explanations closely and to become familiar with the layout of such documents.

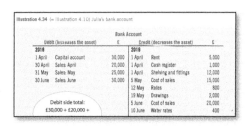

Illustration 4.34 (= Illustration 4.10) Julia's bank account

Bank Account					
Debit (increases the asset)		£	Credit (decreases the asset)		£
2019			2019		
1 April	Capital account	30,000	1 April	Rent	5,000
30 April	Sales: April	20,000	1 April	Cash register	1,000
31 May	Sales: May	25,000	1 April	Shelving and fittings	12,000
30 June	Sales: June	30,000	5 May	Cost of sales	15,000
			12 May	Rates	800
			19 May	Drawings	2,000
Debit side total:			5 June	Cost of sales	20,000
£30,000 + £20,000 +			10 June	Water rates	400

In-text examples

Regular practical examples are presented throughout each chapter to illustrate how accounting material is used in a variety of different business contexts. The diversity in cases demonstrates how accounting information can be interpreted in different ways to achieve different ends according to business needs.

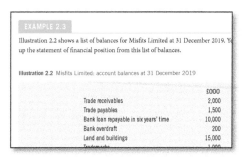

EXAMPLE 2.3

Illustration 2.2 shows a list of balances for Misfits Limited at 31 December 2019. Y up the statement of financial position from this list of balances.

Illustration 2.2 Misfits Limited: account balances at 31 December 2019

	£000
Trade receivables	2,000
Trade payables	1,500
Bank loan repayable in six years' time	10,000
Bank overdraft	200
Land and buildings	15,000
Trademarks	1,000

Accounting in practice

'Give me an example' boxes

Topical examples taken from the *Financial Times*, the BBC and other news outlets and numerous references to financial statements from real companies will help your understanding of how the theory being discussed in the chapter plays out in business practice.

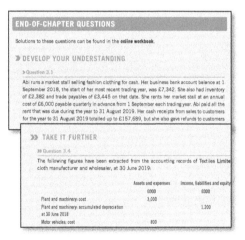

'Why is this relevant to me?' boxes

These short and frequent explanations clarify exactly how the accounting material under discussion will be important and relevant to accounting professionals. They are an important reminder of how important even theoretical accounting knowledge will be in enabling you to succeed in your future career, whether it be as an accountant or as a business professional working with accounting information.

Testing and applying understanding

End-of-chapter questions

There is a set of questions at the end of every chapter designed to test your knowledge of the key concepts and practical examples that have been discussed and illustrated. They are divided into two tiers according to difficulty, allowing you to track your progress. Use them during your course to ensure you fully understand the accounting principles and practice before moving on, or when revising to make sure you can confidently tackle the more difficult questions. The solutions are supplied within the **online workbook**, in an easily printable format.

Chapter summary

Each chapter concludes with a bulleted list linking to the learning outcomes, outlining the key points you should take away from the chapter. This provides another useful method of checking that you have covered the key points when you come to revise each topic.

GUIDED TOUR OF THE ONLINE WORKBOOK

Access the interactive online workbook by visiting www.oup.com/uk/scott_financial/.

Resources in the online workbook have been specifically designed to support you throughout your financial accounting studies. References within the textbook indicate the relevant resource accompanying that section or topic, thereby allowing you to reinforce your learning as you progress through the book and ensuring that you take full advantage of this fantastic package.

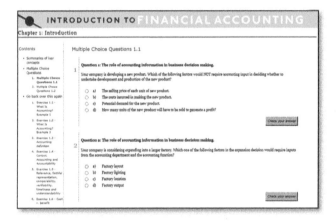

Summaries of key concepts

Key glossary terms are provided in interactive flashcard format.

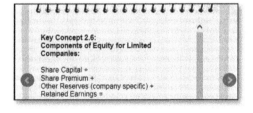

Multiple-choice questions

Interactive multiple-choice questions for every chapter give you instant feedback as well as page references to help you focus on the areas that need further study.

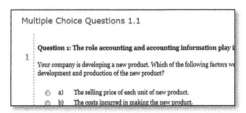

Numerical exercises

These exercises, often based in Excel, give you the opportunity to calculate accounting information from given sets of data, thereby practising what is discussed and illustrated in the book.

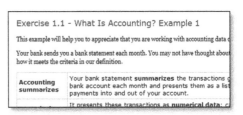

Go back over this again

Containing a mixture of further examples, written exercises, true or false questions and annotated accounting information, this section provides the perfect opportunity for you to revise and revisit any concepts you might be unsure of.

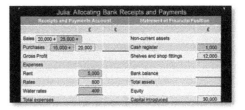

Show me how to do it

Video presentations, accompanied by a voice-over, allow you to watch practical demonstrations of how more complex accounting tasks are dealt with by the author.

Web links

Arranged by chapter, these web links will take you directly to the websites of the companies and organisations covered in the book, as well as websites of more general accounting interest. Follow the links to learn more about how accounting plays out in the real world of business.

Further reading

Arranged by chapter, this section provides you with a list of additional resources you may wish to consult if you'd like to take your learning further, or simply consider a topic from a different perspective.

GUIDE TO THE LECTURER RESOURCES

Test bank

A wealth of additional multiple-choice questions that can be customised to meet your specific teaching needs.

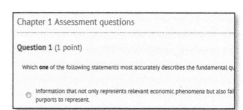

Lecturer examples and solutions

Additional exercises that can be used alongside the PowerPoint slides in lectures or seminars.

Group tutorial exercises

A range of more detailed, workshop-based activities that students can complete prior to and during tutorials.

Lecturer examination questions and answers

Additional problem solving and suggested essay-based exam questions with accompanying answers.

PowerPoint slides

Illustrated PowerPoint slides for each chapter that can be used in lectures or printed as handouts, and can be easily adapted to suit your teaching style.

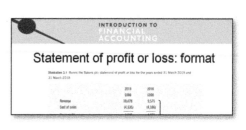

DASHBOARD

Dashboard is a cloud-based online assessment and revision tool. It comes pre-loaded with the resources listed in the 'Guide to the lecturer resources', as well as additional questions to use for assessment and functionality to track your students' progress.

Visit www.oxfordtextbooks.co.uk/dashboard/ for more information.

Simple: With a highly intuitive design, it will take you less than 15 minutes to learn and master the system.

Informative: Assignment and assessment results are automatically graded, giving you a clear view of the class' understanding of the course content.

Mobile: You can access Dashboard from every major platform and device connected to the Internet, whether that's a computer, tablet or smartphone.

Gradebook

Dashboard's Gradebook functionality automatically marks the assignments that you set for your students. The Gradebook also provides heat maps that allow you to view your students' progress and quickly identify areas of the course where your students may need more practice or support, as well as the areas in which they are most confident. This feature helps you focus your teaching time on

the areas that matter. The Gradebook also allows you to administer grading schemes, manage checklists and administer learning objectives and competencies.

INTRODUCTION

INTRODUCTION

Welcome to your study of financial accounting. You are now taking your first steps on the road to qualifying as a member of the accounting profession with a view to building your career in one or more of the varied roles which accountants fulfil in business and the wider economy. In order to help you fulfil your ambition, this book will introduce you to the key techniques and practical applications of financial accounting to provide you with a very strong foundation on which to build your further degree and future professional studies. We shall consider the main financial accounting statements, the statement of financial position (balance sheet), the statement of profit or loss and the statement of cash flows that you will encounter on a daily basis in your professional life. In order to underpin your understanding of financial accounting and its role in business organisations, we shall also be taking an in depth look at how double-entry bookkeeping gathers and analyses information on the transactions that form the building blocks of these financial accounting statements. However, accounting is not just about the mechanics of putting these accounting statements together: it is also about interpreting those accounting statements to understand what they are telling users about the financial performance and financial position of a business. Likewise, accounting does not just look at the past by presenting historical statements relating to past results and outcomes. Accounting information is also used dynamically to plan for the future and to model possible scenarios and outcomes depending on the courses of action taken.

WHAT SKILLS DO I NEED?

Many students find the thought of accounting worrying as they do not feel they have the necessary mathematical ability to be able to understand or apply the subject in practice. However, do be assured that accounting needs no particular mathematical strengths, just some basic applications of arithmetic and an ability to reason. As long as you can add up, subtract, multiply and divide figures you have all the arithmetical skills you will need to undertake the calculations and apply this subject. The ability to reason is a skill that you will need in every subject of study and it will be fundamental to the success of any career, not just to a career in accounting.

Once you have learnt how to apply the basic techniques, accounting is much more about understanding what the figures are telling you and about interpreting the data in front of you—this requires you to think in a logical fashion and to investigate the meaning beneath the surface. Therefore, it is much more accurate to say that accounting requires the ability to communicate and express your ideas in words rather than being dependent upon mathematical skills.

> **WHY IS THIS RELEVANT TO ME?**   Skills needed to study accounting
>
> - To reassure you that the study of accounting requires no further special skills than those you already possess
> - To enable you to appreciate that the study of accounting will further develop the skills you have already acquired in reaching your current level of education

WHAT IS ACCOUNTING?

Let's start with a definition.

Accounting summarises numerical data relating to past events and presents this data as information to managers and other interested parties as a basis for both decision making and control purposes as presented in Figure 1.1.

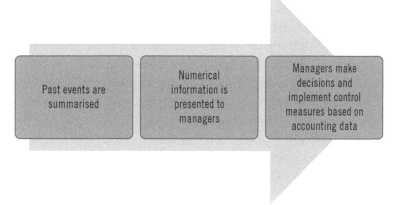

Figure 1.1 What is accounting?

This is quite a lot to take in, so let's unpick the various strands of this definition.

1. Numerical data: accounting information is mostly, but not always, presented in money terms. It could just as easily be a league table of football teams with details of games won, games lost and games drawn, goals for and goals against and points gained, all of which is numerical information. Or it could be a list of schools in a particular area with percentages of pupils gaining five GCSEs grades 1–9 and average A level points at each school. In a business, it could be the number of units of product produced rather than just their cost, or the number of units sold in a given period of time. The critical point here is that accounting data is presented in the form of numbers.

2. Relating to past events: accounting systems gather data and then summarise these data to present details of what has happened. A league table is a summary of past results. Similarly, a total of sales for the month will be a summary of all the individual sales made on each day of that month and relating to that past period of time.

3. Information presented to managers: managers have the power and authority to use accounting information to take action now to maintain or improve future outcomes. In the same way, if a team is in the middle of the league table but aspires to a higher position, the team manager can take steps to hire better coaches, buy in the contracts of players with higher skill levels and sell the contractual rights of underperforming players. If a school wants to improve their examination results, they will take steps to determine what is preventing better performance and try to correct these deficiencies.

4. As a basis for decision making: accounting information is used to determine what went well and which events did not turn out quite as anticipated. For example, demand for a

1

business's product over the past month might not have reached the levels expected. If this is the case, managers can take steps to determine whether the selling price is too high and should be reduced, whether there are defects in the products that require rectification or whether the product is just out of date and no longer valued by consumers. On the other hand, if demand for a product is outstripping supply, then managers can take the decision to divert business resources to increase production to meet that higher demand.

5. Control purposes: businesses prepare budgets prior to the start of an accounting period (usually 12 months) which set out what they aim to achieve in terms of sales, profits and cash flows. A comparison of actual outcomes with the budget will enable managers to decide where the budget was met, where the budget was exceeded and where the budget failed to reach expectations. Then the causes of the last two outcomes can be investigated and action taken to address the reasons behind the underperformance or to take advantage of better than expected results. The future is uncertain, but businesses will still plan by predicting to the best of their ability what they expect to occur in the following months and then compare actual outcomes with what they expected to happen as a means of controlling operations. Published financial statements of companies are used by investors and lenders to determine whether investments should be made in or money lent to those companies.

WHY IS THIS RELEVANT TO ME?   Accounting definition

To enable you as an accounting professional to:

• Understand what accounting is

• Appreciate that the production of accounting information is not an end in itself but is a tool to enable you to understand, direct and control business, investment, lending or other activities

---

SUMMARY OF KEY CONCEPTS   How clearly have you remembered the definition of accounting given earlier? Go to the **online workbook** to revise this definition with Summary of key concepts 1.1.

GO BACK OVER THIS AGAIN!   If this all still seems very complicated, visit the **online workbook** Exercises 1.1 and 1.2 to enable you to appreciate that you are already working with accounting data on a daily basis.

GO BACK OVER THIS AGAIN!   Are you certain you can define accounting? Go to the **online workbook** Exercises 1.3 to make sure you can say what accounting is and what role it performs in a business context.

CONTROL, ACCOUNTING AND ACCOUNTABILITY

The function of accounting information as a mechanism through which to control outcomes and activities can be illustrated further. Representatives are accountable for their actions to those people who have placed them in positions of power or trust. Accounting information is thus provided so that individuals and organisations can render an account of what they have done with the resources placed in their care. Example 1.1 provides an everyday illustration of these ideas.

Your employer pays your salary into your bank account while various payments are made out of your account to pay your bills and other outgoings. Your bank then provides you with a statement (either online or in paper copy) on a regular basis so that you can check whether they have accounted for your money correctly or not.

In the same way, company directors present financial accounts to shareholders and other interested parties on an annual basis to give an account of how they have looked after the money and other resources entrusted to them and how they have used that money to invest and generate income for shareholders. Local and national governments regularly publish information on the taxes collected and how those taxes have been spent. This information enables politicians to render an account of how taxes collected have been used to provide goods and services to citizens.

Where power and resources are entrusted to others, it is important that they are accountable for what they have done with that power and those resources. If your bank makes mistakes in the management of your account or charges you too much for managing your account, then you can change banks. If shareholders are unhappy with their directors' performance, they will not reappoint them as directors of their company. Instead, they will elect other directors to replace them in the expectation that these new directors will manage their investment much more carefully and profitably. Alternatively, they can sell their shares and invest their money in companies that do provide them with higher profits and higher dividends. If voters are unhappy with how their local and national politicians have taxed them or how they have spent their taxes, they will vote for different representatives with different policies more to their liking.

Persons entrusted by others with resources are in the position of stewards, looking after those resources for the benefit of other parties. Providing an account of their stewardship of those resources helps those other parties control the actions of their stewards. At the same time, accounts enable these other parties to make decisions on whether to continue with their current stewards or to replace them with others who will perform more effectively and provide them with a more efficient and profitable service. These relationships are summarised in Figure 1.2.

WHY IS THIS RELEVANT TO ME?   Control, accounting and accountability

To enable you as an accounting professional to:

- Appreciate that accounting functions as a control on the actions of others
- Understand how you will be entrusted with a business's resources and that you will be accountable for your stewardship of those resources

1

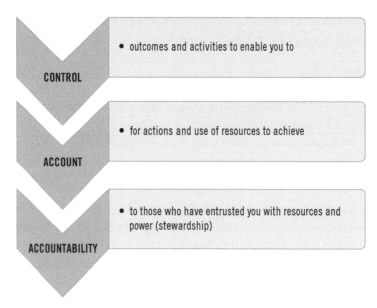

Figure 1.2 Control, accounting and accountability

GO BACK OVER THIS AGAIN!   Are you quite sure you understand how accounting helps with control and accountability? Go to the **online workbook** Exercises 1.4 to make sure you understand the links between accounting, accountability and control.

THE ROLE OF ACCOUNTING INFORMATION IN BUSINESS DECISION MAKING

Businesses are run to make a profit. Businesses that do not make a profit fail and are closed down. In order to achieve this profit aim, businesses need to make and implement decisions on a daily basis. Such decisions might comprise, among others, some or all of the following:

- What products should we produce?
- What services should we provide?
- How much do our products cost to make?
- How much do our services cost to provide?
- What price should we charge for our products or services?
- Should we be taking on more employees?
- How much will the additional employees cost?
- Will the cost of the new employees be lower than the income they will generate?
- Should we be expanding into bigger premises?
- Will the costs of the bigger premises be outweighed by the increase in income?

- How will we finance our expansion?
- Should we take out a bank loan or ask the shareholders to buy more shares?

All of these decisions will require accounting input:

- The marketing department can use reports from sales personnel and consumer evaluations to tell us what the demand for a product is, but it will be up to the accounting staff to tell us what the product costs to make and what the selling price should be in order to generate a profit on each sale.
- The personnel department can tell us about hiring new staff and the legal obligations incurred in doing so, the training required and the market rates for such workers, but it will be the accounting staff who can tell us what level of productivity the new employees will have to achieve in order to generate additional profit for the business.
- The strategy department can tell us what sort of premises we should be looking for, how these new premises should be designed and what image they should present, but it will be the accounting staff who can tell us how many products we will have to make and sell for the new premises to cover their additional costs and the best way in which to finance this expansion.

Accounting is thus at the heart of every decision and every activity that a business undertakes, as shown in Figure 1.3.

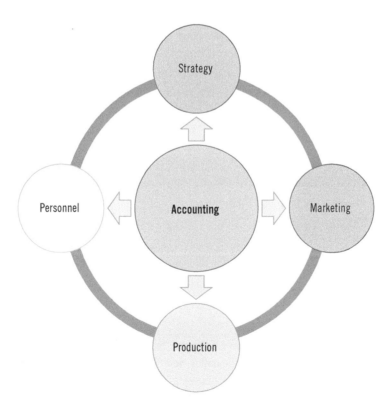

Figure 1.3 Accounting's central role in business activity and business decision making

At this early stage of your studies, it is easy to think of each department in a business just sticking to its own specialist field of expertise, operating in isolation from all the others, concentrating on their own aims and goals. You might reply that you would never think of a business as just a loose grouping of separate departments all doing their own thing with no thought for the bigger picture. But pause for a moment and ask yourself whether you treat all your current year study modules as interlinked or as totally separate subjects? You should see them as interlinked and look to see how all the subjects interact, but it is too easy to adopt a blinkered approach and compartmentalise each different aspect of your studies.

As the previous decisions and discussion illustrate, all business decisions require input from different departments and information from one department has to be integrated with information from other departments before an overall coordinated plan of action is put into operation. Businesses operate as cohesive entities, with all departments pulling in the same direction rather than each following their own individual pathway. Management make decisions and implement strategies, but underpinning all these decisions and strategies is accounting information.

This central role for accountants and accounting information puts accounting staff under pressure to perform their roles effectively and efficiently. After all, if the information presented by the accounting staff is defective in any way, the wrong decision could be made and losses rather than profits might result. Therefore, accountants have to ensure that the information they provide is as accurate and as up to date as possible to enable management to make the most effective decisions. Ideally, accounting staff will always be striving to improve the information they provide to management as better information will result in more informed and more effective decisions.

To illustrate the importance of the accounting function, take a moment to think what would happen if we did not have accounting information. Businesses would be lost without the vital information provided by accounting. If accounting did not exist, there would be no information relating to costs, no indication of what had been achieved in the past as a point of comparison for what is being achieved now, no figures on which to base taxation assessments, no proof that results are as companies claim they are. In short, if accounting did not exist, someone would have to invent it.

WHY IS THIS RELEVANT TO ME?   The role of accounting information in business decision making

To enable you as an accounting professional to:

- Appreciate that business decisions depend upon input from different departments and that decisions are not made in isolation by one department acting on its own
- Appreciate the importance of accounting information in business decision making
- Understand that accounting is not a stand-alone department but an integral part of all organisations

---

MULTIPLE CHOICE QUESTIONS   Are you convinced that you understand what role accounting plays in business decision making? Go to the **online workbook** Multiple choice questions 1.1 to make sure you can suggest how accounting and accounting information would be used in the context of a business decision.

WHAT QUALITIES SHOULD ACCOUNTING INFORMATION POSSESS?

Given the pivotal role of accounting information in business decision making, what sort of qualities should such information possess for it to be useful in making these decisions? Helpfully, the International Accounting Standards Board (IASB) in its *Conceptual Framework for Financial Reporting* provides guidance in this area. The IASB states that financial information should possess the following two fundamental qualitative characteristics:

- Relevance
- Faithful representation

In addition, the IASB's *Conceptual Framework* identifies the following qualitative characteristics that enhance the usefulness of information that is relevant and faithfully represented:

- Comparability
- Verifiability
- Timeliness
- Understandability

This hierarchy of qualitative characteristics is shown in Figure 1.4.

What does each of the above qualitative characteristics represent? Table 1.1 considers the characteristics of each of the two fundamental and four enhancing qualities of financial information.

Let's think about how the qualities considered above apply to accounting information. Taking the bank statement (Example 1.1) considered under control, accounting and accountability earlier in this chapter, our thoughts might be as shown in Table 1.2.

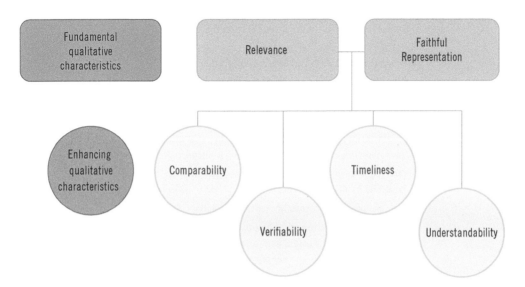

Figure 1.4 The qualitative characteristics of financial information

1

Table 1.1 The qualities of accounting information

Qualitative characteristic	Considerations
Relevance	• Relevant information is capable of making a difference in the decisions made by users. • Relevant information may be predictive and assist users in making predictions about the future or it may be confirmatory by assisting users to assess the accuracy of past predictions. • Relevant information can be both predictive and confirmatory.
Faithful representation	• Financial information must not only represent relevant economic phenomena (transactions and events), but it must also faithfully represent the substance of the phenomena that it purports to represent. • Perfectly faithful representation of economic phenomena in words and numbers requires that the information presented must have three characteristics: it must be complete, neutral and free from error. • Do note that free from error does not mean that information must be perfectly accurate. Much accounting information, as you will see throughout your studies, relies on best estimates or the most likely outcomes. The IASB *Conceptual Framework* makes it clear that 'free from error means there are no errors or omissions in the description of the phenomenon, and the process used to produce the reported information has been selected and applied with no errors in the process. In this context, free from error does not mean perfectly accurate in all respects' (IASB *Conceptual Framework for Financial Reporting* paragraph 2.18).
Comparability	• Information should be comparable over time. • The usefulness of information is enhanced if it can be compared with similar information about other entities for the same reporting period and with similar information about the same entity for other reporting periods. • Where information is comparable, similarities and differences are readily apparent. • Comparability does not mean consistency. However, consistency of presentation and measurement of the same items in the same way from year to year will help to achieve comparability. • Similarly, comparability does not mean that economic phenomena must be presented uniformly. Information about the same phenomena will be presented in similar but not in the same ways by different entities. The differences in the presentation of such phenomena will not be so great as to prevent comparability.
Verifiability	• Verifiability provides users with assurance that information is faithfully presented and reports the economic phenomena it purports to represent. • To ensure verifiability, it should be possible to prove the information presented is accurate in all major respects. • The accuracy of information can be verified by observation or recalculation. • Financial information will often be subject to independent audit and the independent auditors will use various techniques and approaches to verify the financial information presented.

→

Qualitative characteristic	Considerations
Timeliness	• The decision usefulness of information is enhanced if it is available to users in time for it to be capable of influencing their decisions. • The decision usefulness of information generally declines with time although information used in identifying trends continues to be timely in the future.
Understandability	• This characteristic should not be confused with simplicity. • As you will see in your future studies, financial accounting can involve very complex calculations, details and disclosures. Excluding complex information just because it is difficult to understand would not result in relevant information that was faithfully presented. Reports that excluded such information would be incomplete and would thus mislead users. • Readers of financial reports are assumed to have a reasonable knowledge of business and economic activities in order to make sense of what they are presented with. If they are unable to understand the information presented, then the IASB recommends using an adviser. • To help users understand information presented, that information should be classified, characterised and presented clearly.

Table 1.2 How your bank statement fulfils the qualities of accounting information

Relevant?	• Your bank statement is capable of making a difference to the decisions you make. Depending on your current level of cash, you are able to decide to spend less, increase the income into your bank account or decide to invest surplus funds in high interest accounts. • Looking at your current income and expenditure, you can predict what is likely to happen in the future in your bank account. Where you have made predictions about what cash you would have left at the end of each month, you can then confirm how accurate or inaccurate those predictions were and make future predictions about how much you will have left at the end of the next month to decide what you should do with these surplus funds. • Accurate predictions in the past will enable you to be confident that your future predictions will be accurate too.
Faithful representation?	• Your bank statement is presented by your bank, so this should be a faithful representation of your income and expenditure (economic phenomena, transactions and events) over a given period of time. • It is in your bank's interest to ensure that the information presented in your bank statement is complete, neutral (the statement just presents the facts of your income and expenditure) and free from error. Any errors you do pick up can be notified to your bank for correction.

→

Comparable?	• Presentation of your bank statement does not differ over time and is presented in the same format every month so this information is comparable over different periods of time.
	• This consistency of presentation and measurement of income and expenditure in the same way from month to month and year to year will help to achieve the required comparability.
Verifiable?	• The accuracy of your statement can be verified by reference to your list of standing orders, direct debits, debit card transactions, cheques written and income from payslips and other sources.
	• You can add up your bank statement to make sure the balance at the end of each month is correct (recalculation).
	• You are thus the auditor of your own bank account, checking and verifying that the information presented is accurate and free from error to ensure that your statement is faithfully presented and reports the substance of the economic phenomena it purports to represent.
Timely?	• Your bank statement is received each month (or you can access it instantly online), so it is presented in time for it to be capable of influencing your decisions. If your bank statement were to be sent annually, this would be much less relevant information as it would be seriously out of date by the time you received it and much less capable of making a difference to the decisions you make.
	• However, past bank statements are still timely when comparing trends of income and expenditure across different periods of time.
Understandable?	• You can certainly understand your bank statement as it shows you the money going into and out of your account.
	• You have a reasonable knowledge of your finances so you can make sense of what your bank statement presents you with. If you are unable to understand the information presented, then you can always contact your bank for advice.
	• To help you understand the information presented, transactions are classified, characterised and presented clearly in your bank statement.

GO BACK OVER THIS AGAIN!   Are you sure that you can define relevance, faithful representation, comparability, verifiability, timeliness and understandability? Go to the **online workbook** Exercises 1.5 to make sure you can define these qualities of financial information accurately.

SUMMARY OF KEY CONCEPTS   Can you state and define the two fundamental and four enhancing qualities of financial information? Go to the **online workbook** to check your grasp of these qualities with Summary of key concepts 1.2–1.7.

MATERIALITY

A further requirement of financial information for decision making purposes is that it should not be overloaded with unnecessary detail. This leads us on to the concept of materiality. The IASB defines materiality as follows:

> Information is material if omitting it or misstating it could influence decisions that … users … make on the basis of … financial information about a specific reporting entity. In other words, materiality is an entity-specific aspect of relevance based on the nature or magnitude, or both, of the items to which the information relates in the context of an individual entity's financial report.
>
> Source: IASB *Conceptual Framework for Financial Reporting,* paragraph 2.11

How is materiality applied in practice? Example 1.2 provides instances of the circumstances in which an item might be defined as material.

EXAMPLE 1.2

An item could be material by size ('magnitude' in the above definition). If a shop makes £2m of sales a year, then the sale of a 50p carton of milk missed out of those sales will not be material. However, in a steel fabrications business making £2m of sales a year, the omission of a £250,000 sale of a steel frame for a building would be material as it makes up 12.5 per cent of the sales for the year.

As well as size, items can be material by nature. The theft of £5 from the till by a member of staff would be unlikely to be material. However, the theft of £5 from the till by the managing director would be: if you are an investor in the business, this tells you that your investment might not be very safe if the managing director is willing to steal from the business.

MULTIPLE CHOICE QUESTIONS   Are you confident that you can decide whether a piece of information is material or not? Go to the **online workbook** Multiple choice questions 1.2 to make sure you can determine whether information is material or not.

SUMMARY OF KEY CONCEPTS   Can you recall the definition of materiality? Go to the **online workbook** to check your grasp of this definition in Summary of key concepts 1.8.

COST V. BENEFIT

The IASB recognises that there is a cost in collecting, processing, verifying and disseminating financial information (*IASB Conceptual Framework for Financial Reporting*, paragraphs 2.39–2.43). Therefore, information should only be presented if the benefits of providing that information outweigh the costs of obtaining it. Example 1.3 suggests how you might weigh up the costs and benefits in a practical but non-accounting situation.

EXAMPLE 1.3

You know that there is a wonderful quote in a book that you have read that would really enhance your essay and provide you with a brilliant conclusion. However, you have forgotten where to find this quote and you have not written down the name of the book or the page reference. Your essay must be handed in by 4.00 p.m. today and it is already 3.40 p.m. You still have to print off your essay before handing it in. If your essay is handed in after 4.00 p.m. you will be awarded a mark of 0 per cent and so fail the assignment.

The costs of searching for the quote outweigh the benefits of finding it as you will not receive any marks if your essay is late so you print off your essay and hand it in on time and, when it is returned, you have scored 65 per cent and gained a pass on this piece of coursework.

WHY IS THIS RELEVANT TO ME?   The qualities of accounting information

To enable you as an accounting professional to:

• Understand what qualities useful accounting information should possess

• Appreciate the constraints imposed upon the provision of useful accounting information by the materiality concept and the cost/benefit consideration

• Understand the standards against which to measure financial information presented by you

---

GO BACK OVER THIS AGAIN!   Are you quite certain that you understand how cost v. benefit works? Visit the **online workbook** Exercises 1.6 to reinforce your understanding.

SUMMARY OF KEY CONCEPTS   Do you think you can remember how to define cost v. benefit? Go to the **online workbook** to check your grasp of this definition in Summary of key concepts 1.9.

THE USERS OF ACCOUNTING INFORMATION

As we have seen, accounting is all about providing information to interested parties so that they can make decisions on the basis of that information. But who are the users of this accounting information and what decisions do they make as a result of receiving that information?

Accounting is made up of two branches. The first of these branches provides information to external users and the other provides information to internal users. The information needs of both these user groups differ in important ways as we shall see.

Accounting branch 1: financial accounting

Financial accounting is the reporting of past information to users outside the organisation. This information is presented in the annual report and accounts that all companies are obliged to produce by law, publish on their websites and lodge with the Registrar of Companies at Companies House. Directors of companies produce these annual reports and accounts for issue to shareholders to provide an account of how they have used the resources entrusted to them to generate profits, dividends and value for the shareholders. Even if a business entity is not a company and there is no legal obligation to produce accounts, it will still produce financial statements to provide evidence of what it has achieved over the past year. These accounts will also be used as a basis for enabling the business's managers or owners and its lenders and advisers to make decisions based upon them as well as being used by the taxation authorities to determine the tax due on the profits for the year.

What is the aim of these financial accounts and reports and what do they provide? The International Accounting Standards Board states that the objective of financial reporting (not just financial statements) is as follows.

> The objective of general purpose financial reporting is to provide financial information about the reporting entity that is useful to existing and potential investors, lenders and other creditors in making decisions relating to providing resources to the entity. Those decisions involve decisions about:

a) buying, selling or holding equity and debt instruments;

b) providing or settling loans and other forms of credit;

c) or exercising rights to vote on, or otherwise influence, management's actions that affect the use of the entity's economic resources.

Source: IASB *Conceptual Framework for Financial Reporting,* paragraph 1.2

While the IASB focuses on the financial information needs of existing and potential investors, lenders and other creditors, it does envisage that other users might find general purpose financial reports useful:

Other parties, such as regulators and members of the public other than investors, lenders and other creditors, may also find general purpose financial reports useful. However, those reports are not primarily directed to these other groups.

Source: IASB *Conceptual Framework for Financial Reporting,* paragraph 1.10

Financial information is reported to users external to the organisation through three key statements: the statement of financial position, the statement of profit or loss and the statement of cash flows. We shall be studying all three of these financial statements in this book as they will form the bedrock of your professional career in accounting. Chapter 2 will consider the statement of financial position and how this presents the financial position of an entity at a given point in time. Chapter 3 will look at how entities' financial performance is measured and reported in the statement of profit or loss while Chapter 6 will provide a detailed overview of the statement of cash flows. Ways in which users can evaluate these particular financial statements and what they tell them about the performance, the financial stability and the investment potential of entities will be the subject of Chapters 8 and 9. However, our concern at this point is with the users of financial accounts and reports, what those different user groups might use financial reports for and the economic decisions they might base upon them.

As well as the three primary user groups noted by the IASB, other parties who might find general purpose financial statements useful include the following:

- Employees and their representative groups
- Customers
- Governments and their agencies
- The public

What information would each of the identified user groups expect to find in external financial reports that would enable them to make economic decisions? Table 1.3 provides examples of some of the questions that the seven categories of user will ask when looking at financial statements: can you think of additional questions that each user group will ask?

Many questions that users of financial reports ask will be common to all categories of user. For example, investors might ask questions about the ethical and environmental record of the company and whether this is the kind of organisation they would want to be involved with and be seen to be involved with. But ethically and environmentally concerned employees might also ask the same questions and lenders, concerned about their reputation and being seen to do business with

Table 1.3 The external users of financial statements

User group	Examples of questions asked by each user group
Existing and potential investors (this group would include investment advisers)	• What profit has the company made for me in my position as a shareholder/investor? • What financial gains am I making from this company? • Would it be worthwhile for me to invest more money in the shares of this company? • If the company has not done well this year, should I sell my shares or hold onto them? • Does my company comply with all the relevant company and stock market regulations? • Is my company run effectively and efficiently?
Lenders	• Will this company be able to repay what has been lent? • Will this company be able to pay loan instalments and interest as they fall due? • Is this company in danger of insolvency? • What cash resources and cash generating ability does this company have?
Other creditors (this group will include suppliers of goods and services to the entity)	• Will I be paid for goods or services I have supplied? • Will I be paid on time so that I can pay my suppliers? • Will my customer expand so that I can expand, too?
Employees and their representative groups	• How stable is the company I work for? • Is the company I work for making profits? • If the company is making losses, will it survive for the foreseeable future? • What about the continuity of my employment? • Should I be looking for employment elsewhere? • If the company I work for is profitable, will I be awarded a pay rise or a bonus? • What retirement benefit scheme does my company offer to employees? • Is my employer investing in the future prosperity of the business?
Customers	• Will the entity survive in the long term so that it can continue to provide me with goods and services?
Governments and their agencies	• What taxation does this entity pay? • What contribution does this entity make to the economy? • Does this entity export goods to other countries?
The public	• What contribution does this entity make to society? • Does this entity make donations to charity? • If this entity is a major local employer, will they survive into the future to ensure the health of the local economy?

unethical organisations, might be looking for the same information. Suppliers and customers will have similar concerns as their image and reputation will be shaped by those they do business with.

Similarly, all user groups will want to know about the availability of cash with which to pay dividends (investors), salaries (employees), loan interest and loan repayments (lenders), goods supplied on credit (suppliers) and taxes due (governments). Even customers and the public will be concerned about the availability of cash, as, without sufficient inflows of cash from trading, companies will collapse.

While users of external financial statements might legitimately ask the questions mentioned, the extent to which such reports provide this information varies. Some financial reports are very detailed in their coverage, others less so. As you gradually become familiar with the content of published financial reports and accounts, your awareness of shortcomings in these documents will increase.

WHY IS THIS RELEVANT TO ME?   The users of accounting information

To enable you as an accounting professional to understand:

- Who the target audience is for the reports that you will produce
- Which external parties are interested in the financial information provided by business entities
- The kinds of answers users of external financial reports expect from the information provided

---

GO BACK OVER THIS AGAIN!   Are you convinced that you understand what information particular user groups are looking for in published financial reports? Go to the **online workbook** Exercises 1.7 to check your understanding in this area.

SUMMARY OF KEY CONCEPTS   Can you recall the seven user groups of financial accounting information? Go to the **online workbook** to check your knowledge of these user groups with Summary of key concepts 1.10.

SUMMARY OF KEY CONCEPTS   Are you confident that you can state the objective of financial statements? Go to the **online workbook** to check your knowledge of this objective with Summary of key concepts 1.11.

Accounting branch 2: cost and management accounting

Cost and management accounting is concerned with reporting accounting and cost information to users within an organisation. As the name suggests, management accounting information is used to help managers manage the business and its activities. Cost and management accountants are first concerned with the costs that go into producing products and services to determine a selling price for those products and services that will generate a profit for the business. Management accounting information is then used to plan levels of production and activity in the future as well as deciding what products to produce and sell to maximise profits for the business. As well as planning what the business is going to do, management accounting produces reports to evaluate the results of past plans to see whether they achieved their aims and the ways in which improvements could be made.

1

While financial accounting reports what has happened in the past, management accounting is very much concerned with both the present and the future and how accounting information can be used for short-term decision making and longer-term planning. This book will not be considering cost and management accounting beyond this brief introduction.

WHY IS THIS RELEVANT TO ME?   The two branches of accounting

To enable you as an accounting professional to:

- Appreciate the wide range of internal and external users of accounting information
- Distinguish quickly between financial and management accounting

---

THE STRUCTURE AND REGULATION OF THE ACCOUNTING PROFESSION

Professional accounting bodies have been set up in many countries around the world. These professional accounting bodies are responsible for admitting individuals to membership and for regulation and oversight of their conduct as professional people once they have been accepted as members. Admission to the professional bodies is achieved through a combination of examinations and practical experience. The main professional accounting bodies in the United Kingdom and Ireland are:

- The Association of Chartered Certified Accountants (ACCA)
- The Chartered Institute of Management Accountants (CIMA)
- The Chartered Institute of Public Finance and Accounting (CIPFA)
- The Institute of Chartered Accountants in England and Wales (ICAEW)
- The Institute of Chartered Accountants in Ireland (ICAI)
- The Institute of Chartered Accountants in Scotland (ICAS).

Qualified accountants undertake the preparation of financial statements and reports, the audit of financial statements and the provision of taxation and business advice to individuals and organisations. As professionals, qualified accountants are expected to adhere to high standards of conduct to maintain the standing of the profession and to provide a professional service to their clients, employers and the public. Accountants are expected to behave with integrity, being honest in all their professional and business relationships. They are also expected to be objective, to carry out their duties with due care and competence, to maintain the confidentiality of information acquired in the course of fulfilling their duties and to comply at all times with relevant laws and regulations. Where accountants breach these ethical rules of conduct, their professional bodies will take action to discipline them with warnings, fines and, in the most serious cases, exclusion from membership.

As well as adhering to the professional bodies' expected standards of behaviour and ethical conduct, qualified accountants are expected to ensure that accepted accounting standards have been applied correctly in the presentation of financial information. In the European Union and in the UK accounting standards are set by the International Accounting Standards Board (IASB) for companies listed on a Stock Exchange and by the UK Financial Reporting Council (FRC) for smaller unlisted and non-public interest companies. Failure to apply these accounting standards correctly will also result in an accountant's professional body taking disciplinary action against a member.

Poor management and dishonest behaviour on the part of directors in the past led to investors losing a lot of money. Governments and stock exchanges around the world responded by setting up various committees to report on the state of corporate governance, the way in which large companies were run and to make recommendations for improvement. As a result of these recommendations, corporate governance codes were formulated to enshrine best practice and to ensure that large companies were run in an open and honest manner to safeguard shareholders' and the general public's interests in those companies. Professional accountants are expected to adhere to and apply these corporate governance codes in businesses in which they work to ensure the transparency of information presented by these companies. Further consideration of corporate governance will be presented in Chapter 10 and this introduction to the topic will form the basis of your future studies in this area.

WHY IS THIS RELEVANT TO ME?   Structure and regulation of the accounting profession

To provide you as an accounting professional with:

- A quick overview of the accounting profession and the ways in which it is regulated
- An indication of the standards of behaviour to be expected from professional accountants and other persons holding positions of responsibility in companies

---

THE INTERNATIONAL ACCOUNTING STANDARDS BOARD (IASB)

As noted earlier (this chapter, The structure and regulation of the accounting profession), the IASB is responsible for developing and issuing accounting standards. These accounting standards must be adhered to by companies when producing and presenting their annual financial statements. The development process for an accounting standard follows the process outlined in Figure 1.5.

The first step in developing a new standard is the identification of a reporting problem. There may be a variety of different approaches to presenting information about a particular item in financial statements. Such variety will lead to a lack of relevant information due to the lack of comparability between the financial statements of different entities. The IASB then develops a draft accounting standard called an Exposure Draft. This Exposure Draft will propose a single approach to the reporting of the particular item in the financial statements to ensure that reporting differences are eliminated. Interested parties then comment on the proposals in the Exposure Draft,

1

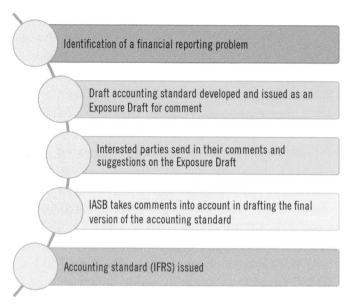

Figure 1.5 The accounting standard development process

supporting or disagreeing with the proposed approach. Once the comment period is complete, the IASB takes all the comments into account when developing the final accounting standard. The standard developed and issued is known as an International Financial Reporting Standard, abbreviated to IFRS. Prior to the establishment of the IASB under its current constitution in 2001, its predecessor body the International Accounting Standards Committee issued statements called International Accounting Standards, abbreviated to IAS. As each IAS is revised in line with current accounting and reporting practice, it is reissued as an IFRS. You will study all the IFRS and IAS in very great detail later on in your degree and professional exams. A complete list of IFRS and IAS in issue at June 2018 is presented in the Appendix to this chapter.

WHY IS THIS RELEVANT TO ME?   The International Accounting Standards Board
To enable you as an accounting professional to: • Appreciate the process of developing and issuing accounting standards • Understand the role of the IASB in the accounting standard development process

THE LIMITATIONS OF ACCOUNTING INFORMATION

We have seen that accounting information plays an anchor role in decision making for businesses and other users. However, there are various aspects of business performance that accounting does not cover. While it is important to know what accounting is and what it does, it is just as important to be aware of what accounting does not do.

First, accounting does not provide you with measures of the quality of an organisation's performance. The quality of what an entity produces or provides is measured by its customers and their level of satisfaction with goods and services delivered, their willingness to recommend an organisation's products and the number of times they return to buy more goods or use more services. While measures can be devised to assess recommendations and repeat business, this is not a function that accounting would normally fulfil.

Similarly, a business entity may make a profit, but accounting does not tell us the time, effort and thought that went into delivering the products and services to generate that profit. In the same way, your team may win, draw or lose, but the bare result does not tell you about the quality of entertainment on offer, whether your team played badly but still managed to scrape a vital goal or whether they played brilliantly and were just unlucky.

Second, accounting does not tell you about the pollution and environmental or social damage an entity has caused. Organisations will report redundancies as an internal cost-saving opportunity for the business while ignoring the wider external effects of their actions. Thus, businesses do not report the destruction of communities built around an organisation's operations and all the burdens that this imposes upon families, social services, the National Health Service and the state. Similarly, while companies use air, water and other natural resources in their production processes, there is no formal, legal requirement that they should report on the damage they cause to these resources. Despite the lack of regulation in this last area, we shall look in more detail in Chapter 10 at the current debate surrounding accounting for the environment and sustainability accounting.

Finally, accounting does not provide any valuation or measure of the skills base and knowledge of organisations. Boards of directors will thank their staff for all their hard work and efforts during the previous financial year, but the monetary value of the employees to the business does not feature in financial statements. This is attributable to the fact that valuing staff is exceptionally complex due to the subjective nature of such valuations and the fact that employees do not meet the asset definition and recognition criteria (Chapter 2, Assets). Thus, you might think your financial accounting lecturer is the most organised and most informative tutor you have seen on your course so far, while your friend is grumbling about how uninteresting the lectures and tutorials are and how she cannot follow them. In the same way, while employees, their skills, knowledge and abilities are the most valuable resources in a business, these resources cannot be measured in money or any other numerical terms and so do not appear in the financial statements. As accounting is about measuring items in financial statements, you might find this omission rather odd given the significance of employees to the success or failure of a business. However, it is important to remember that Albert Einstein's famous dictum is just as applicable to accounting as it is to many other disciplines: 'Not everything that can be counted counts. Not everything that counts can be counted.'

WHY IS THIS RELEVANT TO ME?   The limitations of accounting information

To enable you as an accounting professional to:

- Gain an awareness of the aspects of business performance that accounting does not cover
- Appreciate the limitations of accounting and accounting information
- Understand that accounting and accounting information will not necessarily provide you with all the information you need to make decisions or evaluate an organisation's performance

SUMMARY OF KEY CONCEPTS   Are you confident that you can state the limitations of accounting and accounting information? Go to the **online workbook** to check your knowledge of these limitations with Summary of key concepts 1.12.

APPENDIX: CURRENT IFRS AND IAS IN ISSUE AT JUNE 2018

Listed below are the numbers and titles of all International Financial Reporting Standards and all International Accounting Standards in issue and currently in use at June 2018.

IFRS 1 First-time adoption of International Financial Reporting Standards

IFRS 2 Share-based payment

IFRS 3 Business combinations

IFRS 5 Non-current assets held for sale and discontinued operations

IFRS 6 Exploration for the evaluation of mineral resources

IFRS 7 Financial instruments: disclosures

IFRS 8 Operating segments

IFRS 9 Financial instruments

IFRS 10 Consolidated financial statements

IFRS 11 Joint arrangements

IFRS 12 Disclosure of interests in other entities

IFRS 13 Fair value measurement

IFRS 14 Regulatory deferral accounts

IFRS 15 Revenue from contracts with customers

IFRS 16 Leases

IFRS 17 Insurance contracts

IAS 1 Presentation of financial statements

IAS 2 Inventories

IAS 7 Statement of cash flows

IAS 8 Accounting policies, changes in accounting estimates and errors

IAS 10 Events after the reporting period

IAS 12 Income taxes

IAS 16 Property, plant and equipment

IAS 19 Employee benefits

IAS 20 Accounting for government grants and disclosure of government assistance

IAS 21 The effects of changes in foreign exchange rates

IAS 23 Borrowing costs

CHAPTER SUMMARY

you should now have learnt that:

- Accounting summarises numerical data relating to past events and presents this data as information to managers and other interested parties as a basis for both decision making and control purposes

- Accounting information is the bedrock upon which all business decisions are based

- Financial information should possess the two fundamental characteristics of relevance and faithful representation

- The qualitative characteristics of comparability, verifiability, timeliness and understandability will enhance the usefulness of information that is relevant and faithfully represented

- Financial accounting generates reports for users external to the business

- Financial accounting information is primarily aimed at existing and potential investors, lenders and other creditors who will find this information useful in making decisions about providing resources to the reporting entity

- Other user groups such as employees, customers, governments and the public may also find financial reporting information useful in making decisions and evaluating the performance of organisations

- Management accounting is prepared for internal users in a business to help them manage the business's activities

1

- Accounting does not measure, among other things, quality, pollution, social and environmental damage, human resources and the skills and knowledge base of organisations

---

QUICK REVISION   Test your knowledge with the online flashcards in Summary of key concepts and attempt the Multiple choice questions, all found in the **online workbook**.

END-OF-CHAPTER QUESTIONS

Solutions to these questions can be found in the **online workbook**.

❯Question 1.1

What accounting and other information would the managers of the following organisations require in order to assess their performance and financial position?

- A charity
- A secondary school
- A university
- A manufacturing business

❯Question 1.2

A premier league football club has received an offer for its star striker from Real Madrid. The star striker is eager to leave and join the Spanish team and the board of directors has reluctantly agreed to let him go for the transfer fee offered. The team now needs a new striker and the manager has been put in charge of identifying potential new centre forwards that the club could bid for. You have been asked by the manager to draw up a chart listing the numerical information about potential targets that the manager should take into account when evaluating possible replacements.

THE STATEMENT OF FINANCIAL POSITION

2

LEARNING OUTCOMES

Once you have read this chapter and worked through the questions and examples in both this chapter and the online workbook, you should be able to:

- Define assets and liabilities

- Determine whether an entity should or should not recognise specific resources and obligations on its statement of financial position

- Distinguish between non-current and current assets and liabilities

- State the accounting equation

- Draw up a statement of financial position for organisations in compliance with the International Accounting Standards Board's requirements

- Explain how assets and liabilities are measured in monetary amounts at the statement of financial position date

- State what the statement of financial position does and does not show

- Understand how transactions affect two or more accounts on the statement of financial position (the duality principle)

- Correctly record the effect of transactions on assets, liabilities and equity in the statement of financial position

INTRODUCTION

Figure 2.1 summarises the elements that make up the statement of financial position. All financial statements present a statement of financial position. This is a summary, in money terms, of the assets an organisation controls and the liabilities an organisation owes to outside parties. To enable you to see how this statement is presented in full before we look at the detail, Illustration 2.1 shows the statement of financial position of Bunns the Bakers plc, a regional baker with a bakery and 20 shops in the East Midlands. At first glance, this might look confusing as there are all kinds of seemingly complex words and jargon. However, don't worry as, after working your way through this chapter and the materials in the online workbook, you will soon have a much clearer idea of what the words and jargon mean.

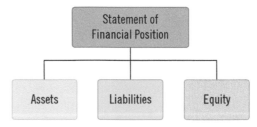

Figure 2.1 The statement of financial position

Notice that there are various headings provided and that these headings contain the words 'assets', 'liabilities' and 'equity'. In this chapter we will be looking at what constitutes an asset and a liability and how equity is calculated. We shall also review the criteria for recognising assets and liabilities and how those assets and liabilities are classified as current or non-current. Just as assets and liabilities can be recognised in an organisation's statement of financial position so, once assets have been used up or liabilities discharged, they are derecognised. This just means that they are removed from the statement of financial position as they are no longer controlled or owed by the entity.

Once the definitions are clear, we shall move on to constructing simple statements of financial position from given data. We shall then consider what the statement of financial position shows us and, equally importantly, what it does not show us. There are many misconceptions about what a statement of financial position represents. This chapter will dispel these misconceptions and provide you with a very precise idea of what the statement of financial position provides by way of information and what it does not.

Finally, at the end of the chapter, we will have a quick look at how new transactions affect the statement of financial position. Double-entry bookkeeping will be dealt with in much greater depth and detail in Chapters 4 and 5, but an early appreciation of how double entry works will give you an insight into the logic of accounting and how new transactions have a two-fold effect on figures in the financial statements of an organisation.

Illustration 2.1 Bunns the Bakers plc: statement of financial position at 31 March 2019

	2019 £000	2018 £000
ASSETS		
Non-current assets		
Intangible assets	50	55
Property, plant and equipment	11,750	11,241
Investments	65	59
	11,865	**11,355**
Current assets		
Inventories	60	55
Trade and other receivables	62	75
Cash and cash equivalents	212	189
	334	**319**
Total assets	**12,199**	**11,674**
LIABILITIES		
Current liabilities		
Current portion of long-term borrowings	300	300
Trade and other payables	390	281
Current tax liabilities	150	126
	840	**707**
Non-current liabilities		
Long-term borrowings	2,700	3,000
Long-term provisions	200	200
	2,900	**3,200**
Total liabilities	**3,740**	**3,907**
Net assets	**8,459**	**7,767**
EQUITY		
Called up share capital (£1 ordinary shares)	2,500	2,400
Share premium	1,315	1,180
Retained earnings	4,644	4,187
Total equity	**8,459**	**7,767**

GO BACK OVER THIS AGAIN!   A copy of this statement of financial position is available in the **online workbook**: you might like to keep this on screen or print off a copy for easy reference while you work your way through the material in this chapter. There is also an annotated copy of this statement of financial position at the back of the book to help you go over the relevant points again to reinforce your knowledge and learning.

2

TERMINOLOGY: STATEMENT OF FINANCIAL POSITION/BALANCE SHEET

International Financial Reporting Standards use the term 'statement of financial position' for what has traditionally been called the balance sheet. In keeping with the international focus of this book, the term 'statement of financial position' will be used throughout. However, you will find the two terms used interchangeably in your wider reading, so you should understand that the terms balance sheet and statement of financial position refer to the same summary statement of assets, liabilities and equity.

ASSETS

Illustration 2.1 shows you the statement of financial position for Bunns the Bakers plc. As noted in the introduction, the first part of this statement of financial position shows you the assets that an entity controls. However, the first questions to ask are: 'What is an asset?' and 'What does an asset represent?'

The International Accounting Standards Board's *Conceptual Framework for Financial Reporting* provides the following definition of an asset:

A present economic resource controlled by the entity as a result of past events.

An economic resource is a right that has the potential to produce economic benefits.

Source: IASB *Conceptual Framework for Financial Reporting*, paragraphs 4.3 and 4.4

This sounds complicated. However, once we consider the words carefully and analyse what they mean, we will find that this definition is actually very simple and presents a very clear set of criteria to determine whether an asset exists or not. So what does this definition tell you? Let's look at the key points:

- Control: 'an entity controls an economic resource if it has the present ability to direct the use of the economic resource and obtain the economic benefits that flow from it' (*IASB Conceptual Framework*, paragraph 4.20). A resource is controlled if it is owned or leased (rented) by an organisation which can enforce its legal rights over that resource. Control is therefore established if an entity can legally prevent anyone else from using that resource and obtaining the economic benefits from it.

- As a result of past events: to gain control of a resource it is likely that a contract has been signed transferring or granting the right to use that resource to the current owner and money has been paid to other parties in exchange for the transfer or rights to use that resource. Contractual rights gained over the resource mean that an entity can enforce its legal rights over that resource.

- Present: firstly, the economic resource must be under the control of an entity at the statement of financial position date. Any economic resource that is not under the control of the entity at the statement of financial position date cannot be included in the entity's statement of financial position. Secondly, the economic resource must have the potential to produce economic benefits at the statement of financial position date. If the economic resource does not have this potential then it cannot be recognised as an asset on the statement of financial position.

- Economic benefits: the economic resource will be used within an organisation to generate cash and profit from the sale of goods or services to other persons.

From this definition it follows that an asset represents a store of potential economic benefits, the ability to use the asset within an organisation to generate cash and profit. Let's see how this definition works in practice in Example 2.1.

2

EXAMPLE 2.1

Let us take the example of Bunns the Bakers. The company bought a city centre shop from a property developer 10 years ago for £500,000, with both the seller and the buyer of the shop signing a contract transferring legal title in the shop to Bunns the Bakers. The shop sells bread, cakes, hot and cold snacks, drinks and sandwiches. Does this constitute an asset of the business? Applying our criteria above:

- Do Bunns the Bakers *control* the shop (the resource)? Yes: the company *owns* the shop and, by virtue of the contract signed at the time the shop was purchased from the property developer, Bunns the Bakers can go to court to assert their legal rights to the shop and to prevent anyone else from using that shop for their own purposes. The company thus has the ability at the statement of financial position date (the present ability) to direct the use of this economic resource (the shop) and to obtain the economic benefits that flow from it.

- Is there *a past event*? Yes: Bunns the Bakers' representatives signed the contract and paid £500,000 to acquire the shop, so this is the *past event* giving rise to control of the economic resource.

- Does the economic resource (the shop) have the potential to produce economic benefits? Yes: Bunns the Bakers is using the shop to sell goods produced by the company and bought in from suppliers to customers in order to generate cash and profits from those sales. You can also view the shop as a store of potential economic benefits for Bunns the Bakers. The company can continue to use the shop to make sales, profits and cash into the future. Alternatively, that store of potential economic benefits could be realised by selling the shop to another company. This would still generate economic benefits as the sale of the shop would release the cash (= the economic benefits) tied up in that shop. Even if Bunns the Bakers did not sell the shop but chose to rent it out to another party, this would still represent potential economic benefits as monthly rental payments would be received in cash from the person or organisation renting the shop.

Thus, the shop represents an asset to the business as it meets the IASB criteria for recognition of an asset.

Assets: faithful representation

Our definition of what constitutes an asset now seems very clear. However, there is one further test to satisfy before an asset (or liability) can be recognised in the statement of financial position.

As we saw in Chapter 1 (What qualities should accounting information possess?), the IASB requires financial information to be relevant and faithfully represented. Faithful representation requires the presentation of information that is complete, neutral and free from error. Since the elements (assets, liabilities and equity) that make up the statement of financial position must be quantified in money terms (IASB, *Conceptual Framework*, paragraph 6.1), these elements must be measured at a monetary value before they can be recognised. While an accurate value for many assets and liabilities can be determined easily from the accounting records of an entity, there will be times when estimates have to be used. When values are estimated, they are subject to measurement uncertainty. In cases where the level of measurement uncertainty is so high that the faithful representation of an asset or liability is in doubt, then no asset or liability is recognised (IASB, *Conceptual Framework*, paragraphs 5.19-5.22). Thus, when the possible range of values for an asset or liability is very wide or when measurement is based on very subjective measures, then the completeness, neutrality and freedom from error required for a faithful

2

representation cannot be achieved and no asset or liability is recognised in the statement of financial position.

Can the cost of the shop be quantified in monetary terms in such a way that it is faithfully represented in the statement of financial position? Yes, as the cost of the shop was £500,000 this is a complete, neutral and error free measurement so the shop can be recognised in Bunns the Bakers' statement of financial position as an asset.

Asset recognition: summary of the steps to follow

Diagrammatically, the steps to follow to determine whether an asset can be recognised on the statement of financial position are shown in Figure 2.2.

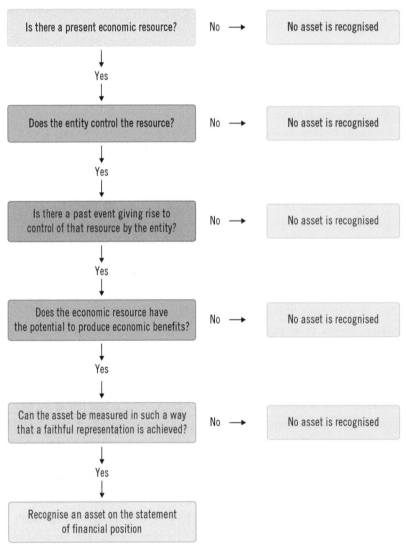

Figure 2.2 Steps in determining whether an asset can be recognised on the statement of financial position or not in accordance with the IASB Conceptual Framework for Financial Reporting

WHY IS THIS RELEVANT TO ME?   Definitions: assets

To enable you as an accounting professional to:

● Understand what assets on the statement of financial position actually represent

● Understand the strict criteria that must be met before an asset can be recognised on the statement of financial position

● Be equipped with the necessary tools to determine whether an asset should be recognised on the statement of financial position or not

SUMMARY OF KEY CONCEPTS   Are you quite convinced that you can define an asset? Go to the **online workbook** to revise this definition with Summary of key concepts 2.1 to reinforce your knowledge.

GO BACK OVER THIS AGAIN!   Are you sure that you have grasped the asset recognition criteria? Go to the **online workbook** Exercises 2.1 to make sure you understand how the asset recognition criteria are used in practice.

ASSETS IN THE STATEMENT OF FINANCIAL POSITION

Now we have found out what assets are and the criteria for their recognition, let's look again at the statement of financial position of Bunns the Bakers plc to see what sort of assets a company might own and recognise.

Illustration 2.1 shows that Bunns the Bakers has two types of assets, non-current assets and current assets. Non-current assets are split into intangible assets, property plant and equipment and investments. Current assets are split into inventories, trade and other receivables and cash and cash equivalents. Total assets are calculated by adding together non-current and current assets as shown in Figure 2.3. What is the distinction between current and non-current assets? Let us look in more detail at these two types of assets and then the categorisation of assets as non-current or current will readily become apparent.

Non-current assets

Non-current assets are those assets that are:

● Not purchased for resale in the normal course of business: this means that the assets are retained within the business for periods of more than one year and are not acquired with the intention of reselling them immediately or in the near future.

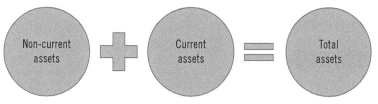

Figure 2.3 The composition of total assets

2

• Held for long-term use in the business to produce goods or services.

An example of a non-current asset would be the shop we considered in Example 2.1. This shop was not purchased with the intention of reselling it, but is held within the business for the long-term purpose of selling bakery goods to customers over many years.

SUMMARY OF KEY CONCEPTS   Are you totally confident that you can define non-current assets? Go to the **online workbook** to revise this definition with Summary of key concepts 2.2 to check your understanding.

Intangible assets are those assets that have no material substance (you cannot touch them). Examples of such assets would be purchased goodwill, patents, trademarks and intellectual property rights. Tangible assets are those assets that do have a material substance (you can touch them) and examples of these would be land and buildings, machinery, vehicles and fixtures and fittings.

Intangible assets are represented on Bunns the Bakers' statement of financial position in Illustration 2.1 and these probably relate to trademarks for the company's products. You would, however, need to consult the notes to the accounts to find out precisely what assets were represented by these figures, as shown in Give me an example 2.1.

GIVE ME AN EXAMPLE 2.1   Intangible assets

Premier Foods plc is the owner of some of the best known grocery brands in the UK, with Mr Kipling, Sharwoods and Oxo among them. On its statement of financial position at 1 April 2017 the company records an amount of £464.0 million under the heading 'Other intangible assets'. The reader of the report and accounts is then referred to Note 13 in the notes to the financial statements for further information. Note 13 shows that the intangible assets recognised are Software and Licences at £37.4 million, Brands, Trademarks and Licences at £422.5 million and Assets under Construction at £4.1 million.

Source: *Premier Foods annual report and accounts for the 52 weeks ended 1 April 2017* www.premierfoods.co.uk

---

The property, plant and equipment heading represents the tangible assets of the business. As this is a bakery retail business, these tangible assets will consist of shops, bakeries, delivery vans, counters, tills and display cabinets in the shops and any other non-current, long-term assets that the company requires to conduct its business.

Investments are just that: holdings of shares or other financial assets (such as loans to other entities) in other companies. These investments represent long-term investments in other companies or operations that are held in order to realise a long-term capital gain when they are eventually sold.

Give me an example 2.2 presents the non-current assets from the statement of financial position of Taylor Wimpey plc.

GO BACK OVER THIS AGAIN!   Do you think you can distinguish between intangible non-current assets, property, plant and equipment and investments? Go to the **online workbook** and complete Exercises 2.2 to make sure you can make these distinctions.

Current assets

Current assets, by contrast, are short-term assets that are constantly changing. On Bunns the Bakers' statement of financial position the following items are found:

- Inventory: inventory is another word for stock of goods. Inventory represents goods held for production or sale. As Bunns the Bakers is a baker, inventories held for production will consist of raw materials such as flour, sugar, eggs and other bakery ingredients. As such raw materials deteriorate rapidly, these inventories will be used and replaced on a regular basis as bakery activity takes place, goods are produced, delivered to the shops and sold to the public. Inventory goods for sale might be bread and cakes produced today and held in cool storage ready for next day delivery to the shops. All inventories thus represent potential cash that will be generated from the production and sales of goods.

GIVE ME AN EXAMPLE 2.2   Non-current assets

We have thought about intangible non-current assets, property, plant and equipment and investments, but what other categories of non-current assets do companies present in their financial statements? The consolidated balance sheet (= statement of financial position) at 31 December 2017 for Taylor Wimpey plc, a large UK residential developer, shows the following non-current assets.

	31 December	
	2017	2016
Non-current assets	£m	£m
Intangible assets	3.9	3.5
Property, plant and equipment	22.8	21.0
Interests in joint ventures	50.9	50.3
Trade and other receivables	60.1	87.2
Deferred tax assets	29.3	57.4
	167.0	219.4

Source: *Taylor Wimpey plc annual report and accounts 2017* www.taylorwimpey.co.uk

Intangible assets are made up of software development costs, while property, plant and equipment consists of land and buildings, plant, equipment and leasehold improvements. Joint ventures are entered into with other companies and Taylor Wimpey's statement of financial position records the share of the joint ventures' net assets attributable to the company. The other companies involved in the joint ventures will record their share of the net assets of the joint ventures in their statements of financial position. It may seem odd to see trade receivables recorded as a non-current asset when Bunns the Bakers shows this as a current asset. However, Taylor Wimpey has provided mortgages to customers to assist them with the purchase of their homes. Mortgages are

→

long-term assets which will be repayable more than 12 months after the statement of financial position date so these mortgages are recorded as non-current trade and other receivables. Deferred tax is a very complex subject which you will consider at a later stage of your studies and can be either an asset (reduced future tax payments) or a liability (increased future tax payments).

- Trade and other receivables: where organisations make their sales on credit terms to customers, customers are given time in which to pay so that the money due from these customers is recognised as money receivable. A moment's thought will convince you that, as Bunns the Bakers sells food products to the public for cash, there will be very few trade receivables. Any trade receivables that there are might arise from a business-to-business contract to supply large quantities of goods to another retailer such as a supermarket chain. As well as small amounts of trade receivables from such contracts, the company will also have other amounts receivable such as tax refunds or amounts paid in advance for services that have yet to be provided (these are called prepayments—see Chapter 3, Prepayments and accruals: recording transactions in the statement of profit or loss and statement of financial position for a detailed discussion of prepayments). While trade and other receivables represent the right to cash in the future, they are not cash yet and so are recognised in this separate category of current assets. You will find some sets of accounts that refer to trade and other receivables as debtors.
- Cash and cash equivalents: this category of current assets comprises of amounts of cash held in tills at the end of the year, cash held in the company's current account at the bank and cash held in short-term deposit accounts with bankers and other financial institutions (for more detail on the components of cash and cash equivalents, see Chapter 6, Cash and cash equivalents).

GIVE ME AN EXAMPLE 2.3   Current assets

When looking at the published financial statements of companies, you will find the same categories of current assets presented on the statement of financial position. The statement of financial position of Nichols plc, an international soft drinks business, at 31 December 2017 shows the same current assets as Bunns the Bakers.

	Years ended 31 December	
	2017	2016
Current assets	£000	£000
Inventories	4,815	6,717
Trade and other receivables	34,740	31,508
Cash and cash equivalents	36,058	39,754
Total current assets	**75,613**	**77,979**

Source: *Nichols plc financial statements 2017* www.nicholsplc.co.uk

MULTIPLE CHOICE QUESTIONS   Are you confident that you can distinguish between different types of current assets? Go to the **online workbook** and have a go at Multiple choice questions 2.1 to make sure you can make these distinctions.

2

The distinction between non-current and current assets

The distinction between non-current and current assets comes down to one of time. As we have seen, non-current assets are held by businesses to provide benefits in accounting periods exceeding one year. On the other hand, current assets are held only for a short time in order to produce goods to be sold to convert into cash which can then be used to buy in more raw materials to produce more goods to convert into more cash in a short but constantly repeating trading cycle.

However, to decide whether a resource is a non-current or current asset it is also important to determine the business in which an entity is engaged. For example, you might think that a car would be a non-current asset in any business, an asset to be used for the long term. But if that car is parked on the premises of a motor trader, is this car an item of inventory, held in stock for resale, a car owned by the motor trading business for long-term use in the business or the property of a member of staff who drives to work each day (and so not a business asset at all)? Further enquiries would have to be made to determine whether the car is a business asset and, if it is, the exact statement of financial position classification of this vehicle.

WHY IS THIS RELEVANT TO ME?   Non-current and current assets

To enable you as an accounting professional to:

- Develop a clear understanding of the different types of assets entities recognise on their statement of financial position

- Distinguish effectively between the two types of assets

- Understand how the different types of assets can be used in evaluating entities' efficiency and working capital management (discussed in detail in Chapters 8 and 9)

GO BACK OVER THIS AGAIN!   How easily do you think you can distinguish between current and non-current assets? Go to the **online workbook** Exercises 2.3 to make sure you can make this distinction.

LIABILITIES

As shown in Illustration 2.1, liabilities appear lower down the statement of financial position and represent amounts that are owed to parties outside the business. As with assets, the first questions to ask are: 'What is a liability?' and 'What does a liability represent?'

The International Accounting Standards Board's *Conceptual Framework for Financial Reporting* provides the following definition of a liability:

A present obligation of the entity to transfer an economic resource as a result of past events.

Source: IASB *Conceptual Framework for Financial Reporting*, paragraph 4.26

2

While this definition again might seem complex, your experience gained in unravelling the meaning of the definition of assets earlier will certainly help you in understanding the various terms employed here. To put it simply, liabilities are the contractual or legal claims of outside parties against an entity. These contractual or legal claims may be short-term (current liabilities) or long-term (non-current liabilities). Again, let's break down this definition into its constituent parts in order to enable us to apply it in determining whether an entity has a liability or not:

- Present obligation: the obligation must exist at the statement of financial position date in order for any liability arising under that obligation to be recognised in the statement of financial position. Therefore, entities cannot recognise just any liability that they think they might incur at any time in the future. The event giving rise to the obligation must have taken place by the statement of financial position date to enable the entity to recognise that liability.

- As a result of past events: to give rise to an obligation, it is likely that a contract has been signed agreeing to pay for goods delivered but not yet paid for from a supplier or to take out a loan or an overdraft at the bank that will have to be repaid at some point in the future.

- Economic resource: the obligation will result in the entity transferring cash to an outside party in order to settle the liability or, possibly, transferring other assets by way of settlement. The term economic resource has exactly the same definition as that provided under Assets (this chapter).

Importantly, the obligation must be unavoidable: if the entity can avoid transferring cash or other economic resources then there is no obligation and no liability exists.

The IASB Conceptual Framework also requires that liabilities measured and presented in the statement of financial position must meet the same standards of faithful representation as required for assets (this chapter, Assets: faithful representation). Where these standards of faithful representation are not met, no liability is recognised in the statement of financial position. Example 2.2 shows how liability recognition works in practice.

EXAMPLE 2.2

Let us take the earlier example of Bunns the Bakers in Example 2.1. When the company bought the city centre shop from the property developer 10 years ago, the purchase was financed by a loan from the bank of £500,000. This loan is currently repayable in full in 8 years' time. Does this loan constitute a liability of the business? Applying our criteria:

- Does Bunns the Bakers have a present obligation at the statement of financial position date? Yes: the loan exists and is outstanding at the current year end. The obligating event (taking out the loan) had taken place by the statement of financial position date.

- Is the obligation to repay the loan unavoidable? Yes: the bank will hold signed documentation from the company agreeing that the loan was taken out and there will be entries in the relevant account at the bank and in bank statements to show the loan being received by the company. Should the company try to avoid repaying the loan, the bank will be able to enforce its legal rights against the company for repayment of the loan.

- Does the obligation arise as a result of past events? Yes: a loan agreement was signed by Bunns the Bakers at the time the loan was taken out and the money transferred to the company with which to buy the shop.

- Will Bunns the Bakers transfer an economic resource? Yes: the company will have to transfer cash to settle the obligation. If the company is unable to meet the obligation in cash, the bank will accept the shop as a suitable substitute for repayment of the loan. The shop embodies the potential to produce economic benefits as we saw in Example 2.1, so taking the shop instead of repayment will still be a transfer of an economic resource.

- Does the measurement of the liability result in a faithful representation? Yes: the loan is measured at £500,000 as a result of the cash transferred. This measurement is complete, neutral and free from error and so is a faithful representation of the amount of the obligation due to the bank.

Thus, the loan represents a liability of the business as it meets the IASB criteria for recognition of a liability.

Liability recognition: summary of the steps to follow

Diagrammatically, the steps to follow to determine whether a liability should be recognised on the statement of financial position are shown in Figure 2.4.

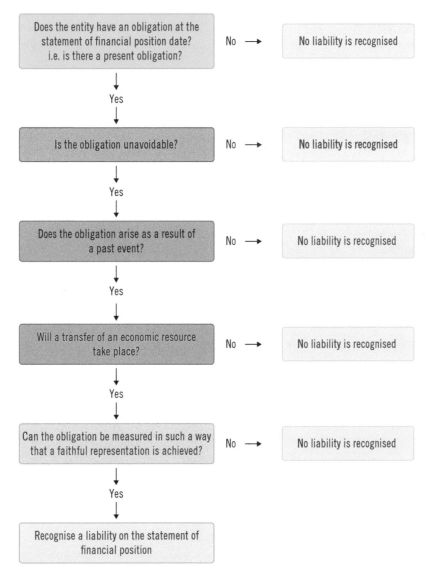

Figure 2.4 Steps in determining whether a liability should be recognised on the statement of financial position or not in accordance with the IASB Conceptual Framework for Financial Reporting

WHY IS THIS RELEVANT TO ME?   Liabilities

To enable you as an accounting professional to:

• Understand what liabilities on the statement of financial position actually represent

• Understand the strict criteria that must be met before a liability can be recognised on the statement of financial position

• Be equipped with the necessary tools to determine whether a liability should be recognised on the statement of financial position or not

SUMMARY OF KEY CONCEPTS   Are you sure that you can define a liability? Go to the **online workbook** to revise this definition with Summary of key concepts 2.3 to reinforce your knowledge.

GO BACK OVER THIS AGAIN!   How well have you grasped the liability recognition criteria? Go to the **online workbook** Exercises 2.4 to make sure you understand how the liability recognition criteria are used in practice.

LIABILITIES IN THE STATEMENT OF FINANCIAL POSITION

Now that we have considered what the term 'liabilities' means and the criteria for liability recognition in the statement of financial position, let us look again at the statement of financial position of Bunns the Bakers plc in Illustration 2.1 to consider what sort of liabilities a company might recognise.

Liabilities, just as in the case of assets, are split into non-current and current. Total liabilities are calculated by adding current and non-current liabilities together, as shown in Figure 2.5.

Non-current liabilities are long-term liabilities that the entity will only have to meet in more than one year's time while current liabilities will have to be paid within the course of the next year. Current liabilities are not due on the day immediately after the statement of financial position date but they will be due for settlement over the course of the next 12 months.

Figure 2.5 The composition of total liabilities

Current liabilities

Just as with current assets, current liabilities are short-term liabilities that are constantly changing. Looking at Bunns the Bakers' statement of financial position the following liabilities are shown:

- Current portion of long-term borrowings: these are the loan instalments due to be repaid to lenders within the next 12 months.

- Trade and other payables: any organisation that is involved in business will trade on credit with their suppliers, consuming services and ordering goods that are both delivered but not paid for immediately. Customers then either use the goods received to produce more goods to sell to the public and businesses or just resell those goods. Suppliers are paid from the proceeds of the sales of goods produced or resold. Normal trading terms are that suppliers are (usually) paid within 30 days of receipt of goods by the customer. Clearly, suppliers will not wait a long time for payment for goods delivered as they have their own suppliers and employees to pay. Therefore, suppliers will expect their cash to be returned to them quickly so trade and other payables are short-term, current liabilities. In the case of Bunns the Bakers, trade payables will consist of amounts of money owed to suppliers for flour, eggs, sugar, salt and other bakery ingredients as well as services provided by, for example, their legal advisers or their accountants.

- Current tax liabilities: Bunns the Bakers plc has made a profit over the course of the year. This profit is subject to tax and the tax liability on this year's profit is recognised as an obligation on the statement of financial position. The government will want the tax due reasonably quickly so that it can meet its own obligations to provide services to the public and contribute to the running of government departments so this, too, is a short-term, current liability.

Non-current liabilities

On Bunns the Bakers' statement of financial position, the following non-current liabilities are represented:

- Long-term borrowings: these are loans and other finance provided by lenders to finance the long-term non-current assets of the business. In the case of Bunns the Bakers, these could be loans used to finance the acquisition of shops (as in Example 2.2 in this chapter), the building of a new state of the art bakery or the purchase of new plant and equipment with which to produce goods. Other companies may take out loans to finance the acquisition of other companies. Long-term borrowings are repayable in accounting periods beyond the next 12 months.

- Long-term provisions: these are liabilities that the entity knows it must meet but which will not be due for payment in the next accounting period but in accounting periods beyond the next 12 months. Examples of such long-term provisions would be deferred taxation and pensions, two highly technical accounting issues that you will consider in depth at a later stage of your studies.

GIVE ME AN EXAMPLE 2.4   Non-current and current liabilities

The group balance sheet (= statement of financial position) at 31 March 2018 of Experian, the credit services, decision analytics, marketing services and consumer services group illustrates the presentation of current and non-current liabilities in practice.

	31 March	
	2018	2017
Current liabilities	US$m	US$m
Trade and other payables	1,294	1,109
Borrowings	956	759
Current tax liabilities	278	150
Provisions	70	50
Other financial liabilities	86	15
	2,684	**2,083**
Non-current liabilities	US$m	US$m
Trade and other payables	44	15
Borrowings	2,558	2,285
Deferred tax liability	206	296
Post-employment benefit obligations	58	54
Other financial liabilities	51	249
	2,917	**2,899**

Source: Experian. *Annual Report 2018* http://www.experianplc.com

As in the case of Bunns the Bakers, Experian's current and non-current liabilities present trade and other payables, borrowings, current tax liabilities and provisions for deferred tax and pension liabilities (post-employment benefit obligations). Other financial liabilities refer to derivative transactions, another complex accounting topic that will be covered at a later stage of your studies.

WHY IS THIS RELEVANT TO ME?   Current and non-current liabilities

To enable you as an accounting professional to:

• Understand the different types of liabilities an entity recognises on its statement of financial position

• Distinguish between the two types of liabilities

• Use the different types of liabilities in assessing an entity's financial position, short-term liquidity and long-term financial stability (discussed in further detail in Chapter 9)

GO BACK OVER THIS AGAIN!   Are you convinced that you can distinguish between current and non-current liabilities? Go to the **online workbook** Exercises 2.5 to make sure you can make this distinction.

THE ACCOUNTING EQUATION

Before we discuss the third element on Bunns the Bakers' statement of financial position, equity, we need to think about the accounting equation. Looking at the statement of financial position, we notice that the net assets (total assets – total liabilities) and the total equity are the same figure. What does this tell us about the relationship between the assets, liabilities and equity in an entity? From this observation, we can draw up the following equations that express the link between the three elements in the statement of financial position:

Either

Total assets = total liabilities + equity

Or:

Total assets – total liabilities = equity

Equity is thus the difference between the total assets (the sum of the current and non-current assets) and the total liabilities (the sum of the current and non-current liabilities). As the two equations add to the same figure, the statement of financial position is said to balance. We shall see in Chapter 4, Double entry and the accounting equation, how this accounting equation forms the foundation upon which double entry and the duality principle are built.

WHY IS THIS RELEVANT TO ME?   The accounting equation

To enable you as an accounting professional to:

- Appreciate how the two halves of the statement of financial position balance
- Balance your own statements of financial position when you draw these up in the future
- Provide the framework within which to understand double-entry bookkeeping

---

SUMMARY OF KEY CONCEPTS   Can you state the accounting equation? Go to the **online workbook** to revise this equation with Summary of key concepts 2.4.

EQUITY

The International Accounting Standards Board defines equity as:

> The residual interest in the assets of the entity after deducting all its liabilities.
>
> Source: IASB *Conceptual Framework for Financial Reporting*, paragraph 4.63

This is exactly the same as the accounting equation above that says assets – liabilities = equity. In theory, equity represents the amount that owners of the entity should receive if the assets were all sold and the liabilities were all settled at their statement of financial position amounts. The

2

cash received from these asset sales less payments made to discharge liabilities would belong to the owners and they would receive this cash on the winding up of the business. As well as the term equity, you will often find the term capital being used to describe this difference between assets and liabilities.

The components of equity

Different forms of business entity present the equity part of the statement of financial position in different ways. We shall discuss the characteristics of different types of business entity in much more detail in Chapter 7. The two ways in which to present the equity section of the statement of financial position that we shall consider at this point are firstly the equity of limited companies and public limited companies (both incorporated businesses) and secondly the equity of sole traders and other unincorporated businesses.

1. The equity section of the statement of financial position: limited companies and public limited companies (plcs)

Bunns the Bakers' (which is a public limited company, a plc) equity is made up of the following elements:

(a) Called up share capital: this is the number of shares issued multiplied by the par value (face value or nominal value) of each share (Chapter 7, Share capital: share issues at par value).

(b) Share premium: where each share is issued for an amount greater than its par value, then any amount received in excess of par value is entered into the share premium account (Chapter 7, Share capital: shares issued at a premium).

(c) Retained earnings: these are profits that the business has earned in past accounting periods that have not been distributed to shareholders as dividends.

You will see many company statements of financial position in practice that have many different accounts (other reserves) under the equity heading (see Give me an example 2.5). Many of these accounts arise from statutory requirements governing transactions entered into by the company and you will look at these at later stages of your studies. The basic calculation of equity for limited companies and plcs is shown in Figure 2.6.

Figure 2.6 Limited companies and plcs: the components of equity

GIVE ME AN EXAMPLE 2.5   Equity

The consolidated balance sheet (= statement of financial position) of First Group plc at 31 March 2018 provides an illustration of the many different accounts that can make up equity. As in the case of Bunns the Bakers, First Group plc reports figures for share capital, share premium and retained earnings.

| | 31 March | |
	2018	2017
EQUITY	£m	£m
Share capital	60.5	60.4
Share premium	681.4	678.9
Hedging reserve	16.5	(17.9)
Other reserves	4.6	4.6
Own shares	(6.3)	(1.2)
Translation reserve	383.5	708.4
Retained earnings	340.6	621.9
	1,480.8	**2,055.1**

Source: *First Group annual report and accounts for the year ended 31 March 2018* www.firstgroupplc.com

2. Sole traders and unincorporated entities

Not all businesses are incorporated as limited companies. Such businesses do not, therefore, have issued share capital, but they still have an equity section. For sole traders and unincorporated entities, this is called the capital account. This comprises of the following headings:

(a) Capital at the start of the year: this is the capital account balance at the end of the previous accounting period. At the beginning of the first accounting period, the first year in which the unincorporated entity starts trading, the balance at the start of the year is £Nil.

(b) Capital introduced: this is the owner's own money that has been introduced into the business during the current accounting period.

(c) Retained profits for the year: any profit retained in the business during the year is added to the capital account as this profit belongs to the business's owner. Where the business makes a loss during the year, then this loss is deducted from the capital account.

(d) Capital withdrawn: the business's owner will draw money out of the business to meet personal rather than business expenses during the year. This is treated as a repayment of part of the capital of the business to the owner. These withdrawals of capital are called drawings and are a deduction from the capital account. This is an application of the business entity convention (Chapter 3, Drawings and the business entity assumption) that states that the business and its owner(s) are totally separate individuals. Only business transactions are included in the financial statements of the business with any non-business, personal transactions excluded.

2

Just as in the case of limited companies and plcs, the amount in the capital account is the amount that would, in theory, be paid out to the owner(s) of the business if all the assets of the business were sold at the amounts recorded in the statement of financial position and all the liabilities of the business were settled at their statement of financial position amounts. The components and calculation of the capital account (equity) balance for sole traders and unincorporated entities are shown in Figure 2.7.

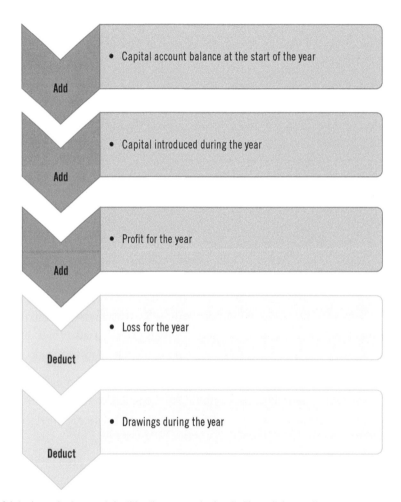

- Capital account balance at the start of the year

  Add

- Capital introduced during the year

  Add

- Profit for the year

  Add

- Loss for the year

  Deduct

- Drawings during the year

  Deduct

Figure 2.7 Sole traders and unincorporated entities: the components of equity (the capital account)

WHY IS THIS RELEVANT TO ME?   Equity and the components of equity

To enable you as an accounting professional to:

- Understand that equity is the difference between an entity's total assets and total liabilities
- Appreciate the different components of equity in incorporated and unincorporated businesses
- Distinguish elements of equity from assets and liabilities

MULTIPLE CHOICE QUESTIONS   Are you quite confident that you could calculate the equity of a business from a given set of information? Go to the **online workbook** and have a go at Multiple choice questions 2.2 to make sure you can make these calculations.

SUMMARY OF KEY CONCEPTS   Are you sure you can state the components of equity? Go to the **online workbook** to revise these components with Summary of key concepts 2.5 and 2.6.

2

DRAWING UP THE STATEMENT OF FINANCIAL POSITION

We now know what assets and liabilities are and how they relate to equity, but what steps should we follow in drawing up the statement of financial position? This section provides a step-by-step approach using Example 2.3 to preparing the statement of financial position from the account balances at the end of the financial year.

EXAMPLE 2.3

Illustration 2.2 shows a list of balances for Misfits Limited at 31 December 2019. You are required to draw up the statement of financial position from this list of balances.

Illustration 2.2 Misfits Limited: account balances at 31 December 2019

	£000
Trade receivables	2,000
Trade payables	1,500
Bank loan repayable in six years' time	10,000
Bank overdraft	200
Land and buildings	15,000
Trademarks	1,000
Fixtures and fittings	2,500
Share capital	1,800
Retained earnings	7,500
Share premium	2,300
Inventories	2,750
Cash in the tills	50

Guidelines on the approach to adopt in drawing up the statement of financial position

1. Decide whether each of the balances is an asset, a liability or an element of equity.

2. Once you have categorised the balances, think about whether the assets and liabilities are current or non-current.

2

3. Some of the balances might need adding together to produce one figure in the statement of financial position. For example, there might be cash in hand or in the safe, cash in the bank current account and cash on deposit in a short-term investment account at the bank. All of these balances would be added together and shown as one figure for cash and cash equivalents.

4. Once you have made all your decisions, slot the figures into the relevant headings (use the headings in Illustration 2.1, adding any additional headings you might need and removing headings you do not need), add it all up and it should balance.

Illustration 2.3 presents the statement of financial position of Misfits Limited at 31 December 2019 using the figures from Illustration 2.2.

Illustration 2.3 Misfits Limited: statement of financial position at 31 December 2019

	£000	Note
ASSETS		
Non-current assets		
Intangible assets	1,000	1
Property, plant and equipment	17,500	2
	18,500	3
Current assets		
Inventories	2,750	4
Trade receivables	2,000	4
Cash and cash equivalents	50	4
	4,800	5
Total assets	**23,300**	6
LIABILITIES		
Current liabilities		
Bank overdraft (you could call this short-term borrowings)	200	7
Trade payables	1,500	7
	1,700	8
Non-current liabilities		
Bank loan (you could call this long-term borrowings)	**10,000**	7
Total liabilities	**11,700**	9
Net assets (total assets – total liabilities)	**11,600**	10
EQUITY		
Called up share capital	1,800	11
Share premium	2,300	11
Retained earnings	7,500	11
Total equity	**11,600**	12

Notes to the above statement of financial position for Misfits Limited:

1. Trademarks are intangible assets, as we noted earlier (this chapter, Non-current assets).

2. Land and buildings and fixtures and fittings are both classified under the heading 'Property, plant and equipment'. The land and buildings are property and the fixtures and fittings are plant and equipment. £15,000,000 for the land and buildings + £2,500,000 for the fixtures and fittings give the total figure of £17,500,000 for Property, plant and equipment.

3. This is the total of the two non-current asset headings £1,000,000 + £17,500,000 = £18,500,000.

4. These figures are as given in the list of balances.

5. £4,800,000 is the total of all the current assets added together.

6. £23,300,000 is the total non-current assets of £18,500,000 added to the total current assets of £4,800,000 to give the figure for total assets.

7. These figures are as given in the list of balances. If you were in any doubt that the loan is a non-current liability, look at the timing of repayment: the loan is due for repayment in six years' time so this liability is repayable more than 12 months after the statement of financial position date. Remember that current liabilities include all obligations payable within 12 months of the year-end date so that any liability payable after this is a non-current liability.

8. £1,700,000 is the total of the bank overdraft of £200,000 and of the trade payables of £1,500,000.

9. £11,700,000 is the total of the current liabilities of £1,700,000 and of the non-current liabilities of £10,000,000.

10. The figure for net assets is given by deducting the total liabilities figure of £11,700,000 from the total assets figure of £23,300,000 to give you net assets (total assets – total liabilities) of £11,600,000.

11. Called up share capital, Share premium and Retained earnings are all as given in the list of balances.

12. This is the total of the three elements of equity added together.

WHY IS THIS RELEVANT TO ME?   Drawing up the statement of financial position

To enable you as an accounting professional to:
- Understand how the statement of financial position is put together from the balances at the year-end date
- Draw up and present your own statements of financial position

---

SHOW ME HOW TO DO IT   Did you understand how Misfits Limited's statement of financial position was drawn up? View Video presentation 2.1 in the **online workbook** to see a practical demonstration of how this statement of financial position was put together.

2

NUMERICAL EXERCISES   Are you sure that you could draw up a statement of financial position from a list of year end balances? Go to the **online workbook** Numerical exercises 2.1 to practice this technique.

HOW ARE ASSETS AND LIABILITIES VALUED?
Historic cost v. fair value

How should we value assets and liabilities for inclusion in the statement of financial position? At their cost price? Selling price? Market value? Or some other amount?

Accounting has traditionally dictated that the value of all assets and liabilities recognised in the statement of financial position should be based on their original cost: this is called the historic cost convention. Thus, for example, inventory is valued at its cost to the business, not its selling price or current market value, while trade payables are valued at their invoice amount and loans are valued at the amount borrowed less any repayments made.

However, this accounting convention has been relaxed over the past 50 years and entities can now choose to value different classes of assets either at their historic cost or at their fair value. Fair value is equivalent to market value, the amount at which an asset could be sold or a liability settled in the open market. However, although the cost or fair value option exists, organisations rarely choose the fair value alternative. The only class of assets that entities might wish to present at their fair value is land and buildings as these assets tend to rise in value over time. For all other assets and liabilities historic cost is preferred.

You will consider the arguments both in favour of and against valuing assets and liabilities at fair value or historic cost at a later stage of your studies. For now, you just need to be aware that these options exist.

A mixture of original cost and fair value: problems

So, users can be presented with a mixture of assets at cost and at fair value. Does this failure to present all assets and liabilities consistently at their fair values cause any problems for users of the statement of financial position?

Historic cost is seen as objective as it is verifiable by reference to a transaction at a fixed point in time. It is thus a reliable measure as it was determined by the market at the date of the transaction. With short-term current assets and liabilities this is not a problem as these assets and liabilities are, as we have seen, always changing and being replaced by new current assets and new current liabilities at more recent, up-to-date values. However, when long-term, non-current assets and liabilities are measured at historic cost these costs gradually become more and more out of date as time moves on. As a result, these costs become less and less relevant in decision making as the market moves forward and asset and loan values rise and fall in real terms with the onward march of the economy.

We will not consider this problem any further in this text, but it is a difficulty of which you should be aware. The cost v. fair/market value debate has been raging for well over a century and an acceptable solution is no nearer than it was when the problem was first pointed out. It is therefore going to be a continuing shortcoming of the statement of financial position for the in-definite future and a limitation that you will need to take into account whenever you are looking at sets of financial statements in your accounting career.

WHY IS THIS RELEVANT TO ME?   Historic cost, valuation and fair/market values

To enable you as an accounting professional to:

- Understand the basis upon which the figures in the statement of financial position are deter-mined
- Gain an early awareness of the limitations of continuing to value non-current assets and non-current liabilities at historic cost
- Appreciate that there are alternative valuation bases for non-current assets and liabilities, but that companies rarely make use of these alternatives

---

WHAT DOES THE STATEMENT OF FINANCIAL POSITION SHOW?

This leads us neatly on to a discussion of what the statement of financial position shows and what it does not show.

Put simply, the statement of financial position shows the financial situation of an entity on the last day of its accounting year. However, it is important to remember that the statement of financial position just shows the financial situation on that one day in the year and it is thus a snapshot of the entity at this one point in time. A totally different view would be shown if the picture were taken on any other day in the year. It is true to say that, at this one point in time, the statement of financial position does show the financially measurable resources (assets) and financially measurable obligations (liabilities) of the business in money terms, but this might seem to present a rather limited view.

In order to gain a better understanding of what the statement of financial position represents, it is useful to consider what the statement of financial position does not show.

WHAT THE STATEMENT OF FINANCIAL POSITION DOES NOT SHOW

The statement of financial position does not show:

- All the assets of the organisation. The statement of financial position does not include or value the most valuable assets of an organisation. These comprise the skills and knowledge of the employees, goodwill, brands, traditions and all the other intangible but extremely difficult to value assets that make an organisation what it is. All entities are so much more than the sum of their financial assets and liabilities. Any attempted valuation of these assets would present values that were so uncertain and subjective that the information presented would lack the relevance and faithful representation required by the IASB in its Conceptual Framework (this chapter, Assets: faithful representation).

- All the liabilities of a business. There might be liabilities for damage caused to the environment or to consumers as a result of product liability legislation, claims for damages or breaches of contract, none of which has come to light by the year-end date: as a result, these additional liabilities will not be reflected in the statement of financial position at the accounting year end.

- The market value of an entity. This is a common misconception about the statement of financial position. The monetary value of any entity is determined by the amount a third party would be willing to pay not only for all the known assets and liabilities but also for the unrecognised assets of the organisation noted previously. However, the amount an outside party would be willing to pay will change on a daily basis as more information comes to light about hidden liabilities or the true value of assets or as the economy moves from a boom to a recession or vice versa.

The IASB recognises these limitations of financial statements in full:

> General purpose financial reports are not designed to show the value of a reporting entity; but they provide information to help existing and potential investors, lenders and other creditors to estimate the value of the reporting entity … The *Conceptual Framework* does not allow the recognition in the statement of financial position of items that do not meet the definition of an asset, a liability or equity. Only items that meet the definition of an asset, a liability or equity are recognised in the statement of financial position.
>
> Source: IASB *Conceptual Framework for Financial Reporting*, paragraphs 1.7, 5.5 and 5.6

You should therefore remember that what the statement of financial position does not recognise is just as or even more important than what it does include.

EXAMPLE 2.4

A moment's thought will show you that this is equally true of your own circumstances. You might know the monetary value of the cash you hold in various bank and savings accounts and you might have a collection of various assets such as a tablet, a mobile phone, digital music and clothing, all of which you could value in money terms. But these assets are not the sum total of what represents you. There are your friends, family, memories and achievements, none of which can be valued or quantified, but which are just as or even more important to you than those tangible items that can be given a monetary value. Give me an example 2.6 demonstrates this further.

GIVE ME AN EXAMPLE 2.6   The statement of financial position does not show the true value of an entity

The published report and accounts for the year ended 31 December 2016 of Ablynx, the Belgian biotech group, showed a net assets (total assets less total liabilities) figure of €103m. In January 2018, Sanofi agreed to pay €3,900m to acquire Ablynx. Sanofi was bidding not for Ablynx's net assets but for its nanobody technology, its drugs in development, patented medicines and research, all of which represent value over and above the value of the net assets in the statement of financial position.

Sources: *Ablynx annual report for the year ended 31 December 2016* www.ablynx.com; *The Financial Times 30 January 2018* and Hargreaves Lansdown http://www.hl.co.uk/shares/stock-market-news/company--news/sanofi-to-buy-belgian-biotech-group-ablynx-for-3.9bn

WHY IS THIS RELEVANT TO ME?   What the statement of financial position shows and does not show

To enable you as an accounting professional to:

- Appreciate the limitations of the monetary information presented in the statement of financial position
- Gain the necessary awareness of what the statement of financial position includes and does not include
- Be aware that the statement of financial position will not provide all the answers needed to evaluate an entity's financial and economic position
- Think outside the parameters of the statement of financial position when assessing an entity's standing in the business world

GO BACK OVER THIS AGAIN!   Do you think that you can say clearly what the statement of financial position does and does not show? Go to the **online workbook** Exercises 2.6 to test your knowledge of this area.

THE DUAL ASPECT CONCEPT

The statement of financial position for Misfits Limited was drawn up from a list of balances at a given point in time. But businesses are not static and new transactions will change the figures on the statement of financial position as they occur. These transactions have an effect on two or more accounts and may cause the balances on those accounts to rise or fall as new assets or liabilities are created or as assets are used up or liabilities settled. Accountants describe this dual aspect as double entry and the entries to the accounts affected by transactions as debits and credits. You might prefer to think of these transactions initially as pluses and minuses or increases and decreases in the various accounts in the following examples and in the online workbook. We will be looking at double entry in much greater depth and detail in Chapters 4 and 5. For the time being, Examples 2.5 and 2.6 together with the end of chapter exercises and the online workbook materials will provide you with a useful introduction to the dual effect that transactions have on the statement of financial position balances.

Firstly, think about how you would record the receipt of goods from a supplier that are to be paid for in 30 days' time. This receipt of goods will increase the inventory that is held by the business, but also increase the amounts owed to trade payables. If the goods were bought for cash, this would still increase the inventory but reduce the cash held in the bank if the company has a positive balance in their account. In both of these examples, two accounts were affected, inventory and trade payables or cash.

The following examples will show you how the dual aspect concept works and how the statement of financial position will still balance after each transaction is completed.

EXAMPLE 2.5

Misfits Limited's statement of financial position at 31 December 2019 is reproduced in Illustration 2.4 in the left hand column. On 2 January 2020 the company receives a £50,000 payment from one of its trade receivables. This payment is paid into the bank account. How would this transaction be recorded in the statement of financial position? Trade receivables go down by £50,000 as this receivable has paid what was owed. The money has been paid into the bank so the bank overdraft (money owed to the bank) also goes down as less money is now owed to the bank. Recording the transactions as shown in Illustration 2.4 gives us the new statement of financial position at 2 January 2020:

Illustration 2.4 Misfits Limited: the effect on the statement of financial position of cash received from a trade receivable

Misfits Limited	Statement of financial position at 31 December 2019	Increase (plus)	Decrease (minus)	Statement of financial position at 2 January 2020
	£000	£000	£000	£000
Non-current assets				
Intangible assets	1,000			1,000
Property, plant and equipment	17,500			17,500
	18,500			18,500
Current assets				
Inventories	2,750			2,750
Trade receivables	2,000		−50	1,950
Cash and cash equivalents	50			50
	4,800			4,750
Total assets	23,300			23,250
Current liabilities				
Bank overdraft	200		−50	150
Trade payables	1,500			1,500
	1,700			1,650
Non-current liabilities				
Bank loan	10,000			10,000
Total liabilities	11,700			11,650
Net assets	11,600			11,600
EQUITY				
Called up share capital	1,800			1,800
Share premium	2,300			2,300
Retained earnings	7,500			7,500
	11,600			11,600

Current assets have reduced by £50,000 and current liabilities have reduced by £50,000 so the statement of financial position still balances.

EXAMPLE 2.6

Let's try another example. On 3 January 2020, the company receives £100,000 of inventory from a supplier, the invoice to be paid in 30 days' time, and acquires a new piece of property, plant and equipment for £75,000 paid for from the bank. How will these transactions be shown in the statement of financial position? Illustration 2.5 shows the account headings affected.

Illustration 2.5 Misfits Limited: the effect on the statement of financial position of cash paid to buy new plant and equipment and inventory acquired on credit

Misfits Limited	Statement of financial position at 2 January 2020 £000	Increase (plus) £000	Decrease (minus) £000	Statement of financial position at 3 January 2020 £000
Non-current assets				
Intangible assets	1,000			1,000
Property, plant and equipment	17,500	+ 75		17,575
	18,500			18,575
Current assets				
Inventories	2,750	+ 100		2,850
Trade receivables	1,950			1,950
Cash and cash equivalents	50			50
	4,750			4,850
Total assets	23,250			23,425
Current liabilities				
Bank overdraft	150	+ 75		225
Trade payables	1,500	+ 100		1,600
	1,650			1,825
Non-current liabilities				
Bank loan	10,000			10,000
Total liabilities	11,650			11,825
Net assets	11,600			11,600
EQUITY				
Called up share capital	1,800			1,800
Share premium	2,300			2,300
Retained earnings	7,500			7,500
	11,600			11,600

Non-current assets increase by £75,000 and the overdraft also increases by £75,000 as a result of the acquisition of the new piece of equipment paid for by cheque from the bank: assets have risen, but more is now owed to the bank as more money has been paid out so the bank overdraft goes up. Similarly, inventory has increased by £100,000, but more is now owed to trade payables so this figure has also risen by £100,000.

2

GO BACK OVER THIS AGAIN!   Are you sure you understand how the dual aspect concept applies to new transactions? Go to the **online workbook** Exercises 2.7 to look at further examples of the dual aspect and the effect of new transactions on the statement of financial position.

NUMERICAL EXERCISES   Are you quite convinced that you could record new transactions accurately in the statement of financial position? Go to the **online workbook** Numerical exercises 2.2 to test out your abilities in this area.

MULTIPLE CHOICE QUESTIONS   Are you confident that you could state the correct entries to record a new transaction in the statement of financial position? Go to the **online workbook** and have a go at Multiple choice questions 2.3 to test your knowledge in this area.

This is probably the first time you have come across the duality principle, so if you are finding this confusing this should not surprise you. Further practice at more examples will help to reduce this confusion and you will gradually appreciate how the duality principle works and how transactions affect two or more accounts on the statement of financial position. Chapters 4 and 5 together with the exercises in the online workbook and the extended case study will give you a wealth of practice in double entry and the dual effect of transactions. Working through these two chapters and the associated exercises will enable you to gain a very firm grasp of this essential technique for recording transactions.

CHAPTER SUMMARY

You should now have learnt that:

• An asset is a present economic resource controlled by the entity as a result of past events

• An economic resource is a right that has the potential to produce economic benefits

• A liability is a present obligation of the entity to transfer an economic resource as a result of past events

• Assets and liabilities are only recognised in the statement of financial position if their monetary values can be faithfully represented

• Non-current assets are resources not purchased for resale in the normal course of business and are held for long-term use in the business to produce goods or services

• Current assets consist of inventory, trade and other receivables and cash and cash equivalents whose economic benefits will be used up within 12 months of the statement of financial position date

• Current liabilities are obligations that will be settled within 12 months of the statement of financial position date, while non-current liabilities are obligations that will be settled in accounting periods beyond the next 12 months

- The accounting equation states that total assets − total liabilities = equity (capital)

- Some assets in the statement of financial position may be shown at historic cost, while some may be shown at fair (market) value

- The statement of financial position only presents figures for monetary resources (assets) whose economic benefits have not yet been consumed and figures for monetary obligations that have not yet been settled

- The statement of financial position does not show all the assets and liabilities of an entity nor does it give a market value for an entity

- Under the dual aspect concept (the duality principle), new accounting transactions affect two or more statement of financial position account headings

QUICK REVISION   Test your knowledge with the online flashcards in Summary of key concepts and attempt the Multiple choice questions, all in the **online workbook**.

END-OF-CHAPTER QUESTIONS

Solutions to these questions can be found in the **online workbook**.

❯ DEVELOP YOUR UNDERSTANDING

❯ Question 2.1

Using the criteria outlined in the summary in Figure 2.2, explain why the following items are assets that entities recognise on the statement of financial position:

(a)   Motor vehicles purchased by an entity.

(b)   Inventory received from suppliers.

(c)   Cash and cash equivalents.

Using the criteria outlined in the summary in Figure 2.2, explain why the following items are *not* assets and why they are not recognised on entities' statements of financial position:

(a)   Redundant plant and machinery that has been replaced by faster, more technologically advanced machinery. This redundant plant and machinery is no longer used in the business or industry and has no resale or scrap value.

(b)   A trade receivable from a customer who is bankrupt and from whom no payment is expected.

(c)   A highly skilled workforce.

❯ Question 2.2

The directors of Oxford Academicals Football Club Limited are discussing whether player registrations can be recognised as assets on the club's statement of financial position. There are two groups of players. The first group consists of those players whose contracts have been bought by the club from other teams in the transfer market. The second group is made up of players who have come up through the youth scheme and who have been playing at various levels for the club since the age of 12. The accounts department has informed the directors that the transfer fees for the bought in contracts amount to £25 million. The directors, however, cannot agree on a valuation for the players that have been developed by the club. The managing director thinks these players should be valued at £30 million, while the finance director thinks this is far too high a figure and would value these players at £15 million. Various offers have been received from other clubs to sign the players developed by the club and the combined values of these offers have ranged from £10 million to £25 million. Advise the directors on whether any of the players' registrations can be recognised in the statement of financial position and, if they can be so recognised, the category of assets that these registrations would appear under and the value that can be recognised.

> **Question 2.3**

The following balances have been extracted from the books of the limited companies Alma, Bella, Carla, Deborah and Eloise at 30 April 2019. Using the statement of financial position format presented in this chapter, draw up the statements of financial position for the five companies at 30 April 2019.

	Alma	Bella	Carla	Deborah	Eloise
	£000	£000	£000	£000	£000
Share capital	1,000	5,000	2,500	3,000	4,500
Cash at bank	—	800	—	550	200
Goodwill	—	—	400	250	500
Inventory	1,000	700	800	750	900
Trade payables	1,450	4,000	1,750	5,600	5,800
Plant and machinery	2,000	9,500	3,750	4,250	5,000
Trade receivables	1,750	3,000	2,750	2,950	3,100
Bank overdraft	800	—	1,250	—	—
Loans due on 30 April 2026	1,000	10,000	1,500	—	—
Loans due by 30 April 2020	200	400	300	—	—
Land and buildings	4,500	17,100	10,200	8,750	15,000
Taxation payable	540	1,100	800	—	—
Cash in hand	10	25	15	8	12
Trademarks	—	—	200	100	450
Motor vehicles	—	1,500	1,950	1,250	1,600
Tax repayment due	—	—	—	250	800
Retained earnings	2,770	4,625	7,465	5,508	8,262
Share premium	1,500	7,500	4,500	5,000	9,000

> Question 2.4

Maria runs a small corner shop. Her statement of financial position at 31 October 2019 is shown below.

	£
Non-current assets	
Property, plant and equipment	**15,000**
Current assets	
Inventory	20,000
Other receivables	3,000
Cash and cash equivalents	500
	23,500
Total assets	**38,500**
Current liabilities	
Bank overdraft	7,000
Trade and other payables	8,000
Taxation	3,000
Total liabilities	**18,000**
Net assets	**20,500**
Capital account	
Balance at 31 October 2019	**20,500**

The following transactions took place in the first week of November 2019:

- Trade payables of £3,500 were paid from the bank account.
- Maria paid £10,000 of her own money into the bank account.
- Inventory of £1,200 was sold for £2,000 cash, a profit of £800 for the week.
- New inventory of £2,500 was purchased on credit from trade payables.
- Maria withdrew £300 from cash for her own personal expenses.

Required

Show how the above transactions would increase or decrease the various balances on the statement of financial position and draw up and balance the new statement of financial position at 7 November 2019.

›› TAKE IT FURTHER

›› Question 2.5

The statement of financial position for Andy Limited at 30 June 2019 is presented below. The following transactions took place in the first week of July 2019:

- 1 July 2019: paid a trade payable with a cheque from the bank for £2,500 and received a cheque for £3,000 from a trade receivable.

- 2 July 2019: took out a bank loan (full repayment is due on 30 June 2022) with which to buy a new vehicle costing £20,000. The vehicle purchase agreement was signed on 2 July 2019.
- 4 July 2019: sold goods which had cost Andy £7,500 to a customer on credit terms, the customer agreeing to pay for those goods on 3 August 2019. The goods were sold for a selling price of £10,000.
- 5 July 2019: sold goods which had cost Andy £2,500 to a customer for £3,250. The customer paid cash for the goods.
- 6 July 2019: received new inventory from a supplier. The new inventory cost £15,000 and Andy Limited has agreed to pay for the inventory on 5 August 2019.
- 7 July 2019: paid tax of £3,000 and a trade payable of £7,000 from the bank account.

Required

Show how the above transactions would increase or decrease the various balances on the statement of financial position and draw up and balance the new statement of financial position at 7 July 2019.

Andy Limited	
Statement of financial position at 30 June 2019	
ASSETS	**£**
Non-current assets	
Property, plant and equipment	**320,000**
Current assets	
Inventories	50,000
Trade receivables	75,000
Cash and cash equivalents	20,000
	145,000
Total assets	**465,000**
LIABILITIES	
Current liabilities	
Trade payables	80,000
Taxation	20,000
	100,000
Non-current liabilities	
Bank loan (long-term borrowings)	250,000
Total liabilities	**350,000**
Net assets	**115,000**
EQUITY	
Called up share capital	20,000
Retained earnings	95,000
Total equity	**115,000**

>> Question 2.6

(a) The following balances have been extracted from the books of Frankie Limited at 31 December 2019.

	£000
Cash at bank	600
Land and buildings	15,500
Loans due for repayment by 31 December 2020	850
Share premium	4,000
Loans due for repayment on 31 December 2028	8,500
Cash in hand	5
Share capital	2,000
Goodwill	1,000
Taxation payable	1,380
Fixtures and fittings	1,670
Trade receivables	4,910
Plant and machinery	10,630
Trade payables	6,720
Retained earnings	13,365
Inventory	2,500

Required

Using the statement of financial position format presented in this chapter, draw up the statement of financial position for Frankie Limited at 31 December 2019.

(b) During January 2020, the following transactions took place:

- Bought £12,200,000 of inventory on credit from suppliers.

- Made sales on credit to customers of £15,500,000. The inventory cost of the sales made was £11,450,000.

- Took out a loan of £2,500,000 with which to purchase new plant and machinery for £2,500,000. The new loan is due for repayment on 31 December 2024.

- Undertook a share issue, which raised cash of £1,500,000. £500,000 of the total amount raised represents share capital while the remaining £1,000,000 represents share premium.

- Made a tax payment from the bank account of £690,000.

- Received £6,450,000 from trade receivables.

- Paid trade payables £8,210,000.

- Sold a surplus piece of land that had cost £2,000,000 for £2,500,000.

- Made a short-term loan repayment of £200,000.

Required

Using the statement of financial position for Frankie Limited drawn up at 31 December 2019, show how the above transactions would increase or decrease the various balances on the statement of financial position and draw up and balance the new statement of financial position at the end of January 2020.

3

THE STATEMENT OF PROFIT OR LOSS

LEARNING OUTCOMES

Once you have read this chapter and worked through the questions and examples in both this chapter and the online workbook, you should be able to:

- Define income and expenses

- Understand the different expense categories and profit figures that are presented in published financial statements

- Understand that revenue and costs in the statement of profit or loss represent income earned and expenditure incurred in an accounting period not just the cash received and cash paid in that period

- Apply the accruals basis of accounting in determining income earned and expenditure incurred in an accounting period

- Calculate prepayments and accruals at the end of an accounting period

- Define and calculate depreciation using both the straight line and reducing balance methods

- Make accounting adjustments to the statement of profit or loss to reflect the effect of irrecoverable debts, the allowance for receivables, sales returns, purchase returns, discounts allowed and discounts received

- Prepare a statement of profit or loss for an accounting period together with the statement of financial position at the end of that accounting period from a given set of information

INTRODUCTION

In the last chapter we looked at the statement of financial position. We noted that this statement just presents an entity's financial position on one day in the year, the financial year-end date. However, many users of financial information turn first of all not to the statement of financial position but to the main source of information about an entity's financial performance during an accounting period, the statement of profit or loss. This statement shows the income and expenditure of the entity for the year. The difference between total income and total expenditure represents the profit or loss that the entity has made during that financial year. It is this profit or loss figure that initially tends to be of most interest to financial statement users. A quick skim through the financial press on any day of the week will show you that profit or loss is one of the most discussed numbers in any set of financial statements. It is this figure, in many people's (and shareholders' and the stock market's) view, that determines whether a company has had a successful or unsuccessful year as shown by the two examples in Give me an example 3.1.

GIVE ME AN EXAMPLE 3.1   The importance of profits for businesses

Compare the stock market's reactions to these announcements from two different companies in late January and early February 2018.

31 January 2018: Capita plc's share price falls in response to lower than expected profits

On 31 January 2018, Capita plc, the outsourcing group, announced that profit before tax for the year to 31 December 2018 would be in the region of £270m–£300m. The market had been expecting a forecast profit for the 2018 calendar year of £400m. In the same announcement, the company said that it was suspending the dividend and looking to raise £700m through an issue of new shares. This news saw the share price fall to 182.50 pence from a closing price on 30 January 2018 of 347.80 pence. On 1 February 2018, the share price of the company fell further to 158.60 pence, a twenty year low.

Source: http://investors.capita.com

8 February 2018: Compass Group's share price rises on revenue growth announcement

On 8 February, Compass Group, the worldwide food services group, announced revenue growth in the three months to 31 December 2017 of 5.9%. Based on this sales growth and other information in the trading update, analysts predicted a rise in profit before tax of over 5% for the year to 30 September 2018. Compass Group's shares rose 76.50 pence to 1,513.50 pence on the day, a rise of 5.32%.

Sources: https://www.compass-group.com and https://uk.webfg.com/news/news-and-announcements/compass-points-towards-north-end-of-growth-targets--3123305.html

---

Illustration 3.1 presents the statement of profit or loss for Bunns the Bakers plc for the years ended 31 March 2019 and 31 March 2018. This statement begins with income (revenue) and then deducts various categories of expenditure to reach the profit for the year. However, income and expenditure are not just simply money received and money spent during the year. There are various accounting conventions that have to be applied in the determination of income and costs for a period. How these conventions are applied to individual items of revenue and expenditure will determine the profit for each accounting period. The application of these conventions will form a large part of this chapter. Careful study of these applications will enable you to understand how income and expenditure are calculated and how, in turn, the profit or loss for a period is determined.

Illustration 3.1 Bunns the Bakers plc: statement of profit or loss for the years ended 31 March 2019 and 31 March 2018

	2019	2018	
	£000	£000	
Revenue	10,078	9,575	
Cost of sales	(4,535)	(4,596)	
Gross profit	5,543	4,979	
			The trading part of the statement of profit or loss
Distribution and selling costs	(3,398)	(3,057)	
Administration expenses	(1,250)	(1,155)	
Operating profit	895	767	
Finance income	15	12	The financing part of the statement of profit or loss
Finance expense	(150)	(165)	
Profit before tax	760	614	
Income tax	(213)	(172)	
Profit for the year	547	442	

GO BACK OVER THIS AGAIN!   A copy of this statement of profit or loss is available in the **online workbook:** you might like to keep this on screen or print off a copy for easy reference while you work your way through the material in this chapter. There is also an annotated copy of this statement of profit or loss at the back of the book to help you go over the relevant points again to reinforce your knowledge and learning.

TERMINOLOGY: STATEMENT OF PROFIT OR LOSS/INCOME STATEMENT/STATEMENT OF FINANCIAL PERFORMANCE/PROFIT AND LOSS ACCOUNT

The statement of profit or loss is also known as the income statement or the profit and loss account. In keeping with the International Financial Reporting Standards approach adopted in this book, the term 'statement of profit or loss' is used throughout, but you will still find entities presenting an 'income statement' or a 'profit and loss account'. Under the IASB *Conceptual Framework for Financial Reporting*, the statement of profit or loss is just one component of the statement of financial performance. This statement of financial performance includes both the statement of profit or loss and a statement of other comprehensive income which presents details of other gains and losses arising in an accounting period from, for example, the revaluation of assets or changes in the valuation of pension liabilities. Consideration of the statement of other comprehensive income is beyond the scope of this book. Our concern in this and subsequent chapters is with the income earned and expenditure incurred in the course of everyday trading operations of businesses that form the basis for the figures presented in the statement of profit or loss.

Note: in Illustration 3.1 income and profit figures are shown without brackets while items of expenditure are shown in brackets. This is to help you understand which items are subtracted and which items are added to determine the result (profit or loss) for the year. Taking revenue (= sales) and finance income as positive figures, subtract the expenses to ensure you understand the relationships between the figures and to make sure that:

- Revenue – cost of sales = gross profit
- Gross profit – distribution and selling costs – administration expenses = operating profit
- Operating profit + finance income – finance expense = profit before tax, and
- Profit before tax – income tax = profit for the year.

DEFINITIONS

Illustration 3.1 shows the statement of profit or loss for Bunns the Bakers plc. As noted in the introduction, the statement of profit or loss contains items of revenue (income) and expenditure (costs incurred in making goods and selling them and in running and financing the company). Before we look at these different items of income and expenditure in more detail, let's start with some definitions.

Income

The International Accounting Standards Board defines income as 'increases in assets, or decreases in liabilities, that result in increases in equity, other than those relating to contributions from holders of equity claims' (IASB *Conceptual Framework for Financial Reporting*, paragraph 4.68). Let's break this definition down to understand what it means. When you make a sale for cash you have increased your cash asset. At the same time, this cash sale transaction also increases the equity of the business. The £s of assets are now higher as a result of the cash generated by the sale made while the £s of liabilities have remained the same (remember that assets – liabilities = equity, Chapter 2, Equity). Similarly, making a sale on credit to a customer who will pay at some later date increases the trade receivables asset while having no effect on liabilities so this increase in assets also increases the equity of the business. Likewise, a reduction in the £s of liabilities while the £s of assets remain the same will also increase equity.

However, not every increase in assets or decrease in liabilities will result in an increase in equity. Taking out a loan increases the cash asset but the borrowings liability rises by an equal and opposite amount so that there is no change in the assets – liabilities figure and, consequently, no increase in equity. Simply paying a trade payable what is owed reduces liabilities but the cash asset also falls by an equal and opposite amount so, again, there is no increase in the equity of the business. To recognise income there must always be an increase in the £s of equity when the £s of liabilities are deducted from the £s of assets.

3

The IASB definition of income also refers to 'increases in equity, other than those relating to contributions from holders of equity claims'. What does this mean? When business owners pay money into their businesses or shareholders subscribe for new shares in companies, these transactions increase both the cash asset and equity (Chapter 2, The components of equity). Assets have increased but these receipts are not income as they are money received from business owners or investors, both holders of equity claims: these amounts are now owed to the business's owners and shareholders and thus do not meet the definition of income.

Expenses

As you might have expected, given the definition of income, the International Accounting Standards Board defines expenses as 'decreases in assets, or increases in liabilities, that result in decreases in equity, other than those relating to distributions to holders of equity claims' (IASB *Conceptual Framework for Financial Reporting*, paragraph 4.69).

Again, let's break this definition down to understand what it means.

When a business pays cash to meet an expense, the cash asset decreases. At the same time, this transaction also decreases the equity of the business. The £s of assets are now lower as a result of the cash paid while the £s of liabilities have remained the same (assets – liabilities = equity, Chapter 2, Equity). Similarly, buying goods or services on credit will increase the trade payables liability while having no effect on the assets of the business, so this increase in liabilities also decreases the equity of the business.

However, not every increase in liabilities or decrease in assets will result in a decrease in equity. Taking out a loan increases the borrowings liability but the cash asset rises by an equal and opposite amount so that there is no change in the equity (assets – liabilities) figure in the statement of financial position and, consequently, no decrease in equity. Likewise, paying cash to settle what is owed to a trade payable reduces the cash asset but it also reduces the trade payables liability by an equal and opposite amount so, again, there is no decrease in the equity of the business. To recognise an expense there must always be a decrease in the £s of equity when the £s of liabilities are deducted from the £s of assets.

The IASB definition of expenses also refers to 'decreases in equity, other than those relating to distributions to holders of equity claims'. What does this mean? When business owners take money out of their businesses or shareholders are paid a dividend, these transactions decrease both the cash asset and equity (Chapter 2, The components of equity). Assets have decreased but these payments are not an expense as they are cash paid out to business owners and shareholders, both holders of equity claims: these amounts have been paid out to the business's owners and shareholders in their capacity as holders of equity claims and thus do not meet the definition of expenses.

WHY IS THIS RELEVANT TO ME?   Definitions: income and expenses

To enable you as an accounting professional to:

- Understand what income and expenditure in the statement of profit or loss represent
- Appreciate how entities meet the definitions by generating income and incurring expenses

---

SUMMARY OF KEY CONCEPTS   Can you remember the income and expenses definitions? Go to the **online workbook** to revise these definitions with Summary of key concepts 3.1 to reinforce your knowledge.

INCOME IN THE STATEMENT OF PROFIT OR LOSS

The first line in Illustration 3.1 refers to Revenue. Revenue represents sales income earned in an accounting period (usually one year) and may be referred to in some sets of accounts as sales or turnover as well as by the term revenue. These three terms all refer to the same type of income, income from trading goods or providing services.

Revenue appears as the first item in the statement of profit or loss and arises from sales made by an entity in the ordinary (everyday) course of business. For Bunns the Bakers plc this will mean selling bread, sandwiches, cakes, hot snacks, drinks and other products associated with their primary (everyday) activity, selling bakery and related goods. Were Bunns the Bakers to sell one of their shops, this would not be a transaction in the ordinary course of business and would not be recorded as part of revenue: selling shops is not what a bakery company would be expected to do on a regular basis. Instead, the profit or loss on the sale of the shop would be recorded in a separate line for exceptional income in the statement of profit or loss below operating profit. The way in which entities record exceptional income in their financial statements is illustrated in Give me an example 3.2.

The first six lines in the statement of profit or loss (from Revenue down to Operating profit) thus consist of items relating to the everyday trading activity of the organisation. Therefore, items of income and expense that do not relate to trading are excluded from the revenue, cost of sales, distribution and selling costs and administration expenses categories in the statement of profit or loss.

Not all income will arise from an entity's regular or trading activities. The other element of income shown in Bunns the Bakers plc's statement of profit or loss is Finance income. This will

---

GIVE ME AN EXAMPLE 3.2   Recording exceptional income in the statement of profit or loss

The following extract from the consolidated income statement (= statement of profit or loss) of Rolls-Royce Holdings plc for the year ended 31 December 2013 shows exceptional income recorded below the operating profit line. Note that such exceptional income is not included in Revenue.

Source: *Rolls-Royce Holdings annual report 2013* www.rolls-royce.com

	£m
Operating profit	1,535
Profit on transfer of joint ventures to subsidiaries	119
Profit on disposal of businesses	216
Profit before financing and taxation	**1,870**

consist of interest income received and receivable from the company's bank on deposits of surplus cash held in Bunns' account(s) or dividends received and receivable from the company's investments. As Bunns the Bakers is not a bank, earning interest is not part of its everyday trading activities in the ordinary course of business, so any interest earned in the period is disclosed on a separate line. This income is disclosed outside the trading part of the statement of profit or loss in its own separate section. Figure 3.1 summarises the three different types of income in the statement of profit or loss.

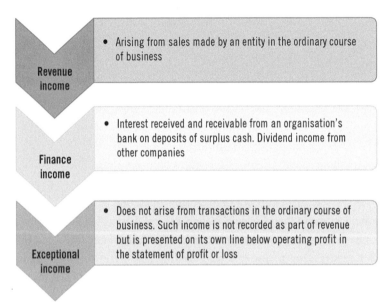

Figure 3.1 The different types of income in the statement of profit or loss

---

WHY IS THIS RELEVANT TO ME?   Income categorised under different headings

To enable you as an accounting professional to:

● Read a published statement of profit or loss and to understand what each category of income represents

● Appreciate that not all income arises from sales made in the ordinary course of business

---

GO BACK OVER THIS AGAIN!   Are you confident that you understand how revenue in the statement of profit or loss is split into income from sales made in the ordinary course of business, finance income and exceptional income? Go to the **online workbook** and complete Exercises 3.1 to make sure you can distinguish between these different types of income.

EXPENDITURE IN THE STATEMENT OF PROFIT OR LOSS

Expenditure in Bunns the Bakers' statement of profit or loss falls under various headings. Let's look at each of these in turn.

Cost of sales

This heading comprises those costs incurred directly in the making or buying in of products for sale. In the case of Bunns the Bakers, there will be the cost of the raw materials such as flour, fat, salt, cream, sugar and all the other ingredients that go into the bread, cakes, hot snacks and sandwiches, as well as goods bought in ready made from other manufacturers such as soft drinks and chocolate bars. In addition, the wages of the bakers, the electricity or gas used in heating the ovens and all the other associated costs of making or buying in the products will be included in cost of sales.

Determining the cost of making the products is important. The cost of the product is usually the starting point for setting a selling price at which customers will buy and to cover all the other costs of the operation so that a profit is made. In smaller entities, as we shall see shortly (this chapter, Statement of profit or loss by nature), cost of sales is usually calculated as: opening inventory of goods at the start of the accounting period + purchases during the accounting period − closing inventory of goods at the end of the accounting period.

Distribution and selling costs

These costs will comprise all those costs incurred in the distribution and selling of the products. For Bunns the Bakers, advertising would fall under this heading, as would the transport of bakery goods produced from the main bakery to each of the individual shops. The wages of shop staff would be part of selling costs, too, as would the costs of running the shops, including shop expenditure on goods and services such as cleaning, repairs, electricity, maintenance, rent, rates and water.

Administration expenses

This category covers all the costs of running the trading operation that do not fall under any other heading. Examples of such costs for Bunns the Bakers (and many other entities) would be legal expenses, accountancy and audit costs, directors' salaries, accounting department costs, bank charges and human resource department expenditure. Such costs are essential in running the business, but they cannot be allocated to the costs of making and producing or distributing and selling the goods sold by the organisation. Figure 3.2 summarises the different types of trading expenditure incurred in running a business.

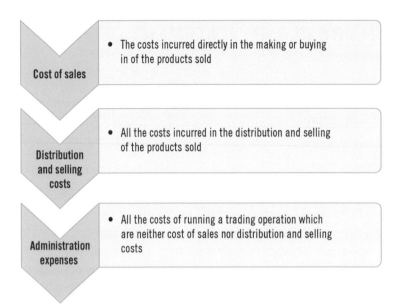

Cost of sales
- The costs incurred directly in the making or buying in of the products sold

Distribution and selling costs
- All the costs incurred in the distribution and selling of the products sold

Administration expenses
- All the costs of running a trading operation which are neither cost of sales nor distribution and selling costs

Figure 3.2 The different types of trading expenditure incurred in running a business

---

GO BACK OVER THIS AGAIN!   Are you convinced that you can distinguish between items that belong in the cost of sales, selling and distribution and administration sections of the statement of profit or loss? Go to the **online workbook** and complete Exercises 3.2 to make sure you can make these distinctions.

Finance expense

As with finance income, this expense is not incurred as part of the trading activities of the business. Finance expense is made up of interest paid on the borrowings used to finance the business. Look back at Illustration 2.1: Bunns the Bakers' statement of financial position shows that the company has borrowings under current and non-current liabilities. The finance expense will be the interest charged on these borrowings.

Income tax

The final expense to be deducted in Bunns the Bakers' statement of profit or loss is income tax. All commercial entities have to pay tax on their profits according to the tax law of the country in which they are resident and in which they operate. The income tax charge is based on the profits of the entity for the accounting period and the entity would expect to pay this tax at some point in the coming financial year. Figure 3.3 presents these five different categories of costs. As you will learn later on in your studies, UK companies pay corporation tax on their profits. However, the IASB presentation format in IAS1 for the statement of profit or loss requires the heading income tax for all taxes paid on company profits.

Figure 3.3 The different categories of costs (expenditure) in a typical statement of profit or loss

3

WHY IS THIS RELEVANT TO ME?   Expenditure categorised under different headings

To enable you as an accounting professional to:

- Appreciate that expenses are categorised according to different types of expenditure
- Read a published statement of profit or loss and understand what each category of expenditure represents

---

MULTIPLE CHOICE QUESTIONS   Are you certain that you can distinguish between items that belong in the various categories of income and expenditure in the statement of profit or loss? Go to the **online workbook** and complete Multiple choice questions 3.1 to make sure you can make these distinctions.

DIFFERENT CATEGORIES OF PROFIT

Bunns the Bakers' statement of profit or loss presents several different lines describing various different numbers as 'profit'. Why are there so many different figures for profit and what does each of them tell us about the profits of the company? The following observations can be made:

- Gross profit = revenue − cost of sales: this is the profit that arises when all the direct costs of production of the goods sold are deducted from the sales revenue earned in the accounting period.
- Operating profit = gross profit − distribution and selling costs − administration expenses: the profit remaining when all the other operating costs not directly associated with the

3

production or buying in of goods are deducted from the gross profit. Alternatively, this is the profit after all the costs of trading, direct (cost of sales) and indirect (distribution and selling costs and administration expenses), are deducted from sales revenue.

• Profit before tax = operating profit + finance income – finance expense: the profit that remains once the costs of financing operations have been deducted and any finance or other income has been added onto operating profit.

• Profit for the year = profit before tax – income tax (also called the profit after tax or the net profit): this is the profit that is left once the tax on the profits for the accounting period has been deducted from the profit before tax. Alternatively, this is the profit that remains once all the expenses have been deducted from the sales revenue and any other income for the accounting period added on. This profit is now available to the company to distribute to the shareholders as a dividend or to retain within the business to finance future expansion. Figure 3.4 presents the different categories of profit.

Figure 3.4 The different categories of profit in a typical company statement of profit or loss

---

WHY IS THIS RELEVANT TO ME?   Different categories of profit

To enable you as an accounting professional to:

• Understand the accounting terminology describing the various categories of profit

• Understand how trading and financing activities have contributed to the results for the accounting period

---

GO BACK OVER THIS AGAIN!   Are you quite sure that you can remember how each different profit figure is calculated and what it represents? Go to the **online workbook** and complete Exercises 3.3 to reinforce your learning.

SUMMARY OF KEY CONCEPTS   Can you state the different profit figure calculations? Go to the **online workbook** to revise these calculations with Summary of key concepts 3.2 to check your understanding.

STATEMENT OF PROFIT OR LOSS BY NATURE

The statement of profit or loss for Bunns the Bakers plc (Illustration 3.1) is presented in the format that you will find in published financial statements for limited and public limited companies which requires the classification of expenses by function (cost of sales, distribution and selling costs, administration expenses, finance expense). However, the rest of this chapter will use examples and exercises based on the statement of profit or loss format in Illustration 3.2, the format that is used every day by traders and companies as a simple way to present income and expenditure to determine whether a profit or loss has been made. Study this format now along with the notes below.

Illustration 3.2 A trader: statement of profit or loss by nature for the year ended 31 March 2019

	£	£
Sales		347,250
Opening inventory	13,600	
Purchases	158,320	
Closing inventory	(17,500)	
Cost of sales (opening inventory + purchases – closing inventory)		154,420
Gross profit (sales – cost of sales)		192,830
Expenses (can be listed in any order required)		
Heat and light	9,500	
Motor expenses	12,250	
Rent and rates	25,685	
Wages and salaries	48,345	
Administration expenses	10,050	
Accountancy	2,000	
Legal expenses	1,950	
Bank interest	6,000	
Depreciation of non-current assets	24,000	
Insurance	7,500	
Miscellaneous	1,890	
Total expenses (all expenses items added together)		149,170
Bank interest received		950
Net profit (gross profit – total expenses + bank interest received)		44,610

GO BACK OVER THIS AGAIN!   How would the income and expenditure in Illustration 3.2 be presented in the published financial statements format which presents expenses by function? Go to the **online workbook** Exercises 3.4 to see how the above information would be summarised ready for publication.

3

Notes to the statement of profit or loss in Illustration 3.2

- The statement of profit or loss by nature consists of three sections: sales, cost of sales and expenses.
- Just as in the case of published statements of profit or loss, sales are made up of all the revenue derived from the ordinary activities of the business.
- Cost of sales is the opening inventory of unsold goods at the start of the year, plus purchases of goods during the year, less the closing inventory of unsold goods at the end of the year.
- Expenses are listed in any order: there is no set order in which expenses have to be presented.
- Expenses would include finance expense if an entity has incurred any interest costs relating to money borrowed to finance the business (Bank interest in Illustration 3.2) while finance income (interest receivable) is shown on a separate line below total expenses (Bank interest received in Illustration 3.2).
- Note the format of the statement: the component parts of Cost of sales and Expenses are listed in the left hand column and then the figures for Cost of sales and Expenses are totalled in the right hand column and deducted from Sales and Gross profit respectively.
- As in Bunns the Bakers' statement of profit or loss, sales − cost of sales = gross profit and gross profit − total expenses = net profit (profit for the year) for the accounting period.

> **WHY IS THIS RELEVANT TO ME?**   Statement of profit or loss by nature
>
> To enable you as an accounting professional to understand:
>
> - That statements of profit or loss for internal use within businesses adopt a different format compared to published statements of profit or loss
> - How to draw up statements of profit or loss by nature for presentation to interested parties
> - What the income and two categories of expenditure represent

NUMERICAL EXERCISES   Do you think that you could prepare statements of profit or loss by nature from a given set of information? Go to the **online workbook** and complete Numerical exercises 3.1 to test out your ability to prepare these statements.

SUMMARY OF KEY CONCEPTS   Are you confident that you can state the calculation for cost of sales? Go to the **online workbook** to revise this calculation with Summary of key concepts 3.3 to check your knowledge.

Now that we have looked at the presentation of the statement of profit or loss and what it contains, it is time to find out how income and expense are determined in an accounting period.

DETERMINING THE AMOUNT OF INCOME OR EXPENSE

At the start of this chapter we noted that income and expenditure are not simply money received and money spent, though cash received and cash paid are the starting point when preparing any set of financial statements. Revenue for an accounting period consists of all the sales made during that period, whether the cash from those sales has been received or not. Where a sale has been made but payment has not been received the entity recognises both a sale and a trade receivable at the end of the accounting period. This trade receivable is money due to the entity from a customer to whom the entity has made a valid sale. Thus, the entity recognises this sale in the statement of profit or loss as part of sales for the period and as a trade receivable in the statement of financial position. Where a sale has been made and the cash received, the entity recognises the sale in the statement of profit or loss and the increase in cash in the statement of financial position.

Diagrammatically, the above transactions can be represented as shown in Table 3.1.

Table 3.1 Cash and credit sales: statement of profit or loss and statement of financial position effects

	Statement of profit or loss effect	Cash received?	Statement of financial position effect
Sale made for cash	Increase revenue	Yes	Increase cash
Sale made on credit, payment due in 30 days	Increase revenue	No	Increase trade receivables
Cash received from trade receivable	No effect: no new revenue	Yes	Increase cash, decrease trade receivables

Give me an example 3.3 illustrates Nestlé's revenue recognition policy which matches exactly the approach outlined in Table 3.1. As soon as goods are sent to a customer, Nestlé recognises the sale whether the cash has been received from the customer or not.

GIVE ME AN EXAMPLE 3.3   At what point in time do commercial organisations recognise revenue in their financial statements?

The following accounting policy regarding the timing of revenue recognition is taken from Nestlé's financial statements for the year ended 31 December 2017.

Revenue

Sales represent amounts received and receivable from third parties for goods supplied to the customers and for services rendered. Revenue from the sales of goods is recognised in the income statement [= the statement of profit or loss] at the moment when the significant risks and rewards of ownership of the goods have been transferred to the buyer, which is mainly upon shipment.

Source: *Nestlé financial statements 2017* www.nestle.com, p.71.

Note that revenue comprises both cash received ('amounts received') and cash receivable (amounts 'receivable'). Revenue is thus not just the cash received in an accounting period, it represents all the revenue that an entity has earned during an accounting period whether the cash has been received or not.

Similarly, expenses are not just the money paid during an accounting period for goods and services received but *all* the expenses incurred in that period whether they have been paid for or not. Where an entity has incurred an expense during an accounting period but not paid this amount by the statement of financial position date, then the entity records the expense along with a trade payable. This trade payable represents a present obligation of the entity at the end of the accounting period for an expense validly incurred during that accounting period. If the expense has been paid then the expense is recognised along with a reduction in cash.

Diagrammatically, these transactions can be represented as shown in Table 3.2.

Table 3.2 Cash and credit expenses: statement of profit or loss and statement of financial position effects

	Statement of profit or loss effect	Cash paid?	Statement of financial position effect
Expense paid for with cash	Increase expenses	Yes	Decrease cash
Expense incurred on credit, payment due in 30 days	Increase expenses	No	Increase trade payables
Cash paid to trade payable	No effect: no new expense	Yes	Decrease cash, decrease trade payables

Give me an example 3.4 illustrates Nestlé's expenses recognition policy which matches exactly the approach outlined in Table 3.2. As soon as goods or service are received, Nestlé recognises the expense whether the cash has been paid by the company or not.

GIVE ME AN EXAMPLE 3.4   When do commercial organisations recognise costs and expenses in their financial statements?

The following accounting policy regarding the timing of expense recognition is taken from Nestlé's financial statements for the year ended 31 December 2017.

Expenses

Cost of goods sold is determined on the basis of the cost of production or of purchase, adjusted for the variation of inventories. All other expenses, including those in respect of advertising and promotions, are recognised when the Group receives the risks and rewards of ownership of the goods or when it receives the services.

Source: *Nestlé financial statements 2017* www.nestle.com, p.72

Note that expenses are recognised not when cash is paid but when goods and services are received and when the company has an obligation to pay for those goods and services (the point at which the risks and rewards of ownership are received, i.e. when the goods or services are delivered to the company).

GO BACK OVER THIS AGAIN!   Are you convinced that you understand how to determine the correct amount of income or expense for a given period? Go to the **online workbook** and complete Exercises 3.5 to reinforce your learning.

THE ACCRUALS BASIS OF ACCOUNTING

The principle that all income earned and expenditure incurred in a period is recognised in that period is referred to as the accruals basis of accounting. Under this basis, the timing of cash payments and receipts is irrelevant as transactions are matched (allocated) to the time period in which they occur not to the time periods in which they are paid for or in which cash is received.

Why is the accruals basis of accounting applied to financial statements? If the accruals basis of accounting did not exist, entities could time their cash receipts and payments to manipulate their cash-based statements of profit or loss to show the picture they wanted to show rather than the portrait of the income actually earned and the expenses actually incurred during an accounting period. Thus, some accounting periods would show high sales receipts, low expense payments and high profits, while other accounting periods would show low sales receipts, high expense payments and low profits or even losses. Results would depend upon money received and money paid out rather than reflecting all the business activity that had actually taken place within a given period of time.

An ability to manipulate the accounts in this way would lead to a lack of comparability between different accounting periods and between different organisations. We saw in Chapter 1 that comparability is an enhancing qualitative characteristic of accounting information. Lack of comparability would make it very difficult for users to gain an understanding of how the entity is making (or failing to make) progress in terms of profits earned or increases in sales made due to the fluctuating nature of cash inflows and outflows. The International Accounting Standards Board recognises the importance of accruals accounting and how this approach to accounting for transactions provides much more useful information relating to an entity's financial performance and financial position to users:

> Accrual accounting depicts the effects of transactions and other events and circumstances on a reporting entity's economic resources and claims in the periods in which those effects occur, even if the resulting cash receipts and payments occur in a different period. This is important because information about a reporting entity's economic resources and claims and changes in its economic resources and claims during a period provides a better basis for assessing the entity's past and future performance than information solely about cash receipts and payments during that period.
>
> Source: IASB *Conceptual Framework for Financial Reporting*, paragraph 1.17

WHY IS THIS RELEVANT TO ME?   The accruals basis of accounting

To enable you as an accounting professional to appreciate that:

● The timing of cash received and cash paid is irrelevant in the preparation of financial statements

● Transactions are reflected in financial statements on the basis of when they took place not on the basis of when the cash was received or paid

SUMMARY OF KEY CONCEPTS   Can you say what the accruals basis of accounting means? Go to the **online workbook** to revise this definition with Summary of key concepts 3.4 to check your learning.

The accruals basis of accounting looks like a difficult concept to grasp, but with practice you will soon be able to apply this concept readily to accounting problems. Let's look at some examples to show how the accruals basis of accounting works in practice. Think about the outcomes you would expect and compare your expectations to the actual answers. Remember that income and expenditure is allocated to an accounting period on the basis of income earned and expenditure incurred in that accounting period not on the timing of cash receipts and payments.

EXAMPLE 3.1

The Traditional Toy Company has an accounting year end of 30 June. On 1 January 2018, the company paid its annual insurance premium of £1,000, giving the company and its activities cover up to 31 December 2018. On 1 January 2019, the company paid its annual insurance premium of £1,200, which covers the company and its activities up to 31 December 2019. What expense should the Traditional Toy Company recognise for insurance for its accounting year 1 July 2018 to 30 June 2019?

The answer is £1,100. How did we arrive at this figure?

The premium paid on 1 January 2018 relates to the 12 months to 31 December 2018. Six of the months for the accounting period 1 July 2018 to 30 June 2019 are covered by this insurance premium, namely July, August, September, October, November and December 2018. Therefore 6/12 of the £1,000 belong in the accounting year to 30 June 2019, the other 6/12 of this payment (January to June 2018) belong in the accounting year 1 July 2017 to 30 June 2018.

Similarly, the premium paid on 1 January 2019 covers the whole calendar year to 31 December 2019. However, as the Traditional Toy Company's accounting year ends on 30 June 2019, only six months of this insurance premium belong in the financial year ended on that date, namely January, February, March, April, May and June 2019. Therefore 6/12 of £1,200 belong in the accounting year to 30 June 2019, the other 6/12 of this payment (July to December 2019) belong to the accounting year 1 July 2019 to 30 June 2020.

The total insurance expense recognised in the statement of profit or loss for the 12 months accounting year to 30 June 2019 is thus:

£1,000 × 6/12 + £1,200 × 6/12 = £1,100

While £1,200 was paid for insurance in the accounting year 1 July 2018 to 30 June 2019, the accruals basis of accounting requires that an expense of £1,100 for insurance is recognised in this financial year as this was the actual cost of insurance during this time period. Figure 3.5 will help you understand how the amounts paid in the above example have been allocated to the different accounting periods.

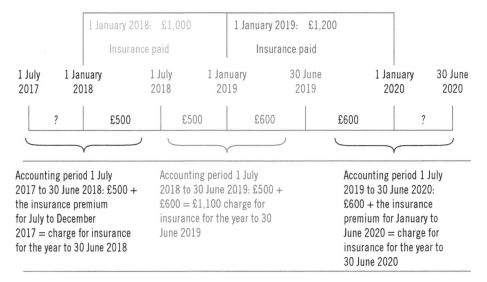

Figure 3.5 The accruals basis of accounting: insurance expense recognised in the Traditional Toy Company's accounting year 1 July 2018 to 30 June 2019

EXAMPLE 3.2

Hand Made Mirrors Limited has an accounting year end of 30 September. On 1 July 2018, the company paid its annual rates bill of £3,000 covering the period 1 July 2018 to 30 June 2019. On 1 July 2019, Hand Made Mirrors Limited received its annual rates bill for £3,600 covering the year to 30 June 2020 but did not pay this bill until 30 November 2019. What expense should the company recognise for rates for its accounting year 1 October 2018 to 30 September 2019?

The answer is £3,150. How did we arrive at this figure?

The rates paid on 1 July 2018 relate to the 12 months 1 July 2018 to 30 June 2019. Nine of the months for the accounting period 1 October 2018 to 30 September 2019 are covered by this rates bill, namely October, November and December of 2018 and January, February, March, April, May and June of 2019. Therefore 9/12 of this £3,000 belong in the accounting year to 30 September 2019.

Similarly, the rates paid on 30 November 2019 cover the whole year from 1 July 2019 to 30 June 2020. However, as Hand Made Mirrors Limited's accounting year ends on 30 September 2019, only three months of this rates bill belong in the accounting year ended on that date, namely July, August and September 2019. Therefore 3/12 of £3,600 belong in the accounting year to 30 September 2019.

The total rates expense recognised in the statement of profit or loss for the year to 30 September 2019 is thus:

£3,000 × 9/12 + £3,600 × 3/12 = £3,150

No rates have been paid in the financial year 1 October 2018 to 30 September 2019, but the accruals basis of accounting requires a cost of £3,150 to be recognised as the rates expense during the year. Again, a diagram as shown in Figure 3.6 will help you understand how the amounts paid in the above example have been allocated to the different accounting periods.

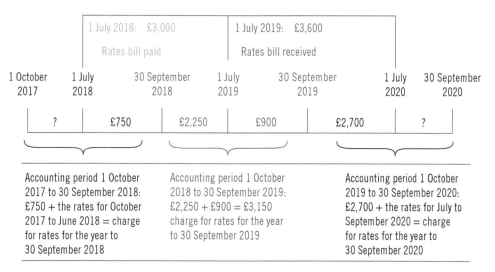

Figure 3.6 The accruals basis of accounting: Hand Made Mirrors Limited's rates expense recognised in the accounting year 1 October 2018 to 30 September 2019

MULTIPLE CHOICE QUESTIONS   Do you think you can allocate costs to accounting periods on an expense incurred basis under the accruals basis of accounting? Go to the **online workbook** and have a go at Multiple choice questions 3.2 to make sure you can make these allocations.

PREPAYMENTS AND ACCRUALS: RECORDING TRANSACTIONS IN THE STATEMENT OF PROFIT OR LOSS AND STATEMENT OF FINANCIAL POSITION

The two scenarios discussed provide us with one example of a prepayment and one example of an accrual at the end of an accounting period.

Prepayments

A prepayment is an expense paid in advance of the accounting period to which it relates. As this expense has been paid in advance, it is an asset of the entity. At 30 June 2019, in the case of the Traditional Toy Company, there is a prepaid insurance premium of £1,200 × 6/12 = £600. This prepayment is an asset as it is a present economic resource controlled by the entity as a result of past events (the payment of the insurance premium) and confers on the company a right that has the potential to produce economic benefits (the right to enjoy the protection provided by payment of the insurance premium in the next six months). While recognising the insurance expense of £1,100 for the accounting year to 30 June 2019, the entity also recognises a prepayment of £600 at the statement of financial position date of 30 June 2019.

At the end of the previous accounting period, at 30 June 2018, the Traditional Toy Company also had an insurance prepayment amounting to £1,000 × 6/12 = £500 (covering the months of July to December 2018 and paid in advance at 30 June 2018) so the insurance expense charge for the year is the £500 prepayment at the end of last year plus the £1,200 paid in the year less the prepayment at the end of the year of £600, thus:

£500 (prepayment at the end of last year) + £1,200 (payment in the year) – £600
(prepayment at the end of this year) = £1,100 insurance expense charge for the year

When attempting the multiple choice questions and exercises in the online workbook (and in real life situations), you can apply the rule presented in Figure 3.7 when you have an expense prepayment at the start and at the end of the financial year.

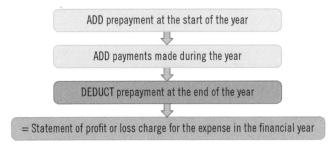

Figure 3.7 Calculating the statement of profit or loss expense for the financial year when there is a prepayment at the start and at the end of the accounting period

Accruals

An accrual is an expense owing at the end of the financial year for goods and services received but not yet paid for. As this expense is owed at the end of the year it represents a liability.

At 30 September 2019, Hand Made Mirrors Limited has a liability for unpaid rates of £3,600 × 3/12 = £900. This is a liability of the company at 30 September 2019 as it is a present obligation of the entity to transfer an economic resource (in the form of a cash payment to the local council on 30 November 2019) as a result of past events (the consumption of services). While recognising the total expense of £3,150 in the statement of profit or loss, Hand Made Mirrors Limited also recognises a £900 liability under trade and other payables in its statement of financial position at 30 September 2019. Remember that this is an expense incurred but not yet paid for, so you should increase the expense and increase the trade payables.

There was no accrual at the end of the previous accounting year. Had there been such an accrual this would have been treated as a deduction in arriving at the expense charge for the current accounting year. This is because an accrual at the end of the previous accounting period is a liability for a cost that was incurred in the previous accounting period but which will be paid in the current accounting period. The payment to discharge this liability has no bearing on the current accounting period's charge for this expense, so it is a deduction from the total payments made in the current accounting period.

When attempting the multiple choice questions and exercises in the online workbook (and in real life situations), you can apply the rule presented in Figure 3.8 when you have an expense accrual at the start and at the end of the financial year to find the amount you should recognise in the statement of profit or loss for that particular expense in the current financial year.

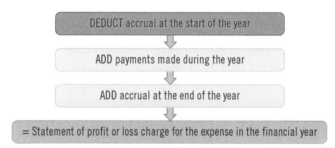

Figure 3.8 Calculating the statement of profit or loss expense for the financial year when there is an accrual at the start and at the end of the accounting period

WHY IS THIS RELEVANT TO ME?   Prepayments and accruals

To enable you as an accounting professional to understand how:

- Costs are allocated to accounting periods in which they are incurred
- To calculate simple accruals and prepayments at the end of an accounting period
- Assets and liabilities arise as a result of prepaid and accrued expenses

MULTIPLE CHOICE QUESTIONS   Are you confident that you can calculate statement of profit or loss expenses when there are prepayments and accruals at the start and end of the financial year? Go to the **online workbook** and have a go at Multiple choice questions 3.3 to test your ability to make these calculations.

3

DEPRECIATION

When we looked at the statement of financial position in Chapter 2, we noted that there are various types of non-current assets such as property, plant and equipment, patents and copyrights, among others. These assets are purchased by business organisations with a view to their long-term employment within the business to generate revenue, profits and cash. Businesses pay money for these assets when they buy them and then place these assets initially on the statement of financial position at their cost to the business.

A problem then arises. How should the cost of these non-current assets be allocated against income generated from those assets? The total cost of these assets is not allocated immediately against the income and profits made from those assets. Instead, the total cost is posted to the statement of financial position when the non-current asset is first acquired. Should we then allocate the cost of the asset to the statement of profit or loss at the end of the asset's life when the asset is worn out and of no further use to the business? Again, this will not happen. Setting the total cost of the asset against profit at the start or at the end of the asset's life would result in a very large one-off expense against profit in the year in which the asset is either bought or scrapped, so there has to be a better way to allocate the cost of non-current assets to accounting periods benefiting from their use. This is where depreciation comes in. Depreciation allocates the cost of a non-current asset to all those accounting periods benefiting from its use.

EXAMPLE 3.3

Pento Printing Press buys a printing machine for £100,000 and expects this non-current asset to be used within the business for the next five years. By simply dividing the asset's cost by the number of years over which the asset will be used in the business, this will give us an annual allocation of the cost of this asset of £100,000 ÷ 5 years = £20,000 per annum. This means that there will be a charge in Pento's statement of profit or loss in year 1 of £20,000 for use of the asset in the business, a charge in the statement of profit or loss of £20,000 in year 2 for use of the asset and so on until the end of the five years when the asset is scrapped and a replacement asset is purchased.

The allocation of depreciation in this way has a dual effect: part of the cost of the asset is charged to the statement of profit or loss each year and at the same time the unallocated cost of the asset on the statement of financial position reduces each year. Table 3.3 shows how the annual depreciation is allocated to each accounting period benefiting from the printing machine's use and the effect that this will have on Pento's statement of financial position figure for this asset at the end of each financial year. In accounting terminology, this is expressed as follows: the original cost of the asset – the accumulated depreciation charged to the statement of profit or loss = the carrying amount of the asset shown on the statement of financial position at the end of each financial year.

The £20,000 depreciation on the asset is charged as an expense in the statement of profit or loss of each annual accounting period in which the asset is used within the business.

The accumulated depreciation charged rises each year as the printing machine ages. At the end of the first year, the accumulated depreciation is the same as the annual depreciation charge. By the end of the second year the accumulated depreciation of £40,000 is made up of the first year's charge of £20,000 plus the second year's charge of £20,000. Then, by the end of year 3, the accumulated depreciation of £60,000 is made up of three years' charges of £20,000 each year and so on until the end of the printing machine's useful life. At the end of year 5, the accumulated depreciation of £100,000 is the same as the original cost of £100,000. As each year progresses, the carrying amount of the printing machine (cost – the accumulated depreciation) gradually falls. Thus, the carrying amount reduces as more of the original cost is allocated against profit each year.

Table 3.3 Straight line depreciation on Pento Printing Press' printing machine costing £100,000 with £Nil value at the end of five years

Year	Statement of profit or loss: annual charge for depreciation on printing machine	Accumulated depreciation	Statement of financial position: carrying amount of printing machine at the end of each financial year
	£	£	£
1	20,000	20,000	80,000
2	20,000	40,000	60,000
3	20,000	60,000	40,000
4	20,000	80,000	20,000
5	20,000	100,000	Nil

WHY IS THIS RELEVANT TO ME?   Depreciation

To enable you as an accounting professional to understand how:

- The use of non-current assets within a business results in an annual depreciation expense in the statement of profit or loss
- The cost of non-current assets is allocated to the statement of profit or loss each year
- The carrying amount of non-current assets is calculated at the end of each financial year

MULTIPLE CHOICE QUESTIONS   How well do you understand the calculation of accumulated depreciation and carrying amount? Go to the **online workbook** and have a go at Multiple choice questions 3.4 to test your understanding of how to make these calculations.

RESIDUAL VALUE AND THE ANNUAL DEPRECIATION CHARGE

In Example 3.3 we assumed that all of the cost of the printing machine would be consumed over the five-year period and that it would have no value at the end of its projected five-year life. This might be a realistic scenario in the case of assets such as computers, which will be completely superseded by advancing technology and so have no value at the end of their useful lives within a business. However, it is just as likely that assets could be sold on to another buyer when the business wishes to dispose of them. A car, for example, will usually have some resale value when a company comes to dispose of it and, in the same way, second-hand machinery will find willing buyers.

3

It is thus normal practice, at the time of acquisition, to estimate a residual value for each non-current asset. Residual value is the amount that the original purchaser thinks that the asset could be sold for when the time comes to dispose of it. When calculating the annual depreciation charge, the residual value is deducted from the original cost so that the asset is depreciated down to this value. If the residual value is estimated at £Nil, then the full cost of the asset is depreciated over its useful life.

EXAMPLE 3.4

The directors of Pento Printing Press now decide that their new printing machine will have an estimated residual value of £10,000 at the end of its five-year life. The annual depreciation charge will now fall to (£100,000 original cost − £10,000 residual value)/5 years = £18,000. Charging £18,000 depreciation each year will depreciate the asset down to its residual value as shown in Table 3.4.

Table 3.4 Pento Printing Press: straight line depreciation of a printing machine costing £100,000 with a £10,000 residual value

Year	Statement of profit or loss: annual charge for depreciation on printing machine	Accumulated depreciation	Statement of financial position: carrying amount of printing machine at the end of each financial year
	£	£	£
1	18,000	18,000	82,000
2	18,000	36,000	64,000
3	18,000	54,000	46,000
4	18,000	72,000	28,000
5	18,000	90,000	10,000

WHY IS THIS RELEVANT TO ME?   Residual value

To enable you as an accounting professional to understand that:

• The estimated residual value of an asset at the end of its useful life will result in a reduction in the annual depreciation charge

• Residual value is just an estimate of expected resale value at the end of a non-current asset's useful life

PROFITS AND LOSSES ON DISPOSAL OF NON-CURRENT ASSETS

You might now wonder what will happen if Pento Printing Press does not sell the asset at the end of the five years for £10,000. If the asset were to be sold for £8,000, £2,000 less than its carrying amount at the end of year 5, then Pento Printing Press would just record a loss (an additional expense) of £2,000 on the disposal of the printing machine in the statement of profit or loss. Profits would be reduced by that additional expense of £2,000. If, on the other hand, the asset were to be sold for £11,000, £1,000 more than the carrying amount at the end of the five years, Pento Printing Press would recognise a profit (a surplus) on the disposal of that asset in the statement of profit or loss. Profits on disposal of non-current assets are recorded as a deduction from expenses and are not recorded as additional revenue in the statement of profit or loss. Where the gain or loss on the disposal is a material amount, this gain or loss would be disclosed separately on the face of the statement of profit or loss as an exceptional item (this chapter, Income in the statement of profit or loss).

There would be no need for Pento Printing Press to go back and recalculate the depreciation for each of the five years in either of these cases as companies accept that the estimation of residual value is just that, a best guess at the time of acquisition of the asset of what the asset might be sold for at the end of its useful life within the business. It is quite normal for companies to recognise small gains and losses on the disposal of assets when they are sold on or scrapped either at the end of their useful lives or during the time that they are being used within the business.

WHY IS THIS RELEVANT TO ME?   Profits and losses on disposal of non-current assets

To enable you as an accounting professional to understand that:

- Profits on the disposal of non-current assets are recognised as income (a deduction from expenses) in the statement of profit or loss in the year of the asset's disposal

- Losses on the disposal of non-current assets are recognised as an expense in the statement of profit or loss in the year of the asset's disposal

- The profit or loss on disposal is calculated as the difference between the sale proceeds and the carrying amount of the asset at the date of disposal

---

MULTIPLE CHOICE QUESTIONS   Are you confident that you can calculate profits and losses arising on the disposal of non-current assets? Go to the **online workbook** and have a go at Multiple choice questions 3.5 to test your ability to make these calculations.

METHODS OF DEPRECIATION: STRAIGHT LINE AND REDUCING BALANCE

The approach used in the Pento Printing Press examples (Examples 3.3 and 3.4) to calculate depreciation resulted in the same depreciation charge for each year of the printing machine's useful life. This is the straight line basis of depreciation as it allocates an equal amount of depreciation to each year that the asset is used within the business.

An alternative method of depreciation that is also used is the reducing balance basis. This approach uses a fixed percentage of the cost in year 1 and the same fixed percentage of the carrying amount in subsequent years to calculate the annual depreciation charge. When using the reducing balance basis, residual value is ignored as the percentage used will depreciate the original cost down to residual value over the number of years in which the asset is used within the business.

EXAMPLE 3.5

Continuing with the Pento Printing Press example, a suitable percentage at which to depreciate the new printing machine on a reducing balance basis would be 36.90 per cent. Let's see how this will work in Table 3.5.
The annual depreciation figures in Table 3.5 were calculated as follows:

- In year 1, depreciation is calculated on cost. This gives a figure of £100,000 × 36.90 per cent = £36,900. This depreciation is then deducted from the original cost of £100,000 to leave a carrying amount at the end of year 1 of £100,000 − £36,900 = £63,100.

- In years 2 and onwards, depreciation is calculated on the carrying amount at the end of the preceding financial year. Carrying amount at the end of year 1 is £63,100, so depreciation for year 2 is £63,100 × 36.90 per cent = £23,284 (rounding to the nearest £). This then gives a carrying amount at the end of year 2 of £63,100 − £23,284 (or £100,000 − £36,900 − £23,284) = £39,816.

- In year 3, depreciation is calculated on the carrying amount at the end of year 2. This gives an annual depreciation charge of £39,816 × 36.90 per cent = £14,692 and a carrying amount at the end of year 3 of £39,816 − £14,692 = £25,124.

Work through the figures for years 4 and 5 to make sure that you understand how reducing balance depreciation works and to reinforce your learning.

Table 3.5 Pento Printing Press: reducing balance depreciation of a printing machine costing £100,000 with a £10,000 residual value

Year	Statement of profit or loss: annual charge for depreciation on printing machine	Accumulated depreciation	Statement of financial position: carrying amount of printing machine at the end of each financial year
	£	£	£
1	36,900	36,900	63,100
2	23,284	60,184	39,816
3	14,692	74,876	25,124
4	9,271	84,147	15,853
5	5,850	89,997	10,003

Figure 3.9 visually represents the annual depreciation charge under both the reducing balance (the blue line) and the straight line (the red line) methods. The straight line method of depreciation charges exactly the same depreciation each year, £18,000 (Table 3.4), so this is a straight line drawn across the graph through the £18,000 mark on the y axis. Reducing balance depreciation charges a high level of depreciation in the first year of the asset's life and this then gradually reduces each year, thereby producing the curved blue line on the graph.

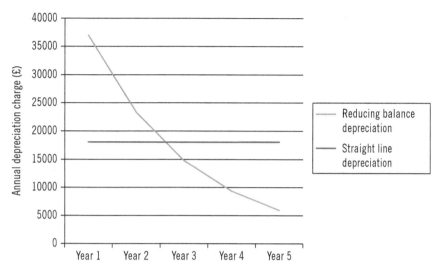

Figure 3.9 Graph representing the annual depreciation charges under both the reducing balance and straight line methods of depreciation for Pento Printing Press' printing machine costing £100,000 with a residual value of £10,000

WHICH DEPRECIATION METHOD IS MOST APPROPRIATE IN PRACTICE?

When selecting a method of depreciation, entities should always ask themselves how the economic benefits of each asset will be consumed. If most of the economic benefits that the asset represents will be used up in the early years of an asset's life, then reducing balance depreciation would be the most suitable method to use. Reducing balance would charge a higher proportion of the cost to the early years of the asset's life, thereby reflecting the higher proportion of economic benefits used up in these early years. Where benefits from the asset's use will be used up evenly over the asset's life, then straight line depreciation is the most appropriate method to use. Straight line and reducing balance depreciation are just two of the methods of depreciation that entities can use in allocating the costs of non-current assets to the accounting periods benefiting from their use. You will come across other methods of depreciation at later stages of your studies.

> **WHY IS THIS RELEVANT TO ME?**　Methods of depreciation: straight line and reducing balance
>
> To enable you as an accounting professional to understand:
>
> - The two main methods of depreciation that are applied in practice
> - How to undertake depreciation calculations to assess the impact of depreciation upon profits in the statement of profit or loss and upon the carrying amounts of assets in the statement of financial position
> - The criteria to be used in the selection of the most appropriate depreciation method for non-current assets

3

What depreciation methods do entities use in practice? Give me an example 3.5 presents the depreciation accounting policy for Finsbury Food Group plc.

GIVE ME AN EXAMPLE 3.5   Depreciation

What sort of depreciation rates and methods do companies use in practice? The following extract from the accounting policies detailed in the report and accounts of Finsbury Food Group plc for the 52 weeks ended 1 July 2017 gives different depreciation rates for different classes of property, plant and equipment assets. Can you decide whether Finsbury Food Group plc uses the straight line or the reducing balance basis to calculate the annual depreciation charge?

Depreciation

Depreciation is provided to write off the cost, less estimated residual value, of the property, plant and equipment by equal instalments over their estimated useful economic lives to the Consolidated Statement of Profit and Loss. When parts of an item of property, plant and equipment have different useful lives, they are accounted for as separate items

(major components) of property, plant and equipment.

The depreciation rates used are as follows:

Freehold buildings	Plant and equipment
2% – 20%	10% – 33%
Leasehold property	Assets under
Up to the remaining life of the lease	construction Nil
Fixtures and fittings	Motor vehicles
10% – 33%	25% – 33%

Source: *Finsbury Food Group plc annual report and accounts 2017* http://www.finsburyfoods.co.uk

Did you notice the words 'equal instalments' in the extract? Equal instalments means that Finsbury Food Group plc uses the straight line basis of depreciation when allocating the cost of non-current assets to the consolidated statement of profit and loss. Equal instalments = the same charge each year, i.e. the straight line basis.

MULTIPLE CHOICE QUESTIONS   Are you totally confident you can calculate depreciation charges on both the straight line and the reducing balance bases? Go to the **online workbook** and have a go at Multiple choice questions 3.6 to test your ability to make these calculations.

WHAT DEPRECIATION IS AND WHAT DEPRECIATION IS NOT

There are many misconceptions about what depreciation is and what it represents. The following notes will help you distinguish between what depreciation is and what it is not:

- Depreciation is a deduction from the cost of a non-current asset that is charged as an expense in the statement of profit or loss each year.

- This depreciation charge represents an allocation of the cost of each non-current asset to the accounting periods expected to benefit from that asset's use by an organisation.

- Depreciation is another application of the accruals basis of accounting. Just as the accruals basis of accounting matches income and expenditure to the periods in which they occurred, so depreciation matches the cost of non-current assets to the periods benefiting from their use.

- Depreciation is NOT a method of saving up for a replacement asset.
- Depreciation does NOT represent a loss in value of a non-current asset.
- Depreciation does NOT represent an attempt to provide a current value for non-current assets at each statement of financial position date.

EXAMPLE 3.6

Think about these last two points. Suppose you were to buy a car today for £15,000 and expect to use that car for five years before buying a replacement. The resale value of that car the next day would not be £15,000 less one day's depreciation, the original cost less a very small charge for the asset's economic benefits used up by one day's travelling. The showroom that sold you the car the day before would probably offer you half of the original cost of £15,000. The car is now second-hand and so worth much less on the open market than you paid for it the day before even if it only has five miles on the clock and is still in immaculate condition. Thus, the carrying amount of non-current assets on a company's statement of financial position is just the original cost of those assets less the depreciation charged to date. This carrying amount represents the store of potential economic benefits that will be consumed by the entity over the remaining useful lives of those assets rather than presenting the current market value of those non-current assets.

WHY IS THIS RELEVANT TO ME?   What depreciation is and what depreciation is not

To enable you as an accounting professional to understand:

- The function of depreciation in accounting statements
- What depreciation does and does not represent

GO BACK OVER THIS AGAIN!   How firmly have you grasped the ideas of what depreciation is and what it is not? Go to the **online workbook** and complete Exercises 3.6 to reinforce your understanding.

FURTHER ADJUSTMENTS TO THE STATEMENT OF PROFIT OR LOSS

We have now looked at how the statement of profit or loss reflects the actual income earned and expenditure incurred in an accounting period rather than just the receipts and payments of cash during that accounting period together with the subject of depreciation. There are some further adjustments that are made to figures in the statement of profit or loss and statement of financial position that you should be aware of before we work through a comprehensive example.

Irrecoverable debts

Where entities trade with their customers on credit, providing customers with goods now and allowing them a period of time in which to pay, there will inevitably be times when some customers are unable or refuse to pay for whatever reason. When this situation arises, an administrative expense is recognised for the amount of the trade receivable that cannot be collected

3

and trade receivables reduced by the same amount. Note that these irrecoverable debts are not deducted from sales (revenue) but are treated as an expense of the business.

Irrecoverable debts are recognised as an expense and a deduction from trade receivables when there is objective proof that the customer will not pay. Usually, this objective proof is in the form of a letter from the customer's administrator advising the company that no further cash will be forthcoming to settle the trade receivable owed.

The allowance for receivables

As well as known irrecoverable debts, organisations will also calculate an allowance for receivables, trade receivables that may not be collected rather than irrecoverable debts, receivables that will definitely not pay. An allowance for receivables is an application of the prudence principle, being cautious and avoiding over optimistic expectations, making a provision for a potential loss just in case. An allowance for receivables thus builds up a cushion against future irrecoverable debts, charging an expense now rather than in the future.

Allowances for receivables are calculated as a percentage of trade receivables after deducting known irrecoverable debts. The allowance for receivables is deducted in its entirety from trade receivables in the statement of financial position while only the increase or decrease in the allowance over the year is charged or credited to administrative expenses (not sales) in the statement of profit or loss. An example will help you understand how an allowance for receivables is calculated and the accounting entries required.

EXAMPLE 3.7

Gemma runs a recruitment agency. She has year-end trade receivables at 30 September 2019 of £300,000. She knows that one trade receivable owing £6,000 will not pay as that company is now in liquidation. Gemma's experience tells her that 5 per cent of the remaining trade receivables will not pay. Her allowance for receivables at 30 September 2018 was £12,000. What is the total amount that she should recognise in her statement of profit or loss for the year to 30 September 2019 for irrecoverable debts and the allowance for receivables? What figure for net trade receivables will appear in her statement of financial position at that date?

Irrecoverable debts and allowance for receivables charge in the statement of profit or loss

	£	£
Irrecoverable debts charged directly to the statement of profit or loss		6,000
Movement in the allowance for receivables:		
Year-end trade receivables (total)	300,000	
Less: known irrecoverable debts charged directly to the statement of profit or loss	(6,000)	
Net trade receivables on which allowance is to be based	**294,000**	
Allowance for receivables on £294,000 at 5%	14,700	
Less: allowance for receivables at 30 September 2018	(12,000)	
Increase in allowance charged to the statement of profit or loss this year		2,700
Total statement of profit or loss charge for irrecoverable debts and allowance for receivables for the year ended 30 September 2019		**8,700**

Trade receivables in the statement of financial position

	£
Total trade receivables at 30 September 2019	300,000
Less: known irrecoverable debts charged directly to the statement of profit or loss	(6,000)
	294,000
Less: allowance for receivables at the start of the year	(12,000)
Less: increase in the allowance for receivables during the year	(2,700)
Net trade receivables at 30 September 2019	**279,300**

The total allowance for receivables is made up of the allowance at the end of last year and the increase (or decrease) during the current year. The total allowance of £14,700 is deducted from trade receivables at the end of the year. The allowance for receivables charge (or credit) for the year in the statement of profit or loss, however, is just the increase (or decrease) during the year.

MULTIPLE CHOICE QUESTIONS   Are you confident that you can calculate allowances for receivables and the amounts to charge or credit to the statement of profit or loss? Go to the **online workbook** and have a go at Multiple choice questions 3.7 to test your ability to make these calculations.

Discounts allowed (early settlement discounts)

To encourage trade receivables to pay what they owe early, companies will offer a discount. As an example, a trade receivable is allowed 30 days in which to pay for goods supplied. However, the seller might offer a discount of, say, 2 per cent if payment is made within 10 days of receipt of the goods. The seller of the goods does not know whether the trade receivable will take up this discount or not. Therefore, the invoice for the goods supplied will present two prices: the first price is after allowing for the early settlement discount, the second is the price if the early settlement discount is not taken up. Thus, if a customer is sold goods with a selling price of £3,000 but offered a 2.5 per cent discount for payment within 10 days, the seller of the goods records a sale and a trade receivable of £3,000 x (100% − 2.5%) = £2,925. If the customer pays within ten days then the seller's cash increases by £2,925 and trade receivables decrease by £2,925. However, should the customer not take up the early settlement discount but pay £3,000 after 30 days, then cash will increase by £3,000, trade receivables will decrease by £2,925 and the additional £75 will be added to sales revenue. Discounts allowed are thus not treated as an expense but are deducted from the initial selling price and then added to sales if the discounts are not taken up.

Discounts received (bulk discounts)

Suppliers will reward their customers with discounts for buying goods in bulk (discounts received). These bulk discounts are a source of income in the statement of profit or loss, a deduction from cost of sales and a deduction from trade payables.

3

Sales returns

Sometimes, goods are just not suitable, are not of the requisite quality or they are faulty. In this case, customers will return these goods to the supplier (sales returns). These returns are treated as a deduction from sales, as the return of goods amounts to the cancellation of a sale, and a deduction from trade receivables.

Purchase returns

Similarly, when entities return goods to their suppliers (purchase returns), suppliers will reduce the amount that is owed to them by the issue of a credit note. As this is the cancellation of a purchase, the purchases part of cost of goods sold and trade payables are reduced.

Closing inventory

At the end of the financial year, entities count up the goods in stock and value them in accordance with the requirements of IAS2 Inventory. This accounting standard requires inventory to be valued at the lower of cost and net realisable value. What do these terms mean?

Cost means the acquisition cost of the inventory, how much it cost the business to acquire or produce the items in stock at the end of the year. For retailers, cost is the purchase price of each product plus, for example, delivery costs and less any bulk discounts received. In manufacturing organisations, cost will be made up of the cost of inputs to a product or process such as materials, labour and other associated costs.

Inventory is valued at net realisable value when goods can only be sold at a price that is lower than the product's original cost. In rapidly changing markets, today's must have product will be superseded very quickly by new, more advanced products and any left-over goods will have to be discounted heavily in order to sell them. When goods can be sold for more than their purchase or production price, closing inventory is not valued at selling price as such a valuation would anticipate profit. This would contravene the realisation principle of accounting which says that profits should not be anticipated until they have been earned through a sale. However, valuing goods at selling price when this is lower than purchase price recognises the losses that will be made on the sale of these goods immediately.

The value of inventory is carried forward to the next accounting period by deducting the cost of this inventory in the statement of profit or loss and recognising an asset in the statement of financial position. This is a further application of the accruals basis of accounting, carrying forward the cost of unsold goods to a future accounting period to match that cost against sales of those goods when these arise.

WHY IS THIS RELEVANT TO ME?   Further adjustments to the statement of profit or loss

To provide you as an accounting professional with:

- Knowledge of additional transactions that affect both income and expenditure and the statement of financial position
- Details of how these adjustments are treated in practice
- An ability to apply these adjustments in practical situations

We will look at how these adjustments are applied in practice in our comprehensive example and in Numerical exercises 3.2.

PREPARING THE STATEMENT OF PROFIT OR LOSS

We have now considered all the building blocks for the statement of profit or loss. It is time to look at a comprehensive example to see how the statement of profit or loss is put together from the accounting records and how it relates to the statement of financial position. You will need to work through this comprehensive example several times to understand fully how all the figures are derived, but this is quite normal. Even those at the top of the accountancy profession today would have struggled with this type of problem when they first started out on their accounting studies. It is just a case of practice and familiarising yourself with the techniques involved in putting a set of accounts together. We shall return to this comprehensive example in demonstrating double-entry bookkeeping in Chapter 4 (Comprehensive example: double entry and the trial balance) so time spent on this example now will make you very familiar with the accounting entries and help you in understanding how double-entry bookkeeping works.

The following list of points is a quick summary of how to prepare a statement of profit or loss and the statement of financial position, starting with a simple list of receipts and payments presented by a business:

- First, summarise the receipts into and payments out of the entity's bank account: this will give you the basic sales receipts and expenses as well as any non-current assets that the entity may have purchased.

- Once you have completed the bank account you will have a difference between the receipts and payments in the period: if receipts are greater than payments, you have a positive cash balance in the bank account, a current asset. If the payments are greater than the receipts, you have a negative balance in the bank account, an overdraft, and this will be recorded as a current liability.

- Using the cash received and paid you should then adjust income and expenditure for the accruals basis of accounting. Add to sales any income earned in the accounting period for which cash has not yet been received and recognise a trade receivable for the outstanding balance due. For expenses, determine what the expense should be based on the time period involved and then add additional expenditure where a particular cost is too low (and add to current liabilities as an accrual, an obligation incurred but not yet paid for) and deduct expenditure where a particular cost is too high (and add to current assets as a prepayment of future expenditure that relates to a later accounting period).

- Remember to depreciate any non-current assets at the rates given, provide for any irrecoverable debts that might have been incurred, make an adjustment for the increase or decrease in the allowance for receivables, adjust sales and purchases for returns and deduct discounts received from purchases.

EXAMPLE 3.8

Your friend Julia started a business on 1 April 2019 buying and selling sports equipment from a shop on the high street. It is now 30 June 2019 and Julia is curious to know how well or badly she is doing in her first three months of trading. She has no idea about accounts and presents you with the list of balances in Illustration 3.3 of the amounts received and paid out of her bank account.

Illustration 3.3 Julia's bank account receipts and payments summary

Date		Receipts £	Payments £
1 April 2019	Cash introduced by Julia	30,000	
1 April 2019	Three months' rent paid on shop to 30 June 2019		5,000
1 April 2019	Cash register paid for		1,000
1 April 2019	Shelving and shop fittings paid for		12,000
30 April 2019	Receipts from sales in April 2019	20,000	
5 May 2019	Sports equipment supplied in April paid for		15,000
12 May 2019	Rates for period 1 April 2019 to 30 September 2019 paid		800
19 May 2019	Cash withdrawn for Julia's own expenses		2,000
30 May 2019	Receipts from sales in May 2019	25,000	
5 June 2019	Sports equipment supplied in May paid for		20,000
10 June 2019	Shop water rates for the year 1 April 2019 to 31 March 2020 paid		400
30 June 2019	Receipts from sales in June 2019	30,000	
30 June 2019	Balance in bank at 30 June 2019		48,800
		105,000	**105,000**

Julia is very pleased with her first three months' trading and regards the additional £18,800 cash in the bank as her profit for the three months. Is she right? Has she really made £18,800 profit in the three months since she started trading? Her argument is that she started with £30,000 and now has £48,800 so she must have made a profit of £18,800, the difference between her opening and closing cash figures. Let us have a look and see how her business has really performed in its first three months of operations.

Our first job is to split the receipts and payments down into trading receipts and payments and statement of financial position (capital) receipts and payments. Have a go at this on your own before you look at the answer presented in Illustrations 3.4 and 3.5. You will need to add up the receipts for sales and the payments for purchases and other expenses: make a list of these individual totals.

You should now have the totals shown in Illustrations 3.4 and 3.5.

Illustration 3.4 Julia's receipts and payments account for the three months ended 30 June 2019

	£	£
Sales £20,000 (April) + £25,000 (May) + £30,000 (June)		75,000
Purchases £15,000 (May) + £20,000 (June)		35,000
Gross surplus (sales – purchases)		**40,000**
Expenses		
Rent £5,000 (April)	5,000	
Rates £800 (May)	800	
Water rates £400 (June)	400	
Total expenses		6,200
Net surplus for the three months		**33,800**

Illustration 3.5 Julia's statement of financial position based on her receipts and payments for her first three months of trading at 30 June 2019

	£
Non-current assets	
Cash register	1,000
Shelving and shop fittings	12,000
	13,000
Bank balance at 30 June 2019	48,800
Total assets	**61,800**
Equity	
Capital introduced by Julia	30,000
Drawings (cash withdrawn from the business for personal expenses)	(2,000)
Surplus for the three months	33,800
	61,800

All we have done in Illustrations 3.4 and 3.5 is restated the figures from Julia's bank account, splitting them into statement of profit or loss and statement of financial position items on a purely receipts and payments basis. Sales and expenses have been entered into the statement of profit or loss, while non-current assets (the cash register and the shelving and shop fittings: those assets that are used long term in the business) have been entered into the statement of financial position. The statement of financial position also shows the cash in the bank, the asset remaining at the end of the financial period, along with the capital introduced by Julia less her drawings in the three-month period plus the surplus the business has made during that period.

3

SHOW ME HOW TO DO IT   Are you completely happy with the way in which Julia's bank receipts and payments were allocated to the receipts and payments account and the related statement of financial position? View Video presentation 3.1 in the **online workbook** to see a practical demonstration of how these allocations were made.

However, there is a problem with receipts and payments accounts. As we have seen in the earlier part of this chapter, what we need to do now is adjust these receipts and payments for the accruals basis of accounting, matching all the income and expenses to the three months in which they were earned and incurred rather than just allocating them to the three-month period on the basis of when cash was received or paid. By doing this we can then determine the actual sales made during the period and what it actually cost Julia to make those sales. This will give her a much clearer idea of the profits she has actually earned in her first three months of trading.

You mention this problem to Julia, who provides you with the following additional information:

- She counted up and valued the inventory at the close of business on 30 June 2019: the cost of this inventory at that date was £10,000.

- At 30 June 2019, Julia owed £25,000 for sports equipment she had purchased from her suppliers on credit in June. She paid this £25,000 on 5 July 2019.

- While her main business is selling sports equipment for cash, Julia has also made sales to two local tennis clubs in June on credit. At 30 June 2019, the two clubs owed £2,500, although one club disputes £50 of the amount outstanding, saying that the goods were never delivered. Julia has no proof that these goods were ever received by the club and has reluctantly agreed that she will never receive this £50.

- During the month of June, Julia employed a part time sales assistant who was owed £300 in wages at the end of June 2019. These wages were paid on 8 July 2019.

- On 5 July 2019, Julia received a telephone bill for £250 covering the three months 1 April 2019 to 30 June 2019 together with an electricity bill for £200 covering the same period.

- Julia expects the cash register and shelving and shop fittings to last for five years before they need replacement. The level of usage of these assets will be the same in each of the next five years. She also expects that the assets will have no residual value at the end of their useful lives and that they will just be scrapped rather than being sold on.

- The cash register contained £500 in cash at 30 June 2019 representing sales receipts that had not yet been banked.

- On 29 June 2019, one of the tennis clubs she trades with on credit returned goods with a sales value of £400. These goods were faulty. Julia returned these goods to her supplier: the goods had originally cost Julia £250.

Taking into account the additional information, together with the transactions through the bank account and our receipts and payments account, Julia's statement of profit or loss and statement of financial position are shown in Illustrations 3.6 and 3.7.

Illustration 3.6 Julia's statement of profit or loss for the three months ended 30 June 2019

	£	£	Note
Sales £75,000 (cash received) + £2,500 (sales invoiced but cash not yet received) − £400 (goods returned: no sale or trade receivable recognised) + £500 (cash in till representing unrecorded sales)		77,600	1
Purchases £35,000 (cash paid) + £25,000 (goods received not yet paid for) − £250 (faulty goods returned to supplier: no cost or liability recognised)	59,750		2
Less: closing inventory (inventory of goods not yet sold at 30 June 2019)	(10,000)		3
Cost of sales (purchases − closing inventory)		49,750	4
Gross profit (sales − cost of sales)		**27,850**	5
Expenses			
Rent	5,000		6
Rates £800 − (£800 × 3/6) (payment is for a 6-month period, therefore three months out of six are prepaid)	400		7
Water rates £400 − (£400 × 9/12) (payment is for a 12-month period, so nine months out of twelve are prepaid)	100		8
Irrecoverable debt £50 (sale made but no cash will be received)	50		9
Wages £300 (work performed for wages in June but paid in July)	300		10
Telephone £250 (service received but paid in July)	250		11
Electricity £200 (electricity received but paid in July)	200		12
Cash register depreciation (£1,000/5 years × 3/12 months)	50		13
Shelving and fittings depreciation (£12,000/5 years × 3/12 months)	600		14
Total expenses		6,950	15
Net profit for the three months		**20,900**	16

Illustration 3.7 Julia's statement of financial position at 30 June 2019

	£	Notes
Non-current assets		
Cash register £1,000 − (£1,000/5 years × 3/12 months)	950	13
Shelving and shop fittings £12,000 − (£12,000/5 years × 3/12 months)	11,400	14
	12,350	
Current assets		
Inventory (inventory of goods not yet sold at 30 June 2019)	10,000	3
Trade receivables £2,500 (sales invoiced but cash not yet received) − £50 (sale made but no cash will be received) − £400 (goods returned: no sale or trade receivable recognised)	2,050	1, 9
Rates prepayment £800 × 3/6 (6 month period, therefore 3/6 prepaid)	400	7
Water rates prepayment £400 × 9/12 (12 month period, 9 months prepaid)	300	8
Bank balance at 30 June 2019	48,800	
Cash in cash register at 30 June 2019 (£500 cash in till representing unrecorded sales, increase sales and increase cash)	500	1
	62,050	
Total assets (£12,350 non-current assets + £62,050 current assets)	**74,400**	

3

	£	Notes
Current liabilities		
Trade payables £25,000 (goods received not yet paid for) – £250 (goods returned to supplier: no cost or liability recognised)	24,750	2
Wages accrual	300	10
Telephone accrual	250	11
Electricity accrual	200	12
Total liabilities	**25,500**	
Net assets (total assets (£74,400) – total liabilities (£25,500))	**48,900**	
Equity (capital account)		
Capital introduced by Julia	30,000	
Drawings (cash paid from the business for personal expenses)	(2,000)	
Net profit for the three months	20,900	
Capital account at 30 June 2019	**48,900**	

Notes to Julia's statement of profit or loss and statement of financial position:

1. This figure consists of the sales represented by cash banked (£75,000) + the additional sales made on credit of £2,500 + the unrecorded cash of £500 representing sales made on 30 June 2019. The £2,500 credit sales are recognised now as they are sales that occurred in the three-month period to 30 June 2019 and so are matched to this accounting period even though the cash from these sales will not be received until after the end of the three-month period. Similarly, the £400 goods returned are recognised as a deduction from the sales total as this sale was cancelled during the three-month period. Money owed by trade receivables is £2,100 (£2,500 credit sales made – £400 selling price of goods returned) while cash rises by £500 as these sales had already been realised in cash. Note that the irrecoverable debt of £50 is not deducted from sales but is disclosed as a separate expense in the statement of profit or loss.

2. Goods purchased on credit in the period and not paid for are likewise matched to the period in which the transaction occurred. Failure to recognise this expense in the period would incorrectly increase the profit for the period and give a completely false picture of how well the business is performing. The receipts and payments account initially showed purchases of £35,000. Once we have added in the additional purchases in the period and deducted the £250 of faulty goods returned to the supplier, the purchases figure has risen to £59,750, a significant increase on the original figure, but one that is required by the accruals basis of accounting. Just as the purchases expense has risen by £24,750 (£25,000 – £250), trade payables have risen by the same amount to reflect the amount owed by the business at 30 June 2019.

3. Closing inventory of goods is treated as a deduction in the statement of profit or loss as the cost of these unsold goods is carried forward to match against future sales of these goods. While cost of sales is thus reduced by £10,000, the statement of financial position reflects the same amount as an asset, a present economic resource the business owns which it can sell in future periods to generate economic benefits for the organisation.

4. Cost of sales, as we noted earlier in the chapter, is calculated as opening inventory (= last year's closing inventory) + purchases during the period – closing inventory. In Julia's case, there is no opening inventory as this is her first trading period, so opening inventory is £Nil.

5. Gross profit is calculated as: sales – cost of sales, income earned less the costs incurred in generating that income. Gross profit is an important figure in assessing the performance of an entity as we shall see in Chapter 8.

6. Rent is one figure that does not need adjusting. As stated in the bank receipts and payments, the rent paid is for the months of April, May and June 2019 and is paid right up to 30 June, so there is no prepayment (money paid in advance for services still to be received) or accrual (unpaid amount for services already received) of rent at the end of the three-month accounting period.

7. The rates are for the half year from 1 April 2019 to 30 September 2019. The whole amount due for the six months has been paid during the period. At 30 June 2019, the payment for July, August and September 2019 has been made in advance so half the £800 is a prepayment at 30 June 2019. The true cost of rates for the three months to 30 June 2019 is 3/6 of £800, so that only £400 is matched as an expense for the quarter.

8. Similarly, the water rates are paid for the whole year from 1 April 2019 to 31 March 2020, so that only three of the twelve months represented by this payment have been used up by 30 June 2019 (April, May and June 2019) leaving the nine months 1 July 2019 to 31 March 2020 prepaid. Again, the water rates expense for the period is only 3/12 of the total paid and this is the expense to match to the three-month period to the end of June 2019. The remainder of this expense is carried forward at the end of the three-month period to match against water usage in future accounting periods.

9. The irrecoverable debt is recognised as an expense and not as a deduction from sales. As well as being charged as an expense in the period to which it relates, it is also deducted from trade receivables. As this £50 will not be received, it no longer represents an asset with the potential to generate economic benefits so it is deducted from trade receivables in the statement of financial position and charged as an expense in the statement of profit or loss.

10. The £300 wages cost has been incurred by 30 June 2019 and, while this amount is not paid until after the end of the three-month period, it is matched with the income that those wages helped to generate during June 2019. Expenses increase by £300 and, as this amount has not been paid by the period end, it is recognised as a liability.

11. Similarly, the telephone service has been received over the three-month accounting period so there is a liability at the end of the period together with an expense of £300 matched to the period in which it was incurred.

12. Again, the electricity has been consumed during the three-month period to 30 June 2019, so that a liability exists at the period end for this amount and this, too, is recognised as an expense matched to the accounting period in which it was incurred.

13. As we saw earlier in this chapter, depreciation is charged on non-current assets to reflect the economic benefits of those assets consumed during each accounting period. Julia expects the same level of usage each year from the cash register and the shelving and shop fittings, so this implies the straight line basis of depreciation, an equal amount charged to the periods benefiting from their use. As there is no residual value, the total cost is used to calculate the depreciation charge for the three-month period. In the case of the cash register, £1,000 divided by five years gives an annual depreciation charge of £200. However, as the accounting period is less than a year, the depreciation charge is spread out over the relevant months to give an expense of £200 × 3/12 = £50.

14. In the same way, the straight line basis of depreciation gives an annual charge of £12,000/5 = £2,400 on the shelving and shop fittings. As the accounting period is only three months long, only 3/12 of this annual depreciation is matched to the current accounting period, so that £2,400 × 3/12 = £600 charged to reflect the economic benefit of these assets used up in the accounting period.

15. Total expenses are the sum of all the expenses from rent down to shelving and fittings depreciation.

16. Net profit for the period is given by the gross profit – total expenses.

Drawings and the business entity assumption

Julia's drawings for her personal expenditure have been deducted from equity. Why are these costs not treated as part of the business's expenditure? Firstly, the business's affairs and the owner's affairs must be kept entirely separate as the business and the owner are treated as two separate entities. Where the owner takes money out of the business for non-business, personal expenditure, any such personal expenditure is deducted from the owner's interest in the business as it is not expenditure incurred on behalf of the business. Secondly, in accordance with the IASB Conceptual Framework, while the payment of cash to Julia represents a decrease in assets and a decrease in equity, this is not an expense but a decrease in equity resulting from a distribution to holders of equity claims (this chapter, Expenses). The owner's interest in the business is represented by the amounts in the capital account, as we saw in Chapter 2 (The components of equity). Any amounts for personal expenditure withdrawn from the business's bank account are treated as repayments of the capital owed to the owner and are not charged as an expense of the business.

SHOW ME HOW TO DO IT Are you certain you understand how Julia's statement of profit or loss and statement of financial position were put together? View Video presentation 3.2 in the **online workbook** to see a practical demonstration of how these two statements were drawn up.

WHY IS THIS RELEVANT TO ME? Comprehensive example: statement of profit or loss and statement of financial position

To enable you as an accounting professional to appreciate:

- How the statement of profit or loss and statement of financial position are drawn up from the receipts and payments for an accounting period together with the application of the accruals basis of accounting

- How you can approach statement of profit or loss and statement of financial position preparation problems

- The principles of accounts preparation before we consider double-entry bookkeeping in Chapter 4

NUMERICAL EXERCISES Are you totally confident that you could prepare statements of profit or loss and statements of financial position from a given set of information? Go to the **online workbook** and complete Numerical exercises 3.2 to test out your ability to prepare these two statements.

CHAPTER SUMMARY

You should now have learnt that:

- Statements of profit or loss and statements of financial position are drawn up on the accruals basis of accounting

- Statement of profit or loss income and expenditure represent income earned and expenditure incurred during an accounting period

- Statement of profit or loss income and expenditure do not just represent cash received and cash paid during an accounting period

- Accruals are expenses incurred in an accounting period but not yet paid

- Accruals give rise to additional expenditure in the statement of profit or loss and a current liability in the statement of financial position

- Prepayments are expenses paid in advance of the accounting period to which they relate

- Prepayments reduce current period expenditure and represent a current asset on the statement of financial position

- Depreciation is the allocation of the cost of non-current assets to the accounting periods benefiting from their use
- Depreciation does not represent a loss in value of non-current assets
- Depreciation is not a way of presenting non-current assets at market values

QUICK REVISION Test your knowledge with the online flashcards in Summary of key concepts and attempt the Multiple choice questions, all in the **online workbook**.

END-OF-CHAPTER QUESTIONS

Solutions to these questions can be found in the **online workbook**.

❯ DEVELOP YOUR UNDERSTANDING

❯ Question 3.1

Abi runs a market stall selling fashion clothing for cash. Her business bank account balance at 1 September 2018, the start of her most recent trading year, was £7,342. She also had inventory of £2,382 and trade payables of £3,445 on that date. She rents her market stall at an annual cost of £6,000 payable quarterly in advance from 1 September each trading year. Abi paid all the rent that was due during the year to 31 August 2019. Her cash receipts from sales to customers for the year to 31 August 2019 totalled up to £157,689, but she also gave refunds to customers for returned goods of £3,789. She paid the outstanding trade payables at 1 September 2018 on 5 September 2018. Her purchases for the year totalled up to £120,465, of which she paid £116,328 during the year to 31 August 2019. At 31 August 2019 Abi valued her inventory of clothing at a cost of £4,638. From 1 September 2018 she employed a part time assistant, Kate, agreeing to pay her £100 a week for the year. At the end of August 2019, while Abi had paid Kate all the amounts due for the first 50 weeks of the year, she still owed her £200 for the last two weeks of August 2019. To improve the presentation of her fashion clothing ranges, Abi paid £600 to buy some display stands on 1 September 2018. Abi reckons that these display stands will last her for three years and that they will have a scrap value of £30. On 31 August 2019, Abi had £650 in cash representing sales that had not yet been banked. Abi withdrew £1,500 a month for her own personal expenses from the business bank account.

Required

1. Calculate Abi's opening capital account (equity) balance (remember the accounting equation) at 1 September 2018.

2. Draw up Abi's bank account for the year to 31 August 2019.

3. Prepare Abi's statement of profit or loss by nature for the year ended 31 August 2019 together with a statement of financial position at that date.

> Question 3.2

Alison runs an online gift shop, trading for cash with individual customers and offering trading on credit terms to businesses. She presents you with the following figures from her accounting records for the year ended 31 December 2019:

	£
Purchases of goods for resale	225,368
Accumulated depreciation on racks, shelving and office furniture at 31 December 2019	14,650
Trade receivables	27,400
Administration expenses	15,265
Racks, shelving and office furniture at cost	33,600
Telephone expenses	5,622
Capital account at 1 January 2019	52,710
Sales	437,990
Accumulated depreciation on computers at 31 December 2019	13,850
Inventory at 1 January 2019	27,647
Purchase returns (already deducted from trade payables)	5,724
Bank balance (asset)	52,315
Trade payables	24,962
Rent on warehouse and office unit	15,000
Business rates	9,325
Computer equipment at cost	20,775
Discounts received (already deducted from trade payables)	2,324
Delivery costs	36,970
Electricity and gas	8,736
Insurance	3,250
Drawings	40,000
Depreciation charge for the year on non-current assets	13,255
Sales returns (already deducted from trade receivables)	17,682

Alison provides you with the following additional information.

- She valued the inventory at 31 December 2019 at a cost of £22,600.
- All depreciation charges on non-current assets for the year to 31 December 2019 are included in the depreciation figures above.
- Rent on the trading unit prepaid at 31 December 2019 amounted to £3,000.
- Rates prepaid at 31 December 2019 amounted to £1,865.
- Accountancy costs of £1,250 had not been paid by the year end and are not included in the figures above.
- There were no other prepaid or accrued expenses at the year end.
- Alison would like to include an allowance for receivables of 10 per cent of year-end trade receivables. There was no allowance for receivables at 31 December 2018.

3

Required

Using the list of figures and the additional information provided prepare Alison's statement of profit or loss by nature for the year ended 31 December 2019 together with a statement of financial position at that date.

> Question 3.3

The following figures have been extracted from the accounting records of Volumes Limited, a book binder, at 30 September 2019:

	Assets and expenses £000	Income, liabilities and equity £000
Plant and machinery: cost	2,000	
Plant and machinery: accumulated depreciation at 30 September 2019		800
Sales		4,750
Trade receivables	430	
Administration expenses	300	
Selling and distribution costs	200	
Production costs	2,600	
Finance expense	100	
Cash at bank	175	
Loan (due 30 September 2028)		500
Trade payables		300
Finance income		25
Called up share capital		250
Share premium		125
Retained earnings at 30 September 2018		155
Inventory at 1 October 2018	100	
Production wages	1,000	
	6,905	**6,905**

Additional information

• Inventory at 30 September 2019 was valued at a cost of £150,000.

• Taxation on the profit for the year has been estimated to be £250,000.

• All depreciation charges for the year to 30 September 2019 have been calculated in the balances above.

Required

Using the list of balances and the additional information prepare the statement of profit or loss and statement of financial position for Volumes Limited in a form suitable for publication.

You will need to produce a working to calculate cost of sales.

You may find that consulting Illustrations 2.1 and 3.1 will assist you in the preparation of the statement of profit or loss and statement of financial position.

>> TAKE IT FURTHER

>> Question 3.4

The following figures have been extracted from the accounting records of Textiles Limited, a cloth manufacturer and wholesaler, at 30 June 2019:

	Assets and expenses	Income, liabilities and equity
	£000	£000
Plant and machinery: cost	3,000	
Plant and machinery: accumulated depreciation at 30 June 2018		1,200
Motor vehicles: cost	800	
Motor vehicles: accumulated depreciation at 30 June 2018		400
Trade receivables	1,050	
Cost of sales	4,550	
Sales returns (already deducted from trade receivables)	150	
Issued share capital		200
Trade payables		300
Finance expense	110	
Purchase returns (already deducted from trade payables)		80
Administration expenses	700	
Bank overdraft		200
Selling and distribution costs	1,000	
Sales		7,550
Discounts received (already deducted from trade payables)		125
Loan (due for repayment on 30 June 2027)		1,000
Retained earnings at 30 June 2018		545
Inventory at 30 June 2019	300	
Allowance for receivables at 30 June 2018		60
	11,860	**11,860**

Additional information

- Audit and accountancy fees (to be charged to administration expenses) of £10,000 have not been taken into account at 30 June 2019.
- Administration expenses include payments for insurance premiums of £30,000 for the 12 months to 31 December 2019.
- Since the year end, a customer of Textiles Limited has gone into liquidation owing £50,000. Textiles Limited does not expect to receive any cash from this trade receivable.

3

- The allowance for receivables is to be adjusted to 4 per cent of trade receivables after deducting known irrecoverable debts. All irrecoverable debts and the change in the allowance for receivables are to be allocated to administration expenses.

- Depreciation for the year to 30 June 2019 still has to be calculated. Plant and machinery is to be depreciated at 20 per cent straight line and motor vehicles are to be depreciated at 25 per cent reducing balance. Plant and machinery depreciation should be charged to cost of sales and motor vehicle depreciation should be charged to distribution and selling expenses.

- Taxation on the profit for the year is to be calculated as 25 per cent of the profit before tax.

Required

Prepare the statement of profit or loss and statement of financial position in a form suitable for publication in accordance with International Financial Reporting Standards.

>> **Question 3.5**

Laura was made redundant on 1 July 2018 and received £50,000 in redundancy pay. With this money, she opened a business bank account and set up a small building company undertaking household and small industrial construction work. She started trading on 1 September 2018 and she has now reached her year end of 31 August 2019. She has produced a summary of payments and receipts into her business bank account along with additional information that she thinks will be useful in preparing her statement of profit or loss and statement of financial position for her first year of trading. The details she has presented you with are as follows:

1. Laura's customers usually pay cash at the end of each job. Cash received and banked from these sales totals up to £112,000. However, her small industrial clients keep her waiting for payment. Her invoices to her small industrial customers add up to a total of £48,000 for work done during the year, but she has only collected £36,000 of this amount by 31 August 2019.

2. Laura buys her construction materials on credit from a local wholesaler. Her total spending on materials this year has been £45,000 of which she had paid £38,000 by 31 August 2019. Her annual trading summary from the wholesaler received on 5 September 2019 tells her that she has qualified for a bulk purchase discount of £1,000 on all her purchases up to 31 August 2019. She will deduct this amount from her next payment to her supplier in September 2019.

3. Since 31 August 2019, a small industrial customer has gone into liquidation, owing Laura £2,500. The liquidator has told Laura that no payment towards this trade receivable will be made. The liquidation of her customer has made Laura think about the solvency of her other trade receivables. She decides that she would like to create an allowance for receivables of 10 per cent of her remaining trade receivables at 31 August 2019.

4. Laura bought a second-hand van for £6,000 on 1 September 2018. She reckons this van will last for three years before she has to replace it. She anticipates that the trade-in value of this van will be £600 in three years' time. Laura expects the van to travel 5,000 miles each year on journeys for business purposes.

5. Van running expenses and insurance for the year amounted to £4,000. All of these expenses were paid from the business bank account. No van running expenses were outstanding or prepaid at 31 August 2019.

6. On 1 September 2018, Laura paid £5,000 for various items of second-hand construction equipment. These assets should last for four years and fetch £60 as scrap when they are

replaced. Laura expects to make the same use of these assets in each of the four years of their expected useful life.

7. Two part-time helpers were employed for 13 weeks during June, July and August 2019. By 31 August 2019, Laura had paid both these helpers 12 weeks of their wages amounting to £9,600 out of the business bank account.

8. Comprehensive business insurance was taken out and paid for on 1 September 2018. As a new business customer, Laura took advantage of the insurance company's discount scheme to pay £1,800 for 18 months' cover.

9. Laura counted up and valued her inventory of building materials at 31 August 2019. She valued all these items at a cost to the business of £4,500.

10. Bank charges of £400 were deducted from Laura's bank account during the year. The bank manager has told her that accrued charges to the end of August 2019 amount to an additional £75. These accrued charges will be deducted from her business bank account during September 2019.

11. Laura's bank account was overdrawn in the early part of her first year of trading. The bank charged her £200 interest on this overdraft. Since then, her bank account has shown a positive balance and she has earned £250 in interest up to 31 July 2019. The bank manager has told her that in August 2019 her interest receivable is a further £50 and this will be added to her account in October 2019.

12. Laura withdrew £2,500 each month from the bank for her personal expenses. As she had so much cash in the bank in August 2019, on 31 August 2019 she used £90,000 from her business bank account to repay half of the mortgage on her house.

Required

1. Prepare Laura's bank account for the year ended 31 August 2019.

2. Prepare a statement of profit or loss by nature for Laura's business for the year to 31 August 2019 and a statement of financial position at that date.

4

DOUBLE-ENTRY BOOKKEEPING 1:
DEBITS, CREDITS, T ACCOUNTS, THE TRIAL BALANCE AND THE FINANCIAL STATEMENTS

LEARNING OUTCOMES

Once you have read this chapter and worked through the questions and examples in both this chapter and the online workbook, you should be able to:

- Define debits and credits
- Understand how double entry is a logical extension of the accounting equation
- Post transactions to T accounts using double entry
- State the double entry to record recurring business transactions and events
- Extract a trial balance from the T accounts at the end of an accounting period
- Use the trial balance to draw up the statement of profit or loss and statement of financial position
- Close off the T accounts, transfer income and expenditure balances to the statement of profit or loss and bring forward asset, liability and capital balances to the new financial year

INTRODUCTION

We considered in Chapter 2 (The dual aspect concept) how transactions have an effect on two or more accounts and how a business's transactions change the figures in the statement of financial position on a day to day or even on a minute to minute basis. It is now time to look in much more detail at this dual aspect concept and to show how transactions are recorded in the double-entry bookkeeping system. This approach to recording transactions will seem strange at first but skills built up through continual practice and experience will enable you to become so familiar with the double-entry approach that it will become as natural as breathing. Double entry is not a subject you will just study in the first year of your Accounting degree and then forget. Double entry will form the bedrock of your professional career in accountancy so you will have to understand how double entry works now and maintain and develop that understanding into the far distant future.

This chapter presents the terminology used in double-entry bookkeeping, debits and credits, together with the T account which is used to record transactions as they occur. We will then see how, once all the transactions and period end adjustments have been recorded in the T accounts, the balances on all the T accounts at the end of the accounting period are used to compile the trial balance which is then used as the foundation from which to produce the statement of profit or loss and the statement of financial position of an organisation. Figure 4.1 summarises the stages in the recording and processing of accounting transactions into the final financial statements.

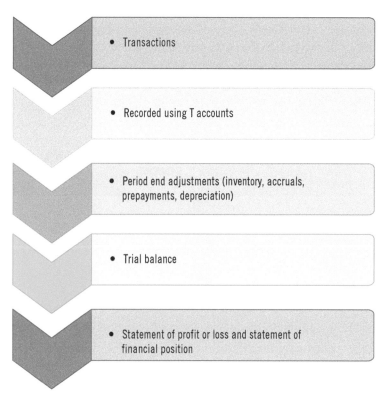

- Transactions

- Recorded using T accounts

- Period end adjustments (inventory, accruals, prepayments, depreciation)

- Trial balance

- Statement of profit or loss and statement of financial position

Figure 4.1 Stages in the recording and processing of transactions into the final financial statements

THE T ACCOUNT

In the double-entry bookkeeping system, a T account is set up for every asset and liability, for every source of income and expense and for every element of capital. The T account is the basic building block for recording accounting transactions and each T account will follow exactly the same pattern as shown in Figure 4.2.

Figure 4.2 The T account

Each and every T account has a title and two sides, one for debit entries and one for credit entries. What do these terms, debits and credits, signify?

Debits

Debit accounts represent assets and expenses. When an asset or expense increases an entry is made to the debit side of the asset or expense T account. Conversely, when an asset or expense decreases, then an entry is made to the credit side of the asset or expense T account. These debit and credit entries for asset and expense accounts are presented in Figure 4.3.

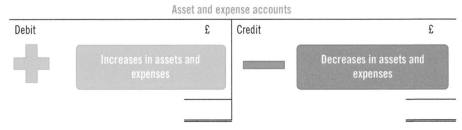

Figure 4.3 Asset and expense entries in the T account

Credits

Credit accounts represent liabilities, income and capital (equity). When there is an increase in a liability, income or capital, an entry is made to the credit side of the liability, income or capital T account. Conversely, when there is a decrease in a liability, income or capital, then an entry is made to the debit side of the liability, income or capital T account. These debit and credit entries for liability, income and capital accounts are presented in Figure 4.4.

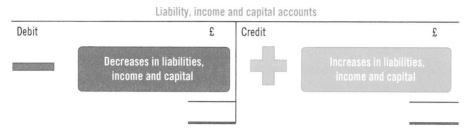

Figure 4.4 Liability, income and capital entries in the T account

We shall see how accounting transactions and events are recorded using T accounts and the debit and credit entry rules shortly. However, the golden rule for double entry states that every debit entry must have a corresponding and equal credit entry. Thus there cannot be two debit entries or two credit entries to record a transaction, there must be a debit entry and a credit entry of equal value otherwise the accounts will not balance. The double-entry rule reflects the dual nature of business transactions and events. Therefore, when one account increases or decreases, another account also increases or decreases as we saw in Chapter 2 (The dual aspect concept) and as we shall also see in this chapter and the next.

WHY IS THIS RELEVANT TO ME?   Recording transactions in T accounts

To enable you as an accounting professional to understand:

- The way in which transactions are recorded in T accounts

- That each and every debit entry must have an equal and opposite credit entry to ensure that the accounts balance

---

GO BACK OVER THIS AGAIN!   Are you quite sure you understand what debits and credits mean and how entries to debit and credit accounts increase or decrease the balance on those accounts? Go to the **online workbook** and have a go at Exercises 4.1 to test your understanding.

SUMMARY OF KEY CONCEPTS   Are you quite certain you can define debit and credit accounts and entries correctly? Go to the **online workbook** to check your understanding of debit and credit accounts with Summary of key concepts 4.1.

DOUBLE ENTRY AND THE ACCOUNTING EQUATION

Double entry is inextricably linked to the accounting equation. Our accounting equation (Figure 4.5 and refer back to Chapter 2, The accounting equation) states that:

Figure 4.5 The accounting equation

However, you might be wondering how income and expenses fit into the accounting equation. We can see assets, liabilities and capital, all of which we have considered as part of the double-entry system, but there is currently no sign of the income and expenses that also form part of the double-entry accounting records. As we saw in Chapter 2 (The components of equity), the capital of a business is made up of the capital introduced by the owner + the profit for the year – any drawings made by the business's owner. Capital introduced by the owner – drawings = equity while profit for the year is calculated by deducting expenses from income. On this basis we can rewrite our accounting equation as shown in Figure 4.6.

Figure 4.6 The accounting equation rewritten to include income and expenses

Moving expenses to the left hand side will then give us our double-entry equation shown in Figure 4.7:

Figure 4.7 The accounting equation rewritten so that debits = credits

WHY IS THIS RELEVANT TO ME?   The accounting equation and the duality principle

To enable you as an accounting professional to understand:
- How the accounting equation reflects the duality principle
- How all the debit entries will be equal to all the credit entries

GO BACK OVER THIS AGAIN!   Are you completely convinced that you can state the expanded accounting equation? Go to the **online workbook** and have a go at Exercises 4.2 to test your understanding.

SUMMARY OF KEY CONCEPTS   Are you certain that you have understood the expanded accounting equation? Go to the **online workbook** to revise this accounting equation with Summary of key concepts 4.2.

POSTING ACCOUNTING TRANSACTIONS TO T ACCOUNTS

Now that we have considered the basis upon which debits and credits work and how the accounts should always be in balance, let's see how accounting transactions and events are posted to the T accounts. We shall do this through a series of examples, Examples 4.1 to 4.6.

EXAMPLE 4.1

Arthur is starting up his own legal practice. He opens a business bank account on 1 June 2019 and pays in £5,000 of his own money to provide him with cash with which to finance transactions in the first few weeks of operations. How should Arthur record this transaction in the T accounts of his legal practice?

Firstly, we have to decide what this £5,000 represents. Is the £5,000 received by the business an asset or an expense (the debit entry)? Is the £5,000 a liability, income or capital (the credit entry)? Once we have made these decisions, then we can post the cash received to the correct T accounts.

As we saw in Chapter 2 (Current assets), cash is a business asset. Cash has been paid into the bank which means that the asset has increased. Therefore, there will be a debit entry to the bank account, an increase in the amount of an asset. Cash introduced by the owner of a business is part of equity (Chapter 2, The components of equity), money owed by the business to the owner, so this will result in a credit entry to the owner's capital account. Cash is not an expense as it is used to buy things for the business, so it is recorded as an asset. The £5,000 that Arthur has paid into the business does not represent a sale by the business or a gift to the business, so it is not income. It is money that Arthur has lent to the business with a view to increasing it so that he can take out a greater amount of money at a later date. Arthur will thus record the transaction as shown in Illustration 4.1. He will debit the bank account (increase the asset) with £5,000 and he will credit the capital account (an increase in capital) with £5,000.

Illustration 4.1 Posting the £5,000 capital introduced to Arthur's books of account

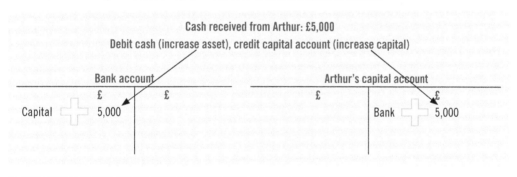

Both assets and capital increase, so both accounts record a plus entry.

Note the way in which the entries are recorded: Arthur notes down the name of the opposite account in each T account to enable him to trace the entries again at a future date. Thus 'capital' is recorded as the opposing entry in the bank account while capital records 'bank' as the other side of the entry. When completing T accounts, you should also follow this approach to enable you to correct entries or to find out where an entry has been posted.

Do the accounts balance? Does the accounting equation still hold true? There is a debit of £5,000 and a credit of £5,000 so the accounts balance. By using the accounting equation, we can check to see if the accounts are in balance. Assets in this case are the cash of £5,000 + £0 expenses = £0 liabilities + £5,000 capital account + £0 income so we can conclude that we have completed the double entry correctly as the accounts balance at £5,000 on each side.

Let's try another example, Example 4.2.

EXAMPLE 4.2

Arthur uses £1,000 of the cash in the bank to pay rent on the office lease he has taken out to provide him with a place from which to run his operations. How should Arthur record this transaction in the T accounts of his business? Again, we have to think about how this transaction will be recorded and which accounts will be affected. The amount of money in the bank account reduces by £1,000, which has now been spent. Thus this reduction in the asset account results in a credit entry to the bank account. Rent is an expense and this expense has increased by £1,000 so the rent account is debited with £1,000 to reflect this increase in the expense account. The double entry for the payment of rent is shown in Illustration 4.2.

Illustration 4.2 Posting the £1,000 payment for rent to Arthur's books of account

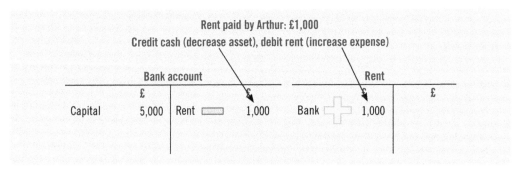

Here there is a reduction in the asset and an increase in the expense.

Do the accounts still balance? A cash asset of £4,000 (£5,000 debit – £1,000 credit) + rent expense of £1,000 = £5,000 capital account + £0 liabilities + £0 income so the accounts are still in balance at £5,000 on each side. Do note that the transactions on each account build up throughout the accounting period: the original cash received in the bank has not disappeared just because we have now moved on to record another transaction.

Let's keep going with more transactions to build up your knowledge and appreciation of how double entry works. These additional transactions are presented in Examples 4.3 to 4.6.

EXAMPLE 4.3

Arthur now buys some computers, desks and chairs from his local office equipment supplier. The cost of the computers, desks and chairs is £2,000. Arthur does not pay for these items of office equipment immediately, but buys them on credit from his supplier. This means that he will pay for these goods at a later date. You might think that Arthur does not need to record this transaction in his books yet as no cash has left the business. However, as we noted in Chapter 3 (The accruals basis of accounting) you must still record the transaction even if the cash has not been paid or received. If this transaction were not recorded immediately, then the debit and credit sides of the accounting equation would both be £2,000 lower than they should be. Think about the double entry for this transaction on credit. What do the computers, desks and chairs represent in accounting terms? These are non-current assets which will be used long-term in the business. Therefore, they will be recorded as assets. The assets increase so this is a debit entry to the office equipment account. We now need to think about the credit entry. No cash has changed hands, so we cannot reduce the asset in the bank account. Careful thought will enable you to realise that Arthur now has a liability, a present obligation to transfer an economic resource (a future payment of cash to settle what is owed to his supplier) as a result of past events (taking delivery of the office equipment). Therefore, Arthur must record a trade payable balance in his books of account. As there is a £2,000 liability, then Arthur must credit the trade payables account because liabilities have increased by this amount. The double entry for this transaction is shown in Illustration 4.3.

Illustration 4.3 Purchase of office equipment on credit posted to Arthur's books of account

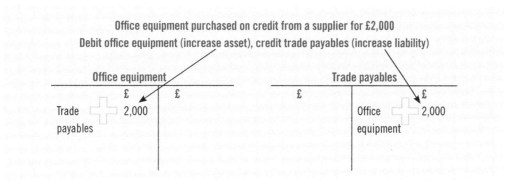

Arthur's assets have increased, but this increase in assets has also given rise to an increase in liabilities so both accounts increase.

Do the accounts still balance? £2,000 office equipment + £4,000 cash at the bank + £1,000 rent expense = £5,000 capital account + £2,000 trade payables + £0 income, so the accounts are still in balance with £7,000 on both the debit and credit sides.

EXAMPLE 4.4

Arthur now goes back to his office equipment supplier to buy £200 of paper and ink cartridges to enable him to print letters and documents. Again, he buys these supplies on credit. Your experience built up in Example 4.3 should enable you to state the double entry for this transaction straight away. Stationery supplies are not a non-current asset, but an expense. These office supplies will be used up quickly in the business so they will have only a short not a long life and so are recognised as an expense. The increase in expenditure gives rise to an increase in liabilities as more is owed to suppliers who will be paid the amounts owed at a later date. Thus the double entry will be debit stationery with £200 and credit trade payables with £200 as shown in Illustration 4.4.

Do the accounts still balance? £200 stationery expense + £2,000 office equipment + £4,000 cash at the bank + £1,000 rent expense = £5,000 capital account + £2,200 trade payables + £0 income, so the accounts are still in balance with £7,200 on the debit side and £7,200 on the credit side of the equation.

Illustration 4.4 Purchase of stationery on credit posted to Arthur's books of account

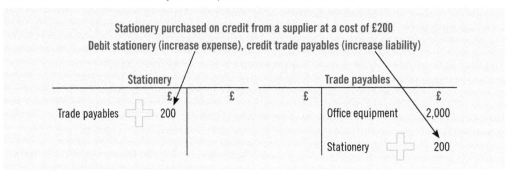

EXAMPLE 4.5

Arthur provides legal services to a client. The client pays Arthur's fee of £500 which Arthur pays into the bank account. Cash paid into the bank account is clearly an increase in an asset, so there is a debit to the bank account. But what is the credit entry? Arthur has generated income for his practice, so he has increased his income. Therefore, he will credit his revenue account with £500. The double entry for this transaction is shown in Illustration 4.5.

Illustration 4.5 Revenue received of £500 posted to Arthur's books of account

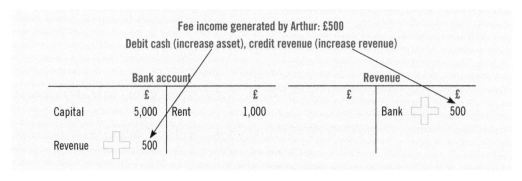

Do the accounts still balance? Let's check. £200 stationery expense + £2,000 office equipment + £4,500 cash at the bank (£5,000 + £500 − £1,000) + £1,000 rent expense = £5,000 capital account + £2,200 trade payables + £500 income, so the accounts are still in balance at £7,700 on each side after the completion of all the double entries.

EXAMPLE 4.6

Arthur now decides to pay £800 off the amounts he owes his trade payables. He uses cash from the bank to make the payment. As we have seen, a payment out of the bank represents a decrease in an asset balance, so there will be a credit entry to the bank of £800 thereby reducing the balance in the bank. What is the debit entry? Arthur is paying off part of what he owes to his trade payables. This means that the amounts owed to trade payables will decrease, so the debit entry will be made in the trade payables account, reducing the amounts owed by £800. The double entry for this transaction is shown in Illustration 4.6.

Illustration 4.6 Trade payable payment of £800 posted to Arthur's books of account

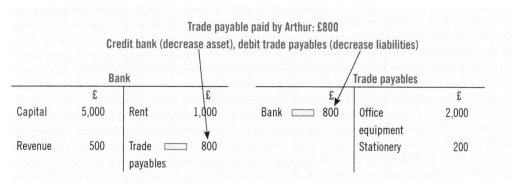

Trade payable paid by Arthur: £800
Credit bank (decrease asset), debit trade payables (decrease liabilities)

Bank					Trade payables		
	£		£		£		£
Capital	5,000	Rent	1,000	Bank	800	Office equipment	2,000
Revenue	500	Trade payables	800			Stationery	200

Do the accounts still balance? Let's check. £200 stationery expense + £2,000 office equipment + £3,700 cash at the bank (£5,000 + £500 − £1,000 − £800) + £1,000 rent expense = £5,000 capital account + £1,400 trade payables (£2,000 + £200 − £800) + £500 income, so the accounts are still in balance at £6,900 on each side after all the double entries have been completed.

WHY IS THIS RELEVANT TO ME?   Using double entry to post transactions to T accounts

To enable you as an accounting professional to understand:

- How double entry works in practical situations
- How the accounts remain in balance after completion of the double entry for each transaction

MULTIPLE CHOICE QUESTIONS   Are you quite sure you have understood the double entry required to record transactions? Go to the **online workbook** and have a go at Multiple choice questions 4.1 to test your ability to make the correct double entry in the accounts.

SHOW ME HOW TO DO IT   Are you completely certain you understood how double entry was used to post the transactions to Arthur's accounts? View Video presentation 4.1 in the **online workbook** to see a practical demonstration of how these entries were made.

THE TRIAL BALANCE

It is hard work balancing the accounts after each transaction has been entered. To make the job of checking whether all the double entry has been completed in full much easier, a trial balance is produced at regular intervals. A trial balance is a listing of all the debit and all the credit balances on the T accounts at any given point in time. If there is a difference on the trial balance then investigations can take place and corrective action can be taken to make the required adjustments to bring everything back into balance.

How is this trial balance drawn up? Firstly, we need to look at all our T accounts and determine what the balance is on each account. Arthur's T accounts after all the transactions have been posted are shown in Illustration 4.7.

Illustration 4.7 Arthur's T accounts after posting his transactions

Arthur's capital account						Bank account			
	£		£			£			£
		Bank	5,000		Capital	5,000	Rent		1,000
Debits =	**0**	Credits =	**5,000**		Revenue	500	Trade payables		800
					Debits =	**5,500**	Credits =		**1,800**

Office equipment						Rent			
	£		£			£			£
Trade payables	2,000				Bank	1,000			
Debits =	**2,000**	Credits =	**0**		Debits =	**1,000**	Credits =		**0**

Revenue						Stationery			
	£		£			£			£
		Bank	500		Trade payables	200			
Debits =	**0**	Credits =	**500**		Debits =	**200**	Credits =		**0**

Trade payables				
	£			£
Bank	800	Office equipment		2,000
		Stationery		200
Debits =	**800**	Credits =		**2,200**

The balance on each account is calculated by adding up the two sides of each account to determine the difference. If there are more debits than credits on the account, then there is a debit balance on that account. If there are more credits than debits on the account, then there is a credit balance on that account. Let's use Arthur's T accounts to illustrate how these rules are applied.

Arthur's capital account has credits of £5,000 and debits of £Nil so there is a credit balance (more credits than debits) of £5,000 on this account (£5,000 credits – £Nil debits). This credit balance is allocated to the credit side of the trial balance as shown in Illustration 4.8.

The bank account has debits of £5,000 and £500 and credits of £1,000 and £800. There is therefore a debit balance (more debits than credits) of £3,700 on the bank account (£5,000 + £500 – £1,000 – £800 = £3,700) and this is added to the debit side of the trial balance as shown in Illustration 4.8.

Office equipment has a debit balance (more debits than credits) of £2,000 as there are debits of £2,000 and credits of £Nil. Similarly, the rent account has a debit balance (more debits than credits) of £1,000, being made up of £1,000 of debits and £Nil credits. Illustration 4.8 shows both of these balances added to the debit side of the trial balance.

The credit balance (more credits than debits) on the revenue account is £500, as there are £500 of credits and £Nil debits so the resulting credit balance is allocated to the credit side of the trial balance (Illustration 4.8).

Stationery is showing a debit balance (more debits than credits) of £200 (£200 of debits – £Nil credits) and appears on the debit side of the trial balance (Illustration 4.8).

Finally, the trade payables account has credit entries of £2,000 and £200 and a debit entry of £800. The credit balance (more credits than debits) on this account is thus £1,400 (£2,000 + £200 – £800) and this balance is added to the credit side of the trial balance (Illustration 4.8).

Illustration 4.8 Arthur's trial balance

Arthur: trial balance at [Date]	Debit £	Credit £
Arthur's capital account		5,000
Bank account	3,700	
Office equipment	2,000	
Rent	1,000	
Revenue		500
Stationery	200	
Trade payables		1,400
	6,900	**6,900**

The debit and credit columns in Arthur's trial balance are added up and both total up to £6,900. This is what would be expected as all the debits should equal all the credits. The trial balance (as we shall see in this chapter, Comprehensive example: double entry and the trial balance) is then used to draw up the statement of profit or loss and statement of financial position for organisations.

Work through the above trial balance again to ensure you have grasped how the trial balance is put together.

WHY IS THIS RELEVANT TO ME?   The trial balance

To enable you as an accounting professional to:

• Understand how the trial balance is compiled from the balances on the T accounts

• Appreciate that the trial balance must balance if all the double entry has been completed in full

• Draw up your own trial balance from a set of T accounts

GO BACK OVER THIS AGAIN!   Are you quite convinced that you understand how the trial balance works? Go to the **online workbook** and have a go at Exercises 4.3 to test your understanding.

NUMERICAL EXERCISES   Are you quite sure you could draw up a trial balance from a given set of information? Go to the **online workbook** and have a go at Numerical exercises 4.1 to test your ability and understanding of how to put a trial balance together.

SHOW ME HOW TO DO IT   Are you completely certain you understood how Arthur's trial balance was put together? View Video presentation 4.2 in the **online workbook** to see a practical demonstration of how Arthur's trial balance was compiled from his T accounts.

COMPREHENSIVE EXAMPLE: DOUBLE ENTRY AND THE TRIAL BALANCE

In Chapter 3 (Example 3.8) we put together Julia's statement of profit or loss and statement of financial position from Julia's receipts and payments account and the further information that Julia provided. We will now use the same information to post the entries to T accounts. From these T accounts we will extract the trial balance and we will use this trial balance to prepare Julia's statement of profit or loss for the three months to 30 June 2019 together with a statement of financial position at that date.

Julia's receipts and payments for the three-month period are presented in Illustration 4.9.

Illustration 4.9 Julia's bank account receipts and payments summary (= Illustration 3.3)

		Receipts £	Payments £
1 April 2019	Cash introduced by Julia	30,000	
1 April 2019	Three months' rent paid on shop to 30 June 2019		5,000
1 April 2019	Cash register paid for		1,000
1 April 2019	Shelving and shop fittings paid for		12,000
30 April 2019	Receipts from sales in April 2019	20,000	
5 May 2019	Sports equipment supplied in April 2019 paid for		15,000
12 May 2019	Rates for period 1 April 2019 to 30 September 2019 paid		800
19 May 2019	Cash withdrawn for Julia's own expenses		2,000
31 May 2019	Receipts from sales in May 2019	25,000	
5 June 2019	Sports equipment supplied in May 2019 paid for		20,000
10 June 2019	Shop water rates for the year 1 April 2019 to 31 March 2020 paid		400
30 June 2019	Receipts from sales in June 2019	30,000	
30 June 2019	Balance in bank at 30 June 2019		48,800
		105,000	**105,000**

Julia's receipts and payments summary is already very much in the T account format with receipts on the left hand side (debit entries) increasing the balance on the bank asset account and payments on the right hand side (credit entries) reducing the balance on the bank asset account. We can rewrite Julia's receipts and payments summary in a T account format. Julia's bank account is shown in Illustration 4.10.

Illustration 4.10 Julia's bank account receipts and payments in T account format

Bank Account

Debit (increases the asset)		£	Credit (decreases the asset)		£
2019			**2019**		
1 April	Capital account	30,000	1 April	Rent	5,000
30 April	Sales (April)	20,000	1 April	Cash register cost	1,000
31 May	Sales (May)	25,000	1 April	Shelving and fittings cost	12,000
30 June	Sales (June)	30,000	5 May	Cost of sales (April)	15,000
			12 May	Rates	800
			19 May	Drawings	2,000
			5 June	Cost of sales (May)	20,000
			10 June	Water rates	400

The receipts of cash from capital and sales (income) increase the asset in the bank (debits) and the payments out of the bank (credits) reduce the asset in the bank. Note that, as well as including the corresponding account in each entry, the date has also been added to each transaction to make the job of tracing transactions through the accounts even easier.

The next step involves deciding which accounts will be credited and which accounts will be debited in order to complete the double entry. We will need the following T accounts to enable us to complete the entries into the accounting records:

- Capital account
- Sales account
- Rent account
- Cash register cost account
- Shelving and fittings cost account
- Cost of sales (opening inventory + purchases – closing inventory) account
- Rates account
- Water rates account

Draw these T accounts up for yourself now and have a go at posting the entries from the bank account into these accounts before you look at the answers presented in Illustrations 4.11 to 4.18. Remember that for every debit entry there must be a credit entry and for every credit entry there must be a debit entry.

Julia has paid £30,000 into the business, so the business owes Julia £30,000. Therefore, this £30,000 increases the capital of the business as shown in Illustration 4.11. If you were in any doubt as to whether this was a debit or credit entry to the capital account, you just had to follow

Illustration 4.11 Julia's capital T account showing the posting of £30,000 capital introduced

Julia's capital account			
Debit (decreases the capital)	£	Credit (increases the capital)	£
2019		**2019**	
		1 April Bank	30,000

4

the double-entry logic: as £30,000 has been debited to the bank account, the other side of the entry must be to the credit side of the capital account. Assets rise by £30,000 and capital rises by £30,000 so the accounts still balance (£30,000 asset + £0 expenses = £30,000 capital + £0 liability + £0 income).

Our next three receipts of cash are for sales. Sales = income so the three receipts of cash from sales are credited to the sales account (Illustration 4.12).

Illustration 4.12 Julia's sales T account showing the cash income from sales in the months of April, May and June 2019

Sales account			
Debit (decreases the income)	£	Credit (increases the income)	£
2019		**2019**	
		30 April Bank (Sales April)	20,000
		31 May Bank (Sales May)	25,000
		30 June Bank (Sales June)	30,000

Again, if you were in any doubt as to whether the sales account should record a debit or a credit entry, you just had to follow the double-entry logic: as £20,000, £25,000 and £30,000 have been debited to the bank account, the other side of the entries must be to the credit side of the sales account. Assets rise by £75,000 and sales rise by the same amount so the accounts still balance (£30,000 + £75,000 assets + £0 expenses = £30,000 capital + £75,000 income + £0 liability).

Now that the debit entries in the bank account have been credited to the relevant income and capital accounts, it is time to turn our attention to the credit entries in the bank. As these are credit entries in the bank, they must be debit entries in their corresponding asset and expense accounts (Illustrations 4.13 to 4.18).

Illustration 4.13 Julia's rent T account showing the cash payment made for rent on 1 April 2019

Rent account

Debit (increases the expense)	£	Credit (decreases the expense)	£
2019		**2019**	
1 April Bank	5,000		

Illustration 4.14 Julia's cash register cost T account showing the cash spent on the cash register on 1 April 2019

Cash register cost account

Debit (increases the asset)	£	Credit (decreases the asset)	£
2019		**2019**	
1 April Bank	1,000		

Illustration 4.15 Julia's shelving and fittings cost T account showing the cash spent on shelving and fittings on 1 April 2019

Shelving and fittings cost account

Debit (increases the asset)	£	Credit (decreases the asset)	£
2019		**2019**	
1 April Bank	12,000		

Illustration 4.16 Julia's cost of sales T account showing the cash paid for purchases in May and June 2019

Cost of sales (opening inventory + purchases − closing inventory)

Debit (increases the expense)	£	Credit (decreases the expense)	£
2019		**2019**	
5 May Bank (purchases April)	15,000		
5 June Bank (purchases May)	20,000		

Illustration 4.17 Julia's rates T account showing the cash spent on rates in the three-month period April to June 2019

Rates account

Debit (increases the expense)	£	Credit (decreases the expense)	£
2019		**2019**	
12 May Bank	800		

Illustration 4.18 Julia's water rates T account showing the cash spent on water rates in the three-month period April to June 2019

Water rates account				
Debit (increases the expense)	£	Credit (decreases the expense)		£
2019		**2019**		
19 May Bank	400			

These accounts show the recording of the assets and expenses in Julia's T accounts. Assets and expenses increase so the entries are all to the debit side of the T accounts. However, there is one more credit in the bank account that still has to be posted to the accounting records. On 19 May, Julia withdrew £2,000 from the business bank account to pay her personal expenses. This is not an asset (this is not an economic resource with the potential to produce economic benefits) and is not a business expense as the payment was to Julia herself (Chapter 3, Drawings and the business entity assumption). In which T account should this £2,000 be recorded? A little thought should enable you to realise that this £2,000 is a repayment of Julia's capital. Any repayment of capital reduces the amount in the capital account so this £2,000 will be debited to Julia's capital account as shown in Illustration 4.19.

Illustration 4.19 Julia's capital T account showing the £30,000 capital introduced and the £2,000 of capital repaid

Julia's capital account				
Debit (decreases the capital)	£	Credit (increases the capital)		£
2019		**2019**		
19 May Bank (Drawings)	2,000	1 April Bank		30,000

Instead of deducting drawings directly from the capital account as we have done, a separate T account can be maintained for drawings. This T account would be headed up Drawings and any drawings made during the accounting period would be debited to this account in the same way. At the end of the accounting period, the balance on the drawings account would be transferred to the capital account (debit capital account, credit drawings account) to reduce the balance on the drawings account to zero.

SHOW ME HOW TO DO IT   Are you quite happy with the double entry for the figures in Julia's receipts and payments summary? View Video presentation 4.3 in the **online workbook** to see a practical demonstration of how the relevant debit and credit entries were made.

Do the accounts still balance? Let's add up all the debits and credits. Debits = £30,000 (bank) + £75,000 (bank) + £5,000 (rent) + £1,000 (cash register) + £12,000 (shelving and fixtures) + £15,000 (cost of sales) + £20,000 (cost of sales) + £800 (rates) + £400 (water rates) = £159,200. Credits = £56,200 paid out of the bank (add up the credit side of the bank account to make sure this is correct) + £30,000 (capital) – £2,000 (drawings) + £75,000 (sales) = £159,200. Therefore, all the debits are equal to all the credits and the accounts balance.

Can we now use the T accounts to draw up Julia's statement of profit or loss and statement of financial position? Not yet. As we saw in Chapter 3 (The accruals basis of accounting and Example 3.8), we must apply the accruals basis of accounting when producing financial statements. Using the T accounts as they currently stand as the basis for Julia's financial statements would mean preparing the figures on a receipts and payments basis, not on the accruals basis as required by accounting principles.

Firstly, let's look at the additional information Julia provided us with in Chapter 3 (Example 3.8):

- She counted up and valued the inventory at the close of business on 30 June 2019: the cost of this inventory at that date was £10,000.

- At 30 June 2019, Julia owed £25,000 for sports equipment she had purchased from her suppliers on credit in June. She paid this £25,000 on 5 July 2019.

- While her main business is selling sports equipment for cash, Julia has made sales to two local tennis clubs in June on credit. At 30 June 2019, the two clubs owed £2,500, although one club disputes £50 of the amount outstanding, saying that the goods were never delivered. Julia has no proof that these goods were ever received by the club and has reluctantly agreed that she will never receive this £50.

- During the month of June, Julia employed a part-time sales assistant who was owed £300 in wages at the end of June. These wages were paid on 8 July 2019.

- On 5 July 2019, Julia received a telephone bill for £250 covering the three months 1 April 2019 to 30 June 2019 together with an electricity bill for £200 covering the same period.

- Julia expects the cash register and shelving and shop fittings to last for five years before they need replacement. The level of usage of these assets will be the same in each of the next five years. She also expects that the assets will have no residual value at the end of their useful lives and that they will just be scrapped rather than being sold on.

- The cash register contained £500 in cash at 30 June 2019 representing sales receipts that had not yet been banked.

- On 29 June 2019, one of the tennis clubs that she trades with on credit returned goods with a sales value of £400. These goods were faulty. Julia returned these goods to her supplier: the goods had originally cost Julia £250.

To satisfy the accruals basis of accounting, all of these transactions must be reflected in Julia's accounting records up to 30 June 2019. But how should the above transactions be recorded in Julia's T accounts? To help you follow the double entry, the debit and credit entries in the following figures have been made in **red**.

• She counted up and valued the inventory at the close of business on 30 June 2019: the cost of this inventory at that date was £10,000.

Closing inventory is a deduction from cost of sales. This deduction will decrease the cost of sales expense. A decrease in an expense requires a credit entry to the expense account. But closing inventory is also an asset at the end of June 2019 as the resource has the potential to produce economic benefits for Julia from sales of this inventory in the next accounting period, therefore there will be a debit to the inventory account. The required double entry is thus debit inventory, credit cost of sales (Illustration 4.20).

Illustration 4.20 T account double entry to record closing inventory in Julia's books at 30 June 2019

Cost of sales (opening inventory + purchases – closing inventory)					
Debit (increases the expense)		£	Credit (decreases the expense)		£
2019			2019		
5 May	Bank (purchases April)	15,000	30 June	Inventory	10,000
5 June	Bank (purchases May)	20,000			

Inventory				
Debit (increases the asset)		£	Credit (decreases the asset)	£
2019			2019	
30 June	Cost of sales	10,000		

• At 30 June 2019, Julia owed £25,000 for sports equipment she had purchased from her suppliers on credit in June. She paid this £25,000 on 5 July 2019.

Julia currently has an unrecognised expense and an unrecognised liability at 30 June. She must recognise both the liability and the expense that this liability represents. At 30 June 2019 she has a present obligation to transfer economic resources (cash) to pay for the sports goods delivered to her in June. This obligation gives rise to a liability for the amount owed and a corresponding expense. Both expenses and liabilities must increase. Therefore she will debit her cost of sales account with £25,000 (a debit to an expense account will increase the balance on the expense account) and credit her trade payables account (this is a new account that needs setting up) with £25,000. A credit to a liability account will increase the balance on the liability account to record the amount owed at the end of the accounting period. These accounting entries are shown in Illustration 4.21.

Illustration 4.21 T account double entry to record the liability for purchases and cost of sales expense for June 2019

Cost of sales (opening inventory + purchases – closing inventory)

Debit (increases the expense)		£	Credit (decreases the expense)		£
2019			**2019**		
5 May	Bank (purchases April)	15,000	30 June	Inventory	10,000
5 June	Bank (purchases May)	20,000			
30 June	Trade payables (June)	25,000			

Trade payables

Debit (decreases the liability)		£	Credit (increases the liability)		£
2019			**2019**		
			30 June	Cost of sales (June)	25,000

- While her main business is selling sports equipment for cash, Julia has made sales to two local tennis clubs in June on credit. At 30 June 2019, the two clubs owed £2,500, although one club disputes £50 of the amount outstanding, saying that the goods were never delivered. Julia has no proof that these goods were ever received by the club and has reluctantly agreed that she will never receive this £50.

In this case, there are two transactions that must be reflected in Julia's books: the trade receivables and the sales that gave rise to those trade receivables and the irrecoverable debt that will result in a reduction in trade receivables and an increase in the irrecoverable debts expense. Let's deal with these two transactions one at a time.

Firstly, recognising the trade receivables (money due to Julia as a result of trading with her customers on credit) will result in an increase (debit) in the asset. The corresponding credit is to the sales account as income also increases (credit) as more sales have been made that require recognition in the three-month accounting period (Illustration 4.22). The double entry to record a sale made on credit is thus debit trade receivables, credit sales.

Secondly, there is a known irrecoverable debt of £50, money which Julia will not receive from her customer. This known irrecoverable debt will decrease the trade receivables asset (a credit to the asset account) by £50 as this asset is derecognised. The asset no longer exists so it is removed (derecognised) from the T account and from the statement of financial position. The known irrecoverable debt represents an expense so the irrecoverable debt expense account will show a debit to reflect this increase (a debit increases the balance on an expense account). The double entry for this event is shown in Illustration 4.23.

4

Illustration 4.22 T account double entry to record the trade receivables asset and sales income at 30 June 2019

Trade receivables

Debit (increases the asset)	£	Credit (decreases the asset)	£
2019		**2019**	
30 June Sales	2,500		

Sales account

Debit (decreases the income)	£	Credit (increases the income)	£
2019		**2019**	
		30 April Bank (Sales April)	20,000
		31 May Bank (Sales May)	25,000
		30 June Bank (Sales June)	30,000
		30 June Trade receivables	2,500

Illustration 4.23 T account double entry to derecognise a trade receivable asset and to charge the derecognised receivable as an irrecoverable debt expense

Trade receivables

Debit (increases the asset)	£	Credit (decreases the asset)	£
2019		**2019**	
30 June Sales	2,500	June 30 Irrecoverable debts	50

Irrecoverable debts

Debit (increases the expense)	£	Credit (decreases the expense)	£
2019		**2019**	
30 June Trade receivables	50		

- During the month of June, Julia employed a part-time sales assistant who was owed £300 in wages at the end of June. These wages were paid on 8 July 2019.

At 30 June, Julia has a liability for wages owed to her part-time sales assistant. At that date, there is a present obligation to transfer economic resources as a result of past events (the work undertaken by the sales assistant and Julia's agreement to pay for this work) which will give rise to the outflow of cash (economic resources) from the business (the payment of the wages on 8 July). Therefore, Julia will recognise a liability for the wages owed, an accrual. To recognise the increase in the liability, she will credit the wages accrual account. The wages payable is an expense so Julia will debit the wages account with this increase in expenses (Illustration 4.24).

Illustration 4.24 T account double entry to recognise a liability to pay wages at 30 June 2019 and the corresponding wages expense

Wages

Debit (increases the expense)	£	Credit (decreases the expense)	£
2019		2019	
30 June Wages accrual	300		

Wages accrual

Debit (decreases the liability)	£	Credit (increases the liability)	£
2019		2019	
		30 June Wages	300

- On 5 July 2019, Julia received a telephone bill for £250 covering the three months 1 April 2019 to 30 June 2019 together with an electricity bill for £200 covering the same period.

In the same way as for the wages payable, Julia has liabilities for both telephone expenses owed to the telephone company and for electricity owed to the electric company. Using the same logic as before, there are two present obligations to transfer economic resources as a result of past events (the usage of the telephone to make business calls and the use of the electricity to light the shop) which will give rise to the outflow of cash (economic resources) from the business to settle the telephone and electricity bills at a later date. Therefore, Julia will recognise a liability for the amounts owed to the telephone and electric companies, two accruals, crediting the telephone accrual and electricity accrual accounts to increase the liabilities of the business at 30 June 2019. The telephone and electricity bills payable are expenses, so Julia will debit the telephone and electricity accounts with these increases in expenses (Illustrations 4.25 and 4.26).

- Julia expects the cash register and shelving and shop fittings to last for five years before they need replacement. The level of usage of these assets will be the same in each of the next five years. She also expects that the assets will have no residual value at the end of their useful lives and that they will just be scrapped rather than being sold on.

We saw in Chapter 3 (Illustration 3.6) that the depreciation on the cash register for the three months was £50 (£1,000/5 years × 3/12 months) while the depreciation on the shelving and fittings was £600 (£12,000/5 years × 3/12 months). Depreciation charges are debited to the

Illustration 4.25 T account double entry to recognise the telephone liability and the corresponding telephone expense at 30 June 2019

Telephone

Debit (increases the expense)	£	Credit (decreases the expense)	£
2019		**2019**	
30 June Telephone accrual	250		

Telephone accrual

Debit (decreases the liability)	£	Credit (increases the liability)	£
2019		**2019**	
		30 June Telephone	250

Illustration 4.26 T account double entry to recognise the electricity liability and the corresponding electricity expense at 30 June 2019

Electricity

Debit (increases the expense)	£	Credit (decreases the expense)	£
2019		**2019**	
30 June Electricity accrual	200		

Electricity accrual

Debit (decreases the liability)	£	Credit (increases the liability)	£
2019		**2019**	
		30 June Electricity	200

depreciation expense account (an increase in an expense) and credited to the accumulated depreciation account (Illustrations 4.27 and 4.28). Netting off the credit balance on the accumulated depreciation account and the debit balance on the non-current assets cost account gives the carrying amount of the non-current assets in the statement of financial position as we shall see (Illustration 4.43). The accumulated depreciation accounts are set up and used to maintain a record of depreciation charged to the statement of profit or loss in different accounting periods. The depreciation charged each year builds up on the accumulated depreciation account and increases each year as more depreciation is charged on the assets, thereby reducing the carrying amount of the non-current assets in the statement of financial position over their estimated useful lives.

Illustration 4.27 T account double entry to recognise the cash register depreciation charge and the accumulated depreciation on the cash register at 30 June 2019

Cash register depreciation charge

Debit (increases the expense)	£	Credit (decreases the expense)	£
2019		2019	
30 June Cash register accumulated depreciation	50		

Cash register accumulated depreciation

Debit (decreases the accumulated depreciation)	£	Credit (increases the accumulated depreciation)	£
2019		2019	
		30 June Cash register depreciation charge	50

Illustration 4.28 T account double entry to recognise the shelving and fittings depreciation charge and accumulated depreciation on shelving and fittings at 30 June 2019

Shelving and fittings depreciation charge

Debit (increases the expense)	£	Credit (decreases the expense)	£
2019		2019	
30 June Shelving and fittings accumulated depreciation	600		

Shelving and fittings accumulated depreciation

Debit (decreases the accumulated depreciation)	£	Credit (increases the accumulated depreciation)	£
2019		2019	
		30 June Shelving and fittings depreciation charge	600

- The cash register contained £500 in cash at 30 June 2019 representing sales receipts that had not yet been banked.

There is an unrecorded asset of £500 cash together with an unrecorded sale of the same amount. Therefore, assets rise by £500 with £500 debited to the cash account (this amount cannot be recorded in the bank account as the cash has not yet been paid into the bank. The cash is therefore maintained in a separate cash account) while income increases by £500, resulting in a credit to the sales account as shown in Illustration 4.29.

Illustration 4.29 T account double entry to recognise the cash asset and additional sales at 30 June 2019

Cash account

Debit (increases the asset)	£	Credit (decreases the asset)	£
2019		2019	
30 June Sales	500		

Sales account

Debit (decreases the income)	£	Credit (increases the income)	£
2019		2019	
		30 April Bank (Sales April)	20,000
		31 May Bank (Sales May)	25,000
		30 June Bank (Sales June)	30,000
		30 June Trade receivables	2,500
		30 June Cash	500

- On 29 June 2019, one of the tennis clubs that she trades with on credit returned goods with a sales value of £400. These goods were faulty. Julia returned these goods to her supplier: the goods had originally cost Julia £250.

There are two transactions represented in this note. Firstly, the trade receivables asset decreases by £400 as a result of the cancelled sale. Therefore, there is a credit entry to the trade receivables account to reflect this reduction in the asset (cash, an economic resource, will no longer be realised from this sale). As the sale has been cancelled, there is a reduction in the sales account, so sales are debited with £400 to reflect the decrease in the sales income as a result of this cancelled sale (Illustration 4.30).

Illustration 4.30 T account double entry to record a reduction in trade receivables and sales arising from a cancelled sale

Sales account

Debit (decreases the income)	£	Credit (increases the income)	£
2019		**2019**	
30 June Trade receivables	400	30 April Bank (Sales April)	20,000
		31 May Bank (Sales May)	25,000
		30 June Bank (Sales June)	30,000
		30 June Trade receivables	2,500
		30 June Cash	500

Trade receivables

Debit (increases the asset)	£	Credit (decreases the asset)	£
2019		**2019**	
30 June Sales	2,500	June 30 Irrecoverable debts	50
		June 30 Sales	400

The second transaction in this note represents a decrease in the amounts owed by Julia to her suppliers: goods to the value of £250 have been returned to the supplier so trade payables will be debited with £250 to reflect this decrease in the liability, the amount that no longer needs to be paid. This return of goods, a cancellation of an obligation, will also have an effect on the cost of sales. £250 less has been spent on purchases, so cost of sales will be credited with this decrease in expenditure (Illustration 4.31).

Illustration 4.31 T account double entry to record the reduction in the trade payables and cost of sales arising from the return of faulty goods to a supplier

Cost of sales (purchases account)

Debit (increases the expense)	£	Credit (decreases the expense)	£
2019		**2019**	
5 May Bank (purchases April)	15,000	30 June Inventory	10,000
5 June Bank (purchases May)	20,000	30 June Trade payables	250
30 June Trade payables (June)	25,000		

Trade payables

Debit (decreases the liability)	£	Credit (increases the liability)	£
2019		**2019**	
30 June Cost of sales	250	30 June Cost of sales	25,000

We have now made all the entries to the T accounts required by the additional information provided by Julia. However, there are still two more entries to complete before our T accounts fully reflect all the transactions that have occurred in Julia's first three months of operation. Look back at Illustration 4.9, Julia's summary of bank receipts and payments. The rates payment of £800 on 12 May represents the rates expense for the months April to September 2019. As our accounts are for the first three months of trading, April to June 2019, this means that three months (July, August and September 2019) have been paid in advance and represent a prepayment of rates. Therefore, £400 (£800 × 3/6) will be deducted from the rates account (a credit) and added to the rates prepayment account (debit). The credit to the rates account represents the decrease in the expense for the accounting period while the increase in the rates prepayment account represents an increase in the assets at the end of the three months. Illustration 4.32 shows the double entry required to reflect this prepayment.

Illustration 4.32 T account double entry to recognise a rates prepayment and the consequent reduction in the rates expense at 30 June 2019

Rates account

Debit (increases the expense)	£	Credit (decreases the expense)	£
2019		**2019**	
12 May Bank	800	30 June Rates prepayment	400

Rates prepayment account

Debit (increases the asset)	£	Credit (decreases the asset)	£
2019		**2019**	
30 June Rates	400		

In the same way, the water rates of £400 were paid for the whole year April 2019 to March 2020. As we are only dealing with the first three months of trading, this means that £300 of water rates have been paid in advance (£400 × 9/12 = £300). Therefore, the prepayment is deducted from the water rates account to reflect the decrease in the expense (credit) and added to the water rates prepayment account to represent the increase in the asset at the end of June 2019 as shown in Illustration 4.33.

Illustration 4.33 T account double entry to recognise a water rates prepayment asset and the consequent reduction in the water rates expense at 30 June 2019

Water rates account

Debit (increases the expense)	£	Credit (decreases the expense)	£
2019		**2019**	
19 May Bank	400	30 June Water rates prepayment	300

Water rates prepayment account

Debit (increases the asset)	£	Credit (decreases the asset)	£
2019		**2019**	
30 June Water rates	300		

MULTIPLE CHOICE QUESTIONS   Convinced you could state the double entry for any given transaction? Go to the **online workbook** and have a go at Multiple choice questions 4.2 to test your ability at making the correct double entry.

JULIA'S TRIAL BALANCE

We have now completed all the entries to the T accounts. Our next step is to check whether all the debits and all the credits have been included by extracting a trial balance. We saw how this worked in the case of Arthur (Illustrations 4.7 and 4.8) and the principles are exactly the same for Julia. The balance on each account is calculated by adding up the two sides of each account to determine the difference. If there are more debits than credits on the account, then there is a debit balance on that account. Whereas more credits than debits on the account means there is a credit balance on that account. Debit balances are posted to the debit side of the trial balance and credit balances are posted to the credit side.

The first account to consider is Julia's bank account, presented in Illustration 4.34.

The debit side of the bank account adds up to £105,000 while the credit side totals up to £56,200. £105,000 has been paid into the bank and only £56,200 has been taken out to acquire assets and pay expenses. There are more debits than credits on the bank account so there is a debit balance of £48,800 (£105,000 debits – £56,200 credits). This debit balance is allocated to the debit side of the trial balance in Illustration 4.41.

Illustration 4.34 (= Illustration 4.10) Julia's bank account

Bank Account

Debit (increases the asset)		£	Credit (decreases the asset)		£
2019			**2019**		
1 April	Capital account	30,000	1 April	Rent	5,000
30 April	Sales: April	20,000	1 April	Cash register	1,000
31 May	Sales: May	25,000	1 April	Shelving and fittings	12,000
30 June	Sales: June	30,000	5 May	Cost of sales	15,000
			12 May	Rates	800
			19 May	Drawings	2,000
			5 June	Cost of sales	20,000
			10 June	Water rates	400

Debit side total:
£30,000 + £20,000 +
£25,000 + £30,000 =
£105,000

Credit side total:
£5,000 + £1,000 +
£12,000 +£15,000 +
£800 + £2,000 +
£20,000 + £400 =
£56,200

Our next account is Julia's capital account (Illustration 4.35). Repeating the same approach on this account as for the bank account we can see that the capital account has £30,000 of credits and £2,000 of debits so there are more credits than debits. The £28,000 (£30,000 – £2,000) credit balance is added to the credit side of the trial balance in Illustration 4.41.

Illustration 4.35 (= Illustration 4.19) Julia's capital account

Julia's capital account

Debit (decreases the capital)		£	Credit (increases the capital)		£
2019			**2019**		
19 May	Bank (Drawings)	2,000	1 April	Bank	30,000

Illustration 4.36 (= Illustration 4.30) Julia's sales account

Sales account

Debit (decreases the income)		£	Credit (increases the income)		£
2019			**2019**		
30 June	Trade receivables	400	30 April	Bank (Sales April)	20,000
			31 May	Bank (Sales May)	25,000
			30 June	Bank (Sales June)	30,000
			30 June	Trade receivables	2,500
			30 June	Cash	500

Julia's sales account (Illustration 4.36) has £78,000 of entries on the credit side of the account and £400 of entries on the debit side of the account. There is therefore a £77,600 credit balance on the sales account (£78,000 of credits – £400 of debits) which is posted to the credit side of the trial balance (Illustration 4.41).

Illustration 4.37 (= Illustration 4.13) Julia's rent account

Rent account

Debit (increases the expense)		£	Credit (decreases the expense)	£
2019			**2019**	
1 April	Bank	5,000		

Our next three accounts (Illustrations 4.37 to 4.39) are debit accounts with only one entry in each on the debit side and no credit balances. The balances on the rent, cash register cost and shelving and fittings cost accounts show debit balances of £5,000, £1,000 and £12,000 respectively and these balances are added to the debit side of the trial balance in Illustration 4.41.

Illustration 4.38 (= Illustration 4.14) Julia's Cash register cost account

Cash register cost account

Debit (increases the asset)		£	Credit (decreases the asset)	£
2019			**2019**	
1 April	Bank	1,000		

Illustration 4.39 (= Illustration 4.15) Julia's shelving and fittings cost account

Shelving and fittings cost account

Debit (increases the asset)		£	Credit (decreases the asset)	£
2019			**2019**	
1 April	Bank	12,000		

Julia's cost of sales account at the end of June 2019 is shown in Illustration 4.40. The cost of sales account shows debits of £60,000 (increases in the expense) and credits of £10,250 (decreases in the expense) so there is a debit (more debits than credits) balance of £49,750 to add to the debit side of the trial balance (Illustration 4.41).

Illustration 4.40 (= Illustration 4.31) Julia's cost of sales account

Cost of sales (purchases account)

Debit (increases the expense)		£	Credit (decreases the expense)		£
2019			**2019**		
5 May	Bank (purchases April)	15,000	30 June	Inventory	10,000
5 June	Bank (purchases May)	20,000	30 June	Trade payables	250
30 June	Trade payables (June)	25,000			

NUMERICAL EXERCISES You should now have gained an appreciation of how to determine whether there is a debit or credit balance on each T account and how to calculate that debit or credit balance for inclusion in the trial balance. Look back at our workings in Illustrations 4.20 to 4.33 to pick up the following balances to include in Julia's trial balance at 30 June 2019:

Rates (Illustration 4.32)
Water rates (Illustration 4.33)
Inventory (Illustration 4.20)
Trade payables (Illustration 4.31)
Trade receivables (Illustration 4.30)
Irrecoverable debts (Illustration 4.23)
Wages (Illustration 4.24)
Wages accrual (Illustration 4.24)
Telephone (Illustration 4.25)
Telephone accrual (Illustration 4.25)

Electricity (Illustration 4.26)
Electricity accrual (Illustration 4.26)
Cash register depreciation charge (Illustration 4.27)
Cash register accumulated depreciation (Illustration 4.27)
Shelving and fittings depreciation charge (Illustration 4.28)
Shelving and fittings accumulated depreciation (Illustration 4.28)
Cash (Illustration 4.29)
Rates prepayment (Illustration 4.32)
Water rates prepayment (Illustration 4.33)

Have a go at constructing and balancing Julia's trial balance at 30 June 2019 before you have a look at Illustration 4.41 to see if you have all the correct answers. To help you construct the trial balance, the grid for completion is given in the **online workbook** in Numerical exercises 4.2.

Once you have completed your summary of the balances on each of Julia's accounts, you should have the trial balance shown in Illustration 4.41. The totals of the debits and credits are equal, so we can be confident that the double entry has been fully and accurately completed.

Illustration 4.41 Julia's trial balance at 30 June 2019

	Debit £	Credit £
Bank account	48,800	
Julia's capital account		28,000
Sales		77,600
Rent	5,000	
Cash register cost	1,000	
Shelving and fittings cost	12,000	
Cost of sales	49,750	
Rates	400	
Water rates	100	
Inventory	10,000	
Trade payables		24,750
Trade receivables	2,050	
Irrecoverable debts	50	
Wages	300	
Wages accrual		300
Telephone	250	
Telephone accrual		250
Electricity	200	
Electricity accrual		200
Cash register depreciation charge	50	
Cash register accumulated depreciation		50
Shelving and fittings depreciation charge	600	
Shelving and fittings accumulated depreciation		600
Cash	500	
Rates prepayment	400	
Water rates prepayment	300	
Totals (must be equal)	**131,750**	**131,750**

MULTIPLE CHOICE QUESTIONS   Are you quite sure you could calculate the debit or credit balance on a T account to add to the trial balance? Go to the **online workbook** and have a go at Multiple choice questions 4.3 to test your ability to make the correct double entry in the accounts.

NUMERICAL EXERCISES   Do you think you could put together a trial balance from a given set of T accounts? Go to the **online workbook** and have a go at Numerical exercises 4.3 to test your ability at drawing up a trial balance.

We can now use the figures from the trial balance to produce Julia's statement of profit or loss for the three months to 30 June 2019 together with a statement of financial position at that date. These financial statements are presented in Illustrations 4.42 and 4.43.

Illustration 4.42 Julia's statement of profit or loss for the three months ended 30 June 2019

	£	£
Sales		77,600
Cost of sales		49,750
Gross profit (sales–cost of sales)		**27,850**
Expenses		
Rent	5,000	
Rates	400	
Water rates	100	
Irrecoverable debt	50	
Wages	300	
Telephone	250	
Electricity	200	
Cash register depreciation	50	
Shelving and fittings depreciation	600	
Total expenses		6,950
Net profit for the three months		**20,900**

Compare Julia's statement of profit or loss and statement of financial position in Illustrations 4.42 and 4.43 with her statement of profit or loss and statement of financial position in Illustrations 3.6 and 3.7. The results are exactly the same. This is completely in line with what we would expect as the financial statements have been produced from exactly the same set of cash receipts and payments and exactly the same set of additional information. However, because all of the entries have been made in the T accounts, the figures can be transferred directly into the statement of profit or loss and the statement of financial position without any need for the additional calculations, narrative and notes that were presented in Illustrations 3.6 and 3.7.

Illustration 4.43 Julia's statement of financial position at 30 June 2019

	£
Non-current assets	
Cash register (£1,000 cost – £50 accumulated depreciation)	950
Shelves and shop fittings (£12,000 – £600 accumulated depreciation)	11,400
	12,350
Current assets	
Inventory	10,000
Trade receivables	2,050
Rates prepayment	400
Water rates prepayment	300
Bank balance	48,800
Cash	500
	62,050
Total assets (£12,350 non-current assets + £62,050 current assets)	**74,400**
Current liabilities	
Trade payables	24,750
Wages accrual	300
Telephone accrual	250
Electricity accrual	200
Total liabilities	**25,500**
Net assets (total assets (£74,400) – total liabilities (£25,500))	**48,900**
Equity (capital account)	
Capital introduced by Julia	30,000
Drawings (cash paid from the business for personal expenses)	(2,000)
Net profit for the three months	20,900
Capital account at 30 June 2019	**48,900**

CLOSING OFF THE T ACCOUNTS AT THE END OF AN ACCOUNTING PERIOD

At the end of each accounting period, each T account is closed off. Where the differences on the T accounts represent assets, liabilities or capital, these differences are carried forward to the next accounting period. Where the differences on the T accounts represent income or expenses, then these differences are transferred to the statement of profit or loss for the accounting period. Income and expenses balances are therefore *not* carried forward to future accounting periods. The difference between the income and the expenses for each accounting period is added to the owner's capital balance as the profit for the year (or deducted from the owner's capital if a loss has been made). This makes sense since the accounting equation states that assets = liabilities +

capital + income − expenses. Income − expenses = profit or loss so the net difference between income and expenses is added to the capital balance in the statement of financial position and carried forward to the next accounting period. Let's see how Julia's accounts are closed off at the end of June 2019.

Our first account is the bank account (Illustration 4.44). The entries on the debit side of the bank account add up to £105,000 while the credit side totals up to £56,200. As we have already seen (this chapter, Illustration 4.34), there are more debits than credits on the bank account so there is a debit balance of £48,800 (£105,000 debits − £56,200 credits). Is the bank account an asset or an expense? Cash is an asset so the debit balance on the bank account is carried forward to the next accounting period. The bank account is closed off as shown in **red** in Illustration 4.44.

Illustration 4.44 Julia's bank account closed off at 30 June 2019 and the carried forward balance brought forward at the start of the new accounting period

Bank Account					
Debit (increases the asset)		£	Credit (decreases the asset)		£
2019			**2019**		
1 April	Capital account	30,000	1 April	Rent	5,000
30 April	Sales: April	20,000	1 April	Cash register	1,000
31 May	Sales: May	25,000	1 April	Shelving and fittings	12,000
30 June	Sales: June	30,000	5 May	Cost of sales	15,000
			12 May	Rates	800
			19 May	Drawings	2,000
			5 June	Cost of sales	20,000
			10 June	Water rates	400
			30 June	Balance c/f	48,800
		105,000			105,000
1 July	Balance b/f	48,800			

Points to note about closing off T accounts:

- The accounts are balanced by adding in the debit or credit balance to the side of the account that is lower than the other. In Illustration 4.44 the credit side of the bank account is lower so £48,800 is added to the credit side of the account so that both sides total up to £105,000.

- The totals on both the debit and credit sides of each T account must be equal at the end of each accounting period.

- As both sides now equal £105,000, the account is said to balance.

- The abbreviation c/f means carried forward, a balance transferred to the next accounting period.

- The abbreviation b/f means brought forward, a balance transferred from the end of the last accounting period.

- The brought forward balance appears in the bank account on the opposite side to the balance carried forward. This is logical: the bank balance is an asset so it must appear on the debit side of the bank account at the start of the next accounting period. This balance is an asset because more cash has been paid into the bank than has been paid out. Assets, as we have seen, are debits.

- Asset, liability and capital accounts will have balances carried forward at the end of the accounting period. These balances are then brought forward on the first day of the next accounting period on either the debit side (assets) or the credit side (liabilities and capital) ready for the next set of entries to be made to the accounts in the next accounting period.

Think about these points as we work our way through the remaining accounts.

Our next account is Julia's capital account. This account is balanced off as shown in Illustration 4.45.

Illustration 4.45 Julia's capital account closed off at 30 June 2019 and the carried forward balance brought forward at the start of the next accounting period

Julia's capital account					
Debit (decreases the capital)		£	Credit (increases the capital)		£
2019			**2019**		
19 May	Bank (Drawings)	2,000	1 April	Bank	30,000
30 June	Balance c/f	48,900	30 June	Profit for 3 months	20,900
		50,900			50,900
			1 July	Balance b/f	48,900

Before we can close off Julia's capital account, we must add in the profit for the three months. As we saw in Illustrations 4.42 and 4.43 this profit was £20,900. £20,900 is debited to the statement of profit or loss and credited to Julia's capital account as the business now owes Julia an additional £20,900. Julia's capital account has £50,900 of credits and £2,000 of debits. The credits are greater than the debits, so there is a £48,900 (£50,900 – £2,000) credit balance on Julia's capital account. This is posted to the debit side of the account so that both sides total up to £50,900. The brought forward balance appears on the credit side of the account. £48,900 is owed to Julia in her capacity as owner of the business so you would expect this to be a credit balance as it is the capital owed to the owner.

Our next account is the sales account. This account is balanced off as shown in Illustration 4.46.

The sales account has £80,000 of credits and £400 of debits so there is a £77,600 (£80,000 – £400) credit balance on this account. All of this income has been earned in the three-month accounting period so the £77,600 balance on the sales account is recognised as income for the three-month accounting period and transferred to the statement of profit or loss. There is thus no balance carried forward or brought forward on the sales account.

Illustration 4.46 Julia's sales account closed off at 30 June 2019 and the balance transferred to the statement of profit or loss for the period

Debit (decreases the income)		£	Credit (increases the income)		£
2019			**2019**		
30 June	Trade receivables	400	30 April	Bank	20,000
30 June	Statement of profit or loss	77,600	31 May	Bank	25,000
			30 June	Bank	30,000
			30 June	Trade receivables	2,500
			30 June	Cash	500
		80,000			80,000

Sales account

NUMERICAL EXERCISES   At this point, you might like to have a go at balancing off all the remaining T accounts before you check your answers against the T accounts presented in Illustrations 4.47 to 4.69. To help you in making this attempt, the **online workbook** Numerical exercises 4.4 presents the T accounts as they stand at 30 June 2019 after posting all the transactions up to that date but before the accounts are closed off and the balances either carried forward or transferred to the statement of profit or loss.

Julia's rent account is balanced and closed off as shown in Illustration 4.47.

Illustration 4.47 Julia's rent account closed off at 30 June 2019 and the balance transferred to the statement of profit or loss for the period

Rent account

Debit (increases the expense)		£	Credit (decreases the expense)		£
2019			**2019**		
1 April	Bank	5,000	30 June	Statement of profit or loss	5,000
		5,000			5,000

There is a debit balance on the account of £5,000, £5,000 of debits – £0 credits. The rent paid covered the three months of April, May and June 2019 so all the economic benefits of this payment have been consumed during the three-month period. This expense is transferred to the statement of profit or loss to be matched against the income generated from this expenditure to determine the net profit or loss for the accounting period.

Our next two accounts are the cash register cost and the shelving and fittings cost accounts, shown in Illustrations 4.48 and 4.49.

Illustration 4.48 Julia's cash register cost account closed off at 30 June 2019 and the carried forward balance brought forward at the start of the new accounting period

Cash register cost account

Debit (increases the asset)		£	Credit (decreases the asset)		£
2019			**2019**		
1 April	Bank	1,000	30 June	Balance c/f	1,000
		1,000			1,000
1 July	Balance b/f	1,000			

4

Illustration 4.49 Julia's shelving and fittings cost account closed off at 30 June 2019 and the carried forward balance brought forward at the start of the new accounting period

Shelving and fittings cost account

Debit (increases the asset)		£	Credit (decreases the asset)		£
2019			**2019**		
1 April	Bank	12,000	30 June	Balance c/f	12,000
		12,000			12,000
1 July	Balance b/f	12,000			

The cash register and shelving and fittings have a useful life of five years. Therefore, these are non-current assets which have the potential to produce economic benefits for more than one year. Both accounts show debit balances with debits of £1,000 and £12,000 and zero credits. These represent debit balances which are carried forward at the period end (30 June) and brought forward on the first day of the next accounting period 1 July.

The next three T accounts (Illustrations 4.50, 4,51 and 4.52) are debit accounts with more debits than credits. Cost of sales, rates and water rates are expense accounts whose balances are transferred to the statement of profit or loss. In this way the revenue generated is matched with the costs incurred to produce that revenue.

Illustration 4.50 Julia's cost of sales account closed off at 30 June 2019 and the balance transferred to the statement of profit or loss for the period

Cost of sales (opening inventory + purchases – closing inventory)

Debit (increases the expense)		£	Credit (decreases the expense)		£
2019			**2019**		
5 May	Bank	15,000	30 June	Inventory	10,000
5 June	Bank	20,000	30 June	Trade payables	250
30 June	Trade payables	25,000	30 June	Statement of profit or loss	49,750
		60,000			60,000

4

Illustration 4.51 Julia's rates account closed off at 30 June 2019 and the balance transferred to the statement of profit or loss for the period

Rates account				
Debit (increases the expense)	**£**	**Credit (decreases the expense)**		**£**
2019		**2019**		
12 May Bank	800	30 June	Rates prepayment	400
		30 June	Statement of profit or loss	400
	800			800

Illustration 4.52 Julia's water rates account closed off at 30 June 2019 and the balance transferred to the statement of profit or loss for the period

Water rates account				
Debit (increases the expense)	**£**	**Credit (decreases the expense)**		**£**
2019		**2019**		
19 May Bank	400	30 June	Water rates prepayment	300
		30 June	Statement of profit or loss	100
	400			400

Inventory at the end of the three months is an asset which is carried forward to the next accounting period to match against the revenue that Julia expects to generate from the sale of that inventory. The entries required to close off the inventory account are shown in Illustration 4.53.

Illustration 4.53 Julia's inventory account closed off at 30 June 2019 and the carried forward balance brought forward at the start of the new accounting period

Inventory				
Debit (increases the asset)	**£**	**Credit (decreases the asset)**		**£**
2019		**2019**		
30 June Cost of sales	10,000	30 June	Balance c/f	10,000
	10,000			10,000
1 July Balance b/f	10,000			

The balance on the trade payables account is a credit balance as there are more credits than debits on this account. Trade payables are a liability, a present obligation for Julia which has arisen from trading with her suppliers on credit. This balance is carried forward to the next accounting period as shown in Illustration 4.54.

Illustration 4.54 Julia's trade payables account closed off at 30 June 2019 and the carried forward balance brought forward at the start of the new accounting period

Trade payables					
Debit (decreases the liability)		**£**	**Credit (increases the liability)**		**£**
2019			**2019**		
30 June	Cost of sales	250	30 June	Cost of sales	25,000
30 June	Balance c/f	24,750			
		25,000			25,000
			1 July	Balance b/f	24,750

4

Trade receivables are the opposite of trade payables, money owed to the business rather than money owed by the business. The debit side of the account totals up to £2,500 while the credit side reflects reductions in the asset of £450 as a result of irrecoverable debts and sales returns. Therefore, the debit balance on the account is £2,050 (£2,500 – £50 – £400) which is carried forward to the next accounting period as an asset to be realised in the following months (Illustration 4.55) when customers pay what is owed.

Illustration 4.55 Julia's trade receivables account closed off at 30 June 2019 and the carried forward balance brought forward at the start of the new accounting period

Trade receivables					
Debit (increases the asset)		**£**	**Credit (decreases the asset)**		**£**
2019			**2019**		
30 June	Sales	2,500	June 30	Irrecoverable debts	50
			June 30	Sales	400
			June 30	Balance c/f	2,050
		2,500			2,500
1 July	Balance b/f	2,050			

Julia's irrecoverable debts account (Illustration 4.56) is a debit account with more debits than credits. Irrecoverable debts are an expense account whose balances are transferred to the statement of profit or loss so that revenue generated is matched with the costs incurred to produce that revenue.

Illustration 4.56 Julia's irrecoverable debts account closed off at 30 June 2019 and the balance transferred to the statement of profit or loss for the period

		Irrecoverable debts			
Debit (increases the expense)		£	Credit (decreases the expense)		£
2019			**2019**		
30 June	Trade receivables	50	30 June	Statement of profit or loss	50
		50			50

Illustrations 4.57 to 4.62 show three expense accounts (Illustrations 4.57, 4.59 and 4.61) with debit balances that are transferred to the statement of profit or loss for the three months to match against the revenue generated. There are also three liability accounts for accrued expenses, costs incurred but not yet paid, which show more credits than debits. The balances on these three liability accounts (Illustrations 4.58, 4.60 and 4.62) are carried forward to match against the cash payments that will be made in the next accounting period to extinguish these liabilities.

Illustration 4.57 Julia's wages account closed off at 30 June 2019 and the balance transferred to the statement of profit or loss for the period

		Wages			
Debit (increases the expense)		£	Credit (decreases the expense)		£
2019			**2019**		
30 June	Wages accrual	300	30 June	Statement of profit or loss	300
		300			300

Illustration 4.58 Julia's wages accrual account closed off at 30 June 2019 and the carried forward balance brought forward at the start of the new accounting period

		Wages accrual			
Debit (decreases the liability)		£	Credit (increases the liability)		£
2019			**2019**		
30 June	Balance c/f	300	30 June	Wages	300
		300			300
			1 July	Balance b/f	300

Illustration 4.59 Julia's telephone account closed off at 30 June 2019 and the balance transferred to the statement of profit or loss for the period

Telephone

Debit (increases the expense)		£	Credit (decreases the expense)		£
2019			**2019**		
30 June	Telephone accrual	250	30 June	Statement of profit or loss	250
		250			250

Illustration 4.60 Julia's telephone accrual account closed off at 30 June 2019 and the carried forward balance brought forward at the start of the new accounting period

Telephone accrual

Debit (decreases the liability)		£	Credit (increases the liability)		£
2019			**2019**		
30 June	Balance c/f	250	30 June	Telephone	250
		250			250
			1 July	Balance b/f	250

Illustration 4.61 Julia's electricity account closed off at 30 June 2019 and the balance transferred to the statement of profit or loss for the period

Electricity

Debit (increases the expense)		£	Credit (decreases the expense)		£
2019			**2019**		
30 June	Electricity accrual	200	30 June	Statement of profit or loss	200
		200			200

Illustration 4.62 Julia's electricity accrual account closed off at 30 June 2019 and the carried forward balance brought forward at the start of the new accounting period

Electricity accrual

Debit (decreases the liability)		£	Credit (increases the liability)		£
2019			**2019**		
30 June	Balance c/f	200	30 June	Electricity	200
		200			200
			1 July	Balance b/f	200

Illustrations 4.63 to 4.66 present the two depreciation charge and the two accumulated depreciation accounts. Illustrations 4.63 and 4.65 show debit balances as there are more debits than credits on these accounts so these expense balances are charged to the statement of profit or loss, matching this expenditure with sales to determine the profit for the three months. Illustrations 4.64 and 4.66 present accounts with credit balances, more credits than debits, and these accumulated depreciation balances are carried forward to the next accounting period to set off against the cost of the associated non-current assets.

Illustration 4.63 Julia's cash register depreciation charge account closed off at 30 June 2019 and the balance transferred to the statement of profit or loss for the period

Cash register depreciation charge			
Debit (increases the expense)	£	Credit (decreases the expense)	£
2019		2019	
30 June Cash register accumulated depreciation	50	30 June Statement of profit or loss	50
	50		50

Illustration 4.64 Julia's cash register accumulated depreciation account closed off at 30 June 2019 and the carried forward balance brought forward at the start of the new accounting period

Cash register accumulated depreciation			
Debit (decreases the accumulated depreciation)	£	Credit (increases the accumulated depreciation)	£
2019		2019	
30 June Balance c/f	50	30 June Cash register depreciation charge	50
	50		50
		1 July Balance b/f	50

Illustration 4.65 Julia's shelving and fittings depreciation charge account closed off at 30 June 2019 and the balance transferred to the statement of profit or loss for the period

Shelving and fittings depreciation charge			
Debit (increases the expense)	£	Credit (decreases the expense)	£
2019		2019	
30 June Shelving and fittings accumulated depreciation	600	30 June Statement of profit or loss	600
	600		600

Illustration 4.66 Julia's shelving and fittings accumulated depreciation account closed off at 30 June 2019 and the carried forward balance brought forward at the start of the new accounting period

Shelving and fittings accumulated depreciation

Debit (decreases the accumulated depreciation)		£	Credit (increases the accumulated depreciation)		£
2019			**2019**		
30 June	Balance c/f	600	30 June	Shelving and fittings depreciation charge	600
		600			600
			1 July	Balance b/f	600

There is a debit balance on the cash account (Illustration 4.67). Cash is an asset which is carried forward to the next accounting period.

Illustration 4.67 Julia's cash account closed off at 30 June 2019 and the carried forward balance brought forward at the start of the new accounting period

Cash account

Debit (increases the asset)		£	Credit (decreases the asset)		£
2019			**2019**		
30 June	Sales	500	30 June	Balance c/f	500
		500			500
1 July	Balance b/f	500			

Illustrations 4.68 and 4.69 are prepayment accounts. There are debit balances on these accounts, more debits than credits. Prepayments are expenditure paid in advance and are treated as assets at the end of each accounting period so these balances are carried forward at 30 June 2019.

Illustration 4.68 Julia's rates prepayment account closed off at 30 June 2019 and the carried forward balance brought forward at the start of the new accounting period

Rates prepayment account

Debit (increases the asset)		£	Credit (decreases the asset)		£
2019			**2019**		
30 June	Rates	400	30 June	Balance c/f	400
		400			400
1 July	Balance b/f	400			

Illustration 4.69 Julia's water rates prepayment account closed off at 30 June 2019 and the carried forward balance brought forward at the start of the new accounting period

Water rates prepayment account					
Debit (increases the asset)		£	Credit (decreases the asset)		£
2019			**2019**		
30 June	Water rates	300	30 June	Balance c/f	300
		300			300
1 July	Balance b/f	300			

WHY IS THIS RELEVANT TO ME?   Closing off the T accounts at the end of an accounting period

To enable you as an accounting professional to understand:

- How the asset, liability, capital, income and expense balances are treated at the end of each accounting period
- How the opening balances for each new accounting period arise

All our accounts have now been closed off, the income and expenditure balances transferred to the statement of profit or loss and the asset, liability and capital balances carried forward to the next accounting period. Extracting a trial balance at 1 July will enable Julia to make sure that her accounting records are still in balance and that no errors have crept into her books of account during the closing off process.

NUMERICAL EXERCISES   Make sure that the opening balances on Julia's accounts do balance by attempting Numerical exercises 4.5 in the **online workbook**.

APPENDIX: SEPARATE T ACCOUNTS FOR INVENTORY AND PURCHASES

In this chapter, we have posted transactions relating to inventory and to purchases to the same cost of sales account. This has enabled us to produce one single cost of sales account, adding opening inventory to purchases and deducting closing inventory from the total of opening inventory + purchases. However, two separate T accounts can be set up, one for inventory and one for purchases, to record the same transactions.

Purchases are recorded in the purchases T account as normal by debiting purchase invoices or cash payments to the purchases account and crediting goods returned to suppliers to the same account.

The double entry for inventory follows three steps.

Step 1 Opening inventory at the start of the accounting period

Opening inventory is the figure brought forward from the end of the previous accounting period. This is recorded on the debit side of the inventory account to reflect the inventory asset at the start of the new financial period. This opening inventory is shown in Illustration 4.70 (note that the figure of £35,000 is used purely as an example and does not refer to any previous example in this chapter).

Illustration 4.70 The inventory T account showing inventory at the start of the accounting period

Inventory				
Debit (increases the asset)	£	Credit (decreases the asset)	£
2019		**2019**	
1 Jan Balance b/f	35,000		

Step 2 Opening inventory at the end of the accounting period

As we saw in Chapter 3 (Statement of profit or loss by nature), cost of sales = opening inventory + purchases – closing inventory. The purchases figure is the purchases – purchase returns figure on the purchases T account. At the end of the accounting period, opening inventory is no longer an asset and so is charged to cost of sales at the end of the accounting period by debiting the statement of profit or loss and crediting inventory with the opening inventory figure as shown in Illustration 4.71.

Illustration 4.71 The inventory T account showing opening inventory charged to the statement of profit or loss at the end of the accounting period

Inventory				
Debit (increases the asset)	£	Credit (decreases the asset)	£
2019		**2019**	
1 Jan Balance b/f	35,000	31 Dec Statement of profit or loss	35,000

4

Step 3 Closing inventory at the end of the accounting period

Closing inventory is a credit in the statement of profit or loss (a deduction from cost of sales) and a debit in the statement of financial position (an asset). The double entry required to record closing inventory is:

> Debit inventory account, credit statement of profit or loss to record the removal of closing inventory from cost of sales for the accounting period.

This leaves a debit balance on the inventory account which is the closing inventory asset carried forward at the end of the accounting period.

The double entry for these transactions is shown in the inventory account in Illustration 4.72.

Illustration 4.72 The inventory T account showing the recording of closing inventory at the end of the accounting period

Inventory					
Debit (increases the asset)		£	**Credit (decreases the asset)**		£
2019			**2019**		
1 Jan	Balance b/f	35,000	31 Dec	Statement of profit or loss	35,000
31 Dec	Statement of profit or loss	42,500	31 Dec	Balance c/f	42,500
		77,500			**77,500**
2020			**2020**		
1 Jan	Balance b/f	42,500			

Using a cost of sales T account or separate purchases and inventory T accounts will produce exactly the same cost of sales figure in the statement of profit or loss and inventory asset in the statement of financial position.

CHAPTER SUMMARY

You should now have learnt that:

- Accounting transactions and events are recorded in T accounts using the double-entry system
- The double-entry system uses debits and credits in the posting of transactions and events
- For every debit entry there must be an opposite credit entry of equal value to ensure that the accounts remain in balance
- Increases in assets and expenses are entered on the debit side of the T account
- Decreases in assets and expenses are entered on the credit side of the T account
- Increases in liabilities, income and capital are entered on the credit side of the T account
- Decreases in liabilities, income and capital are entered on the debit side of the T account
- Where the monetary value of the debits is greater than the monetary value of the credits on a T account, then there is a debit balance on that account

- Where the monetary value of the credits is greater than the monetary value of the debits on a T account, then there is a credit balance on that account
- Debit and credit balances on an entity's accounts are summarised in the trial balance at the end of each accounting period
- The sum of all the debit balances and the sum of all the credit balances on the trial balance will be equal if the double entry has been completed in full
- T accounts are closed off and balanced at the end of each accounting period
- At the end of each accounting period, income and expenses account balances are transferred to the statement of profit or loss and are not carried forward to future accounting periods
- At the end of each accounting period, assets, liabilities and capital account balances are carried forward to the next accounting period

QUICK REVISION   Test your knowledge with the online flashcards in Summary of key concepts and attempt the Multiple choice questions, all in the **online workbook**.

END-OF-CHAPTER QUESTIONS

Solutions to these questions can be found in the **online workbook**.

≫ DEVELOP YOUR UNDERSTANDING

≫ Question 4.1

State the double entry for the following transactions made by the TC Company Limited during September:

1. Cash sales of £35,225.

2. Credit sales of £125,750.

3. Received goods from suppliers on credit. The goods received had a cost of £62,894.

4. Insurance premium of £6,000 paid from the bank account.

5. Cash received from credit customers of £140,362.

6. Cash paid to suppliers for purchases made on credit of £55,574.

7. New plant and machinery purchased with a cash payment from the bank. The new plant and machinery cost £150,000.

8. Taxation paid of £27,450.

9. Loan instalment paid of £5,500.

10. Bank interest received of £250.

You are not required to produce T accounts to reflect the above transactions. Your answer should state which account will be debited and which account will be credited with the stated amounts.

> Question 4.2

Primrose is a market trader selling fabrics. She rents her market stall on a monthly basis from the local council. At 1 September 2019 she has inventory at a cost of £3,540. Her only other assets are cash in hand of £200 and a business bank account with a balance of £6,825. At 1 September 2019, Primrose owed her fabric suppliers £4,690. Her transactions during September were as follows:

1. She made total sales of £25,642. All sales made were for cash.

2. She paid £23,057 of her cash receipts into her bank account.

3. Her fabric suppliers delivered fabrics at a cost to Primrose of £12,300.

4. She paid her fabric suppliers a total of £13,460 during the month. All payments to the fabric suppliers were made from the business bank account.

5. She paid rent on her market stall to the local council of £250 in cash.

6. She made cash refunds to her customers of £1,985.

7. Her inventory at 30 September 2019 was counted up. The cost of this inventory at the end of the month was £2,695.

8. During the month, Primrose withdrew £1,200 from the business bank account and £300 from cash to pay her personal expenses.

Required

1. Calculate Primrose's capital account balance at 1 September 2019.

2. Enter the opening balances at 1 September 2019 into T accounts.

3. Enter the transactions for the month of September 2019 into the T accounts. You will need T accounts for cash, bank account, trade payables, cost of sales, capital account, sales, rent and inventory.

4. Extract a trial balance from the T accounts you have prepared.

5. Draw up Primrose's statement of profit or loss and statement of financial position at 30 September 2019 from the trial balance you have extracted.

6. Enter the profit for the month into Primrose's capital account and close off the T accounts at 30 September 2019.

7. Bring forward the balances on the T accounts at 1 October 2019.

>> TAKE IT FURTHER

>> Question 4.3

Laura was made redundant on 1 July 2018 and received £50,000 in redundancy pay. With this money, she opened a business bank account on 1 September 2018 and set up a small building company undertaking household and small industrial construction work. She started trading on 1 September 2018 and she has now reached her year end of 31 August 2019. She has produced a summary of payments and receipts into her business bank account along with additional information that she thinks will be useful in preparing her statement of profit or loss and statement of financial position for her first year of trading. The details she has presented you with are as follows:

1. Laura's customers usually pay cash at the end of each job. Cash received and banked from these sales totals up to £112,000. However, her small industrial clients keep her waiting for payment. Her invoices to her small industrial customers add up to a total of £48,000 for work done during the year, but she has only collected £36,000 of this amount by 31 August 2019.

2. Laura buys her construction materials on credit from a local wholesaler. Her total spending on materials this year has been £45,000 of which she had paid £38,000 by 31 August 2019. Her annual trading summary from the wholesaler received on 5 September 2019 tells her that she has qualified for a bulk purchase discount of £1,000 on all her purchases up to 31 August 2019. She will deduct this amount from her next payment to her supplier in September 2019.

3. Since 31 August 2019, a small industrial customer has gone into liquidation, owing Laura £2,500. The liquidator has told Laura that no payment towards this trade receivable will be made. The liquidation of her customer has made Laura think about the solvency of her other trade receivables. She decides that she would like to create an allowance for receivables of 10 per cent of her remaining trade receivables at 31 August 2019.

4. Laura bought a second hand van for £6,000 on 1 September 2018. She reckons this van will last for three years before she has to replace it. She anticipates that the trade-in value of this van will be £600 in three years' time. Laura expects to use the van to travel 5,000 miles each year on journeys for business purposes.

5. Van running expenses and insurance for the year amounted to £4,000. All of these expenses were paid from the business bank account. No van running expenses were outstanding or prepaid at 31 August 2019.

6. On 1 September 2018, Laura paid £5,000 for various items of second hand construction equipment. These assets should last for four years and fetch £60 as scrap when they are replaced. Laura expects to make the same use of these assets in each of the four years of their expected useful life.

7. Two part-time helpers were employed for 13 weeks during June, July and August 2019. By 31 August 2019, Laura had paid both these helpers 12 weeks of their wages amounting to £9,600 out of the business bank account.

8. Comprehensive business insurance was taken out and paid for on 1 September 2018. As a new business customer, Laura took advantage of the insurance company's discount scheme to pay £1,800 for 18 months cover.

9. Laura counted up and valued her inventory of building materials at 31 August 2019. She valued all these items at a cost to the business of £4,500.

10. Bank charges of £400 were deducted from Laura's bank account during the year. The bank manager has told her that accrued charges to the end of August 2019 amount to an additional £75. These accrued charges will be deducted from her business bank account during September 2019.

11. Laura's bank account was overdrawn in the early part of her first year of trading. The bank charged her £200 interest on this overdraft. Since then, her bank account has shown a debit balance and she has earned £250 in interest up to 31 July 2019. The bank manager has told her that in August 2019 her interest receivable is a further £50 and this will be added to her account in October 2019.

12. Laura withdrew £2,500 each month from the bank for her personal expenses. As she had so much cash in the bank in August 2019, on 31 August 2019 she used £90,000 from her business bank account to repay half the mortgage on her house.

Required

1. Open as many T accounts as you require and post all the above transactions into the T accounts you have opened.

2. Extract a trial balance from the T accounts you have produced.

3. Produce Laura's statement of profit or loss and statement of financial position for the year ended 31 August 2019.

4. Compare your statement of profit or loss and statement of financial position with Answer 3.5 to make sure that you have the same results.

5. Add the profit for the year to Laura's capital account and close off the T accounts for the year ended 31 August 2019. Income and expenditure balances are written off to the statement of profit or loss for the year whereas asset, liability and capital balances are carried forward at 31 August 2019. Bring forward the asset, liability and capital account balances at 1 September 2019.

6. Extract a trial balance at 1 September 2019 to ensure that Laura's accounts are in balance at the start of the new financial year.

DOUBLE-ENTRY BOOKKEEPING 2: BOOKS OF PRIME ENTRY, ACCOUNTING SYSTEMS AND OTHER DOUBLE-ENTRY APPLICATIONS

5

LEARNING OUTCOMES

Once you have read this chapter and worked through the questions and examples in both this chapter and the online workbook, you should be able to:

- Outline the transactions generated by the sales, purchases and payroll systems

- Describe the functions of and the details presented in the books of prime entry, the sales day book, the sales returns day book, the purchase day book, the purchase returns day book, the payroll, the cash book and the petty cash book

- Make the double entry from the books of prime entry into the T accounts in the nominal ledger

- Understand how the sales ledger records sales transactions with and cash received from individual credit customers

- Understand how the purchase ledger records purchases of goods and services from and payments to individual suppliers providing goods on credit

- Appreciate the effect of value added tax and payroll taxes on transactions undertaken by businesses and other organisations

- Understand how the trade receivables and trade payables control accounts help to ensure that trade receivables and trade payables figures are correct at the end of each financial period
- Undertake bank reconciliations to prove that the bank account and the cash book are in agreement
- Make the double entry required to record the disposal of non-current assets
- Use the logic of the double-entry system to reconstruct T accounts to find missing figures required to produce the financial statements
- Use journal entries to make corrections in the nominal ledger when transactions are recorded incorrectly or are omitted completely from the accounting records

INTRODUCTION

In the last chapter, we looked at the way in which double-entry bookkeeping works by recording Julia's accounting transactions in the relevant T accounts. The number of transactions was limited and it was easy to make these postings either on a monthly or three-monthly basis into the books of account. Julia's sales were made almost entirely for cash and her suppliers paid monthly.

However, many businesses buy and sell goods and services on credit many times each day, receive and pay out large sums of cash on a daily basis and trade frequently with large numbers of customers and suppliers of goods and services. Such businesses require much more detailed accounting records to ensure that each and every business transaction is captured and summarised. Transactions are initially captured and summarised in daily listings of sales, purchases, wages and salaries and cash. These daily listings (summaries of transactions) are then used to make the relevant double entries in the books of account, the nominal ledger.

While even the smallest businesses now use computers which complete the double entry automatically, it is very important for you to understand how these records are compiled and the ways in which the software packages in use summarise the accounting transactions to post to the books of account. Auditors test the logic of clients' computer systems to ensure that all transactions have been posted correctly and in full. As a result of this testing auditors can be confident that the financial statements present a true and fair view of the income and expenditure for the financial period and that the assets, liabilities and capital present a true and fair view of the financial position of an entity at the end of each and every accounting period. Without a detailed knowledge of double-entry bookkeeping and how it works, auditors would be unable to follow transactions through the computer systems to determine whether they had been correctly accounted for or not. As an accountant in practice, in industry, in the public or in the charitable sector, you, too, will want to be certain that the information you are working with has been correctly compiled from the source data to enable you to make valid decisions. Therefore, an understanding of double-entry principles and practice will be essential to your future career in accounting. Careful study to understand double entry now will make you a much more valuable accountant in the future.

In this chapter we will look at accounting systems. These accounting systems use day books or listings to record transactions on a daily basis. These daily listings are referred to as the books of prime entry, the first point at which transactions are recorded in the accounting system. These books of prime entry are then used to complete the double entry to the accounting records which form the basis for the preparation of the financial statements. This process is illustrated in Figure 5.1.

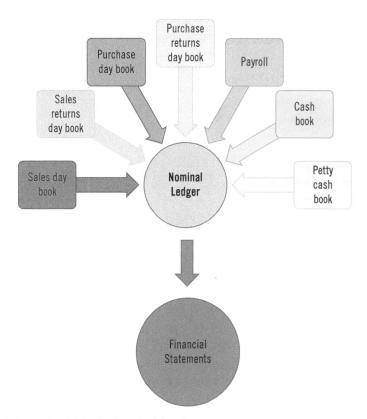

Figure 5.1 Processing transactions into the final financial statements

TRANSACTIONS AND TRANSACTION SYSTEMS

As we saw in Chapter 1 (What is accounting?), accounting involves the recording of transactions in money terms. All businesses use the following three systems which generate transactions that require recording in the books of account:

- The sales system: this system covers the selling of goods and services to customers and the collection of cash from those customers for the goods and services supplied.

- The purchases system: this system covers the buying in of goods and services from suppliers and the payment of cash to those suppliers for the goods and services provided.

- The payroll system: this system covers payments to employees for the time they have spent working for their organisations. In addition, organisations act as tax collection agencies for the state and they pay the income tax and national insurance deducted from employees' pay over to the tax authorities on a regular basis.

WHY IS THIS RELEVANT TO ME?   Transactions and transaction systems

To enable you as an accounting professional to:

- Appreciate that all organisations operate three main transaction systems: sales, purchases and wages

- Understand what each of these three main transaction systems involves

- Appreciate that these three transaction systems collect and record the information that builds up into the income and expenditure and the assets, liabilities and capital recorded in the financial statements

---

THE SALES AND CASH RECEIVED SYSTEM

All accounting systems generate records as evidence that transactions have taken place. These records can be in either paper or electronic form. The sales and cash received system has four transactions that require recording. The transactions in the sales system are presented in Figure 5.2.

Sales

When a sale occurs, a sales invoice is raised, recording the value of the goods or services supplied, any sales taxes such as value added tax (abbreviated henceforth to VAT) and the total amount owed by the customer (value of the sale made + the sales taxes). Illustration 5.1 shows an example of a sales invoice. Most businesses trade with their business customers on credit, so the cash due from each business customer for goods and services supplied will be received at a later date. The most common credit terms expect business customers to pay their invoices within 30 days of the invoice date. Where businesses make sales for cash, sales invoices are still produced to provide evidence that a transaction has occurred. Without evidence that a transaction has occurred, these cash sales might not be recorded in the accounting records and thus be omitted from the financial statements.

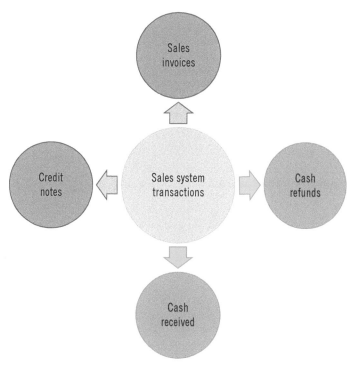

Figure 5.2 Transactions in the sales system

Illustration 5.1 An example of a sales invoice

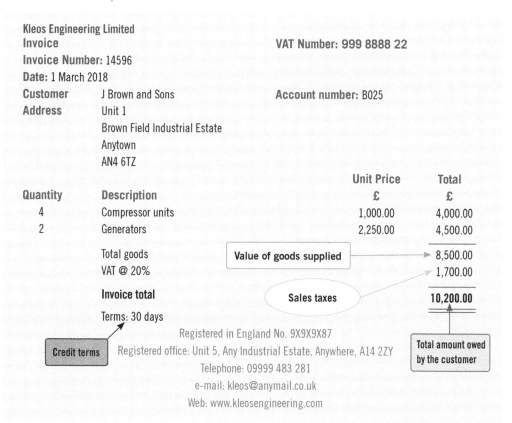

Credit notes

Credit notes are a negative sale. Goods supplied may be damaged on arrival, they may not meet the customer's requirements or there may just be an error on the invoice that requires correction. Damaged goods or goods that are not required are returned to the seller and a credit note issued to cancel the sales transaction either in part or in full. Credit notes record the value of the cancelled sale together with any cancelled sales taxes and show the total amount that is no longer owed by the customer (value of sale cancelled + the sales taxes). Illustration 5.2 shows an example of a credit note. Credit notes represent sales returns (Chapter 3, sales returns).

Illustration 5.2 An example of a credit note

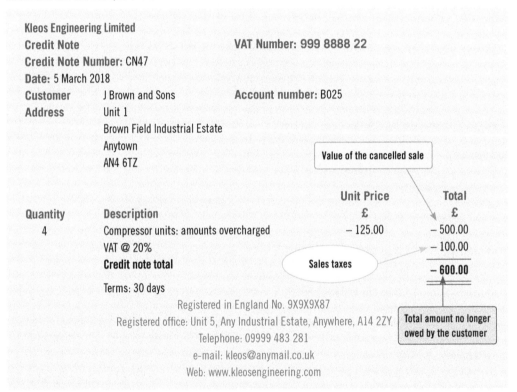

Cash received

When a customer pays what is owed, the receiving company receives cash either as physical cash or more commonly as a cheque or as a direct payment into the company's bank account. A payment from a credit customer relates to one or more invoices for goods or services supplied at an earlier date. Cash customers pay what is owed immediately with the cash received being recorded in the till.

Cash refunds

When customers return goods that they have already paid for, then they receive a cash refund. These refunds are made through cash taken from the till, by cheque sent to the customer or as a direct credit to the customer's bank account.

WHY IS THIS RELEVANT TO ME?   The sales and cash received system

To enable you as an accounting professional to:

- Familiarise yourself with the transactions in the sales and cash received system
- Understand how each transaction works in the sales system
- Understand the flow of transactions in the sales system

GO BACK OVER THIS AGAIN!   Are you quite happy that you understand the role of the different transactions in the sales system? Go to the **online workbook** and complete Exercises 5.1 to check your understanding.

RECORDING DAILY SALES: THE SALES DAY BOOK

Sales invoices produced for sales made to customers are recorded each day in the sales day book. The sales day book is also known as the sales listing but we shall use the term sales day book to refer to this transaction record throughout this chapter. The sales day book is the book of prime entry for sales, the first point at which sales are recorded in the accounting system. The sales day book is a daily record of all sales made on each trading day of the year. The sales day book for Kleos Engineering Limited for 1 March 2018 is presented in Illustration 5.3.

Illustration 5.3 Kleos Engineering Limited: sales day book for 1 March 2018

Date	Invoice number	Customer	Total £	VAT £	Net sales £
1 3 2018	14596	J Brown and Sons	10,200.00	1,700.00	8,500.00
1 3 2018	14597	Vivanti plc	4,346.40	724.40	3,622.00
1 3 2018	14598	Vodravid Limited	6,553.62	1,092.27	5,461.35
1 3 2018	14599	Mangonese plc	682.50	113.75	568.75
1 3 2018	14600	Tiddle and Toddle	375.36	62.56	312.80
1 3 2018	14601	F Smith and Co	9,300.00	1,550.00	7,750.00
Totals for day			**31,457.88**	**5,242.98**	**26,214.90**

As you can see, the sales day book is just a list of sales invoices categorised by customer with totals for net sales, VAT and the total value of each invoice. Each sales invoice has a date and is given a unique sequential number (Illustrations 5.1 and 5.3, Invoice number column) to enable companies to ensure that all their sales invoices have been recorded and to enable each invoice to be traced quickly and efficiently if a question or query relating to the invoice ever arises. The sales day book is not part of the double-entry system, but is used to make the double entry into the accounting records (this chapter, The double entry to record sales listed in the sales day book).

WHY IS THIS RELEVANT TO ME?   Recording daily sales: the sales day book

To ensure you as an accounting professional understand:

- The function of the sales day book as the book of prime entry for sales, the first point at which an organisation records details of the sales made in the accounting system

- The information that is recorded in the sales day book

GO BACK OVER THIS AGAIN!   Are you convinced that you can say what is included in the sales day book? Go to the **online workbook** and complete Exercises 5.2 to test your knowledge.

Where organisations sell more than one type of product, the sales day book may analyse the sales further into different categories of sales. Give me an example 5.1 shows the categories that Rolls Royce plc analyses its sales into in its annual report and accounts. Such an analysis helps organisations determine the performance of each division and whether divisional objectives and targets are being achieved.

GIVE ME AN EXAMPLE 5.1   Different categories of sale

Rolls Royce plc categorises sales as follows in its annual report and accounts for the year ended 31 December 2017:

Civil Aerospace—development, manufacture, marketing and sales of commercial aero engines and aftermarket services.

Defence Aerospace—development, manufacture, marketing and sales of military aero engines and aftermarket services.

Power Systems—development, manufacture, marketing and sales of reciprocating engines and power systems.

Marine—development, manufacture, marketing and sales of marine-power propulsion systems and aftermarket services.

Nuclear—development, manufacture, marketing and sales of nuclear systems for civil power generation and naval propulsion systems.

Source: www.rolls-royce.com

VALUE ADDED TAX (VAT)

Value Added Tax is a tax on the value of sales. It is a very complex tax which you will learn much more about later on in your studies and throughout your professional career. For now, all you need to know is that VAT is charged on the value of each sale made by entities that are liable to registration for VAT (which is nearly all business organisations in the UK). The current standard rate of VAT in the UK is 20 per cent. The sales value of the goods sold to J Brown and Sons (Illustrations 5.1 and 5.3) is £8,500.00. VAT on £8,500.00 at the rate of 20 per cent is £1,700.00 (£8,500.00 × 20 per cent). The sales value of £8,500.00 + the VAT of £1,700.00 results in a total invoice value of £10,200.00 (Illustrations 5.1 and 5.3). £10,200 is the amount that John Brown and Sons will pay to Kleos Engineering Limited to settle the invoice. VAT is collected on behalf of the government and paid over to HM Revenue and Customs every three months. The amount paid over at the end of each three-monthly period is the difference between the VAT charged and collected on sales and the VAT paid on purchases from other VAT registered businesses. A purchase from another business is a sale by that business, so VAT has to be charged on that sale. We shall see later on in this chapter how the VAT account summarises VAT on sales and purchases to generate a net amount payable at the end of each quarter.

5

WHY IS THIS RELEVANT TO ME?   Value Added Tax

To provide you as an accounting professional with:

- A very brief introduction to Value Added Tax
- An appreciation of how Value Added Tax is calculated on sales of goods and services
- An understanding of how the net amounts due to HM Revenue and Customs are calculated

MULTIPLE CHOICE QUESTIONS   Do you think you understand how VAT works and how it is calculated? Go to the **online workbook** and have a go at Multiple choice questions 5.1 to test your understanding.

THE DOUBLE ENTRY TO RECORD SALES LISTED IN THE SALES DAY BOOK

Given that the sales day book is not part of the double-entry system, how are the sales, VAT and total figures posted into the accounting records? What are the debit and what are the credit entries required to record these sales transactions? You should apply your knowledge of double-entry bookkeeping gained in Chapter 4 to determine the answers to these questions.

5

Making a sale generates an asset, either cash from sales made for cash or trade receivables if sales are made to customers on credit terms. Therefore, the cash or trade receivables account (we shall henceforth refer to the trade receivables account as the trade receivables control account) are debited with the daily sales day book total thereby increasing the balance on the asset account: the sales day book total for each day is the amount of economic benefits that will be received by the organisation. Sales are income so the sales value net of VAT or any other sales taxes is credited to the sales account. VAT, on the other hand, is a liability, the tax collected on sales which has to be paid over to the tax authorities. Therefore, the VAT liability account is credited with the VAT payable. VAT is not classified as revenue as it will never belong to the entity making the sale, it belongs to HM Revenue and Customs. VAT is therefore not an increase in assets or a decrease in liabilities that results in an increase in equity (the IASB definition of income, see Chapter 3, Income) so it is not revenue; it is an obligation to transfer an economic resource (cash) as a result of past events (the act of making each sale). The double entry for each daily sales day book total is shown in Illustration 5.4: in this illustration, it is assumed that all the sales in the sales day book have been made on credit to customers. Only credit sales are debited to the trade receivables control account. Cash sales are debited to the cash or bank account.

Do the double-entry postings balance? Yes. There is a debit of £31,457.88 and two credits totalling to £31,457.88 (£5,242.98 VAT + £26,214.90 net sales = £31,457.88). All the debits are equal to all the credits so the accounts are in perfect balance.

WHY IS THIS RELEVANT TO ME?   Double entry from the sales day book

To enable you as an accounting professional to:

● Understand how the daily sales day book totals are posted to the accounting records

● Make the required double entry to the accounting records to reflect the daily sales transactions in full

---

SUMMARY OF KEY CONCEPTS   Are you quite sure you can make the double entry to record daily sales day book totals in the books of account? Go to the **online workbook** to revise the required double entry in Summary of key concepts 5.1.

MULTIPLE CHOICE QUESTIONS   Are you completely confident you understand what the entries in the sales day book represent and how to make the required entries into the accounting records from the sales day book? Go to the **online workbook** and attempt Multiple choice questions 5.2 to test your abilities in this area.

Illustration 5.4 The double entry to record the daily sales day book totals in the books of account of Kleos Engineering Limited

Date	Invoice Number	Customer	Total £	VAT £	Net Sales £
1 3 2018	14596	J Brown and Sons	10,200.00	1,700.00	8,500.00
1 3 2018	14597	Vivanti plc	4,346.40	724.40	3,622.00
1 3 2018	14598	Vodravid Limited	6,553.62	1,092.27	5,461.35
1 3 2018	14599	Mangonese plc	682.50	113.75	568.75
1 3 2018	14600	Tiddle and Toddle	375.36	62.56	312.80
1 3 2018	14601	F Smith and Co	9,300.00	1,550.00	7,750.00
Totals for day			**31,457.88**	**5,242.98**	**26,214.90**

Trade receivables control account

2018		£	2018		£
1 March	Sales day book	31,457.88			

Debit trade receivables, increase the asset with monies owed by customers

VAT account

2018	£	2018		£
		1 March	Sales day book	5,242.98

Credit VAT, increase the liability for monies owed to HM Revenue and Customs

Sales account

2018	£	2018		£
		1 March	Sales day book	26,214.90

Credit sales, increase the revenue earned by the entity

SALES RETURNS DAY BOOK

The sales returns day book is also known as the sales returns listing but we shall use the term sales returns day book to refer to this transaction record throughout this chapter. The sales returns day book uses exactly the same headings as the sales day book. As there are fewer returns than sales, the sales returns day book is a much shorter record of daily transactions. The sales returns day book for Kleos Engineering Limited for 5 March 2018 and the illustration of how the entries from this record are recorded in the double-entry system are shown in Illustration 5.5.

Illustration 5.5 Sales returns day book for Kleos Engineering Limited for 5 March 2018 and the double entry to record the daily sales returns day book totals in the company's books of account

Date	Credit Note Number	Customer	Total £	VAT £	Net Credit £
5 3 2018	CN47	J Brown and Sons	600.00	100.00	500.00
5 3 2018	CN48	Vodravid Limited	410.70	68.45	342.25
Totals for day			**1,010.70**	**168.45**	**842.25**

VAT account

2018		£	2018		£
5 March	Sales returns	168.45	1 March	Sales day book	5,242.98

Debit VAT, decrease the liability as less money is now owed to HM Revenue and Customs

Sales account

2018		£	2018		£
5 March	Sales returns	842.25	1 March	Sales day book	26,214.90

Debit sales, decrease the revenue earned by the entity as a result of returns

Trade receivables control account

2018		£	2018		£
1 March	Sales day book	31,457.88	5 March	Sales returns	1,010.70

Credit trade receivables, decrease the asset as less is now owed by customers

THE DOUBLE ENTRY TO RECORD SALES RETURNS LISTED IN THE SALES RETURNS DAY BOOK

The double entries from the sales returns day book are the reverse of the double entry used to record sales. The sales returns reduce both assets and equity, so the sales (income) account is debited (decrease in income) as a result of these cancelled sales. A smaller amount of VAT is now owed to the tax authorities due to the cancellation of a sale so the liability is debited (a decrease) to reflect this reduction in the obligation. Less money is now owed by trade receivables so the trade receivables control account is credited (a decrease in an asset) by the total in the sales returns day book. Do the totals balance? Yes. There is a debit of £1,010.70 (£168.45 + £842.25 = £1,010.70) and a credit of £1,010.70 so the double entry is complete and the accounts continue to be in perfect balance.

5

WHY IS THIS RELEVANT TO ME?   Sales returns day book

To enable you as an accounting professional to:

* Understand how the sales returns day book totals are posted to the accounting records
* Make the required double entry to the accounting records to reflect the daily sales returns transactions in full

---

SUMMARY OF KEY CONCEPTS   Do you think that you know how to make the double entry to record daily sales returns day book totals in the books of account? Go to the **online workbook** to check your recollection in Summary of key concepts 5.2.

GO BACK OVER THIS AGAIN!   Are you convinced that you understand what sales returns represent and how to make the required entries into the accounting records from the sales returns day book? Go to the **online workbook** and attempt Exercises 5.3 to test your abilities in this area.

SHOW ME HOW TO DO IT   Did you completely understand how the double entry was made from the sales day book and from the sales returns day book into the books of account? View Video presentation 5.1 in the **online workbook** to see a practical demonstration of how the double entry was completed in the trade receivables, VAT and sales accounts.

THE SALES LEDGER

As we have seen, the total value of daily sales is recorded in the trade receivables control account. However, with only one total figure for trade receivables, how will entities know what each trade receivable owes and whether individual customers are paying for the goods or services they have received? Control must be maintained over each and every trade receivable on an individual basis to ensure that sales are being paid for regularly and that certain customers are not building up an excessively large debt that they might not be able to pay in the future. In order to keep track of the activity on each customer's account, a sales ledger (trade receivable) account is maintained for each customer. The total balance on each customer's sales ledger account will be calculated at the end of each month. The total on each of these individual sales ledger accounts added together will be equal to the total on the trade receivables control account. Each individual customer's sales ledger account is debited with the total sales invoice value for each invoice raised and credited with any credit notes issued and any cash received (see this chapter, The sales ledger and cash receipts). Using our examples from Illustrations 5.3 and 5.5 for sales invoices and sales returns, the sales ledger accounts for the six customers of Kleos Engineering Limited are shown in Illustration 5.6. Note that the sales ledger accounts are listed in alphabetical order not invoice order so that each account can be found quickly and easily.

Illustration 5.6 Kleos Engineering Limited: individual sales ledger balances

J Brown and Sons sales ledger account

2018		£	2018		£
1 March	14596	10,200.00	5 March	CN47	600.00

Mangonese plc sales ledger account

2018		£	2018		£
1 March	14599	682.50			

F Smith and Co sales ledger account

2018		£	2018		£
1 March	14601	9,300.00			

Tiddle and Toddle sales ledger account

2018		£	2018		£
1 March	14600	375.36			

Vivanti plc sales ledger account

2018		£	2018		£
1 March	14597	4,346.40			

Vodravid Limited sales ledger account

2018		£	2018		£
1 March	14598	6,553.62	5 March	CN48	410.70

Adding up the balances on each sales ledger account gives us the following totals:

- Total debit balances on the individual sales ledger accounts: £10,200.00 + £682.50 + £9,300.00 + £375.36 + £4,346.40 + £6,553.62 = £31,457.88.
- Credit balances: £600.00 + £410.70 = £1,010.70.

Do these equal the totals on the trade receivables control account? Yes, they do, as shown in Illustration 5.7.

Illustration 5.7 (= Illustration 5.5) Trade receivables control account for Kleos Engineering Limited

Trade receivables control account					
2018		£	**2018**		£
1 March	Sales day book	31,457.88	5 March	Sales returns day book	1,010.70

The sales ledger is maintained as a separate record of what each customer owes the business. Note that each sale and credit note transaction is recorded using the invoice number and the credit note number from the sales day book and the sales returns day book. Reference can thus be made quickly and easily to the source documents for each transaction should a query arise at a later date.

WHY IS THIS RELEVANT TO ME?   The sales ledger

To enable you as an accounting professional to:

- Appreciate the control exercised through maintaining individual trade receivable accounts for each customer
- Understand how the totals of all the individual sales ledger balances add up to the total on the trade receivables control account
- Understand the need for a sales ledger to record individual balances owed by each customer

NUMERICAL EXERCISES   Are you confident that you could complete the sales ledger accounts for a company's trade receivables and post the sales invoices and sales returns accurately and in full? Go to the **online workbook** and complete Numerical exercises 5.1 to test your abilities in this area.

CASH RECEIVED

Businesses use a cash book to record transactions made through the bank account, namely cash received and cash paid. The cash book is another book of prime entry, the first point at which an entity records individual amounts of cash received and cash paid. The cash book is in effect one large T account with cash received on the left hand side (debit, increase the cash asset) and cash paid on the right (credit, decrease the cash asset). Cash received and cash paid is analysed into various headings to reflect the different categories of cash received and cash paid out by a business. An example of the cash received side of the cash book for Kleos Engineering Limited is shown in Illustration 5.8. The main column in the cash received side will be the cash received (in the form of cheques or direct payments into the bank account) from trade receivables with other columns for cash from sources such as interest received and cash sales. When a business makes cash sales, the cash received from these cash sales is split into sales revenue and the liability to pay VAT on those cash sales to HM Revenue and Customs. In Illustration 5.8, the total cash receipt of £432.00 from cash sales is split into £360.00 for cash sales and £72.00 owed for VAT on those sales. The net sales and VAT on cash received from trade receivables do not require splitting in the same way as the net sales and VAT have already been recorded in the sales day book (Illustration 5.3) and in the sales returns day book (Illustration 5.5).

Illustration 5.8 Kleos Engineering Limited: cash book: cash received

Date	Detail	Total	Trade receivables	Cash sales	Interest received	VAT
2018		£	£	£	£	£
2 April	Interest received	26.21			26.21	
2 April	J Brown and Sons	8,400.00	8,400.00			
2 April	Tiddle and Toddle	375.36	375.36			
3 April	Cash sales	432.00		360.00		72.00
4 April	Vivanti plc	4,346.40	4,346.40			
Totals		**13,579.97**	**13,121.76**	**360.00**	**26.21**	**72.00**

How are these cash receipts recorded in the double-entry system? As we saw in Chapter 4, cash received is an increase in an asset, so any cash received is debited to the bank account. To complete the double entry, there has to be a credit to various other accounts as shown in Illustration 5.9. The credits represent increases in income (cash sales and interest received), an increase in liabilities (VAT) and a decrease in an asset (trade receivables).

Illustration 5.9 The double entry to record cash receipts in the books of account of Kleos Engineering Limited

	Total	Trade receivables	Cash sales	Interest received	VAT
Cash receipts totals	13,579.97	13,121.76	360.00	26.21	72.00

Bank account

2018		£	2018		£
4 April	Cash book	13,579.97			

Debit bank, increase asset with cash received

Trade receivables control account

2018		£	2018		£
1 March	Sales day book	31,457.88	5 March	Sales returns	1,010.70
			4 April	Cash book	13,121.76

Credit trade receivables, decrease the asset as less is now owed by customers

Sales account

2018		£	2018		£
5 March	Sales returns	842.25	1 March	Sales day book	26,214.90
			3 April	Cash book	360.00

Credit sales, increase the revenue earned by the entity

Interest received account

2018		£	2018		£
			2 April	Cash book	26.21

Credit interest received, increase the income earned by the entity

VAT account

2018		£	2018		£
5 March	Sales returns	168.45	1 March	Sales day book	5,242.98
			3 April	Cash book	72.00

Credit VAT, increase the liability for monies owed to HM Revenue and Customs

To enable you as an accounting professional to:

- Understand how the cash received is posted to the accounting records
- Make the required double entry to the accounting records to record the cash received transactions in full

SUMMARY OF KEY CONCEPTS Are you certain you know what the double entry to record cash received in the books of account is? Go to the **online workbook** to check your recollection in Summary of key concepts 5.3.

GO BACK OVER THIS AGAIN! Are you convinced you understand how to make the required entries into the accounting records from the cash received records? Go to the **online workbook** and attempt Exercises 5.4 to test your understanding.

THE SALES LEDGER AND CASH RECEIPTS

The individual sales ledger accounts are also updated for the cash received from individual trade receivables. Each trade receivable is an asset, so the receipt of cash reduces the amounts owed by each trade receivable as shown in Illustration 5.10 while increasing the cash asset (debit cash, increase the cash asset, credit trade receivables, reduce the trade receivable asset).

Illustration 5.10 Kleos Engineering Limited: individual sales ledger balances showing the posting of trade receivables cash received on 2 April 2018

J Brown and Sons sales ledger account

2018		£	2018		£
1 March	14596	10,200.00	5 March	CN47	600.00
			2 April	Cash book	8,400.00

Tiddle and Toddle sales ledger account

2018		£	2018		£
1 March	14600	375.36	2 April	Cash book	375.36

Vivanti plc sales ledger account

2018		£	2018		£
1 March	14597	4,346.40	2 April	Cash book	4,346.40

J Brown and sons have not paid the full amount of their invoice less the credit note, so company staff might want to contact this customer to find out whether there is a problem. Tiddle and Toddle and Vivanti plc have paid what is owed in full, but there are three other trade receivables that have not yet paid their March 1 invoices. The company can now start to chase these trade receivables for payments which are overdue (more than 30 days since the invoice date). Maintaining individual sales ledger accounts for each customer makes it much easier for the company to know who has and who has not paid and to control the amounts owed by individual trade receivables.

WHY IS THIS RELEVANT TO ME?   The sales ledger and cash receipts

To enable you as an accounting professional to:

- Understand how the cash received from trade receivables is posted to the individual sales ledger accounts

- Appreciate how maintaining individual sales ledger accounts for each customer enables entities to identify customers who are not paying so that action to recover outstanding debts can be taken

---

NUMERICAL EXERCISES   Do you think that you could complete the sales ledger accounts to reflect cash received from trade receivables? Go to the **online workbook** and complete Numerical exercises 5.2 to test your ability to make these entries.

SHOW ME HOW TO DO IT   Did you completely follow how the double entry was made from the cash book to the accounting records and to the individual sales ledger accounts? View Video presentation 5.2 in the **online workbook** to see a practical demonstration of how the double entry was completed in the relevant T accounts and the individual sales ledger accounts.

EXERCISING CONTROL: THE TRADE RECEIVABLES CONTROL ACCOUNT

The trade receivables control account summarises the transactions in the sales system for sales made on credit. As we have seen, total credit sales are debited to this account as the trade receivables asset increases while cash or sales returns are credited as trade receivables pay what is owed or sales are cancelled thereby reducing the asset. What other entries are made in the trade receivables control account? Illustration 5.11 presents all the entries that you would expect to find in this account (figures given are for illustration purposes only).

Illustration 5.11 The trade receivables control account

Trade receivables control account					
2018		**£**	**2018**		**£**
1 Jan	Balance b/f	52,867	31 Dec	Sales returns day book	15,742
31 Dec	Sales day book	408,383	31 Dec	Cash book	382,621
			31 Dec	Irrecoverable debts	2,600
			31 Dec	Balance c/f	60,287
		461,250			**461,250**

The left hand side of the account represents increases in the asset. The balance brought forward at the start of the year is made up of the trade receivables at the end of the previous accounting period. This balance represents money still owed by customers as a result of accepting goods and services from the organisation up to the end of the previous financial year. On the right hand side of the account, we find transactions and events that will reduce the trade receivables asset. As well as sales returns and cash received from trade receivables, irrecoverable debts (cash that will never be collected from trade receivables who cannot or will not pay, Chapter 3, Irrecoverable debts) will also reduce the amount of the trade receivables asset while increasing the corresponding expense account. Do note that the allowance for receivables does not form part of the trade receivables control account. The allowance for receivables is made for those trade receivables that might not pay what they owe rather than being trade receivables which will never pay the amounts due (Chapter 3, The allowance for receivables). As a result, the allowance for receivables is carried forward as a balance on a separate account which is netted off against the trade receivables carried forward at the end of the accounting period in the statement of financial position.

The balance brought forward + the sales – the sales returns – the cash received – the irrecoverable debts should then give us the trade receivables balance at the end of the accounting period. The trade receivables control account provides a quick summary of transactions and a total balance for amounts owed to the business at the end of the accounting period. As we have seen, the total transactions (sales, cash received, sales returns and irrecoverable debts) should be equal to the totals on each of the individual sales ledger accounts. At the end of the accounting period, the trade receivables balance carried forward at the end of the period should be equal to the total of all the individual sales ledger balances. Time will be spent making sure that this is the case. If it is not and there is a difference between the balance on the trade receivables control account and the total of all the individual balances on each of the sales ledger accounts, then there is an error and time will have to be devoted to finding and correcting this error. As the trade receivables control account balances carried forward and the total of the individual sales ledger balances should be the same, control is exercised through the two sets of figures which enables organisations to track down and correct errors as they arise. An irrecoverable debt may have been recorded in the individual sales ledger account which has not been added to the trade receivables control account or cash, sales returns or sales may have been missed out of the individual sales ledger accounts. Whatever the cause of the error, the comparison of the two independent records will ensure that the trade receivables figure at the end of the accounting period is correct.

WHY IS THIS RELEVANT TO ME?   Exercising control: the trade receivables control account

As an accounting professional you will be expected to be able to:

- Understand which entries are made in the trade receivables control account
- Compile the trade receivables control account from the available data on sales, sales returns, cash received and irrecoverable debts
- Reconcile the trade receivables control account balance at the end of an accounting period with the total of the individual trade receivable balances on the sales ledger

---

SUMMARY OF KEY CONCEPTS   Are you completely certain that you can say what the entries in the trade receivables control account are? Go to the **online workbook** to check your recollection with Summary of key concepts 5.4.

GO BACK OVER THIS AGAIN!   Are you quite sure you understand how the trade receivables control account works? Go to the **online workbook** and have a go at Exercises 5.5 to check your understanding.

THE PURCHASES AND CASH PAID SYSTEM

As well as selling goods and services, organisations buy in goods and services from other entities. As in the case of the sales system, the purchases and cash paid system has four transactions that require recording. These transactions are shown in Figure 5.3.

Purchases

When an entity buys in goods or services, a purchase invoice is received from the supplier of those goods or services. This purchase invoice shows the value of goods or services supplied,

5

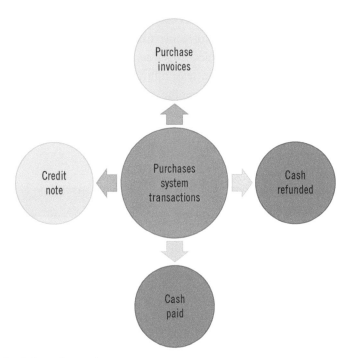

Figure 5.3 Transactions in the purchases system

any VAT charged on that supply of goods and services and the total amount owed by the entity (value of the goods or services supplied + the VAT). Purchase invoices will follow the same format as Illustration 5.1, the only difference being that the name and address of each supplier will be different on each purchase invoice while the customer's name, the buying company, and address will always be the same. Most businesses trade with their suppliers on credit, so the cash due to each supplier for goods and services supplied will be paid at a later date.

Credit notes

Credit notes received from suppliers represent negative purchases. When goods supplied are damaged on arrival, do not meet the buying entity's requirements or there is just an error on the invoice from the supplier, a credit note will be issued. Damaged or unsuitable goods are returned to the supplier and a credit note issued to cancel the purchase transaction either in part or in full. Credit notes record the value of the cancelled purchase together with any VAT and show the total amount that is no longer owed by the organisation (value of purchase cancelled + VAT). Credit notes from suppliers of goods and services will follow the same format as the example of a credit note shown in Illustration 5.2 with the name and address of the supplier being different on each and every credit note received while the name and address of the buying company will always be the same. Credit notes represent purchase returns (Chapter 3, Purchase returns).

Cash paid

When an organisation pays what is owed to its suppliers, physical cash or more commonly a cheque or a direct payment into the supplier's bank account is made. Organisations will pay one or more purchase invoices for goods or services supplied at an earlier date.

Cash refunds

When an organisation returns goods that they have already paid for, then they receive a cash refund. These refunds are made by the supplier and will be recorded as a receipt of cash in the buying entity's books as this is cash coming in to the business. Cash refunds from suppliers are rare but you should be aware that they can arise.

WHY IS THIS RELEVANT TO ME?   The purchases and cash paid system

To enable you as an accounting professional to:

- Familiarise yourself with the transactions in the purchases and cash paid system
- Understand how each transaction works in the purchases system
- Understand the flow of transactions in the purchases system

GO BACK OVER THIS AGAIN!   Are you quite happy that you understand the role of the different transactions in the purchases system? Go to the **online workbook** and complete Exercises 5.6 to check your understanding.

RECORDING DAILY PURCHASES: THE PURCHASE DAY BOOK

Purchases made each day are recorded in the purchase day book. The purchase day book may also be called the purchase listing but we shall use the term purchase day book to refer to this transaction record throughout this chapter. The purchase day book is the book of prime entry for purchases and is a daily record of all purchases made on each trading day of the year. The purchase day book of Kleos Engineering Limited for 1 March 2018 is presented in Illustration 5.12.

Illustration 5.12 Kleos Engineering Limited's purchase day book for 1 March 2018

Date	Internal invoice number	Supplier	Total £	VAT £	Raw materials £	Office supplies £	Legal fees £
1 3 2018	2460	Optimo Ltd	6,900.00	1,150.00	5,750.00		
1 3 2018	2461	Fuzzy Ltd	1,200.00	200.00	1,000.00		
1 3 2018	2462	Doric plc	210.24	35.04		175.20	
1 3 2018	2463	Ionic Ltd	477.00	79.50	397.50		
1 3 2018	2464	Legal Bee	825.00	137.50			687.50
Totals for day			**9,612.24**	**1,602.04**	**7,147.50**	**175.20**	**687.50**

As was the case with the sales day book, the purchase day book is not part of the double-entry system, it is just a list of purchases made analysed by supplier and by expenditure type. While there may be a limited number of categories for sales, the classification of purchase expenditure is much wider. The purchase day book will therefore analyse purchase invoices into the categories of expenditure most frequently made by the entity. On receipt, each purchase invoice is given a unique internally generated sequential number (Illustration 5.12, Internal invoice number column) to enable companies to ensure that all their purchase invoices have been recorded and to enable each invoice to be traced quickly and efficiently if ever a query or a question about an invoice arises.

WHY IS THIS RELEVANT TO ME?   Recording daily purchases: the purchase day book

To ensure that you as an accounting professional understand:

* The function of the purchase day book as the book of prime entry for purchases, the first point at which each purchase is recorded by an organisation in the accounting system
* The information that is recorded in the purchase day book

GO BACK OVER THIS AGAIN!   Do you think that you can say what is included in the purchase day book? Go to the **online workbook** and complete Exercises 5.7 to test your knowledge.

THE DOUBLE ENTRY TO RECORD PURCHASES LISTED IN THE PURCHASE DAY BOOK

As the purchase day book is not part of the double-entry system, how are the purchases, VAT and figures for each category of expenditure posted into the accounting records? Making a purchase on credit from a supplier creates a liability, an obligation to transfer an economic resource (cash) to settle the liability. Therefore, the trade payables control account (we have called this account the trade payables account up to this point but will henceforth refer to it as the trade payables

Illustration 5.13 The double entry to record the daily purchase day book totals in the books of account of Kleos Engineering Limited

Date	Internal invoice number	Supplier	Total £	VAT £	Raw materials £	Office supplies £	Legal fees £
1 3 2018	2460	Optimo Ltd	6,900.00	1,150.00	5,750.00		
1 3 2018	2461	Fuzzy Ltd	1,200.00	200.00	1,000.00		
1 3 2018	2462	Doric plc	210.24	35.04		175.20	
1 3 2018	2463	Ionic Ltd	477.00	79.50	397.50		
1 3 2018	2464	Legal Bee	825.00	137.50			687.50
Totals for day			**9,612.24**	**1,602.04**	**7,147.50**	**175.20**	**687.50**

Trade payables control account

2018		£	2018		£
			1 March	Purchase day book	9,612.24

Credit trade payables with the increase in liabilities

VAT account

2018		£	2018		£
5 March	Sales returns	168.45	1 March	Sales day book	5,242.98
1 March	Purchase day book	1,602.04	3 April	Cash book	72.00

Debit VAT, decrease the liability for monies owed to HM Revenue and Customs

Raw materials account

2018		£	2018		£
1 March	Purchase day book	7,147.50			

Debit expense accounts with the increases in costs

Office supplies account

2018		£	2018		£
1 March	Purchase day book	175.20			

Legal fees account

2018		£	2018		£
1 March	Purchase day book	687.50			

5

control account) is credited with the daily total as the liability, the amount owed to suppliers, increases. Purchases represent an increase in expenditure so the various totals on each category of purchases are debited to the various expenditure accounts. VAT on purchases is recoverable as a deduction from the VAT payable on sales, so the VAT liability account is debited with the reduction in the VAT payable. VAT incurred on expenditure is not classified as an expense as it is not a cost to a business. VAT on purchases is not a decrease in assets or an increase in liabilities that results in a decrease in equity (Chapter 3, Expenses). VAT on purchases is a reduction in a liability which is debited to the VAT account. As noted previously (this chapter, Value Added Tax (VAT)), the difference between the VAT charged on sales and the VAT recovered on purchases is paid to HM Revenue and Customs at the end of every quarter (three-monthly period). The double entry for the daily totals in the purchase day book is shown in Illustration 5.13.

Do the double-entry postings balance? Yes. There is a credit of £9,612.24 and four debits totalling to £9,612.24 (£1,602.04 + £7,147.50 + £175.20 + £687.50 = £9,612.24). All the debits are equal to all the credits so the accounts are in perfect balance.

WHY IS THIS RELEVANT TO ME?   Double entry from the purchase day book

To enable you as an accounting professional to:

- Understand how the purchase day book totals are posted to the accounting records
- Make the required double entry to the accounting records to reflect the daily purchase transactions in full

---

SUMMARY OF KEY CONCEPTS   Are you convinced that you can state the double entry to record purchase day book totals in the books of account? Go to the **online workbook** to revise the required double entry in Summary of key concepts 5.5.

MULTIPLE CHOICE QUESTIONS   Are you completely confident you understand what the entries in the purchase day book represent and how to make the double entry into the accounting records from the purchase day book? Go to the **online workbook** and have a go at Multiple choice questions 5.3 to test your abilities in this area.

PURCHASE RETURNS DAY BOOK

The purchase returns day book is also known as the purchase returns listing but we shall use the term purchase returns day book to refer to this transaction record throughout this chapter. The purchase returns day book uses exactly the same headings as the purchase day book. As there are fewer returns than purchases, the purchase returns day book is a much shorter record of daily transactions. The purchase returns day book for Kleos Engineering Limited for 5 March 2018 and the illustration of how the entries from this record are recorded in the double-entry system are shown in Illustration 5.14.

Illustration 5.14 The purchase returns day book of Kleos Engineering Limited for 5 March 2018 and the double entry to record the daily purchase returns day book totals in the books of account of the company

Date	Internal invoice number	Supplier	Total £	VAT £	Raw materials £	Office supplies £	Legal fees £
5 3 2018	PR79	Optimo Ltd	510.00	85.00	425.00		
5 3 2018	PR80	Doric plc	30.30	5.05		25.25	
5 3 2018	PR81	Ionic Ltd	23.88	3.98	19.90		
Totals for day			**564.18**	**94.03**	**444.90**	**25.25**	—

Trade payables control account

2018		£	2018		£
5 March	Purchase returns	564.18	1 March	Purchase day book	9,612.24

Debit trade payables with the decrease in liabilities

Raw materials account

2018		£	2018		£
1 March	Purchase day book	7,147.50	5 March	Purchase returns	444.90

Credit expense accounts with the decrease in costs

Office supplies account

2018		£	2018		£
1 March	Purchase day book	175.20	5 March	Purchase returns	25.25

VAT account

2018		£	2018		£
5 March	Sales returns	168.45	1 March	Sales day book	5,242.98
1 March	Purchase day book	1,602.04	3 April	Cash book	72.00
			5 March	Purchase returns	94.03

Credit VAT, increase the liability for monies owed to HM Revenue and Customs

5

5

THE DOUBLE ENTRY TO RECORD PURCHASE RETURNS LISTED IN THE PURCHASE RETURNS DAY BOOK

The double entries from the purchase returns day book are the opposite of the double entry used to record purchases. The purchase returns decrease liabilities and so increase equity as expenditure is reduced, so the purchase (expense) accounts are credited (decrease in expense) as a result of these cancelled purchases. A smaller amount of VAT is reclaimed from the tax authorities so the liability is credited (an increase) to reflect this additional obligation. Less money is now owed to trade payables so the trade payables control account is debited (a decrease in a liability) with the total in the purchase returns day book. Do the totals balance? Yes. There is a debit of £564.18 and credits of £564.18 (£94.03 + £444.90 + £25.25 = £564.18) so the double entry is complete and the accounts continue to balance perfectly.

WHY IS THIS RELEVANT TO ME?   Purchase returns day book

To enable you as an accounting professional to:

● Understand how the purchase returns day book totals are posted to the accounting records

● Make the required double entry to the accounting records to reflect the daily purchase returns transactions in full

---

SUMMARY OF KEY CONCEPTS   Are you confident that you can state the double entry required to record purchase returns day book totals in the books of account? Go to the **online workbook** to revise the required double entry in Summary of key concepts 5.6.

GO BACK OVER THIS AGAIN!   Are you convinced that you understand what purchase returns represent and how to make the required entries into the accounting records from the purchase returns day book? Go to the **online workbook** and attempt Exercises 5.8 to test your understanding.

SHOW ME HOW TO DO IT   Did you completely appreciate how the double entry was made from the purchase day book and from the purchase returns day book? View Video presentation 5.3 in the **online workbook** to see a practical demonstration of how the double entry was completed in the trade payables, VAT and expense accounts.

THE PURCHASE LEDGER

As we have seen, the total value of purchases is recorded in the trade payables control account. However, with only one total figure for trade payables, how will entities know what is owed to each trade payable, whether the correct amounts are being paid to each supplier and that the entity is not paying more than once for goods and services supplied? In order to keep track of the activity on each supplier's account, a purchase ledger account is maintained for each provider of goods and services. The total balance on each supplier's purchase ledger account will be calculated at the end of each month. The total on each of the individual purchase ledger accounts added together will be equal to the total on the trade payables control account. Each supplier's purchase ledger account is credited with the total value of each purchase invoice received and debited with any credit notes received and any cash paid (see this chapter, The purchase ledger and cash payments). Using our examples from Illustrations 5.12 and 5.14 for the purchase day book and the purchase returns day book, the purchase ledger accounts for the five suppliers of Kleos Engineering Limited are shown in Illustration 5.15. Note that the purchase ledger accounts, just like the sales ledger accounts, are listed in alphabetical order rather than invoice order so that each account can be found quickly and easily should any queries or questions arise.

Illustration 5.15 Kleos Engineering Limited's individual purchase ledger accounts for suppliers

Doric plc purchase ledger account

2018		£	2018		£
5 March	PR80	30.30	1 March	2462	210.24

Fuzzy Limited purchase ledger account

2018		£	2018		£
			1 March	2461	1,200.00

Ionic Limited purchase ledger account

2018		£	2018		£
5 March	PR81	23.88	1 March	2463	477.00

Legal Bee purchase ledger account

2018		£	2018		£
			1 March	2464	825.00

Optimo Limited purchase ledger account

2018		£	2018		£
5 March	PR79	510.00	1 March	2460	6,900.00

Adding up the balances on each purchase ledger account gives us the following totals:

- Total credit balances on the individual purchase ledger accounts: £210.24 + £1,200.00 + £477.00 + £825.00 + £6,900.00 = £9,612.24.

- Total debit balances on the individual purchase ledger accounts: £30.30 + £23.88 + £510.00 = £564.18.

Do these equal the totals on the trade payables control account? Yes, they do, as shown in Illustration 5.16.

Illustration 5.16 (= Illustration 5.14) Trade payables control account for Kleos Engineering Limited

	Trade payables control account				
2018		**£**	**2018**		**£**
5 March	Purchase returns	564.18	1 March	Purchase day book	9,612.24

The purchase ledger is maintained as a separate record of what a business owes each supplier. Note that each purchase invoice and credit note transaction is recorded using the internal invoice number and the internal credit note number from the purchase day book and the purchase returns day book. Reference can thus readily be made to the source documents for each transaction should any questions or queries arise.

WHY IS THIS RELEVANT TO ME?   The purchase ledger

To enable you as an accounting professional to:

- Appreciate the control exercised over purchases, purchase returns and cash payments through maintaining individual accounts for each supplier

- Understand how the totals of all the individual purchase ledger balances add up to the total on the trade payables control account

- Understand the need for a purchase ledger to record individual balances owed to each supplier

---

NUMERICAL EXERCISES   Do you think that you could complete the purchase ledger accounts for a company's trade payables and post the purchase invoices and purchases returns accurately and in full? Go to the **online workbook** and complete Numerical exercises 5.3 to make sure you can.

CASH PAYMENTS

As noted in this chapter, Cash received, the right hand side of the cash book is used to record cash payments. These payments represent reductions in the cash asset. As in the case of cash received, cash paid is analysed into various headings to reflect the different categories of cash payments made by a business. An example of the cash paid side of the cash book for Kleos Engineering Limited is shown in Illustration 5.17. The main column in the cash paid side will be the cash paid to trade payables but there are other significant outgoings such as payments for wages and salaries, payments to HM Revenue and Customs for tax and national insurance (PAYE and NIC) as well as for VAT. Any cash purchases will be split into the net purchases figure and the VAT recoverable on those purchases. The purchases and VAT on cash paid to trade payables do not require splitting in the same way as the net purchases and VAT have already been recorded in the purchase day book (Illustration 5.12) and in the purchase returns day book (Illustration 5.14).

Illustration 5.17 Kleos Engineering Limited: cash book: cash payments

Date 2018	Detail	Total £	Trade payables £	Wages and salaries £	PAYE and NIC £	Petty cash £
28 March	Optimo Limited	6,390.00	6,390.00			
28 March	Week 51 wages	19,341.36		19,341.36		
29 March	Fuzzy Limited	1,200.00	1,200.00			
29 March	Legal Bee	825.00	825.00			
29 March	HMRC Week 51	8,220.08			8,220.08	
29 March	Petty cash	100.00				100.00
Totals		**36,076.44**	**8,415.00**	**19,341.36**	**8,220.08**	**100.00**

How are these cash payments recorded in the double-entry system? As we saw in Chapter 4 (Posting accounting transactions to T accounts), cash paid is a decrease in an asset, so any cash paid is credited to the bank account. To complete the double entry, there has to be a debit to various other accounts as shown in Illustration 5.18. The debits represent increases in expenses (for example, bank charges or interest, which are not illustrated here), increases in other assets (petty cash) or decreases in liabilities (trade payables, wages control account and PAYE and NIC control).

Illustration 5.18 The double entry to record cash payments in the books of account of Kleos Engineering Limited

Date	Detail	Total	Trade payables	Wages and salaries	PAYE and NIC	Petty cash
Totals		**36,076.44**	**8,415.00**	**19,341.36**	**8,220.08**	**100.00**

Bank account

2018		£	2018		£
4 April	Cash book	13,579.97	30 March	Cash book	36,076.44

Credit bank, decrease asset with cash paid

Trade payables control account

2018		£	2018		£
5 March	Purchase returns	564.18	1 March	Purchase day book	9,612.24
30 March	Cash book	8,415.00			

Debit trade payables with the decrease in liabilities

Wages and salaries control account

2018		£	2018		£
30 March	Cash book	19,341.36			

Debit wages control with the decrease in liabilities

PAYE and NIC control account

2018		£	2018		£
30 March	Cash book	8,220.08			

Debit PAYE and NIC control with the decrease in liabilities

Petty cash account

2018		£	2018		£
29 March	Cash book	100.00			

Debit petty cash with the increase in the asset

To enable you as an accounting professional to:

- Understand how the cash paid is posted to the accounting records
- Make the required double entry to the accounting records to reflect the cash paid transactions in full

SUMMARY OF KEY CONCEPTS   Are you totally sure you can state the double entry to record cash payments in the books of account? Go to the **online workbook** to revise the required double entry in Summary of key concepts 5.7.

GO BACK OVER THIS AGAIN!   Convinced you understand how to make the required entries into the accounting records from the cash paid records? Go to the **online workbook** and attempt Exercises 5.9 to test your understanding.

THE PURCHASE LEDGER AND CASH PAYMENTS

The individual purchase ledger accounts are also updated for the cash paid to individual trade payables. Each trade payable is a liability, so the payment of cash reduces the amounts owed to each trade payable as shown in Illustration 5.19 (credit cash, decrease the cash asset, debit trade payables, decrease the trade payable liability).

Illustration 5.19 Kleos Engineering Limited: individual purchase ledger balances reflecting cash paid in March 2018

Fuzzy Limited purchase ledger account

2018		£	2018		£
29 March	Cash book	1,200.00	1 March	2461	1,200.00

Legal Bee purchase ledger account

2018		£	2018		£
29 March	Cash book	825.00	1 March	2464	825.00

Optimo Limited purchase ledger account

2018		£	2018		£
5 March	PR79	510.00	1 March	2460	6,900.00
28 March	Cash book	6,390.00			

Everything owed to the three trade payables in Illustration 5.19 has been paid. When reviewing the trade payables for unpaid amounts, the company's staff will see that these accounts have been paid in full and so will not pay these invoices again.

WHY IS THIS RELEVANT TO ME?   The purchase ledger and cash payments

To enable you as an accounting professional to:

- Understand how the cash paid to trade payables is posted to the individual purchase ledger accounts

- Appreciate how maintaining individual purchase ledger accounts for each supplier enables entities to identify suppliers who have and who have not been paid thereby avoiding double payments to suppliers

---

NUMERICAL EXERCISES   Do you think you could complete the purchase ledger accounts to reflect cash paid to trade payables? Go to the **online workbook** and complete Numerical exercises 5.4 to test your ability to make these entries.

SHOW ME HOW TO DO IT   Did you completely follow how the double entry was made from the cash paid records to the accounting records and to the individual purchase ledger accounts? View Video presentation 5.4 in the **online workbook** to see a practical demonstration of how the double entry was completed in the relevant T accounts and the individual purchase ledger accounts.

EXERCISING CONTROL: THE TRADE PAYABLES CONTROL ACCOUNT

The trade payables control account summarises all the credit transactions in the purchases system. We have seen how total purchases are credited to the trade payables control account as the trade payables liability increases and how cash is debited to the account as trade payables are paid what is owed thereby reducing the liability. What other entries are made in the trade payables control account? Illustration 5.20 presents all the entries that you would expect to find in the trade payables control account with figures for illustration purposes only.

The right hand side of the account represents increases in the liability. The balance brought forward at the start of the year is the trade payables at the end of the previous accounting

Illustration 5.20 The trade payables control account

Trade payables control account

2018		£	2018		£
31 Dec	Purchase returns day book	1,998	1 Jan	Balance b/f	47,789
31 Dec	Discounts received	2,765	31 Dec	Purchase day book	344,622
31 Dec	Cash paid	339,325			
31 Dec	Balance c/f	48,323			
		392,411			**392,411**

period representing money still owed to suppliers as a result of trading on credit with these suppliers up to the end of the previous accounting period. On the left hand side of the account, we find transactions and events that will reduce the trade payables liability. As well as cash paid to suppliers, purchase returns and discounts received from suppliers for bulk buying (Chapter 3, Discounts received) will also reduce the amount of the trade payables liability while decreasing the corresponding expense accounts and increasing the corresponding income account.

The balance brought forward + purchases – cash paid – discounts received – purchase returns should then give us the trade payables balance at the end of the accounting period. The trade payables control account provides a quick summary of transactions and a total balance for amounts owed by the business at the end of the accounting period. As we have seen, the total transactions (purchases, cash paid, purchase returns and discounts received) should be equal to the totals on each of the individual purchase ledger accounts. At the end of the accounting period, the trade payables balance carried forward at the end of the period should be equal to the total of all the individual purchase ledger balances. Time will be spent making sure that this is the case. If it is not and there is a difference between the balance on the trade payables control account and the total of all the individual balances on each of the purchase ledger accounts, then there is an error and time will have to be allocated to finding and correcting this error. As the trade payables control account balances carried forward and the total of the individual purchase ledger balances should be the same, control is exercised through the two sets of figures which enables organisations to track down and correct errors as they arise. A discount received may have been recorded in the individual purchase ledger account which has not been added to the trade payables control account or cash or purchases may have been missed out of the individual purchase ledger accounts. Whatever the cause of the error, the comparison of the two independent records will ensure that the trade payables figure at the end of the accounting period is correct.

EXERCISING CONTROL: THE BANK RECONCILIATION

We have considered how the sales and purchase ledger control accounts enable entities to ensure that their sales and purchase records are correct and to make corrections where they are not. Control over the cash book (= the bank acount) is exercised through checking cash book receipts and payments with the bank statements provided regularly by the bank. Sometimes, there is no entry in the cash book for items such as bank charges or bank interest or trade receivables may have made direct payments into an organisation's bank account which are not recorded in the cash book. Additional entries are then made in the cash book to ensure that the cash book and the bank account are in full agreement with each other and that the cash book presents a true and complete record of transactions through the bank account. At the end of any financial period, the cash book balance and the bank account balance are compared to ensure that they agree. However, there will also be entries in the cash book for cash received and cash paid that are not included in the bank statement at the end of any accounting period. This is because receipts paid in at the month end have not yet been cleared by the bank (this usually takes around three days) and payments to suppliers have been sent and recorded in the cash book but they have not yet cleared through the company's bank account. At the end of each period of account, therefore, organisations have to complete a bank reconciliation to ensure that the cash book balance (opening balance + receipts – payments) and the bank balance are in complete agreement after taking into account any uncleared or unrecorded items. Let's look at an example to see how the bank reconciliation works.

Illustration 5.21 shows the cash book receipts and payments total columns for Kleos Engineering Limited for the last week of June 2018.

Illustration 5.21 The cash book for the final week of June 2018 for Kleos Engineering Limited

Receipts: June 2018			Payments: June 2018		
Date	**Detail**	**Total £**	**Date**	**Detail**	**Total £**
25 June	J Brown and Sons 110670	10,800.00	25 June	Optimo 005995	6,240.00
26 June	Tiddle and Toddle 110671	499.20	26 June	Wages and salaries BACS	32,462.10
27 June	Cash sales 110672	458.64	27 June	HMRC BACS	36,880.42
29 June	Vivanti plc 110673	632.64	29 June	Doric plc 005996	1,320.78
29 June	Vodravid 110674	2,429.80	29 June	Fuzzy Limited 005997	6,480.72
			29 June	Bodgitt and Leggott 005998	480.00

The balance in the bank, according to the cash book, is £25,200.42. Illustration 5.22 shows the bank statement for Kleos Engineering Limited for the final week of June 2018.

Illustration 5.22 Bank statement for the final week of June 2018 for Kleos Engineering Limited

Covetous Bank plc
Sort code: 99-99-99
Account number: 11112222

Kleos Engineering Limited
Unit 5
Any Industrial Estate
Anywhere
A14 2ZY

	Date 2018	Withdrawn	Paid in	Balance
Balance forward				94,244.16
DD BPower	25 June	400.00		93,884.16
BACS F Smith and Co	25 June		750.00	94,594.16
BACS	26 June	32,462.10		62,132.06
BACS HMRC	27 June	36,880.42		25,251.64
110672	27 June		458.64	25,710.28
110670	28 June		10,800.00	36,510.28
005995	28 June	6,240.00		30,270.28
110671	29 June		499.20	30,769.48

There is clearly a difference between the cash book balance of £25,200.42 and the bank statement balance of £30,769.48. How do these two figures reconcile with each other? Firstly we have to tick off those items that appear in both the cash book and in the bank statement to find out where the differences arise. The items that appear in both the cash book and in the bank statement are ticked and highlighted in **red** in Illustration 5.23.

Illustration 5.23 Highlighted items appearing in both the cash book and the bank statement for Kleos Engineering Limited for the final week of June 2018

Receipts: June 2018			Payments: June 2018		
Date	Detail	Total £	Date	Detail	Total £
25 June	J Brown and Sons 110670	✓10,800.00	25 June	Optimo 005995	✓6,240.00
26 June	Tiddle and Toddle 110671	✓499.20	26 June	Wages and salaries BACS	✓32,462.10
27 June	Cash sales 110672	✓458.64	27 June	HMRC BACS	✓36,880.42
29 June	Vivanti plc 110673	632.64	29 June	Doric plc 005996	1,320.78
29 June	Vodravid 110674	2,429.80	29 June	Fuzzy Limited 005997	6,480.72
			29 June	Bodgitt and Leggott 005998	480.00

	Date 2018	Withdrawn	Paid in	Balance
Balance forward				94,244.16
DD BPower	25 June	400.00		93,884.16
BACS F Smith and Co	25 June		750.00	94,594.16
BACS	26 June	✓32,462.10		62,132.06
BACS HMRC	27 June	✓36,880.42		25,251.64
110672	27 June		✓458.64	25,710.28
110670	28 June		✓10,800.00	36,510.28
005995	28 June	✓6,240.00		30,270.28
110671	29 June		✓499.20	30,769.48

The items that only appear in one of the two records are the reconciling items: these remain in black in the bank statement and in the cash book in Illustration 5.23. The first step in the bank reconciliation is to update the cash book balance for amounts paid in and withdrawn from the bank that do not appear in the cash book. This will produce the correct cash book balance to compare to the balance in the bank statement. In the bank statement, there is the receipt from F Smith and Co for £750 to add on to the cash book balance and the £400 direct debit to BPower to deduct. Illustration 5.24 shows the corrected cash book balance at 29 June 2018.

Illustration 5.24 Corrected cash book balance for Kleos Engineering Limited at 29 June 2018

	£
Cash book balance at 29 June 2018	25,200.42
Add: direct credit not in the cash book (25 June)	750.00
Deduct: direct debit to BPower (25 June)	(400.00)
Corrected cash book balance at 29 June 2018	**25,550.42**

Now that the cash book balance takes into account all the receipts and payments for the period, the cash book balance and the bank balance can be reconciled. The bank reconciliation starts with the balance in the bank statement. Receipts in the cash book that do not appear in the bank statement are then listed, totalled and added on to the bank account balance. Payments in the cash book that do not appear in the bank statement are listed, totalled and deducted from the bank statement balance. The final figure should be the balance as shown in the cash book. The bank reconciliation is presented in Illustration 5.25.

Illustration 5.25 Bank reconciliation for Kleos Engineering Limited at 29 June 2018

	£	£
Balance per bank statement (Illustration 5.22)		30,769.48
Add: cash book receipts not in the bank statement (Illustration 5.23)		
110673 29 June Vivanti plc	632.64	
110674 29 June Vodravid	2,429.80	
		3,062.44
Deduct: cash book payments not in the bank statement (Illustration 5.23)		
005996 29 June Doric plc	1,320.78	
005997 29 June Fuzzy Limited	6,480.72	
005998 29 June Bodgitt and Leggott	480.00	
		(8,281.50)
Balance per the cash book (Illustration 5.24)		**25,550.42**

Through regular checking of the cash book records to the bank statement, entities ensure that their bank balance is accurate and reflects the actual cash available for investment or making payments to clear liabilities. The bank reconciliation is another example of the ways in which organisations operate controls to ensure their financial figures are correct and up to date.

WHY IS THIS RELEVANT TO ME?   Exercising control: the bank reconciliation

As an accounting professional you will be expected to be able to:

• Understand how bank reconciliations are put together

• Compare the cash book and bank statements to identify unrecorded and reconciling items

• Produce and present bank reconciliation statements for the organisations you work for

SUMMARY OF KEY CONCEPTS   Are you quite sure you know what steps to follow to put the bank reconciliation together? Go to the **online workbook** to check your recollection with Summary of key concepts 5.9.

NUMERICAL EXERCISES   Do you think that you could reconcile the cash book balance and the bank statement balance? Go to the **online workbook** and complete Numerical exercises 5.5 to test your ability to make these entries.

SHOW ME HOW TO DO IT   Did you completely understand how the bank reconciliation was put together? View Video presentation 5.5 in the **online workbook** to see a practical demonstration of how the bank reconciliation was compiled.

PETTY CASH

As well as the main cash book which tracks the cash received and cash paid from the bank account, entities will also maintain a petty cash book. The petty cash book is another book of prime entry which makes the first record of small sums of cash paid out of the business on a day-to-day basis. Petty cash is a store of actual cash with which to meet small day-to-day expenses such as the purchase of, for example, tea and coffee for the office, postage stamps, items of stationery and so on. Suppliers would be unwilling to supply such small items on credit terms, so businesses use cash to make these purchases directly. The petty cash is topped up on a regular basis with money from the bank (Illustration 5.18) and this cash is then used to pay for small purchases in cash on a daily basis. Just like the bank account, the petty cash book is already a double-entry record with receipts of cash from the bank on the left hand side and payments of cash on the right. At any point in time, total receipts – total payments should be equal to the amount left in the petty cash box. Illustration 5.26 presents the petty cash book of Kleos Engineering Limited and the record of the double entry for the cash paid. Cash received is debited to the petty cash as the petty cash asset increases while the bank account is credited as the bank account asset decreases (Illustration 5.18). Cash paid out is credited to petty cash as the cash asset decreases and debited to expenditure as expenses increase (Illustration 5.26).

Illustration 5.26 The petty cash book of Kleos Engineering Limited for April 2018 and the double entry to record petty cash payments in the books of account of the company

Date	Supplier	Total £	VAT £	Tea and Coffee £	Postage £	Petrol £
3 4 2018	J and J Stores	10.20		10.20		
4 4 2018	Samoco plc	15.00	2.50			12.50
5 4 2018	Post office	12.60			12.60	
		37.80	2.50	10.20	12.60	12.50

Petty cash account

2018		£	2018		£
29 March	Cash book	100.00	5 April	Petty cash expenses	37.80

Credit petty cash, decrease asset with cash paid

VAT account

2018		£	2018		£
5 March	Sales returns	168.45	1 March	Sales day book	5,242.98
1 March	Purchase day book	1,602.04	3 April	Cash book	72.00
4 April	Petty cash	2.50	5 March	Purchase returns	94.03

Debit VAT, decrease the liability for monies owed to HM Revenue and Customs

Tea and coffee account

2018		£	2018		£
3 April	Petty cash	10.20			

Debit tea and coffee, increase the expense with cash paid

Postage account

2018		£	2018		£
5 April	Petty cash	12.60			

Debit postage, increase the expense with cash paid

Petrol account

2018		£	2018		£
5 April	Petty cash	12.50			

Debit petrol, increase the expense with cash paid

WHY IS THIS RELEVANT TO ME?   Petty cash

To enable you as an accounting professional to:

- Understand how petty cash is used to pay for small day-to-day expenses
- Make the relevant double entries in the accounting records to record receipts into petty cash
- Make the relevant double entries in the accounting records to record payments from petty cash
- Understand how the balance on the petty cash account at any point in time is calculated by deducting total payments from total receipts

MULTIPLE CHOICE QUESTIONS   Are you confident that you understand accounting for petty cash? Go to the **online workbook** and have a go at Multiple choice questions 5.4 to test your understanding.

THE PAYROLL SYSTEM

Employees provide their time in return for payment in the form of wages and salaries. Wages and salaries can be paid weekly or monthly. The rate of pay is agreed with employers in each employee's contract of employment, but employees do not receive this amount of money each week or each month. This is because employees' remuneration is subject to deductions for income tax and national insurance as well as other deductions for items such as pension contributions, trade union subscriptions and student loan repayments among others. The weekly payroll for Kleos Engineering Limited for week 51 is shown in Illustration 5.27.

Illustration 5.27 The weekly payroll for Kleos Engineeing Limited

Employee name	Works number	Gross pay	PAYE (Income tax)	Employee's national insurance	Pension	Net	Employer's national insurance
		£	£	£	£	£	£
Afzal	167	700.00	86.85	65.40	35.00	512.75	74.52
Barrow	145	550.00	58.35	46.80	27.50	417.35	53.82
Begum	109	606.00	68.99	53.52	30.30	453.19	61.55
Carr	135	724.00	91.41	67.68	36.20	528.71	77.83
Desai	121	688.00	84.57	63.36	34.40	505.67	72.86
...	...	...	...	...	...	...	...
Totals for week 51		26,144.00	3,121.36	2,374.08	1,307.20	19,341.36	2,724.64

How does the payroll work? As Illustration 5.27 shows, there are various numbers that need to be considered and explained. Let's think about each of the headings and numbers in the payroll and what each of these represents.

Gross pay

Gross pay for employees with an annual salary is calculated by dividing the annual salary by 12. For example, the monthly gross pay of an employee with an annual salary of £30,000 will be £30,000 ÷ 12 = £2,500.00. Gross pay for weekly paid employees is the number of hours worked multiplied by the agreed hourly rate. Thus, for Afzal (Illustration 5.27), if she worked for 40 hours at an hourly rate of £17.50 this would give gross pay for the week of £700.00. Alternatively, £700.00 would be the gross pay for working 35 hours during the week at a rate of £20 per hour. The starting point for any payroll is the gross pay for each employee.

Income tax (PAYE)

Each employee's weekly or monthly gross pay is subject to income tax. This is often referred to as PAYE which is an abbreviation for pay-as-you-earn: employers make a deduction from each employee's gross pay for the tax that is due on their earnings each week or each month. This enables each employee to meet their obligation to pay the income tax on what they earn each year rather than being asked to pay all of the tax due for the year at the end of the tax year. The deductions for tax made by employers are paid over to HM Revenue and Customs on a regular basis throughout the financial year. Your future studies will show you how each employee's annual tax liability is calculated and how this translates into a weekly or monthly tax deduction. For now, you just need to be aware of the deduction that is made for tax and how this is accounted for each week or each month in the weekly or monthly payroll.

Employee's national insurance

As well as a weekly or monthly deduction for income tax, employees' gross pay is also subject to a deduction for national insurance contributions. These national insurance contributions are the basis for determining an individual's future rights to various state benefits such as a state pension. You will frequently see the abbreviation NIC, which is commonly used to refer to national insurance contributions. NIC deductions are made by employers and paid over to HM Revenue and Customs on a regular basis along with the deductions made for PAYE. Again, your future studies will explain how national insurance contributions are calculated and how much each individual pays on their earnings. For now, just be aware of the deductions made for national insurance and how these are accounted for on a weekly or monthly basis.

Pension contributions

Employees are not limited to just the state pension when they retire. Employers set up company pension schemes for their workforce and invite each employee to join the entity's own pension scheme when they take up employment with the organisation. Employees then make weekly or monthly contributions to the pension scheme from their wages and salaries. These contributions build up into a retirement fund for each employee over a number of years which is then used to pay each employee a pension on their retirement. The contributions made by employees are

5

5

deducted from their gross pay and paid over to the pension scheme on a regular basis. You will cover pension schemes and pension accounting in much greater detail in your later studies. For now you just need to understand that these deductions are made from the payroll and the way in which they are accounted for.

Net pay

Net pay is what is left after all the deductions have been made from gross pay. For Afzal (Illustration 5.27), the gross pay of £700.00 − £86.85 (PAYE: tax) − £65.40 (NIC) − £35.00 (pension contribution) = the net pay of £512.75. £512.75 is the amount of money that Afzal will receive for week 51. As noted above, the tax, national insurance and pension contributions are collected by the employing company and paid over to HM Revenue and Customs (tax and national insurance) and to the pension scheme (pension contribution) on Afzal's behalf.

Employer's national insurance

As well as each employee paying their own national insurance contribution each week or each month, employers also have to pay a national insurance contribution on the basis of what each employee earns each week or each month. These employer's national insurance contributions are an additional expense for the company over and above the gross pay that is paid to each employee. The employer's national insurance contributions are calculated each week or each month and paid over regularly to HM Revenue and Customs along with the PAYE and NIC deducted from employees' gross pay. You will, again, learn much more about these employer's national insurance contributions in your later studies. You should just understand for now how these employer national insurance contributions are accounted for.

WHY IS THIS RELEVANT TO ME?   The payroll system

To ensure you as an accounting professional understand:

- How gross and net pay are calculated
- What the various deductions from gross pay mean
- How employer's national insurance is an additional expense for each employing entity

---

GO BACK OVER THIS AGAIN!   Are you completely certain that you understand the various parts of the payroll system? Go to the **online workbook** and complete Exercises 5.11 to check your grasp of these different elements in the payroll system.

THE DOUBLE ENTRY TO RECORD THE WEEKLY/ MONTHLY PAYROLL

Just as in the case of the sales day book, the sale returns day book, the purchase day book, the purchase returns day book, the cash book and the petty cash book, the weekly and monthly payroll is not part of the double-entry system. The weekly and monthly payroll is the book of prime entry for wages and salaries, the first point of recording expenditure made on remunerating employees for work undertaken. Therefore, the double entry still has to be completed from each weekly and monthly payroll. Three sets of double entries are required to record the payroll expenses and the additional obligations that are created when paying wages and salaries to employees.

The first double entry records the liability for gross pay and the expense that arises from the payment of wages and salaries. The liability for gross wages and salaries is credited to the wages control account as shown in Illustration 5.28. Employees have given their time in exchange for their earnings, so the giving of employees' time in the service of the entity creates a liability to pay wages and salaries. The gross wages and salaries expense is debited to the wages (expense) account (Illustration 5.28) to reflect the total expenditure incurred by the employing entity in paying their employees for the work they have undertaken.

5

Illustration 5.28 The double entry to record gross wages and salaries cost in the books of account of Kleos Engineering Limited

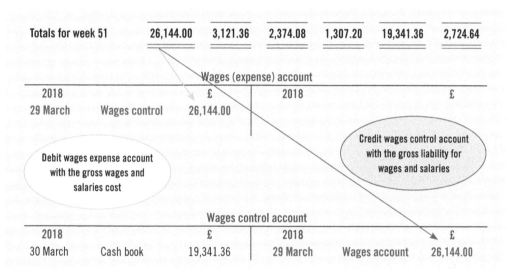

Once the double entry to record gross wages and salaries figures is complete, entries can be made to record the deductions for PAYE, employees' NIC and pensions. These deductions are debited to the wages control account as these deductions decrease the obligation to pay wages and salaries to the employees (Illustration 5.29): only the net amount (gross wages and salaries – deductions) is paid to employees. However, while these deductions from gross wages and salaries decrease the obligation to make payments to employees, they in turn create new obligations. The amounts deducted must be paid over to HM Revenue and Customs and to the pension scheme. Therefore the PAYE and employee NIC deductions are credited to the PAYE and NIC control account and the pension deductions are credited to the pensions control account to reflect this increase in liabilities (Illustration 5.29).

Illustration 5.29 The double entry to record deductions from gross wages and salaries in the books of account of Kleos Engineering Limited

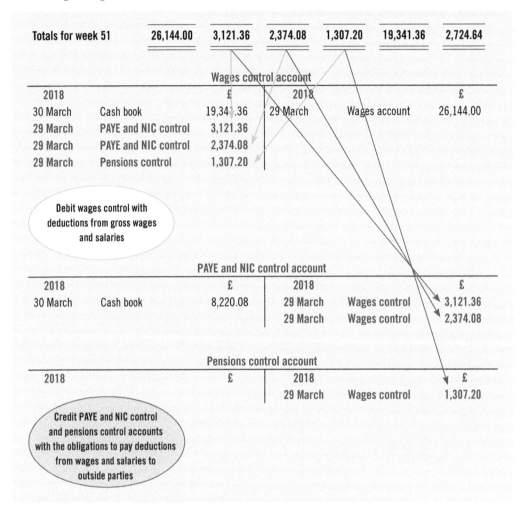

| Totals for week 51 | | 26,144.00 | 3,121.36 | 2,374.08 | 1,307.20 | 19,341.36 | 2,724.64 |

Wages control account

2018		£	2018		£
30 March	Cash book	19,341.36	29 March	Wages account	26,144.00
29 March	PAYE and NIC control	3,121.36			
29 March	PAYE and NIC control	2,374.08			
29 March	Pensions control	1,307.20			

Debit wages control with deductions from gross wages and salaries

PAYE and NIC control account

2018		£	2018		£
30 March	Cash book	8,220.08	29 March	Wages control	3,121.36
			29 March	Wages control	2,374.08

Pensions control account

2018		£	2018		£
			29 March	Wages control	1,307.20

Credit PAYE and NIC control and pensions control accounts with the obligations to pay deductions from wages and salaries to outside parties

The final double entry records the additional obligation and expense arising from the requirement to pay employer's national insurance on the gross wages and salaries of each employee. As we have seen, employer's national insurance is an expense over and above the expenditure on gross wages and salaries. This obligation creates a liability to pay more money to HM Revenue and Customs so this liability is credited to the PAYE and NIC control account. The increase in the liability is reflected as an expense which is debited to the employer's national insurance account. These entries are shown in Illustration 5.30.

Illustration 5.30 The double entry to record employer's national insurance contributions in the books of account of Kleos Engineering Limited

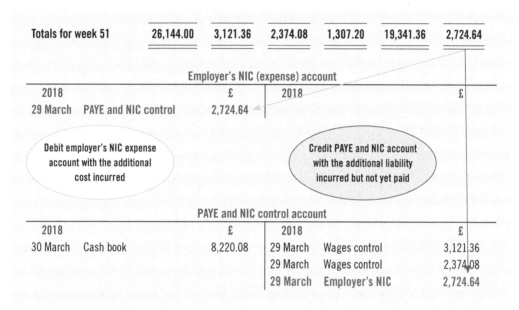

| Totals for week 51 | 26,144.00 | 3,121.36 | 2,374.08 | 1,307.20 | 19,341.36 | 2,724.64 |

Employer's NIC (expense) account

2018		£	2018	£
29 March	PAYE and NIC control	2,724.64		

Debit employer's NIC expense account with the additional cost incurred

Credit PAYE and NIC account with the additional liability incurred but not yet paid

PAYE and NIC control account

2018		£	2018		£
30 March	Cash book	8,220.08	29 March	Wages control	3,121.36
			29 March	Wages control	2,374.08
			29 March	Employer's NIC	2,724.64

To ensure you as an accounting professional can:

- Make the required double entries to record the payroll expense in the books of account
- Recognise how the various expenses and liabilities associated with the payroll arise and how they are recorded in the books of account

Are you quite certain that you can state the double entry to record payroll expenses and liabilities in the books of account? Go to the **online workbook** to revise the required double entry in Summary of key concepts 5.10.

Are you convinced that you can make the required double entry to record the payroll in the books of account? Go to the **online workbook** and complete Exercises 5.12 to make sure that you can.

Did you completely follow how the double entry was made from the payroll to the accounting records? View Video presentation 5.6 in the **online workbook** to see a practical demonstration of how the double entry was completed in the relevant T accounts.

THE NOMINAL LEDGER

Throughout both Chapters 4 and 5 we have referred frequently to the books of account to describe the various T accounts that make up the total of the accounting records of an organisation. All these accounts in their entirety make up what is called the nominal ledger (you will also find the nominal ledger referred to as the general ledger). The nominal ledger is a list of all the double-entry transactions in all the asset, liability, capital, income and expenditure T accounts of an organisation. The nominal ledger lists each account in alphabetical order and represents the books of account of the organisation. When a trial balance is extracted, this trial balance presents the balances on all the accounts in the nominal ledger. As the nominal ledger only records all the double entries made to record an organisation's transactions, it does not include the books of prime entry (which are not part of the double-entry system) or the sales and purchase ledgers (a record of individual amounts owed by customers and owed to suppliers that operate outside the double-entry system). You will find many references throughout your studies and your professional career to the nominal ledger, the record of all the double entries made by an organisation to record each and every transaction during the financial period which provide the foundation upon which the financial statements are built.

WHY IS THIS RELEVANT TO ME?   The nominal ledger

To ensure that you as an accounting professional understand that:

- The nominal ledger presents all the books of account of an organisation
- The nominal ledger records all the double-entry transactions of an organisation during a financial period
- The trial balance is extracted from the balances in the nominal ledger
- The books of prime entry and the sales and purchase ledgers are records separate from the nominal ledger
- The balances in the nominal ledger represent the figures that appear in the financial statements

---

SUMMARY OF KEY CONCEPTS   Are you quite certain that you understand the function and purpose of the nominal ledger? Go to the **online workbook** to check your understanding with Summary of key concepts 5.11.

GO BACK OVER THIS AGAIN!   Are you totally sure that you can describe the nominal ledger, its function and contents? Go to the **online workbook** and complete Exercises 5.13 to check your knowledge.

THE DOUBLE ENTRY TO RECORD DISPOSALS OF NON-CURRENT ASSETS

In Chapter 4 (Comprehensive example: double entry and the trial balance), we saw how Julia recorded her purchase of non-current assets (debit non-current assets with the cost of each asset, credit cash with the payment made) and the way in which depreciation of non-current assets is recorded (debit depreciation expense, credit accumulated depreciation). As we saw in Chapter 3 (Profits and losses on disposal of non-current assets), non-current assets can be sold, generating a profit or a loss on their sale if they are sold for more or less than their carrying amount. What is the double entry required when there is a disposal of non-current assets? The asset disposed of is no longer owned by the company, so the asset must be derecognised in the books of account. This derecognition must be made in both the asset cost account and the accumulated depreciation account so that the carrying amount of the asset is completely removed from the accounting records in the nominal ledger. The carrying amount of the asset disposed of is compared to the sale proceeds (if any) to determine whether there is a profit or loss on disposal. This profit or loss on disposal is recorded as either income (profit) or expense (loss) in the statement of profit or loss in the accounting period in which the disposal takes place. Let's have a look at the entries required to record an asset disposal in the books of account in Example 5.1.

EXAMPLE 5.1

Kleos Engineering Limited sells a piece of machinery on 28 February 2018 for £20,000. The machinery had originally cost £75,000. Depreciation of £60,000 had been charged on this piece of machinery up to the date of disposal.

There are three entries that have to be made on the disposal of any non-current asset. The first is to record any cash received from the disposal. The double entry to record this cash is to:

- Debit the cash asset as the cash asset has now increased (Illustration 5.31).

- Credit the non-current asset disposal account (Illustration 5.31). Cash has been received so the credit balance on this income account increases. Note that cash received from the sale of non-current assets is not recorded in sales as this is not a sale made in the ordinary course of business (Chapter 3, Income in the statement of profit or loss).

Illustration 5.31 Double entry to record the receipt of cash from the disposal of a non-current asset

Bank account

2018		£	2018		£
28 Feb	Non-current asset disposals	20,000			

Non-current asset disposals

2018		£	2018		£
			28 Feb	Bank	20,000

Step 2 is to derecognise the cost of the asset in the non-current assets cost account. The double entry to record the derecognition of cost is:

- Debit the non-current asset disposals account with the original cost of the asset (Illustration 5.32). The carrying amount of the asset at the date of disposal is compared with the cash received to determine the profit or loss on disposal. As we saw in Chapter 3, Depreciation, carrying amount = the cost of an asset − the accumulated depreciation charged on that asset.

Therefore, moving the cost of the asset disposed of to the non-current asset disposals account is the first step in determining the carrying amount of the asset at the date of disposal.

- Credit the non-current asset cost account (Illustration 5.32) with the original cost of the asset. The cost of the assets still in use in the business has now decreased as a result of the disposal, so the credit to the cost account reduces the cost of the assets still employed within the business.

Illustration 5.32 Double entry to record the derecognition of the cost of a non-current asset disposed of

Non-current asset disposals

2018		£	2018		£
28 Feb	Machinery	75,000	28 Feb	Bank	20,000

Machinery account

2018		£	2018		£
			28 Feb	Non-current asset disposals	75,000

Step 3 then removes the accumulated depreciation on the asset disposed of from the accumulated depreciation account. The double entry required to remove this accumulated depreciation is to:

- Debit accumulated depreciation with the depreciation on the asset to the date of disposal (Illustration 5.33). Accumulated depreciation is a credit balance. Debiting this account will reduce the accumulated depreciation. The accumulated depreciation left on this account is then just the accumulated depreciation on assets that are still employed within the business.

- Credit the non-current asset disposal account (Illustration 5.33) with the accumulated depreciation on the asset to the date of disposal.

Illustration 5.33 Double entry to record the derecognition of the accumulated depreciation on a non-current asset disposed of

Non-current asset disposals

2018		£	2018		£
28 Feb	Machinery	75,000	28 Feb	Bank	20,000
			28 Feb	Machinery accumulated depreciation	60,000

Machinery accumulated depreciation account

2018		£	2018		£
28 Feb	Non-current asset disposals	60,000			

Is there a profit or loss on this disposal? Illustration 5.33 shows that the credit side of the non-current asset disposals account totals up to £80,000 (£20,000 cash received + £60,000 accumulated depreciation) while the debit side totals up to £75,000 (machinery cost). The total of the credits on the account is higher than the total of the debits, so the non-current asset disposals account has a credit balance of £5,000 (£80,000 – £75,000). A credit balance on an income or expense account means that this is a profit of £5,000 on disposal and this £5,000 will be recorded as a non-trading income in the statement of profit or loss in the year of disposal. Had the balance on the non-current assets disposals account been a debit balance (a higher total on the debit side of the account than on the credit side), then this would have been a loss not a profit on disposal, an additional expense in the statement of profit or loss.

Does this result make sense? You can look at this disposal from a different point of view to check that the conclusion of a profit is correct. The carrying amount of the asset disposed of is £15,000 (£75,000 cost – £60,000 accumulated depreciation). The cash received for this asset was £20,000. Therefore, a receipt of £20,000 for an asset with a carrying amount of £15,000 gives a profit of £5,000, indicating that our profit on disposal from the T account is correct.

At the end of the financial period (30 June 2018), the non-current asset disposals account is closed off as shown in Illustration 5.34.

Illustration 5.34 Closing off the non-current asset disposals account at the end of the financial period

Non-current asset disposals

2018		£	2018		£
28 Feb	Machinery	75,000	28 Feb	Bank	20,000
30 June	Statement of profit or loss	5,000	28 Feb	Machinery accumulated depreciation	60,000
		80,000			**80,000**

WHY IS THIS RELEVANT TO ME?   The double entry to record disposals of non-current assets

To make sure you as an accounting professional can:

- Make the required double entries to record the disposal of non-current assets
- Understand why these entries are required when non-current assets are disposed of

SUMMARY OF KEY CONCEPTS   Are you totally sure that you can state the double entry to record the disposal of non-current assets in the books of account? Go to the **online workbook** to revise the required double entry in Summary of key concepts 5.12.

MULTIPLE CHOICE QUESTIONS   Are you confident that you can make the required double entry to record the disposal of non-current assets in the books of account and calculate profits and losses on disposal? Go to the **online workbook** and have a go at Multiple choice questions 5.5 to test your ability in this area.

FINDING MISSING FIGURES BY USING T ACCOUNTS: INCOMPLETE RECORDS

Sometimes, certain figures required to produce a set of accounts are not available as they have not been recorded. This is a common situation when preparing financial statements for cash-based businesses. However, we can find a missing figure by using the logic of T accounts as shown in Example 5.2.

Madge is a market trader selling fruit and vegetables for cash. She provides you with the following information:

- Cash in the till counted up at 31 December 2017: £529.
- Cash in the till counted up at 31 December 2018: £380.
- Cash paid into her business bank account during the year: £85,242. This figure can be verified by totalling up the receipts for the year in her business bank statements.
- Cash used to pay suppliers for goods received during the year: £50,647. This figure can be verified by reference to her purchase invoices stamped 'paid in cash' or 'cash received'.
- Total sales during the year to 31 December 2018: no records have been kept of daily cash takings on the market stall.

To complete Madge's accounts, we need to find the sales figure. As she has not kept any records of her daily cash takings, we will have to reconstruct her sales figure using the information we already have and which we can verify from other independent sources. How can we do this?

Using a T account, we can reconstruct the cash account as shown in Illustration 5.35.

Illustration 5.35 Using a T account to find an unknown or missing figure

2018		£	2018		£
1 Jan	Balance b/f	529	31 Dec	Bank account	85,242
31 Dec	Balancing figure = sales	135,740	31 Dec	Purchases	50,647
			31 Dec	Balance c/f	380
		136,269			136,269

Madge: cash account

How was the cash account shown in Illustration 5.35 reconstructed to determine the sales figure?

- The £529 cash in hand at 31 December 2017 is the closing balance of cash for that year and forms the opening cash balance at the start of the current financial year. Cash is an asset, so the opening balance of £529 will be brought down on the debit side of the cash account.
- Money paid into the bank is an increase in the bank asset (debit bank) but a decrease in the cash asset. Decreases in assets are posted to the credit side of asset accounts, so £85,242 of payments out of cash into the bank are credited to the cash account to reflect this reduction in the cash balance.
- Similarly, payments to suppliers represent a decrease in cash as money is paid out of the cash account to pay for purchases. Therefore, £50,647 is posted to the credit side of the cash account and

debited to the purchases account, a reduction (credit) in cash and an increase (debit) in expenses (cost of sales).

- The balance left in the cash account at the end of the financial year is an asset, a debit balance: for a debit balance to arise on the cash account, the total on the debit side of the account has to be greater than the total on the credit side of the account. Total cash received – total cash paid out = the balance on the cash account at the end of the financial year. This cash at the end of the year is added to the credit side of the account to balance the account for the year and is carried forward as an asset transferred from the current financial year into the next financial year.

- The total on the credit side of the account is £136,269 (£85,242 of cash paid into the bank out of cash + £50,647 of cash paid for purchases from cash + £380 remaining at the end of the year to transfer to the next financial year). The only figure on the debit side of the account is the cash at the start of the year, a figure of £529. This cash existed at the start of the year, so cannot be part of cash receipts from sales for the current year. To balance the account at £136,269, a figure of £135,740 is added to the debit side. If there are £136,269 of credits, then sales of £135,740 (£136,269 – £529) must have been made to increase (debit) the cash account in order to meet the actual payments out of cash during the year and still have £380 left over at 31 December 2018.

You can use this technique to find other missing figures when putting accounting statements together. In Illustration 5.35 we found the figure for sales by using the logic of T accounts. We could also use the same logic to find missing figures for purchases or drawings among others. We shall return to this technique in Chapter 6 (Using T accounts to calculate cash flows and Appendix) to see how missing figures for cash received from sales, cash paid to suppliers and other figures can be determined from numbers given in the financial statements in order to prepare statements of cash flows.

WHY IS THIS RELEVANT TO ME?   Finding missing figures by using T accounts: incomplete records

To provide you as an accounting professional with:

- A way to use the logic and discipline of T accounts to reconstruct accounting figures
- A method to use in examinations to calculate figures that are not given in a question
- An awareness of the techniques you can use in practice to find missing figures

---

MULTIPLE CHOICE QUESTIONS   Do you think that you can use T accounts to determine missing numbers required to complete a set of financial statements? Go to the **online workbook** and have a go at Multiple choice questions 5.6 to make sure you can apply this technique in practice.

POTENTIAL ERRORS

Once all the double entries have been made, the trial balance is extracted from the nominal ledger accounts. If the trial balance balances, then it is tempting to assume that all the double entry has been completed correctly and that the financial statements drawn up from the nominal ledger accounts are totally accurate. However, you should be aware that various errors might arise that will require correction, even if the trial balance balances perfectly. These errors fall into six categories. These six categories are presented in Table 5.1. Think about the double entry that would be required to correct these errors.

Table 5.1 Potential double-entry errors

Category of error	Description
Error of omission	A transaction is completely missed out. For example, omitting sales for a day would understate sales income, the VAT liability and the trade receivables or cash asset. The trial balance will still balance as the debits and the credits will both be understated by exactly the same figure. Once any omissions are discovered, then the double entry must be completed with debits and credits to the relevant accounts to make the correction and to ensure that all transactions are recorded accurately and in full.
Error of commission	A transaction is posted to the correct type of account (income, expense, asset, liability or capital) but the wrong account is debited or credited. For example, recording rent as motor expenses records the rent in the correct type of account, an expense account, but in the wrong account: rent is not a motor expense. In this case, the motor expenses account would be credited and the rent account debited to record the expense in the correct account. Again, the trial balance will balance but the amounts recorded on the two expense accounts will be incorrect.
Error of principle	This is where a transaction is posted to the wrong type of account. For example, a sale is recorded as a credit to an expense account instead of a credit to the sales account. Correcting this entry would require a debit to the expense account and a credit to the sales account. The trial balance will still balance but both sales and expenses will be understated by the same amount.
Error of original entry	The correct accounts are debited and credited, but the wrong amount is recorded. For example, sales of £17,280 are recorded instead of the correct amount of £17,820. These errors are also called transposition errors as the wrong figures are entered due to two figures in the transaction total being transposed. When a transposition error occurs, the difference is divisible exactly by 9: £17,820 – £17,280 = £540 ÷ 9 = £60. Where both double entries record the incorrect figure, then the trial balance will still balance. However, where one figure is recorded correctly while the other is subject to a transposition error, then the trial balance will not balance. Should the difference on your trial balance divide by 9, then look out for a transposition error in the double entry in your T accounts. This will require methodical checking of all the double entries made to find and correct the source of the error.
Compensating error	These arise when two or more errors cancel each other out. Thus, the property, plant and equipment account might be incorrectly added up, resulting in an understatement of £1,000. An expense account is then also incorrectly added up and produces an overstatement of £1,000. These two errors will cancel each other out as one debit is £1,000 too high and another debit is £1,000 too low.
Complete reversal of entries	Transactions are posted to the correct accounts, but the debit and credit entries are reversed. For example, sales are debited with £10,000 while cash is credited with £10,000. To correct this error, the sales will be credited with £20,000 and the bank account will be debited with £20,000. The first £10,000 adjustment on both accounts will reverse the incorrect entry to bring the balances back to zero and the second £10,000 on both accounts will enter the correct amounts on the correct sides of each account.

WHY IS THIS RELEVANT TO ME?   Potential errors

To enable you as an accounting professional to:

- Be aware of errors that might arise while making double entries to the books of account
- Identify and correct any errors that do arise

SUMMARY OF KEY CONCEPTS   Are you confident that you can define the six types of double-entry error? Go to the **online workbook** to check your ability to do so with Summary of key concepts 5.13.

GO BACK OVER THIS AGAIN!   Are you sure that you know which of the six types of double-entry error is which? Test your ability to describe these errors with Exercises 5.14.

MULTIPLE CHOICE QUESTIONS   How certain are you that you can make the required double entry to correct accounting errors? Go to the **online workbook** and have a go at Multiple choice questions 5.7 to test your ability in this area.

5

THE TRIAL BALANCE DOES NOT BALANCE

If all the double entry has been completed correctly, then the trial balance will balance. However, when the trial balance does not balance, then there is a problem with the double entry. The trial balance may not balance for the following reasons:

- A transaction has been entered as two debits or two credits instead of one debit and one credit.
- Only the debit or the credit entry to record the transaction has been made and the double entry is incomplete.

When the trial balance fails to balance, then the difference is recorded in a suspense account. If the debits in the trial balance are lower than the credits, then the balance on the suspense account is a debit balance. If the credits in the trial balance are lower than the debits, then a credit balance is recorded in the suspense account. The T accounts are then subjected to detailed scrutiny to find and correct the trial balance difference and to reduce the balance on the suspense account to zero.

EXAMPLE 5.3

The trial balance of Kleos Engineering Limited at 30 June 2018 shows total debits of £34,491,950 and total credits of £34,500,650, a difference of £8,700. The total credits are larger than the total debits, so the difference is recorded on the debit side of the suspense account as shown in Illustration 5.36.

Illustration 5.36 Kleos Engineering Limited: the suspense account used to record the difference on the trial balance

			Suspense account			
2018			**£**	**2018**		**£**
30 June	Trial balance difference		8,700			

A detailed review of the nominal ledger shows that a payment for rates in the cash book of £5,850 on 1 April was credited correctly to the bank account and credited (instead of being debited) to the rates account. Rates of £5,850 are paid quarterly in advance on 1 July, 1 October, 1 January and 1 April. The total rates charge for the year should be £23,400 (£5,850 × 4 = £23,400), but the rates account currently shows a balance of £11,700 (£17,550 debits – £5,850 credits) as presented in Illustration 5.37.

Illustration 5.37 Kleos Engineering Limited's rates account at 30 June 2018 before any corrections have been made

		Rates account				
2018		**£**	**2018**			**£**
1 July	Cash book	5,850	1 April	Cash book		5,850
1 Oct	Cash book	5,850				
1 Jan	Cash book	5,850				

In addition, a further error was uncovered. Cash sales of £3,000 (including VAT of £500) had been correctly debited to the bank account but not credited to the sales account or to the VAT account. How should these errors be corrected?

The current rates expense account balance is £11,700 lower than it should be (£23,400 – the current balance of £11,700). Therefore, the rates account is debited with £11,700 and the suspense account credited with £11,700 to correct this error (Illustration 5.38). The first £5,850 of this correction eliminates the credit entry to the account and the remaining £5,850 adds the expense on to the correct side of the account. The balance on the rates account is now £23,400 (£29,250 on the debit side – £5,850 on the credit side). This leaves a balance of £3,000 credit on the suspense account (£8,700 debit balances – £11,700 credit balances). As the double entry relating to sales and VAT has been omitted from the sales and VAT account, then completing the credit entries to these accounts while debiting the suspense account will reduce the suspense account balance to zero (Illustration 5.38). There should always be a zero balance on the suspense account at the end of every financial period so that the financial statements present a complete and accurate picture of the results and financial position of an entity with no unresolved differences.

Illustration 5.38 Kleos Engineering Limited: correction of the errors on the rates, sales and VAT accounts and the cancellation of the suspense account balance

			Suspense account			
2018			**£**	**2018**		**£**
30 June	Trial balance difference		8,700	30 June	Rates (correction)	11,700
30 June	Sales (correction)		2,500			
30 June	VAT (correction)		500			
			11,700			**11,700**

Rates account

2017		£	2018		£
1 July	Cash book	5,850	1 April	Cash book	5,850
1 Oct	Cash book	5,850	30 June	Statement of profit or loss	23,400
2018					
1 Jan	Cash book	5,850			
30 June	Suspense (correction)	11,700			
		29,250			**29,250**

Sales account

2018		£	2018		£
			30 June	Suspense (correction)	2,500

VAT account

2018		£	2018		£
			30 June	Suspense (correction)	500

WHY IS THIS RELEVANT TO ME?   The trial balance does not balance

To enable you as an accounting professional to:

- Understand how a balance on the suspense account arises
- Make corrections to eliminate the suspense account balance
- Understand that the balance on the suspense account must be reduced to zero at the end of each financial period

MULTIPLE CHOICE QUESTIONS   Are you confident that you can state the required double entry to eliminate the balance on the suspense account? Go to the **online workbook** and have a go at Multiple choice questions 5.8 to test your understanding.

JOURNALS

Corrections and changes to the books of account in the nominal ledger must be recorded to provide a record of all the changes made. These changes are recorded through entries called journals. Each journal consists of details of the account or accounts to be debited and credited together with a brief explanation of the changes made by the journal entries. Journal entries are given a unique sequential number and a date to enable other users of the accounting system and books of account to trace any changes made and to ensure that all journals are recorded and that they are recorded in the correct accounting period. The journal for the corrections made in Example 5.3 would be as follows:

Journal number: 1	Debit	Credit
Date: 30 June 2018	£	£
Rates account	11,700	
Suspense account		11,700
Suspense account	2,500	
Suspense account	500	
Sales account		2,500
VAT account		500
Journal totals (must be equal)	**14,700**	**14,700**

Being entries to correct the suspense account balance on the trial balance.

WHY IS THIS RELEVANT TO ME? Journals

To provide you as an accounting professional with:

- Knowledge of how corrections and changes to accounts in the nominal ledger are recorded
- A suitable journal format to use in practice now and in your future career

CHAPTER SUMMARY

You should now have learnt that:

- There are three transaction streams that give rise to financial data that requires recording, sales, purchases and payroll
- Day books are the books of prime entry which are used to make the first record of accounting transactions
- Double entries are made into the nominal ledger from the books of prime entry
- Control is exercised over the sales ledger and purchase ledger through the use of control accounts reconciled to the totals on the individual sales and purchase ledger balances
- Control is exercised over the bank account through regular reconciliations with the bank statements
- Sales and purchase transactions give rise to a net liability to pay VAT to HM Revenue and Customs
- Employing staff gives rise to liabilities to pay income tax and national insurance to HM Revenue and Customs

- Disposals of non-current assets require the cost and accumulated depreciation on those assets to be removed from the nominal ledger cost and accumulated depreciation accounts

- T accounts can be used to reconstruct accounting records to discover missing financial information

- Accountants cannot assume that nominal ledger accounts are correct as errors can arise in the preparation of accounting records

---

QUICK REVISION   Test your knowledge with the online flashcards in Summary of key concepts and attempt the Multiple choice questions, all in the **online workbook**.

5

END-OF-CHAPTER QUESTIONS

Solutions to these questions can be found in the **online workbook.**

❯ DEVELOP YOUR UNDERSTANDING

❯ Question 5.1

Maria sets up in business on 1 April 2019 as a provider of plumbing services. She employs three members of staff. Her firm carries out work for the following customers in April, May and June:

Date 2019	Invoice number	Customer	Sales value £
16 April	0001	Benzo Limited	5,000
23 April	0002	Zorro	8,000
30 April	0003	Cotoneaster Limited	3,500
8 May	0004	Tramp Limited	2,750
11 May	0005	Dingdongbell plc	9,500
15 May	0006	Jerry Builders Limited	6,100
21 May	0007	Benzo Limited	3,400
30 May	0008	Cotoneaster Limited	5,000
6 June	0009	D-Day Builders Limited	1,300
14 June	0010	Zorro	18,000
18 June	0011	Jerry Builders Limited	9,200
26 June	0012	Dingdongbell plc	8,300
29 June	0013	Monzo plc	2,350

Maria invoiced all the above customers, adding on 20 per cent VAT to the sales value on each invoice. In addition, she issued the following credit notes (adding 20 per cent VAT on to each credit note) to reflect amounts overcharged on invoices:

Date	Credit note number	Customer	Credit note value
2019			£
28 May	CN001	Benzo Limited	500
15 June	CN002	Zorro	1,000
20 June	CN003	Jerry Builders Limited	800
28 June	CN004	Dingdongbell plc	750

Maria trades on credit with her customers, allowing them 30 days in which to pay what is owed. During April, May and June, she received the following amounts from her trade receivables:

Date	Customer	Cash Received
2019		£
16 May	Benzo Limited	6,000
23 May	Zorro	9,000
31 May	Cotoneaster Limited	4,200
12 June	Dingdongbell plc	11,400
13 June	Jerry Builders Limited	7,320
18 June	Tramp Limited	3,000
29 June	Benzo Limited	3,480

In addition, there were cash receipts from cash sales to domestic customers of £720 on 29 April, £900 on 30 May and £840 on 28 June. The amounts received from these cash sales include VAT at 20 per cent.

Maria paid £20,000 of her own money into her business bank account on 3 April 2019.

Required:

1. Write up the sales day book, the sales returns day book and the cash book for April, May and June 2019.

2. Post the entries from the sales day book, the sales returns day book and the cash book into the nominal ledger accounts, using as many T accounts as you require.

3. Post the relevant entries from the sales day book, the sales returns day book and the cash book into individual sales ledger accounts for each customer.

4. Extract the balance on each sales ledger account (total debits – total credits), add up the individual balances and agree the total of the individual balances to the trade receivables control account.

5. Without closing off the T accounts for the three months, extract a trial balance at 30 June 2019.

> Question 5.2

Maria's plumbing services business makes the following purchase transactions on credit with the suppliers listed below in April, May and June 2019:

Date	Internal invoice number	Supplier	Plumbing materials	Stationery	Other
2019			£	£	£
1 April	P001	Such a Wrench Limited			1,440
5 April	P002	Honest Autos Limited			2,736
7 April	P003	Tapz n Pipez Limited	6,000		
8 April	P004	Washerz plc	1,182		
8 April	P005	Pens and Paper		300	
30 April	P006	Tapz n Pipez Limited	4,500		
4 May	P007	Washerz plc	3,000		
8 May	P008	Tapz n Pipez Limited	3,840		
23 May	P009	Tapz n Pipez Limited	5,250		
1 June	P010	PCUK			576
8 June	P011	Washerz plc	1,314		
14 June	P012	Tapz n Pipez Limited	5,400		
18 June	P013	Washerz plc	5,250		
20 June	P014	Tapz n Pipez Limited	3,906		

All the above purchase invoices include VAT at 20 per cent. The other purchases are as follows:

- P001: tools and tool boxes with an estimated useful life of 4 years.
- P002: second hand van with an estimated useful life of 3 years.
- P010: a laptop for recording business information which has an estimated useful life of 2 years.

Maria made returns of goods only once during the three months and received the following credit note from her supplier:

Date 2019	Credit note number	Supplier	Credit note value £
15 June	PR01	Tapz n Pipez Limited	204

This credit note from Tapz n Pipez Limited includes VAT at 20 per cent.

During April, May and June, Maria made the following payments to her trade payables from her bank account:

Date 2019	Supplier	Cash paid £
20 April	Such a Wrench Limited	1,440
30 April	Honest Autos Limited	2,736
8 May	Washerz plc	1,182
10 May	Pens and Paper	300

Date	Supplier	Cash paid
2019		£
25 May	Tapz n Pipez Limited	10,500
4 June	Washerz plc	3,000
20 June	Tapz n Pipez Limited	9,090
29 June	PC UK	576

In addition, there were payments from the bank for plumbing materials of £480 on 25 April, £360 on 18 May and £540 on 22 June: all these payments include VAT at 20 per cent.

Cash withdrawn from the bank for petty cash was £200 on 10 April, £250 on 16 May and £300 on 14 June. Petty cash payments for petrol for the van were £180 for April, £240 for May and £312 for June. The payments for petrol include VAT at 20 per cent.

Maria paid the VAT due to HM Revenue and Customs on 30 June 2019 (use the balance on the VAT account (total credits − total debits) to calculate Maria's payment on 30 June).

Payments to her employees for wages were £7,036 on 30 April, £7,172 on 31 May and £6,560 on 29 June. PAYE and NIC payments of £3,030 were made on 15 May and £3,122 on 18 June.

Required:

1. Write up the purchase day book, the purchase returns day book, the cash book and the petty cash book for April, May and June 2019.

2. Post the entries from the purchase day book, the purchase returns day book, the cash book and the petty cash book into the nominal ledger accounts, adding as many new T accounts as you require. You should use the relevant accounts you set up in your answers to Question 5.1 and add in additional entries where required.

3. Post the relevant entries from the purchase day book, the purchase returns day book and the cash book into individual purchase ledger accounts for each supplier.

4. Extract the balance on each purchase ledger account (total credits − total debits), add up the individual balances and agree the total of the individual balances to the trade payables control account.

5. Without closing off the T accounts for the three months, extract a trial balance at 30 June 2019. You should include the T accounts relating to sales transactions from Question 5.1 in your trial balance.

> Question 5.3

Maria pays her employees monthly and presents you with the following payroll information for April, May and June 2019:

Month	Gross	PAYE	Employee's NIC	Net	Employer's NIC
	£	£	£	£	£
April	9,100	1,221	843	7,036	966
May	9,300	1,261	867	7,172	994
June	8,400	1,081	759	6,560	869

Required:

1. Post the entries from the monthly payroll into the nominal ledger accounts, adding as many new T accounts as you require. You should use the relevant accounts you set up in your answers to Question 5.2 and add in additional entries where required.

2. Using the information on non-current assets and their expected useful lives given in Question 5.2, calculate depreciation on the non-current assets for the three months to 30 June 2019. Opening as many new T accounts as you require, post the depreciation charges to the relevant accounts.

3. Without closing off the accounts, extract Maria's trial balance at 30 June 2019.

4. Using the trial balance, prepare Maria's statement of profit or loss for the three months ended 30 June 2019 together with a statement of financial position at that date. Maria had no inventory at 30 June 2019 and there was no prepaid expenditure and no accrued expenditure at 30 June 2019.

5

≫ TAKE IT FURTHER

≫ Question 5.4

Question 5.4 is an extended case study, building up a full set of T accounts and final financial statements. After attempting each task, you should check your answer with the solutions presented in the **online workbook** to make sure that your answers are correct before moving on to the next task.

ABC Limited is a manufacturing company which produces and sells Bodgets. Opening balances at 1 May 2018 are as follows:

	Debit £	Credit £
Factory cost	650,000	
Factory accumulated depreciation		78,000
Motor vehicles cost	220,000	
Motor vehicles accumulated depreciation		88,000
Plant and machinery cost	275,000	
Plant and machinery accumulated depreciation		137,500
Inventory at 1 May 2018	112,280	
Trade receivables control account	2,056,918	
Allowance for receivables		30,854
Prepayments: insurance	1,000	
rates	1,600	
equipment hire	1,850	
Bank account	132,158	
Petty cash	290	
Trade payables control account		1,222,955
Accruals: audit fee		3,000
bank charges		180
rent		4,500
wages		3,000

	Debit £	Credit £
PAYE and NIC control account		31,216
VAT		378,599
Taxation payable		199,800
Share capital		600,000
Share premium		90,000
Retained earnings at 1 May 2018		583,492
	3,451,096	**3,451,096**

Task 1

Set up nominal ledger T accounts and post the opening balances to these nominal ledger T accounts.

You should post opening inventory to the cost of sales account.

*****

An analysis of the books of prime entry for the year to 30 April 2019 shows the following details:

	£
Sales day book	
Sales (net of VAT)	9,435,600
VAT	1,887,120
Sales day book total	**11,322,720**
Sales returns day book	
Sales returns (net of VAT)	385,600
VAT	77,120
Sales returns day book total	**462,720**
Purchase day book	£
Raw materials	4,451,920
Motor expenses	39,200
Plant and machinery	70,000
Motor vehicle	25,000
Audit and accountancy	9,000
Legal expenses	5,000
Printing and stationery	12,000
Postage	5,400
VAT	922,424
Purchase day book total	**5,539,944**
Purchase returns day book	
Raw materials	111,300
Motor expenses	450
VAT	22,350
Purchase returns day book total	**134,100**

Petty cash book payments	£
Postage	1,875
Office refreshments	4,214
Entertaining customers	2,632
Stationery	1,642
Petrol	8,600
VAT	3,410
Total petty cash expenditure	**22,373**

Petty cash receipts	£
From bank	22,500
Stamps sold	20
Total petty cash receipts	**22,520**

Cash book receipts	£
Trade receivables	10,994,382
Receipt from sale of motor vehicle	5,500
Receipt from sale of plant and machinery	4,800
VAT on asset sales	960
Bank interest	800
Total cash book receipts	**11,006,442**

Cash book payments	£
Trade payables	5,524,932
Wages payments	2,163,488
Salaries payments	434,976
PAYE and NIC	1,063,732
VAT	1,059,206
Pension payments	161,750
Petty cash	22,500
Taxation	199,800
Dividends	60,000
Bank charges	1,988
Total cash book payments	**10,692,372**

Wages and salaries	Wages	Salaries
	£	£
Gross wages	2,929,100	600,000
PAYE	352,529	78,000
Employees NIC	266,628	57,024
Pension	146,455	30,000
Net wages and salaries paid to employees	**2,163,488**	**434,976**
Employers NIC	**306,622**	**65,578**

The bank statement shows the following items not in the cash book at the year end:

	£
Bank charges	50
BACS receipt from a trade receivable customer	750

Task 2

Post all the transactions from the books of prime entry to the nominal ledger T Accounts. In addition to the T accounts already set up with the opening balances, you will need to open T accounts with the following headings:

- Bank interest
- Dividends
- Employers' NIC salaries
- Employers' NIC wages
- Entertaining customers
- Legal expenses
- Motor expenses
- Non-current asset disposals
- Office refreshments
- Pension control
- Postage
- Printing and stationery
- Salaries
- Sales
- Wages control

Raw materials figures should be posted to the cost of sales T account.

***

Task 3

Adjustments

1 Non-current asset disposals

The non-current assets sold during the year had an original cost of £20,000 (plant and machinery) and £19,000 (motor vehicle). The plant and machinery had been purchased 4 years ago and had been depreciated at the rate of 20 per cent per annum straight line. The motor vehicle had been purchased 3 years ago and had been depreciated at the rate of 30 per cent per annum reducing balance. Adjustments to remove these assets have not yet been made in the books of the company.

2 Depreciation

Depreciation is to be provided at the following rates:

Plant and machinery	20% per annum straight line on cost at the end of the financial year
Motor vehicles	30% per annum reducing balance on carrying amount at the end of the financial year
Factory	2% per annum straight line on cost

Land is not depreciated.

The factory buildings have a cost of £490,000 and land a cost of £160,000.

3 Prepayments

Prepayments at 30 April 2019 were as follows:

	£
Insurance	750
Rates	500

You should set up a prepayments account in which to record all the prepayments at 30 April 2019.

4 Accruals

Accruals for the following expenses are required:

	£
Audit and accountancy	5,000
Bank charges	100
Legal expenses	750
Rent	2,750
Wages	2,500

You should set up an accruals account in which to record all the accruals at 30 April 2019.

5 Irrecoverable debts and allowance for receivables

The allowance for receivables is to be adjusted to 1.50 per cent of trade receivables at 30 April 2019 after allowing for specific irrecoverable debts at the year end of £17,786. You should set up a combined irrecoverable debts and allowance for receivables expense account in which to record both irrecoverable debts and changes in the allowance for receivables balance.

6 Inventory

Inventory at the year end was counted and had a cost of £125,228.

7 Taxation

A provision for taxation on the profit for the year of £118,285 is to be made in the accounts.

8 Errors/mispostings

The following expenditure has been posted to raw materials and requires reallocating to the correct expenditure heading:

Insurance: £20,000

Rates: £15,000

Rent: £11,000

Post the above adjustments to the nominal ledger T accounts, opening any new T accounts required.

***

Task 4

Extract the trial balance at 30 April 2019.

***

Task 5

Prepare a statement of profit or loss for the year ended 30 April 2019 and a statement of financial position for the company at that date. Expenditure in the statement of profit or loss should be allocated to the following headings:

Cost of sales

- Cost of sales
- Employer's NIC wages
- Equipment hire
- Factory annual depreciation charge
- Plant and machinery annual depreciation charge
- Rates
- Rent
- Wages

Distribution and selling costs

- Employer's NIC salaries (50 per cent)
- Entertaining customers
- Motor expenses
- Motor vehicle annual depreciation charge
- Salaries (50 per cent)

Administration expenses

- Audit and accountancy
- Bank charges
- Employer's NIC salaries (50 per cent)
- Insurance
- Irrecoverable debts and allowance for receivables expense
- Legal expenses
- Profit or loss on non-current asset disposals
- Office refreshments
- Postage
- Printing and stationery
- Salaries (50 per cent)

Finance income

- Bank interest

***

Task 6

Close off all the T accounts and bring down the opening balances at 1 May 2019.

***

THE STATEMENT OF CASH FLOWS

6

LEARNING OUTCOMES

Once you have read this chapter and worked through the questions and examples in both this chapter and the online workbook, you should be able to:

- Understand that profit does not equal cash

- Appreciate that without a steady cash inflow from operations an entity will not be able to survive

- Describe the make up of operating, investing and financing cash flows

- Prepare statements of cash flows using both the direct and indirect methods

- Use T accounts to calculate figures for use in preparing statements of cash flows

- Explain the importance of statements of cash flows as the third key accounting statement alongside the statement of profit or loss and statement of financial position

- Understand why statements of cash flows on their own would be insufficient to present a clear picture of an entity's performance and financial position

- Summarise and describe the conventions upon which accounting is based

INTRODUCTION

Chapters 2 and 3 considered two of the three main accounting statements that entities publish relating to each accounting period. The statement of financial position gives us a snapshot of an entity's assets and liabilities at the end of each accounting period, while the statement of profit or loss shows us the profit or loss based on the income generated and expenditure incurred within each accounting period. This chapter will consider the third key accounting statement, the statement of cash flows, which presents users of financial information with details of cash inflows and outflows for an accounting period. As we shall see, the statement of cash flows links together the statement of profit or loss and statement of financial position to demonstrate changes in an entity's financial position over each accounting period arising from operating, investing and financing activities.

Without a steady inflow of cash, businesses cannot survive. Thus, if cash is not generated from sales, there will be no money with which to pay liabilities owed, to pay wages to employees to produce or sell goods, to pay rent on facilities hired, to pay returns to investors or to finance growth and expansion. Over time, cash inflows must exceed cash outflows in order for an entity to remain a going concern, a business that will continue into the foreseeable future. The ability of a business to generate cash is thus critical to its survival as, without a steady inflow of cash, the business cannot carry on, no matter how profitable. It is hugely important to appreciate that profit does not represent cash. To illustrate this fact, Give me an example 6.1 presents the case of Salesforce.com which generates a modest profit while enjoying very strong cash inflows from its daily operations.

GIVE ME AN EXAMPLE 6.1   Salesforce.com

In the financial year to 31 January 2018, Salesforce.com, the customer relationship management software business, reported a net profit of $127.5m. However, cash generated from operations amounted to $2,738.0m, a difference of $2,610.5m. How does this difference arise? Many if not all customers pay in full for the services they buy when they sign the contract. However, the sales income and profit from each contract are recognised over the life of that contract which may extend for several months or even years. Cash is thus received far in advance of the point in time at which services are provided.

Source: http://investor.salesforce.com

WHY IS THIS RELEVANT TO ME?   The importance of cash

To enable you as an accounting professional to understand that:

- Profit is not equivalent to cash
- Turning profits into cash is a most important task for businesses
- Without cash, businesses will not be able to meet their commitments or fund their expansion plans and will fail

GO BACK OVER THIS AGAIN!   Do you really appreciate how important cash and cash inflow are? Go to the **online workbook** Exercises 6.1 to make sure you have grasped this critical lesson.

STATEMENT OF CASH FLOWS: THE IAS7 PRESENTATION FORMAT

What format does the statement of cash flows take? International Accounting Standard 7 (IAS7) sets out the format in which the statement of cash flows should be presented. Illustration 6.1 shows the statement of cash flows for Bunns the Bakers plc for the years ended 31 March 2019 and 31 March 2018 in the IAS7 required format. As with the statement of financial position and the statement of profit or loss, we shall look at the statement of cash flows in its entirety before considering how each part of the statement is constructed and what the terminology means.

6

Note: cash inflows (money coming in) are shown without brackets while cash outflows (money going out) are shown in brackets. Work through the statement of cash flows, adding the figures without brackets and deducting the figures in brackets to help you understand how the cash inflows and outflows add up to the subtotals given.

The net increase in cash and cash equivalents for the year ended 31 March 2019 of £23,000 is given by adding the net cash inflow from operating activities (+ £1,219,000) and then subtracting the net cash outflow from investing activities (– £891,000) and subtracting the net cash outflow from financing activities (– £305,000). Check back to the statement of financial position for Bunns the Bakers plc (Chapter 2, Illustration 2.1) to make sure that the figure given for cash and cash equivalents at 31 March 2019 is £212,000. Repeat the calculations for 2018 to make sure you understand how the figures in the statement of cash flows are derived.

SUMMARY OF KEY CONCEPTS   Are you certain that you know how to calculate the net increase/ (decrease) in cash and cash equivalents? Go to the **online workbook** to check your knowledge with Summary of key concepts 6.1.

GO BACK OVER THIS AGAIN!   A copy of this statement of cash flows (Illustration 6.1) is available in the **online workbook**. You might like to keep this on screen or print off a copy for easy reference while you work your way through the material in this chapter. There is also an annotated copy of this statement of cash flows at the end of the book to help you go over the relevant points again to reinforce your knowledge and learning.

Illustration 6.1 Bunns the Bakers plc statement of cash flows for the years ended 31 March 2019 and 31 March 2018

	2019 £000	2018 £000
Cash flows from operating activities		
Profit for the year	547	442
Income tax expense	213	172
Finance expense	150	165
Finance income	(15)	(12)
(Increase)/decrease in inventories	(5)	8
Decrease in trade and other receivables	13	9
Increase/(decrease) in trade and other payables	109	(15)
Amortisation of intangible non-current assets	5	7
Depreciation of property, plant and equipment	394	362
(Profit)/loss on the disposal of property, plant and equipment	(3)	4
Cash generated from operations	1,408	1,142
Taxation paid	(189)	(154)
Net cash inflow from operating activities	1,219	988
Cash flows from investing activities		
Acquisition of property, plant and equipment	(910)	(600)
Acquisition of investments	(6)	(11)
Proceeds from the sale of property, plant and equipment	10	47
Interest received	15	12
Net cash outflow from investing activities	(891)	(552)
Cash flows from financing activities		
Proceeds from the issue of ordinary share capital	235	148
Dividends paid	(90)	(72)
Repayment of the current portion of long-term borrowings	(300)	(300)
Interest paid	(150)	(165)
Net cash outflow from financing activities	(305)	(389)
Net increase in cash and cash equivalents	23	47
Cash and cash equivalents at the start of the year	189	142
Cash and cash equivalents at the end of the year	212	189

CONSTRUCTING THE STATEMENT OF CASH FLOWS

Illustration 6.1 shows that Bunns the Bakers' statement of cash flows consists of three sections:

- Cash flows from operating activities
- Cash flows from investing activities
- Cash flows from financing activities.

These three sections represent the inflows and outflows of cash for all entities. Let us look at each of these categories in turn.

CASH FLOWS FROM OPERATING ACTIVITIES

All entities operate with a view to generating cash with which to finance their day-to-day operations, their operating activities, and with the intention and expectation of generating surplus cash for future investment and expansion. This cash generated will consist of the cash from sales less the cash spent in both generating those sales and in running the organisation.

As we have already seen, Bunns the Bakers produces bakery goods and buys in other goods for resale in the shops. Operating cash inflows will thus consist of money received from sales in the shops while operating cash outflows will be made up of the money spent on:

- Producing the goods
- Buying goods in for resale
- Distributing the goods to shops
- Selling those goods in the shops
- Administration expenses incurred in the running of the business.

The difference between the trading and operating cash flowing into the business and the trading and operating cash flowing out of the business will give the net operating cash inflows or outflows for each accounting period, the cash generated from operations. Any taxation paid by the entity will also be deducted from operating cash flows as shown in Illustration 6.1. Tax arises as a consequence of profits made from operating activities, so any tax paid in an accounting period will be deducted from the cash generated from operations.

Bunns the Bakers' statement of cash flows is an example of the indirect method of cash flow preparation. This approach requires that the profit for the year is subjected to certain adjustments: these adjustments are given in the Cash flows from operating activities calculation in the first part of Illustration 6.1. These adjustments to the profit firstly add back the income tax expense, finance expense and finance income to arrive at the operating profit line in the statement of profit or loss. Further adjustments then represent the effect of non-cash income and expenses in the statement of profit or loss alongside movements in working capital (changes in inventory, trade and other receivables and trade and other payables over the course of the accounting period) and are made in order to work back to the actual cash generated from operating activities. These adjustments and how they are derived are explained in more detail later in this chapter, The indirect method. Give me an example 6.2 presents the Cash flows from operating activities for Greggs plc to illustrate many of the adjustments made to the profit for the year to determine the cash flows from operating activities that you will come across in practice.

6

GIVE ME AN EXAMPLE 6.2   Cash flows from operating activities

What sort of cash flows from operating activities do companies present in their annual reports and accounts? The following extract is taken from the statements of cash flows of Greggs plc for the 52 weeks ended 30 December 2017 and the 52 weeks ended 31 December 2016.

Cash flow statement—cash generated from operations

	2017	2016
	£000	£000
Profit for the financial year	56,906	57,993
Amortisation	3,435	2,100
Depreciation	50,044	43,453
(Reversal of impairment)/Impairment	(415)	488
Loss on sale of property, plant and equipment	2,719	2,476
Release of government grants	(472)	(472)
Share-based payment expenses	1,835	1,994
Finance expense	368	26
Income tax expense	15,039	17,149
(Increase) in inventories	(2,754)	(490)
(Increase) in receivables	(2,652)	(3,066)
Increase in payables	4,497	11,845
Increase in provisions	5,920	277
Cash from operating activities	**134,470**	**133,773**

Source: *Greggs plc annual report and accounts 2017* https://corporate.greggs.co.uk/investors

Just as in the case of Bunns the Bakers, Greggs plc presents the movements in working capital (changes in inventory, receivables and trade payables as well as provisions), adds back amortisation and depreciation charged on non-current assets together with losses on the sale of non-current assets and adds back the income tax and finance expenses deducted from operating profit in calculating the profit for the year. In addition, Greggs makes an entry for the impairment of non-current assets: this is a loss in the carrying value of non-current assets over and above the regular charge for depreciation that is added to the statement of profit or loss as an expense as soon as it is known: charges for (or reversals of) impairment are an expense (income) in the statement of profit or loss which do not involve any cash inflow or outflow. Companies that receive government grants record the cash received in the year of receipt as a cash inflow from financing activities but release a portion of each grant to the statement of profit or loss each year: as this allocation to the statement of profit or loss is not a cash flow, the income is deducted from operating profit to arrive at cash flows from operating activities. Payments in shares are an expense but do not involve cash as shares are used to make the payments, so these share-based payment expenses are also added back to profit for the year in calculating cash flows from operating activities.

GO BACK OVER THIS AGAIN!   Are you convinced that you can distinguish between cash inflows and cash outflows from operating activities? Go to the **online workbook** and complete Exercises 6.2 to make sure you can make these distinctions.

CASH FLOWS FROM INVESTING ACTIVITIES

In order to expand a business, entities must invest in new capacity in the form of non-current assets. Any cash paid out to buy new property, plant and equipment or intangible assets such as trademarks will appear under this heading as this represents investment of cash into new long-term assets with which to generate new income by expanding and improving the business. Where an entity has surplus funds that cannot currently be used to invest in such assets, it will place those funds in long-term investments to generate interest or dividend income that will increase the profits of the organisation. Thus, any investment in non-current asset investments will also appear under this heading. Note that both of these uses of cash represent outflows of cash as cash is leaving the business in exchange for new property, plant and equipment or new long-term investments.

In addition to these outflows of cash, investing activities also give rise to inflows of cash. When buying new property, plant and equipment, it is quite likely that some other non-current assets will be sold or scrapped at the same time, as these are now worn out or surplus to requirements. Selling or scrapping these assets will result in a cash inflow and any cash raised in this way will be classified under investing activities. Likewise, any interest or dividends received from investing surplus funds in current or non-current asset investments are also cash inflows under investing activities: the investments were made with a view to generating investment income, so such cash inflows are logically included under this heading. Cash inflows and outflows from investing activities are summarised in Figure 6.1 while Give me an example 6.3 presents the Cash flows from investing activities for Greggs plc to provide a real life illustration of these cash inflows and outflows.

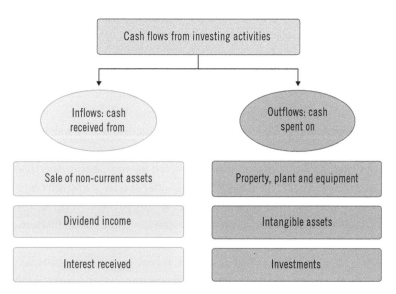

Figure 6.1 Cash inflows and outflows from investing activities

---

GIVE ME AN EXAMPLE 6.3   Cash flows from investing activities

What sort of cash flows from investing activities do companies present in their annual reports and accounts? The following extract is taken from the statements of cash flows of Greggs plc for the 52 weeks ended 30 December 2017 and the 52 weeks ended 30 December 2016.

Investing activities

	2017	2016
	£000	£000
Acquisition of property, plant and equipment	(68,646)	(74,016)
Acquisition of intangible assets	(3,918)	(6,106)
Proceeds from sale of property, plant and equipment	2,171	4,698
Interest received	249	124
Net cash outflow from investing activities	**(70,144)**	**(75,300)**

Source: *Greggs plc annual report and accounts 2017* https://corporate.greggs.co.uk/investors

All the above entries should be familiar to you from the statement of cash flows of Bunns the Bakers.

GO BACK OVER THIS AGAIN!   Are you quite sure that you could say whether a transaction is a cash inflow or cash outflow from investing activities? Go to the **online workbook** and complete Exercises 6.3 to make sure you can make these decisions correctly.

CASH FLOWS FROM FINANCING ACTIVITIES

There are three main sources of finance for a business. The first of these is cash generated from operations. This source of cash has already been dealt with earlier under 'Cash flows from operating activities'.

The second source of finance for business is from the issue of share capital. Bunns the Bakers have issued shares during the year for cash and so this is recorded as a cash inflow to the business: money has been paid into the company in return for new shares. Shareholders expect a return on their investment in the company: the cash outflows related to share capital are the dividends paid out to shareholders (Chapter 7, Dividends). The payment of dividends is an outflow of cash and is recorded under financing activities as it relates to the cost of financing the business through share capital.

The third source of finance is provided by lenders, money borrowed from banks or the money markets to finance expansion and the acquisition of new non-current assets. As the expansion/

new non-current assets generate cash from their operation, these cash inflows are used to repay the borrowings over the following years, much as a taxi driver might borrow money to buy a taxi and then repay that loan from monthly fares earned. This is the case for Bunns the Bakers this year. While no new borrowings have been taken out (this would be an inflow of cash) part of the money previously borrowed has now been repaid from cash generated from operations in the current year. Repayments of borrowings are an outflow of cash. Any interest paid that arises from borrowing money is recorded as an outflow of cash under financing activities. Just as dividends are the cost of financing operations or expansion through the issue of share capital, interest is the cost of financing operations or expansion through borrowing and so is matched to the financing activities section of the statement of cash flows. Figure 6.2 summarises the cash inflows and outflows from financing activities while Give me an example 6.4 presents the Cash flows from financing activities for Greggs plc to provide a real life example of these cash inflows and outflows.

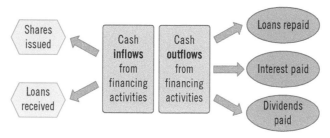

Figure 6.2 Cash inflows and cash outflows from financing activities

GIVE ME AN EXAMPLE 6.4   Cash flows from financing activities

What sort of cash flows from financing activities do companies present in their annual reports and accounts? The following extract is taken from the statements of cash flows of Greggs plc for the 52 weeks ended 30 December 2017 and the 52 weeks ended 31 December 2016.

Financing activities

	2017 £000	2016 £000
Sale of own shares	5,358	4,063
Purchase of own shares	(11,352)	(12,398)
Dividends paid	(32,187)	(30,936)
Net cash outflow from financing activities	**(38,181)**	**(39,271)**

Source: *Greggs plc annual report and accounts 2017* https://corporate.greggs.co.uk/investors

→

Just as in the case of Bunns the Bakers, cash from the sale of shares is an inflow of cash to the business while dividends paid are an outflow. Why would Greggs buy its own shares? As noted under Give me an example 6.2, Cash flows from operating activities, Greggs incurs share-based payment expenses. The company buys shares in the stock market and then uses these shares to make the share-based payments. As we noted in Give me an example 6.2, share-based payments do not involve a cash outflow. Instead, the cash outflow occurs when the company buys its shares with which to meet the share-based payments.

GO BACK OVER THIS AGAIN!   How easily can you distinguish between cash inflows and cash outflows from financing activities? Go to the **online workbook** and complete Exercises 6.4 to make sure you can make these distinctions.

CASH AND CASH EQUIVALENTS

The sum of all three cash flow sections will equal the movement in cash and cash equivalents during the accounting period. The meaning of cash is quite clear, but you might be puzzled by the phrase cash equivalents. Is there really an equivalent to cash?

What this means is anything that is close to cash, a source of cash that could be called upon immediately if required. Such a source might be a bank deposit account rather than money held in the current account for immediate use. Where money held in bank deposit accounts is readily convertible into cash then this is a cash equivalent. Thus, cash held in a deposit account requiring 30 days' notice would be a cash equivalent as the cash can easily be converted into a fixed sum of cash in a maximum of 30 days. However, cash currently held in a bond with a maturity date in two years' time would not be a cash equivalent as it cannot be converted easily to cash now or in the very near future. The International Accounting Standards Board allows any deposit of cash with a notice term of 90 days or less to be classified as a cash equivalent alongside money held in current accounts and held as cash on the business premises.

WHY IS THIS RELEVANT TO ME?   Cash flows from operating activities, investing activities and financing activities

To enable you as an accounting professional to:

• Understand the different sources from which cash flows into and out of an entity

• Read statements of cash flows and understand what the various cash inflows and outflows of an organisation represent, along with the transactions behind them

MULTIPLE CHOICE QUESTIONS Do you think that you can say to which category of cash flows a cash inflow or outflow belongs? Go to the **online workbook** and complete Multiple choice questions 6.1 to make sure you can identify these accurately.

GO BACK OVER THIS AGAIN! Are you confident you can categorise cash inflows and outflows correctly? Go to the **online workbook** and complete Exercises 6.5 to check your understanding.

SUMMARY OF KEY CONCEPTS Are you quite sure that you can say how cash flows from operating activities, investing activities and financing activities are made up? Go to the **online workbook** to revise these categories with Summary of key concepts 6.2–6.4.

PROFIT ≠ CASH

We have already touched upon the idea—both in the Julia example in Chapter 3 (Preparing the statement of profit or loss) and at the start of this chapter—that profit does not equal cash. It is now time to show how true this statement is with the detailed example presented in Example 6.1.

EXAMPLE 6.1

Start Up begins a wholesale trading business on 1 January and makes sales of £20,000 in January, £30,000 in February and £40,000 in March. The cost of purchases is £15,000 in January, £22,500 in February and £30,000 in March. All goods purchased each month are sold in that month so that cost of sales equals cost of purchases.

The statement of profit or loss for Start Up for each month and in total for the three months will be as follows:

	January £	February £	March £	Total £
Sales	20,000	30,000	40,000	90,000
Cost of sales	15,000	22,500	30,000	67,500
Gross profit	**5,000**	**7,500**	**10,000**	**22,500**

Start Up makes a profit each month. Profit is rising so the owners of Start Up will be pleased. However, to show that profit is not cash, let's look at two alternative scenarios for the way in which Start Up collects its cash from customers and pays cash to its suppliers.

Start Up's cash flow: scenario 1

Start Up is unable to gain credit from its suppliers and so pays for goods in the month of purchase. In order to build up trade with its customers, Start Up offers generous credit terms and allows its customers to pay for goods delivered two months after sales are made. There is no cash in the bank on 1 January and each month that the company is overdrawn a charge of 1 per cent of the closing overdraft is incurred on the first day of the following month. Each month that the company is in credit (has a surplus in its account) the bank pays interest of 0.5 per cent on the credit balance at the end of the month on the first day of the following month. The cash flow for the three months ended 31 March will be as follows:

	January	February	March	Total
	£	£	£	£
Opening cash balance	—	(15,000)	(37,650)	—
Cash receipts from sales	—	—	20,000	20,000
Cash paid to suppliers	(15,000)	(22,500)	(30,000)	(67,500)
Interest received	—	—	—	—
Overdraft charges (1%)	—	(150)	*(377)	(527)
Closing cash balance	**(15,000)**	**(37,650)**	**(48,027)**	**(48,027)**

*Rounded to the nearest whole £.

Despite the profit made according to the statement of profit or loss, look how poorly trading has turned out from a cash flow point of view. All the purchases have been paid for in the month in which they were made, but the company is still owed £70,000 by customers (£30,000 for February + £40,000 for March: might any of these trade receivables become irrecoverable debts?) at the end of March. In addition, Start Up has incurred overdraft charges of £527 in February and March with the prospect of another £480 to pay in April (£48,027 × 1 per cent).

Clearly, the £22,500 gross profit for the three months has not translated into surplus cash at the end of the three-month period. Start Up's bank manager might begin to worry about the increasing overdraft and put pressure on the company to reduce this. But, with cash being paid out up front to suppliers while customers enjoy a two-month credit period in which to pay, a reduction in the overdraft in the near future looks highly unlikely. Many small businesses when they start up offer generous credit terms to customers while being forced to pay quickly by their suppliers, so it should come as no surprise that many small businesses collapse within a year of starting to trade as their cash flow dries up and banks close them down to recover what they are owed.

Start Up's cash flow: scenario 2

Facts are as in Scenario 1, except that this time Start Up pays for its supplies one month after the month of purchase and collects cash from its customers in the month in which sales are made. The three-month cash flow will now be as shown in the table below.

	January	February	March	Total
	£	£	£	£
Opening cash balance	—	20,000	35,100	—
Cash receipts from sales	20,000	30,000	40,000	90,000
Cash paid to suppliers	—	(15,000)	(22,500)	(37,500)
Interest received	—	100	*176	276
Overdraft charges	—	—	—	—
Closing cash balance	**20,000**	**35,100**	**52,776**	**52,776**

*Rounded to the nearest whole £.

What a difference a change in the terms of trade makes. By requiring customers to pay immediately for goods received and deferring payments to suppliers for a month, the cash flow has remained positive throughout the three months and additional interest income has been received from the bank by keeping cash balances positive. Suppliers are still owed £30,000, but there is more than enough cash in the bank to meet this liability and still have money available with which to keep trading.

Notably, the cash in the bank again bears no relationship to the gross profit of £22,500, so, once again, this example illustrates the key point that profit does not equal cash. The lesson to learn here is clear: if you can make sure that your customers pay before cash has to be paid to suppliers, the business will survive. In situations in which customers pay what is owed after suppliers have been paid, then the business will struggle to maintain cash inflows and be in danger of being closed down by the banks to which the business owes money.

6

WHY IS THIS RELEVANT TO ME?   Profit ≠ cash

To enable you as an accounting professional to:

- Appreciate that profit does not equal cash in an accounting period
- Realise that the timing of cash inflows and cash outflows has to be finely balanced to ensure that positive cash inflows are achieved
- Understand that positive cash inflows are critical to a business's ability to survive

NUMERICAL EXERCISES   Are you quite convinced that you could calculate cash flows from given terms of trade? Go to the **online workbook** Numerical exercises 6.1 to test out your abilities in this area.

CASH IS CASH IS CASH: THE VALUE OF STATEMENTS OF CASH FLOWS

The statement of profit or loss and the two cash flows for Start Up in Example 6.1 also illustrate the advantages and the true value of the statement of cash flows when making comparisons between entities. If two companies presented exactly the same statement of profit or loss figures, it would be very difficult, if not impossible, to choose between the two and to say which company enjoyed the more stable, cash generative financial position. However, by looking at the statements of cash flows, we could say instantly that the company that presented the cash flow shown in scenario 2 was in a much better position financially compared to the company presenting the cash flow in scenario 1. Without the statement of cash flows we would not see that one company is doing very well from a cash management point of view while the other is doing very poorly. Hence the value of the statement of cash flows in enabling users to determine the financial position of an entity, information that is not available from just the statement of profit or loss.

However, the two statements of cash flows above illustrate further advantages of this statement. As we saw in Chapter 3 (The accruals basis of accounting and Preparing the statement of profit or loss), the statement of profit or loss is drawn up on the accruals basis of accounting, which requires income and expenditure to be recognised in the period in which it was earned and incurred. The statement of cash flows just presents the cash inflows and outflows relating to that period. As we have seen, profit, the difference between income earned and expenditure incurred, does not equate to cash. Therefore, the provision of a statement of cash flows enables users to see much more clearly how quickly profit is turned into cash: in scenario 2 cash is clearly being generated very effectively whereas in scenario 1 the company looks as though it is about to collapse. While the accrual of expenses and income into an accounting period can produce the impression of an excellent result from a profit point of view, since cash is cash is cash it does not suffer from any distortion that might arise in the timing of income and expenditure recognition.

WHY IS THIS RELEVANT TO ME?   The value of statements of cash flows

To enable you as an accounting professional to appreciate how statements of cash flows:

- Enable users to discriminate between different entities with the same levels of profit
- Are not distorted by the effect of the accrual of income and expenditure into different accounting periods

GO BACK OVER THIS AGAIN!   Are you quite sure that you appreciate why statements of cash flows are so valuable? Go to the **online workbook** Exercises 6.6 to test your grasp of their value.

IS THE STATEMENT OF CASH FLOWS ENOUGH ON ITS OWN?

If statements of cash flows are so useful, why do entities have to present the statement of profit or loss and the statement of financial position as well? Why not just require all organisations to produce the statement of cash flows only? This is a valid question and it leads us into thinking about why the statement of cash flows in isolation does not actually tell us very much beyond the cash generated and spent during an accounting period. Let's think first about how useful the statement of financial position and the statement of profit or loss are.

In Chapter 2 we saw that the statement of financial position provides us with details of:

- Liabilities to be paid
- Assets employed within the organisation.

Users of financial statements can look at an entity's assets and make an assessment of whether they will be able to generate the cash necessary to meet the liabilities as they fall due. If only a statement of cash flows were to be presented, then there would be no details of either assets or liabilities and so no assessment of an entity's cash generating potential would be possible.

In Chapter 3 we saw that the statement of profit or loss presents details of:

- Income earned
- Expenditure incurred.

Users of financial statements can then assess how profitable an organisation is and, in conjunction with the statement of cash flows, how effectively it can turn profits into cash with which to meet operating expenses and liabilities as they fall due. Without a statement of profit or loss, the statement of cash flows cannot tell us how profitable an organisation is or how quickly profits are being turned into cash.

A statement of cash flows on its own could be subject to manipulation. Entity owners or directors could time their cash inflows and outflows to present the most flattering picture of their organisation (Chapter 3, The accruals basis of accounting). Therefore, just as a statement of profit or loss or statement of financial position in isolation does not tell us very much, so a statement of cash flows presented as the sole portrait of performance would also be much less informative without its fellow financial statements.

The IASB's Conceptual Framework recognises that all three statements are essential in providing information to users about the cash generating potential of businesses and that a statement of cash flows on its own is insufficient:

> Accrual accounting [in the statement of profit or loss and statement of financial position] depicts the effects of transactions and other events and circumstances on a reporting entity's economic resources and claims in the periods in which those effects occur, even if the resulting cash receipts and payments occur in a different period. This is important because information about a reporting entity's economic resources and claims [the statement of financial position] and changes in its economic resources and claims during a period [the statement of profit or loss] provides a better basis for assessing the entity's past and future performance than information solely about cash receipts and payments during that period. Information about a reporting entity's financial performance during a period [the statement of profit or loss], reflected by changes in its economic resources and claims … is useful in assessing the entity's past and future ability to generate net cash inflows. That information indicates the extent to which the reporting entity has increased its available economic resources, and thus its capacity for generating net cash inflows through its operations … Information about a reporting

entity's cash flows during a period also helps users to assess the entity's ability to generate future net cash inflows … It [the statement of cash flows] indicates how the reporting entity obtains and spends cash, including information about its borrowing and repayment of debt, cash dividends or other cash distributions to investors, and other factors that may affect the entity's liquidity or solvency. Information about cash flows helps users understand a reporting entity's operations, evaluate its financing and investing activities, assess its liquidity or solvency and interpret other information about financial performance.

Source: IASB *Conceptual Framework for Financial Reporting*, paragraphs 1.17, 1.18 and 1.20

Thus, any one (and indeed any two) of the three financial statements on their own will not provide all the information that users require to make the necessary evaluations. Figure 6.3 summarises the interactions between and the interconnected nature of the three main financial statements.

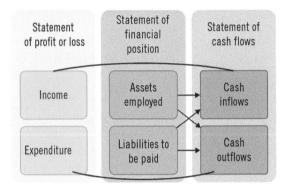

Figure 6.3 The three main financial statements and the ways in which they interact

---

WHY IS THIS RELEVANT TO ME?   Is the statement of cash flows enough on its own?

To enable you as an accounting professional to appreciate how:

● Statements of cash flows would not on their own provide sufficient useful information about an entity's financial position and performance

● The three main financial statements work together to provide useful information to users

---

GO BACK OVER THIS AGAIN!   Are you convinced that you understand how statements of cash flows work in conjunction with the other two financial statements? Go to the **online workbook** Exercises 6.7 to test your grasp of the value of cash flow statements.

GO BACK OVER THIS AGAIN!   Can you see how the statement of cash flows explains the changes in the financial position of an entity? Go to the **online workbook** Exercises 6.8 to see how the one statement explains the changes in the other.

PREPARING THE STATEMENT OF CASH FLOWS:
THE DIRECT METHOD

We shall illustrate the direct method of preparation of the statement of cash flows through Illustration 6.2 and Example 6.2.

Illustration 6.2 Julia's bank account receipts and payments summary (= Illustration 3.3)

Date		Receipts £	Payments £
1 April 2019	Cash introduced by Julia	30,000	
1 April 2019	Three months' rent paid on shop to 30 June 2019		5,000
1 April 2019	Cash register paid for		1,000
1 April 2019	Shelving and shop fittings paid for		12,000
30 April 2019	Receipts from sales in April 2019	20,000	
5 May 2019	Sports equipment supplied in April paid for		15,000
12 May 2019	Rates for period 1 April 2019 to 30 September 2019 paid		800
19 May 2019	Cash withdrawn for Julia's own expenses		2,000
30 May 2019	Receipts from sales in May 2019	25,000	
5 June 2019	Sports equipment supplied in May paid for		20,000
10 June 2019	Shop water rates for the year 1 April 2019 to 31 March 2020 paid		400
30 June 2019	Receipts from sales in June 2019	30,000	
30 June 2019	Balance in bank at 30 June 2019		48,800
		105,000	**105,000**

EXAMPLE 6.2

There are two approaches to preparing the statement of cash flows, the direct and indirect methods. We will use the example of Julia from Chapter 3 (Preparing the statement of profit or loss) to illustrate both methods. Julia's bank summary for the three months ended 30 June 2019 from Chapter 3 (Example 3.8, Illustration 3.3) is shown again in Illustration 6.2.

While Illustration 6.2 is already almost a complete statement of cash flows, showing cash received and cash paid out, all these transactions (together with the cash not yet banked from sales on 30 June 2019) would be presented in the required format as shown in Illustration 6.3.

Illustration 6.3 Julia: statement of cash flows for the three months ended 30 June 2019 using the direct method

	£	£
Cash flows from operating activities		
Receipts from sales banked 20,000 + 25,000 + 30,000	75,000	
Cash sales not yet banked	500	
Payments to trade payables for sports equipment 15,000 + 20,000	(35,000)	
Payments for expenses 5,000 (rent) + 800 (rates) + 400 (water)	(6,200)	
Net cash inflow from operating activities		34,300
Cash flows from investing activities		
Payments to acquire shop fittings and shelving	(12,000)	
Payments to acquire cash register	(1,000)	
Net cash outflow from investing activities		(13,000)
Cash flows from financing activities		
Cash introduced by Julia	30,000	
Cash withdrawn by Julia	(2,000)	
Net cash inflow from financing activities		28,000
Net increase in cash and cash equivalents		49,300
Cash and cash equivalents at the start of the period		—
Cash and cash equivalents at the end of the period		**49,300**

The figure for cash and cash equivalents at the end of the period is exactly the same as the bank balance plus the cash in the till at 30 June 2019 as shown in Julia's statement of financial position in Chapter 3, Illustration 3.7.

NUMERICAL EXERCISES   Are you certain that you could prepare statements of cash flows using the direct method? Go to the **online workbook** Numerical exercises 6.2 to test out your ability to prepare these statements.

Using T accounts to calculate cash flows

Under normal circumstances, users of financial statements will not have access to the cash books of the entities they are assessing. Without an organisation's cash book, how can users work out the cash inflows generated by sales and the cash outflows arising from payments to suppliers and providers of services in order to produce the statement of cash flows using the direct method? By using T accounts, these cash flows can be calculated from the information provided in the statement of profit or loss and the statement of financial position. Suppose that we just have Julia's statement of profit or loss and statement of financial position as shown in Illustrations 6.4 and 6.5 (= Illustrations 3.6 and 3.7).

Illustration 6.4 (= Illustration 3.6) Julia's statement of profit or loss for the three months ended 30 June 2019

	£	£
Sales		77,600
Purchases	59,750	
Less: closing inventory	(10,000)	
Cost of sales (purchases – closing inventory)		49,750
Gross profit (sales – cost of sales)		**27,850**
Expenses		
Rent	5,000	
Rates	400	
Water rates	100	
Irrecoverable debt	50	
Wages	300	
Telephone	250	
Electricity	200	
Cash register depreciation	50	
Shelving and fittings depreciation	600	
Total expenses		6,950
Net profit for the three months		**20,900**

Illustration 6.5 (= Illustration 3.7) Julia's statement of financial position at 30 June 2019

	£
Non-current assets	
Cash register	950
Shelves and shop fittings	11,400
	12,350
Current assets	
Inventory	10,000
Trade receivables	2,050
Rates prepayment	400
Water rates prepayment	300
Bank balance	48,800
Cash	500
	62,050
Total assets	**74,400**

	£
Current liabilities	
Trade payables	24,750
Wages accrual	300
Telephone accrual	250
Electricity accrual	200
Total liabilities	**25,500**
Net assets	**48,900**
Equity (capital account)	
Capital introduced by Julia	30,000
Drawings	(2,000)
Net profit for the three months	20,900
Capital account at 30 June 2019	**48,900**

In the statement of profit or loss and the statement of financial position we have sufficient information from which to reconstruct the trade receivables control account, the trade payables control account and the expenses account so that we can calculate the cash received from customers, the cash paid to suppliers and the cash paid for expenses. By adding in the known numbers, the missing number, the balancing figure, in each account will be the cash received or paid.

Calculating cash received from the trade receivables control account

The trade receivables control account, as we saw in Chapter 5 (Exercising control: the trade receivables control account and Illustration 5.3), is made up as shown in Illustration 6.6.

Illustration 6.6 The trade receivables control account

Trade receivables control account			
	£		£
Trade receivables brought forward	X	Cash received	X
Sales	X	Irrecoverable debts	X
		Sales returns	X
		Trade receivables carried forward	X
	XX		XX

Which of these figures are already available in the statement of profit or loss and the statement of financial position? As this is Julia's first year of trading, trade receivables brought forward are £Nil. Trade receivables carried forward are £2,050 while irrecoverable debts are £50. Sales in the statement of profit or loss amount to £77,600. After entering these figures into the trade receivables control account, we now have the position shown in Illustration 6.7.

Illustration 6.7 Julia's trade receivables control account for the three months ended 30 June 2019 showing the figures available in the statement of profit or loss and the statement of financial position

Trade receivables control account

	£		£
Trade receivables brought forward	0	Cash received	?
Sales	*78,000	Irrecoverable debts	50
		Sales returns	*400
		Trade receivables carried forward	2,050
	78,000		**78,000**

*Illustration 3.6 shows gross sales of £78,000 – £400 sales returns = sales of £77,600. Net sales of £77,600 can be used instead of £78,000 debits – £400 credits.

The total on both sides of the trade receivables control account must be £78,000 so that the account balances. Therefore, cash received, the missing number, is £78,000 – £50 irrecoverable debt – £400 sales returns – £2,050 trade receivables carried forward = £75,500. Is this figure correct? Illustration 6.3 shows cash received from sales of £75,000 banked + £500 cash in the till but not yet banked = £75,500.

WHY IS THIS RELEVANT TO ME?   Calculating cash received from the trade receivables control account

To enable you as an accounting professional to:

• Understand how the trade receivables control account can be used to calculate the missing figure for cash received from sales

• Use the trade receivables control account to reconstruct cash flows from sales when preparing the statement of cash flows using the direct method

SHOW ME HOW TO DO IT   Quite sure you understand how Julia's cash received from sales was calculated using the trade receivables T account? View Video presentation 6.1 in the **online workbook** to see a practical demonstration of how this calculation was made from the information presented in the statement of profit or loss and statement of financial position.

MULTIPLE CHOICE QUESTIONS   Do you think you can use the trade receivables control account to calculate missing figures for use in the statement of cash flows? Go to the **online workbook** and complete Multiple choice questions 6.2 to test your ability to apply these calculations.

Calculating cash paid to suppliers from the trade payables control account

The trade payables control account, as we saw in Chapter 5 (Exercising control: the trade payables control account), is made up as shown in Illustration 6.8.

Illustration 6.8 The trade payables control account

Trade payables control account				
	£			£
Purchase returns	X	Trade payables brought forward		X
Cash paid	X	Purchases		X
Discounts received	X			
Trade payables carried forward	X			
	XX			XX

Unlike the sales figure, the purchases figure is not instantly available from the statement of profit or loss. Our first step therefore is to calculate the figure for purchases. Illustration 6.4 shows purchases before deducting closing inventory, so we could just use the figure of £59,750 as our purchases in Julia's case. However, most sets of accounts will only show a single figure for cost of sales. How, then, can we calculate purchases from this cost of sales number? Cost of sales, as we saw in Chapter 3 (Statement of profit or loss by nature), is calculated by adding opening inventory to purchases and deducting closing inventory (cost of sales = opening inventory + purchases – closing inventory). Rearranging this equation will enable us to calculate purchases as follows:

Purchases = cost of sales + closing inventory – opening inventory

If we take Julia's cost of sales figure from the statement of profit or loss of £49,750 and the closing inventory of £10,000 from the statement of financial position, this gives us a figure for purchases of £59,750:

£49,750 (cost of sales) + £10,000 (closing inventory) – £Nil (opening inventory—
this is Julia's first period of trading so there is no opening inventory) = £59,750 purchases

Trade payables brought forward are also £Nil as this is Julia's first period of trading while trade payables carried forward are £24,750. Entering these figures into the trade payables control account gives us the account shown in Illustration 6.9.

Illustration 6.9 Julia's trade payables control account for the three months ended 30 June 2019 showing the known numbers derived from the statement of profit or loss and the statement of financial position

Trade payables control account			
	£		£
Purchase returns	*250	Trade payables brought forward	0
Cash paid	?	Purchases	*60,000
Trade payables carried forward	24,750		
	60,000		60,000

*Illustration 3.6 shows gross purchases of £60,000 – £250 purchase returns = purchases of £59,750. Net purchases of £59,750 can be used instead of £60,000 credits – £250 debits.

The total on both sides of the trade payables control account must be £60,000 so that the account balances. Therefore, cash received, the missing number, is £60,000 purchases – £250 purchase returns – £24,750 trade payables carried forward = £35,000. Is this figure correct? Illustration 6.3 shows cash paid to suppliers of £35,000 so our calculation is correct.

WHY IS THIS RELEVANT TO ME?   Calculating cash paid to suppliers from the trade payables control account

To enable you as an accounting professional to:

- Understand how the trade payables control account can be used to calculate the missing figure for cash paid to suppliers

- Use the cost of sales calculation and the trade payables control account to reconstruct cash outflows when preparing the statement of cash flows under the direct method

---

SHOW ME HOW TO DO IT   Quite sure you understand how Julia's cash paid to suppliers was calculated using the trade payables control account? View Video presentation 6.2 in the **online workbook** to see a practical demonstration of how this calculation was made from the information presented in the statement of profit or loss and statement of financial position.

MULTIPLE CHOICE QUESTIONS   Are you quite sure that you could use the cost of sales calculation and the trade payables control account to calculate missing figures for use in the statement of cash flows? Go to the **online workbook** and complete Multiple choice questions 6.3 to test your ability to make these calculations.

Calculating cash paid for expenses using the expenses T account

The final step in calculating cash inflows under the direct method is to determine how much cash has been paid out as expenses. This calculation is also made using a T account, but one that we have not come across before. This T account will consider the different elements of expenses, some of which involve cash flows and some which do not, and summarise these into one account. Illustration 6.10 presents the expenses T account.

Illustration 6.10 The expenses T account

Expenses account

	£		£
Prepayments brought forward	x	Accruals brought forward	x
Depreciation	x	Statement of profit or loss expenses total	x
Increase in allowance for receivables	x	Decrease in allowance for receivables	x
Irrecoverable debts	x	Prepayments carried forward	x
Cash paid (balancing figure)	x		
Accruals carried forward	x		
	XX		**XX**

The debit side of this account builds up those expenses which do not result in a cash out-flow during the current financial period. Prepayments brought forward from the previous accounting period are expenses for the current period which arose from cash outflows in the previous period. There is therefore no cash outflow associated with these brought forward prepayments in the current accounting period. Depreciation is not a cash outflow so this is also posted to the debit side of the account as an addition to expenditure that does not generate any cash outflows. Likewise, an irrecoverable debt and an increase in the al-lowance for receivables are expenses that do not arise from cash outflows. Finally, accruals at the end of an accounting period are expenses that have not resulted in a cash outflow in the period under review but which will generate an outflow of cash in the following accounting period.

The credit side of the expenses account on the other hand presents those items increasing cash outflows in the current accounting period. Accruals at the start of the year will result in a cash outflow as these expenses charged in a previous period are paid in the current period. Prepay-ments carried forward at the end of the current period represent costs that belong to a future accounting period but which have been paid in the current accounting period. A decrease in the allowance for receivables represents a reduction in an expense that does not relate to an inflow of cash from expenses but to an inflow of cash from sales.

Entering the known figures from Julia's statement of profit or loss and statement of financial position in Illustrations 6.4 and 6.5 results in the expenses T account shown in Illustration 6.11.

Illustration 6.11 Julia's expenses account for the three months ended 30 June 2019 showing the known num-bers derived from the statement of profit or loss and the statement of financial position

Expenses account

	£		£
Prepayments brought forward	0	Accruals brought forward	0
Depreciation (£600 + £50)	650	Statement of profit or loss expenses	6,950
Irrecoverable debts	50	Prepayments c/f (£400 + £300)	700
Cash paid (balancing figure)	?		
Accruals c/f (£300 + £250 + £200)	750		
	7,650		**7,650**

As this is Julia's first year of trading, there are no prepayments or accruals brought forward at the start of the year. The irrecoverable debt expense of £50, the two depreciation charges of £600 (shelving and fittings) and £50 (the cash register) and the total expenses of £6,950 for the three months are given in Julia's statement of profit or loss. The accruals and prepayments carried forward are shown under current assets and current liabilities in the statement of financial pos-ition. The total expenses of £6,950 are made up of all the charges to the statement of profit or loss on each of the expense accounts in Chapter 4 (Closing off the T accounts at the end of an accounting period). Check that the individual expenses charged to the statement of profit or loss on these T accounts do total up to £6,950 as shown in Illustration 6.4.

The cash outflow from expenses is thus £6,950 (statement of profit or loss expenses) + £700 (prepayments carried forward) – £650 (depreciation) – £50 (irrecoverable debts) – £750 (accruals carried forward) = £6,200. Is this correct? Yes, Illustration 6.3 shows payments for expenses of £6,200.

Further applications of T accounts to calculate missing figures for inclusion in the statement of cash flows are presented in the appendix to this chapter.

WHY IS THIS RELEVANT TO ME?   Calculating cash paid for expenses using T accounts

To enable you as an accounting professional to:

* Understand how the expenses T account can be used to calculate the missing figure for cash paid for expenses

* Use the expenses T account to reconstruct cash outflows when preparing the statement of cash flows under the direct method

6

SHOW ME HOW TO DO IT   Convinced that you followed how Julia's cash paid for expenses was calculated using the expenses T account? View Video presentation 6.3 in the **online workbook** to see a practical demonstration of how this calculation was made from the information presented in Julia's statement of profit or loss and statement of financial position.

MULTIPLE CHOICE QUESTIONS   Are you convinced that you could use the expenses T account to calculate missing figures for use in the statement of cash flows? Go to the **online workbook** and complete Multiple choice questions 6.4 to test your ability to make these calculations.

PREPARING THE STATEMENT OF CASH FLOWS: THE INDIRECT METHOD

The statement of cash flows for Julia in Illustration 6.3 represents an example of the direct method of cash flow preparation: this takes all the cash inflows and outflows from operations and summarises them to produce the net cash inflow from operating activities. Thus, receipts from sales are totalled up to give the cash inflow from sales and payments to suppliers and payments for expenses are totalled up to give a figure for payments to trade payables and other suppliers of goods and services in the period. The difference between the inflows of cash from sales and the outflows of cash for expenses represents the operating cash inflows for the three months.

However, as we noted in this chapter in the Cash flows from operating activities section, the example of Bunns the Bakers' statement of cash flows in Illustration 6.1 represents an example of the indirect method of cash flow preparation. Under this method, the total inflows and outflows from operations are ignored and the operating profit for a period is adjusted for increases or decreases in inventory, receivables, prepayments, payables and accruals and for the effect of non-cash items such as depreciation. As we saw in Chapter 3 (Depreciation), depreciation is an accounting adjustment that allocates the cost of non-current assets to the accounting periods benefiting from their use. The actual cash flows associated with non-current assets are the cash paid to acquire the assets in the first place and the cash received on disposal of those assets when they are sold or scrapped at the end of their useful lives.

Illustration 6.12 Julia: statement of cash flows for the three months ended 30 June 2019 using the indirect method

	£	£
Cash flows from operating activities		
Net profit for the 3 months to 30 June 2019 (Illustrations 3.6 and 6.4)		20,900
Add: depreciation on shelving and fittings (Illustrations 3.6 and 6.4)		600
Add: depreciation on the cash register (Illustrations 3.6 and 6.4)		50
Deduct: increase in inventory		(10,000)
Deduct: increase in receivables		(2,050)
Deduct: increase in prepayments		(700)
Add: increase in payables		24,750
Add: increase in accruals		750
Net cash inflow from operating activities (= Illustration 6.3)		34,300
Cash flows from investing activities		
Payments to acquire shop fittings and shelving	(12,000)	
Payments to acquire cash register	(1,000)	
Net cash outflow from investing activities (= Illustration 6.3)		(13,000)
Cash flows from financing activities		
Cash introduced by Julia	30,000	
Cash withdrawn by Julia	(2,000)	
Net cash inflow from financing activities (= Illustration 6.3)		28,000
Net increase in cash and cash equivalents		49,300
Cash and cash equivalents at the start of the period		—
Cash and cash equivalents at the end of the period		**49,300**

Let's look at how using the indirect method would affect the preparation of Julia's statement of cash flows. While the direct method of cash flow preparation is very easy to understand and put together from summaries of cash receipts and payments, most entities use the indirect method. For Julia, the cash flow for the three months ended 30 June 2019 under the indirect method would be as shown in the accounting statement in Illustration 6.12.

Not surprisingly, both the direct and the indirect method give the same answer for net cash inflow for the three months, £49,300. The only differences between the two cash flows are in the calculation of the cash flow from operating activities.

In the cash flow from operating activities section, depreciation on the shelving and fittings and on the cash register is exactly the same as the depreciation charged in the statement of profit or loss for the three months ended 30 June 2019 (Chapter 3, Illustration 3.6 = this chapter, Illustration 6.4). The changes in the amounts for inventory, receivables, prepayments, payables and accruals are usually the difference between the current period end's figures and the figures at the end of the previous accounting period. As this is Julia's first trading period, the figures for the changes in these amounts are exactly the same as the figures from her statement of financial position (Chapter 3, Illustration 3.7 = this chapter, Illustration 6.5). The figures at the start of the business were all £Nil. Thus, for example, in the case of inventory £10,000 − £Nil = an increase of £10,000.

WHY IS THIS RELEVANT TO ME?   Preparing the statement of cash flows: direct and indirect methods

To enable you as an accounting professional to:

- Prepare cash flow statements for a given period using either the direct or indirect method
- Understand that the two different methods used to prepare statements of cash flows produce the same results

6

SHOW ME HOW TO DO IT   Are you certain that you understand how Julia's statement of cash flows using the indirect method was put together? View Video presentation 6.4 in the **online workbook** to see a practical demonstration of how this statement of cash flows was drawn up.

NUMERICAL EXERCISES   Do you reckon that you could prepare statements of cash flows using the indirect method? Go to the **online workbook** Numerical exercises 6.3 to test out your ability to prepare these statements.

THE INDIRECT METHOD: CASH FLOWS FROM OPERATING ACTIVITIES: INFLOWS OR OUTFLOWS?

Why are the cash flows associated with Julia's inventory, receivables and prepayments treated as outflows of cash (appearing in brackets) while the cash flows associated with payables and accruals are all inflows of cash (appearing without brackets)? The answer lies in the fact that the statement of profit or loss is prepared on the accruals basis of accounting, recognising income and expenses in the period in which they are earned or incurred rather than in the periods in which cash is received or paid. Some income has thus been recognised in the statement of profit or loss that has not yet resulted in a cash inflow. Similarly, some expenses have been recognised in the statement of profit or loss without the corresponding cash outflow. Therefore, adjustments for these 'non-cash' figures have to be made to operating profit to determine the actual cash flows from operating activities under the indirect method. Let's look at each of these adjustments in turn.

Inventory

An increase in inventory is an increase in an asset. This represents an outflow of cash as more money will have been spent on acquiring this additional inventory. Hence the deduction from operating profit. On the other hand, if the cost of inventory decreases over the year, this would mean that more inventory had been sold, resulting in larger cash inflows. Such a fall in inventory would result in an inflow of cash and be added to operating profit.

Receivables

An increase in receivables means additional sales have been recognised in the statement of profit or loss, but that cash has not yet been received from this additional income. As no cash inflow relating to these additional sales has occurred yet, the increase in receivables is treated as a deduction from operating profit to reflect this reduction in cash inflows. As in the case of inventory, if the amount of receivables falls, this means more money has been generated from receivables so this is treated as an increase in cash inflows and is added to cash flows from operating activities.

Trade payables

On the other hand, if trade payables have increased, you have spent less money on paying your suppliers. An increase in trade payables means that cash has not flowed out of the business, so this reduction in payments is added to operating profit. Where trade payables have decreased, this means more cash has been spent on reducing liabilities, so this is treated as a decrease in cash and a deduction is made from operating profit to reflect this outflow of cash.

Prepayments and accruals

Prepayments represent expenses paid in advance so an increase in prepayments means that more cash has flowed out of the business due to an increase in payments made in the current year. This increase is deducted from operating profit. An increase in accruals on the other hand, as with the increase in payables, means that while an expense has been recognised no cash has yet been paid out so this increase is added to operating profit. Where prepayments fall, this is treated as an increase in operating cash flows as less cash has been spent on paying expenses in advance, while a decrease in accruals would represent increased cash outflows as more money would have been spent on reducing these liabilities.

Initially these rules will seem confusing, but practice will enable you to become familiar with them and to apply them confidently in the preparation of statements of cash flows. To assist you in applying these rules, Table 6.1 shows which adjustments should be added and which adjustments should be deducted from operating profit in arriving at the cash flows from operating activities when applying the indirect method. Keep this table handy when you are working through the online examples and the questions at the end of this chapter.

Table 6.1 Figures to add to and figures to deduct from operating profit to determine the cash flow from operating activities when preparing statements of cash flows using the indirect method

Starting point: operating profit in the statement of profit or loss	
Add	Deduct
Depreciation of non-current assets	
Amortisation of intangible non-current assets	
Loss on disposal of non-current assets	Profit on disposal of non-current assets
Decrease in inventory	Increase in inventory
Decrease in receivables	Increase in receivables
Decrease in prepayments	Increase in prepayments
Increase in payables	Decrease in payables
Increase in accruals	Decrease in accruals
Increase in provisions	Decrease in provisions

GO BACK OVER THIS AGAIN!   How well can you remember Table 6.1? Go to the **online workbook** and complete Exercises 6.9 to check your recollection.

The only items in Table 6.1 that we have not dealt with in our cash flow studies to date are the profits and losses on the disposal of non-current assets. The actual cash flow associated with the disposal of non-current assets is the actual cash received. Just as depreciation, which was treated as an expense in arriving at operating profit, is added back to operating profit to determine the cash flows from operating activities, so losses on disposal are added as they, too, have been treated as an additional expense in arriving at operating profit. Profits on disposal, on the other hand, have been treated as income in determining operating profit and so have to be deducted in arriving at the cash flows from operating activities.

WHY IS THIS RELEVANT TO ME?   The indirect method: cash flows from operating activities: inflows or outflows?

To enable you as an accounting professional to understand how:

- Adjustments under the indirect method of preparing the statement of cash flows have been calculated
- Movements in the working capital (inventory, receivables and payables) impact upon the cash flows from operating activities

---

MULTIPLE CHOICE QUESTIONS   Could you calculate profits and losses on the disposal of non-current assets? Say what the cash inflow or outflow was on a non-current asset disposal? Go to the **online workbook** and complete Multiple choice questions 6.5 to make sure you can make these calculations correctly.

ACCOUNTING PRINCIPLES AND CONVENTIONS

We have now worked through the three key accounting statements, the statement of profit or loss, the statement of financial position and the statement of cash flows, and shown how double-entry bookkeeping is used to record all the transactions that form the basis of the figures in the financial statements. On our journey this far, we have noted various accounting principles and conventions that apply in the preparation of the three key financial statements. These principles and conventions are summarised below:

Accruals (also known as matching)

The accruals basis of accounting was covered in Chapter 3 (The accruals basis of accounting). This principle states that all income earned and expenditure incurred in an accounting period is recognised in that period irrespective of when cash is received or paid.

Business entity

Under the business entity principle, the affairs of the business and the affairs of the owner are kept entirely separate. The business and the owner are thus treated as two separate entities. This principle requires that personal and business transactions are not mixed together so that the financial statements of the business present just the results and financial position of the business (Chapter 3, Drawings and the business entity assumption).

Consistency

Presentation and measurement in the financial statements of the same items in the same way from year to year will assist users in understanding the information presented and in making comparisons between different accounting periods and between different business entities. Consistency in presentation and measurement will help achieve comparability (Chapter 1, What qualities should accounting information possess?).

Dual aspect

This principle states that every transaction has a dual effect on the financial statements. As assets are created, this gives rise to an increase in liabilities, income or capital. Similarly, as liabilities are assumed this causes assets or expenditure to increase. An increase in one asset can cause a reduction in another asset or both assets and liabilities can decrease. (Chapter 2, The dual aspect concept, Chapter 4 Double entry and the accounting equation).

Going concern

The financial statements of an entity are drawn up on the basis that the entity will continue in existence for the foreseeable future. In preparing the financial statements for publication, it is assumed that an entity does not intend to cease trading and that it will not be entering into liquidation. If an organisation does intend to cease trading or enter into liquidation, it is not a going concern and the financial statements will be drawn up on an entirely different basis.

Historic cost

The historic cost convention dictates that the assets and liabilities of a business should be valued at their original (historic) cost to the organisation. This convention has been relaxed over the years and the IASB now allows (and sometimes requires) the recognition of assets and liabilities at their fair value (Chapter 2, How are assets and liabilities valued?).

Materiality

Information is material if its omission or misstatement could influence the decisions of users based on the financial information provided by an entity. Information can be material by virtue of its size, its nature or both its size and nature (Chapter 1, Materiality).

Money measurement

Money is the unit of measurement in financial statements. Figures presented in the statement of profit or loss, statement of financial position and statement of cash flows must be measured in money terms.

Periodicity

Entities report their financial performance and their financial position at regular intervals. The usual reporting period for business organisations is at yearly intervals to allow users to assess how well the organisation is performing and to enable the tax authorities to tax each entity on the basis of its financial performance.

Prudence

'Prudence is the exercise of caution when making judgements under conditions of uncertainty' (IASB *Conceptual Framework for Financial Reporting*, paragraph 2.16). This means that preparers of financial statements should take care to ensure that assets, expenses, liabilities and income are neither overstated nor understated. The exercise of excessive prudence in the valuation of items in financial statements should be avoided as this will introduce bias into financial reporting and mean that the financial information presented is no longer faithfully represented or relevant. Note that prudence only applies to judgements made under conditions of uncertainty: when there is no uncertainty, there is no requirement to exercise prudence.

Realisation

Profits should not be anticipated until they have been earned through a sale (Chapter 3, Closing inventory). Until a sale has been completed through the delivery of goods to and the acceptance of those goods by a customer no sale or profit should be recognised as the customer can change their mind up until that point. Once goods have been delivered to and accepted by a customer then the sale and the associated profit can be recognised by an entity.

WHY IS THIS RELEVANT TO ME?   Accounting principles and conventions

To enable you as an accounting professional to understand the principles and conventions:

• Upon which financial statements are based

• Which you will have to apply when you are required to produce sets of financial statements

---

GO BACK OVER THIS AGAIN!   How well have you remembered what these principles and conventions state and how they are applied? Go to the **online workbook** and complete Exercises 6.10 to check your recollection.

MULTIPLE CHOICE QUESTIONS   Do you think that you can distinguish between different accounting principles and conventions? Go to the **online workbook** and complete Multiple choice questions 6.6 to test your ability to make these distinctions.

APPENDIX: FURTHER USES FOR T ACCOUNTS IN THE CALCULATION OF FIGURES TO INCLUDE IN THE STATEMENT OF CASH FLOWS

As we noted earlier (this chapter, Calculating cash paid for expenses using the expenses T account) T accounts can be used in various other situations to calculate missing numbers for inclusion in the statement of cash flows. While the detail provided in this appendix may be beyond the scope of your current studies, you will find these notes helpful when preparing statements of cash flows in the future.

1 Property, plant and equipment

Figures may need to be calculated in three situations:

• Cash paid to acquire property, plant and equipment

• Depreciation charged during the accounting period on property, plant and equipment

• The carrying amount of disposals of property, plant and equipment

To calculate any one of these figures, the property, plant and equipment T account in Illustration 6.13 will be used.

Illustration 6.13 The property, plant and equipment T account

Property, plant and equipment account

	£		£
Carrying amount brought forward	X	Disposals at carrying amount	X
Additions at cost	X	Depreciation charged in year	X
		Carrying amount carried forward	X
	XX		**XX**

The carrying amounts brought forward and carried forward will be presented in the statements of financial position provided in the question. Information given about the sale of property, plant and equipment will require some thought to work out the carrying amount of the property, plant and equipment disposed of. Details of either additions at cost or depreciation will then be provided, leaving you to calculate the missing figure using the framework shown in the T account in Illustration 6.13. The left hand side of the T account shows transactions that will result in increases in the carrying amount of the asset (additions), while the right hand side shows transactions that will result in decreases in the carrying amount of the asset (disposals and depreciation charged in the year).

To show how these calculations work in practice, let's look at the financial statements of Bunns the Bakers. Illustration 2.1 shows property, plant and equipment with a carrying amount at 31 March 2018 of £11,241,000 and of £11,750,000 at 31 March 2019. There is a difference of £509,000 between the figures at the two dates. But how much of this difference is due to cash spent on new property, plant and equipment, how much is due to the depreciation charge for the year and how much is due to disposals of property, plant and equipment assets during the year? The statement of cash flows for the company (Illustration 6.1) provides us with the following relevant information:

- Depreciation of property, plant and equipment in the year to 31 March 2019 amounted to £394,000.

- The profit on disposal of property, plant and equipment during the year was £3,000.

- Acquisition costs of property, plant and equipment in the year to 31 March 2019 amounted to £910,000.

- The proceeds from the sale of property, plant and equipment were £10,000.

We now have all the information required to draw up our property, plant and equipment T account. This T account is presented in Illustration 6.14.

Illustration 6.14 Bunns the Bakers' property, plant and equipment T account

Property, plant and equipment account			
	£000		£000
Carrying amount brought forward at 1 April 2018	11,241	Disposals at carrying amount	7
Additions at cost	910	Depreciation charged in year	394
		Carrying amount carried forward at 31 March 2019	11,750
	12,151		12,151

The carrying amount of the disposals is £7,000. How was this figure calculated? £10,000 was received for the assets disposed of and this resulted in a profit of £3,000. To generate a £3,000 profit from a selling price of £10,000 means that the item sold must have had a carrying amount of £7,000 (£10,000 selling price – £3,000 profit = £7,000 carrying amount). £910,000 additions at cost – £7,000 carrying amount of disposals – £394,000 depreciation = £509,000, the difference between the opening and closing carrying amounts calculated above. When tackling questions that require the preparation of a statement of cash flows, you will be provided with information to calculate four of the numbers shown in Illustrations 6.13 and 6.14. The missing number will then be the balancing figure for additions at cost, depreciation charged for the year or the carrying amount of disposals. Work through the figures in Illustration 6.14, omitting one of the figures each time to prove to yourself that the missing figure is the balancing figure.

MULTIPLE CHOICE QUESTIONS   Are you convinced that you can calculate property, plant and equipment figures for inclusion in the statement of cash flows? Go to the **online workbook** and complete Multiple choice questions 6.7 to test your ability to calculate these figures correctly.

2 Tax paid during the year

When preparing the statement of cash flows, there is only one question with respect to taxation that requires answering: how much tax was paid during the year? This question is answered by preparing the T account shown in Illustration 6.15.

Illustration 6.15 The taxation T account

Taxation account			
	£		£
Balancing figure = cash paid	x	Taxation liability brought forward	x
Taxation liability carried forward	x	Statement of profit or loss income tax charge	x
	XX		XX

Taxation is a liability so the balance brought forward appears on the credit side of the T account. The balance on the T account once payments have been made and the taxation liability to carry forward has been calculated is charged to the statement of profit or loss as the income tax charge. Questions will provide the balances brought forward and carried forward in the statement of financial position and the income tax charge for the year in the statement of profit or loss. Entering these figures into the taxation T account will then provide the cash paid figure for taxation. Again, let's illustrate this process using the statement of financial position and statement of profit or loss of Bunns the Bakers (Illustrations 2.1 and 3.1). Illustration 6.16 presents the relevant figures from Bunns the Bakers' statement of financial position and statement of profit or loss.

Illustration 6.16 Bunns the Bakers' taxation T account showing the figures known from the statement of financial position (Illustration 2.1) and the statement of profit or loss (Illustration 3.1)

Taxation account

	£000		£000
Balancing figure = cash paid	?	Taxation liability brought forward at 1 April 2018 (Illustration 2.1)	126
Taxation liability carried forward at 31 March 2019 (Illustration 2.1)	150	Statement of profit or loss income tax charge (Illustration 3.1)	213
	339		**339**

The credit side of the account adds up to £339,000 while the debit side shows only the liability carried forward at the end of the year of £150,000. To balance the account, the cash paid figure of £189,000 (£339,000 – £150,000) is debited to the taxation account. How can we be sure that cash paid is a debit figure in this account? A payment from the bank account is a credit to the bank account, so to complete the double entry there must be a debit figure. As the payment of tax is the reduction of a liability, the tax paid is debited to the taxation account to reflect this reduction in the taxation liability. The completed taxation account is shown in Illustration 6.17.

Illustration 6.17 Bunns the Bakers' taxation T account showing the cash paid as the balancing figure

Taxation account

	£000		£000
Balancing figure = cash paid	189	Taxation liability brought forward at 1 April 2018 (Illustration 2.1)	126
Taxation liability carried forward at 31 March 2019 (Illustration 2.1)	150	Statement of profit or loss income tax charge (Illustration 3.1)	213
	339		**339**

The taxation paid figure of £189,000 is added to Bunns the Bakers' statement of cash flows (Illustration 6.1).

MULTIPLE CHOICE QUESTIONS   Do you think that you can calculate the taxation paid figure for inclusion in the statement of cash flows? Go to the **online workbook** and complete Multiple choice questions 6.8 to test your ability to calculate this figure correctly.

---

3 Dividends paid

Dividends paid are deducted directly from retained earnings. Retained earnings fall and the bank balance also falls with the reduction in the asset as a result of the payment made. The double entry for the payment of dividends is debit retained earnings, credit bank account. The retained earnings T account is shown in Illustration 6.18.

Illustration 6.18 The retained earnings T account

Retained earnings account			
	£		£
Balancing figure = dividends paid	X	Retained earnings brought forward	X
Retained earnings carried forward	X	Profit for the year (statement of profit or loss)	X
	XX		XX

Using the retained earnings figures from Bunns the Bakers' statement of financial position (Illustration 2.1) and the profit for the year in the statement of profit or loss (Illustration 3.1), the retained earnings account is presented in Illustration 6.19.

Illustration 6.19 Bunns the Bakers' retained earnings T account showing the figures known from the statement of financial position (Illustration 2.1) and the statement of profit or loss (Illustration 3.1)

Retained earnings account			
	£000		£000
Balancing figure = dividends paid	90	Retained earnings brought forward at 1 April 2018 (Illustration 2.1)	4,187
Retained earnings carried forward at 31 March 2019 (Illustration 2.1)	4,644	Statement of profit or loss profit for the year (Illustration 3.1)	547
	4,734		4,734

The balancing figure of £90,000 (£4,734,000 – £4,644,000) represents the dividends paid during the year. Again, looking at the statement of cash flows for the company (Illustration 6.1), cash flows from financing activities shows a figure of £90,000 for dividends paid.

MULTIPLE CHOICE QUESTIONS Do you think that you can calculate the dividends paid figure for inclusion in the statement of cash flows? Go to the **online workbook** and complete Multiple choice questions 6.9 to test your ability to calculate this figure correctly.

4 Interest received (finance income)

Bunns the Bakers' statement of profit or loss (Illustration 3.1) and statement of cash flows (Illustration 6.1) both show finance income/interest of £15,000. There is thus no difference between the income recognised in the statement of profit or loss and actual cash inflow from this interest received during the year. However, for most entities the receipt of cash from interest does not coincide exactly with the accounting period end. As a result of the accruals basis of accounting, organisations record a receivable at each year end for finance income that has accrued since the last cash receipt from this source of income. To calculate the cash actually received from finance income during the year, the T account presented in Illustration 6.20 is used.

Illustration 6.20 The interest receivable T account

Interest receivable account

	£		£
Interest receivable brought forward	X	Balancing figure = cash received	X
Finance income in the statement of profit or loss	X	Interest receivable carried forward	X
	XX		**XX**

Let's see how the cash received from interest receivable would be calculated in Example 6.3.

EXAMPLE 6.3

At 30 April 2018 CHY Limited had interest receivable of £24,000. At 30 April 2019, interest receivable was £27,000 and the statement of profit or loss showed finance income (all from interest) for the year to 30 April 2019 of £92,000. How much cash was received from interest during the year to 30 April 2019? We can use our T account in Illustration 6.20 to calculate the cash received from interest during the year. The results of these calculations are shown in Illustration 6.21.

Illustration 6.21 CHY Limited interest receivable T account

Interest receivable account

	£000		£000
Interest receivable brought forward at 1 May 2018	24	Balancing figure = cash received	89
Finance income in the statement of profit or loss	92	Interest receivable carried forward at 30 April 2019	27
	116		**116**

MULTIPLE CHOICE QUESTIONS Are you quite sure that you can calculate the cash received from finance income figure for inclusion in the statement of cash flows? Go to the **online workbook** and complete Multiple choice questions 6.10 to test your ability to calculate this figure correctly.

5 Interest paid (finance expense)

The same approach applies to interest paid. Bunns the Bakers' statement of profit or loss (Illustration 3.1) and statement of cash flows (Illustration 6.1) both show finance expense/interest paid of £150,000. There is thus no difference between the expense recognised in the statement of profit or loss and actual cash outflow to lenders during the year. Again, most entities find that they have an accrual for interest at the end of each accounting period, an interest cost that has been incurred but not paid by the accounting period end. Organisations thus record a payable (a liability) at each year end for interest that has accrued since the last payment. To calculate the finance expense cash actually paid during the year, the T account presented in Illustration 6.22 is used.

Illustration 6.22 The interest payable T account

Interest payable account				
	£			£
Balancing figure = cash paid	x	Interest payable brought forward		x
Interest payable carried forward	x	Finance expense in the statement of profit or loss		x
	XX			**XX**

Example 6.4 shows how this interest paid T account is used in practice to determine the cash paid during an accounting period.

EXAMPLE 6.4

At 30 April 2018 CHY Limited had an interest payable liability of £35,000. At 30 April 2019, the interest payable liability stood at £32,000 and the statement of profit or loss showed finance expense (all interest paid) for the year to 30 April 2019 of £160,000. How much cash was paid in interest during the year to 30 April 2019? We can use our T account in Illustration 6.22 to calculate the cash paid in interest during the year. The results of these calculations are shown in Illustration 6.23.

Illustration 6.23 CHY Limited interest payable T account

Interest payable account				
	£000			£000
Balancing figure = cash paid	163	Interest payable brought forward		35
Interest payable carried forward	32	Finance expense in the statement of profit or loss		160
	195			**195**

MULTIPLE CHOICE QUESTIONS   Are you convinced that you can calculate the finance expense (interest) cash paid figure for inclusion in the statement of cash flows? Go to the **online workbook** and complete Multiple choice questions 6.11 to test your ability to calculate this figure correctly.

CHAPTER SUMMARY

You should now have learnt that:

- Organisations' cash flows are made up of cash flows from operating activities, cash flows from investing activities and cash flows from financing activities
- Cash generated during an accounting period is not the same as profit
- Cash flow is critical to the survival of an organisation
- Statements of cash flows can be prepared using both the direct and indirect methods
- A statement of cash flows is not sufficient on its own to provide users of financial statements with all the information they will need to assess an entity's financial position, performance and changes in financial position
- T accounts can be used to calculate missing figures for inclusion in the statement of cash flows
- Various accounting principles and conventions apply in the preparation of financial statements

QUICK REVISION   Test your knowledge with the online flashcards in Summary of key concepts and attempt the Multiple choice questions, all in the **online workbook**.

END-OF-CHAPTER QUESTIONS

Solutions to these questions can be found in the **online workbook**.

❯ DEVELOP YOUR UNDERSTANDING

❯ Question 6.1

Look up the answer to End of chapter questions 3.1. Using details of Abi's assets and liabilities at the start of the trading year, her statement of profit or loss, her statement of financial position and her bank account summary for the year, present Abi's statement of cash flows using both the direct and the indirect method for the year ended 31 August 2019.

❯ Question 6.2

Alison runs an online gift shop, trading for cash with individual customers and offering trading on credit terms to businesses. Alison provides you with the following list of statement of financial position balances at 31 December 2018:

	£
Non-current assets	
Computer equipment at cost	12,775
Less: accumulated depreciation on computer equipment at 31 December 2018	(7,245)
Racks, shelving and office furniture at cost	24,000
Less: accumulated depreciation on racks, shelving and office furniture at 31 December 2018	(8,000)
	21,530
Current assets	
Inventory	27,647
Trade receivables	27,200
Rent prepayment	2,500
Rates prepayment	1,965
Cash and cash equivalents	3,682
	62,994
Total assets	**84,524**
Current liabilities	
Trade payables	30,314
Telephone, electricity and gas accruals	1,500
Total liabilities	**31,814**
Net assets	**52,710**
Capital account	**52,710**

Alison provides you with the following additional information:

- During the year to 31 December 2019, Alison spent £8,000 on buying new computer equipment and £9,600 on new racks, shelving and office equipment as her business expanded.
- There were no disposals of non-current assets during the year.

Required

Using the statement of financial position at 31 December 2018 and the additional information above, together with the answer to Question 3.2, prepare Alison's statement of cash flows for the year ended 31 December 2019 using both the direct and the indirect method. For your calculation of cash flows from operating activities under the direct method you will need to prepare the trade receivables control account (Illustration 6.6), the trade payables control account (Illustration 6.8) and the expenses T account (Illustration 6.10)

> Question 6.3

Look up the answer to End of chapter questions 3.5. Using the statement of profit or loss, the statement of financial position and the bank account, present the statement of cash flows for Laura for the year ended 31 August 2019 using both the indirect and direct method.

>> TAKE IT FURTHER

>> Question 6.4

The statements of financial position for Potters Limited, together with relevant notes, are given below. Potters Limited produces crockery for sale to shops and through its site on the Internet.

Potters Limited: statements of financial position at 30 June 2019 and 30 June 2018

	2019 £000	2018 £000
ASSETS		
Non-current assets		
Intangible assets: trademarks	100	120
Property, plant and equipment	10,200	8,600
	10,300	**8,720**
Current assets		
Inventories	1,000	1,100
Trade and other receivables	1,800	1,550
Cash and cash equivalents	200	310
	3,000	**2,960**
Total assets	**13,300**	**11,680**
LIABILITIES		
Current liabilities		
Trade and other payables	1,200	1,000
Current tax liabilities	300	250
	1,500	**1,250**
Non-current liabilities		
Long-term borrowings	**3,200**	**2,600**
Total liabilities	**4,700**	**3,850**
Net assets	**8,600**	**7,830**
EQUITY		
Called up share capital (£1 ordinary shares)	1,000	800
Share premium	2,500	2,150
Retained earnings	5,100	4,880
Total equity	**8,600**	**7,830**

During the year to 30 June 2019:

- Potters Limited paid £2,500,000 to acquire new property, plant and equipment
- Depreciation of £800,000 was charged on property, plant and equipment
- Plant and equipment with a carrying amount of £100,000 was sold for £150,000
- Amortisation of £20,000 was charged on the trademarks
- Dividends of £100,000 were paid
- Taxation of £275,000 was paid
- £200,000 interest was paid on the long-term borrowings
- Operating profit for the year was £845,000
- 200,000 new ordinary shares were issued for cash at a price of £2.75 each
- Potters Limited received no interest during the year to 30 June 2019

Required

Prepare the statement of cash flows for Potters Limited for the year ended 30 June 2019 using the indirect method.

>> **Question 6.5**

Statements of financial position for Metal Bashers plc, together with the statement of profit or loss for the current year and relevant notes, are given below. Metal Bashers plc produces machine tools for industrial use.

Metal Bashers plc: statements of financial position at 30 September 2019 and 30 September 2018

	2019 £000	2018 £000
ASSETS		
Non-current assets		
Intangible assets: patents	200	150
Property, plant and equipment	21,800	18,850
	22,000	**19,000**
Current assets		
Inventories	1,400	1,200
Trade receivables	2,000	2,100
Prepayments	350	300
Cash and cash equivalents	750	400
	4,500	**4,000**
Total assets	**26,500**	**23,000**

	£000	£000
LIABILITIES		
Current liabilities		
Current portion of long-term borrowings	500	500
Trade payables	1,800	2,050
Accruals	200	250
Current tax liabilities	400	350
	2,900	3,150
Non-current liabilities		
Long-term borrowings	**6,500**	**7,000**
Total liabilities	**9,400**	**10,150**
Net assets	**17,100**	**12,850**
EQUITY		
Called up share capital (£1 ordinary shares)	3,600	2,000
Share premium	5,600	2,400
Retained earnings	7,900	8,450
Total equity	**17,100**	**12,850**

Metal Bashers plc: statement of profit or loss for the year ended 30 September 2019

	2019 £000
Revenue	12,196
Cost of sales	9,147
Gross profit	3,049
Distribution and selling costs	425
Administration expenses	899
Operating profit	1,725
Finance income	100
Finance expense	870
Profit before taxation	955
Income tax	425
Profit for the year	**530**

During the year to 30 September 2019:

- Metal Bashers plc paid total dividends of £1,080,000
- New patents costing £70,000 were acquired
- Amortisation charged on patents was £20,000. This amortisation was charged to administration expenses

- 1.6 million new shares were issued during the year for cash at a price of £3 each
- Finance income and finance expense represent the actual cash received and paid during the year
- Income tax of £375,000 was paid during the year
- New property, plant and equipment costing £5,000,000 was purchased during the year for cash
- Redundant property, plant and equipment with a carrying amount of £250,000 was sold for £175,000. Profits and losses on disposal of non-current assets are credited or charged to administration expenses
- Depreciation of £1,800,000 was charged on property, plant and equipment during the year. This depreciation was charged to cost of sales
- Administration expenses include a charge for an irrecoverable debt of £125,000

Required

Prepare the statement of cash flows for Metal Bashers plc for the year ended 30 June 2019 using both the direct and indirect method. For your calculation of cash flows from operating activities under the direct method you will need to prepare the trade receivables control account (Illustration 6.6), the trade payables control account (Illustration 6.8) and the expenses T account (Illustration 6.10).

BUSINESS ORGANISATIONS AND THE FINANCING OF BUSINESS

LEARNING OUTCOMES

Once you have read this chapter and worked through the questions and examples in both this chapter and the online workbook, you should be able to:

- Understand the different forms of business organisation and the advantages and disadvantages of each format

- Describe the various sources of finance available to the different forms of business organisation

- Discuss the returns to each source of finance

- Describe the features of ordinary and preference share capital

- Understand how cash is raised from an issue of shares

- Understand how bonus issues and rights issues work

- Understand how limited companies make dividend distributions and whether they have the capacity to make such distributions

INTRODUCTION

So far we have studied various examples of accounting statements produced by a variety of different organisations. While the financial statements of these organisations seem to adopt basically the same formats, we have not yet formally considered the different types of business entity and the ways in which they differ one from the other. Bunns the Bakers is a public limited company, while Julia set up her sports equipment shop and started trading as a sole trader. What are the distinctions between these two business formats? Are there any other business formats that are commonly adopted in practice? Why is one format preferable to another and why do all businesses not follow the same format? Quite commonly, what starts off as a small business trading as a sole trader becomes a limited company later on in that business's life. This chapter will deal with the different features of each type of business organisation and the advantages and disadvantages of each format.

At the same time, the two business formats we have looked at seem to adopt different methods through which to finance their operations. Julia introduced her own money into her sports equipment retailing business and was allocated all the profit from that activity at the end of the accounting year. Bunns the Bakers is financed by share capital, but how is the profit from that business allocated to its investors? In this chapter we will also be looking at how different businesses finance their operations and the requirements that each different financing method imposes upon each different business format.

WHY IS THIS RELEVANT TO ME?   Types of business organisation and organisational finance

To introduce to you as an accounting professional:

- The various different types of business organisation you will be dealing with in practice
- The ways in which different types of business organisation are set up and the powers that each type enjoys
- The different types of finance that are available to different types of business organisation and how each type of organisation raises finance to fund their operations

---

TYPES OF BUSINESS ORGANISATION

Let's start with a review of each of the three main types of business organisation. These comprise sole traders, partnerships and limited companies.

Sole traders

Simple businesses require a simple format. As the name implies, sole traders run their businesses on their own. Sole traders set their businesses up and, while they might employ other people to assist them in the day-to-day running of operations, they take all the business decisions themselves and assume total responsibility for the success or failure of their businesses. Sole traders have unlimited liability for the debts incurred by their businesses and they could lose everything in a business failure. These losses would extend not only to business assets but also to personal assets such as houses, cars, investments, in fact anything that those sole traders own.

The sole trader format for organising a business is most effective where operations are straightforward and where there are no complexities that could be more efficiently dealt with by adopting a different structure. Examples of sole traders would be Julia, our stand-alone retailer in Chapters 3, 4 and 6, childminders, hairdressers, market traders, taxi drivers, sports coaches, barristers and accountants working as sole practitioners. All these people operate their businesses on their own and plough a lone furrow as they make their way in the world. There are no special requirements for setting up in business as a sole trader: just start trading. The features of the sole trader business format are summarised in Figure 7.1.

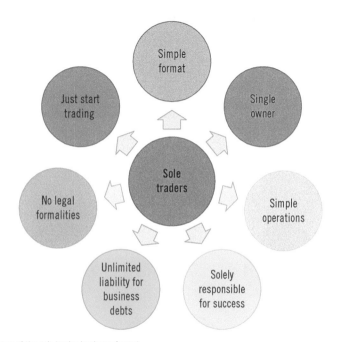

Figure 7.1 The features of the sole trader business format

GO BACK OVER THIS AGAIN!   Are you quite sure that you understand how sole traders operate? Go to the **online workbook** and have a go at Exercises 7.1 to reinforce your understanding of sole traders and how they operate.

Partnerships

Where two or more individuals own and run a business together, then a partnership structure will be adopted for that business. Partnerships are more complex undertakings than sole traders and reflect the fact that one person cannot know everything or be talented in every activity. Thus, in a building firm partnership, one partner might be skilled as a bricklayer and plasterer, one as a plumber and heating engineer, one as an electrician. Similarly, in an accounting partnership,

7

one partner might be knowledgeable in accounts preparation and audit, one in tax and one in insolvency.

The principle in a partnership is that all the partners take part in running the business and enjoy a share of the profits or suffer a share of the losses from that business. You might say that a partnership is two or more sole traders coming together to make a bigger business, with each partner enjoying a share of management and reward from that enlarged business. The problem in a partnership is that the partners have to be certain that they will all be able to work together effectively and that no personality clashes or disputes will cause disruption to the business. Sole traders, of course, do not have this problem. Partnerships, like sole traders, can be set up informally and just start trading. However, given the possibility that there will be disagreements between the partners, it is usual to set out the key terms of the partnership in a written agreement signed by all the partners at the start of the partnership. As was the case with sole traders, partnerships have unlimited liability for the debts incurred by the partnership. This unlimited liability is joint and several which means that each partner is liable collectively for the partnership debts incurred not just by themselves but by their fellow partners as well. Limited liability partnerships (LLPs) can now be set up in the UK as a result of the Limited Liability Partnerships Act 2000. Under this Act partners in an LLP can place limits on their liability for partnership debts. Further consideration of limited liability partnerships is beyond the scope of the current book. The features of the partnership business format are summarised in Figure 7.2.

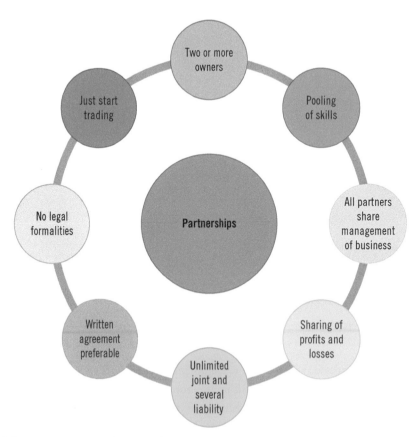

Figure 7.2 The features of the partnership business format

GO BACK OVER THIS AGAIN!   Are you confident that you know how partnerships work? Go to the **online workbook** and have a go at Exercises 7.2 to reinforce your understanding of partnerships and how they operate.

Limited companies

Limited companies are much more complex organisations and are subject to much greater regulation and oversight. Given this complexity, let's look at the distinguishing features of limited liability companies (summarised in Figure 7.3) one by one, comparing and contrasting limited companies with sole traders and partnerships.

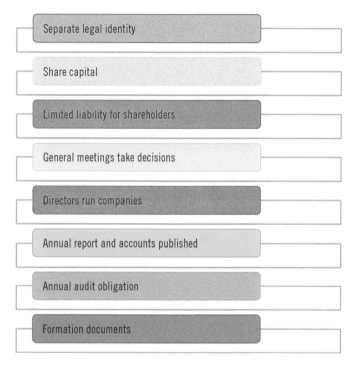

Figure 7.3 The features of the limited liability company business format

Separate legal identity

Limited companies are regarded as separate legal entities with their own name and a perpetual life. Businesses that operate as sole traders or partnerships are considered to be an extension of those individuals and the businesses and their owners are not regarded as distinct legal beings. This separate legal identity means that limited companies can sue and be sued, sign undertakings and enter into contractual obligations in their own name. Sole trader and partnership businesses tend to cease when the owners retire or die, but limited companies carry on indefinitely no matter how many of their directors or shareholders leave the company.

Share capital

Businesses can incorporate themselves as limited companies. Incorporation requires a detailed formal process (see this chapter, Formation documents). On incorporation of a business, shareholders subscribe for shares in the limited company. When individuals subscribe for shares, this gives limited companies a source of finance. While sole traders and partners provide the financing for their businesses and record this in their statements of financial position as capital introduced, shareholders pay money into the company's bank account and receive shares in proportion to the capital they have invested. This share capital is recorded as issued share capital in the limited company's statement of financial position.

Limited liability

The great advantage of limited companies over sole traders and partnerships is that the liability of the shareholders to meet the debts of the limited company is restricted to the amount they have subscribed for their shares. If a limited company were to fail and go out of business, then shareholders will not have to provide any more money towards clearing the debts of the company than they have already paid for their shares. Shareholders lose the money they have already paid to acquire their shares, but they have no further liability beyond this. Thus, if a shareholder agreed to purchase one hundred £1 shares on the formation of a company, then, once the £100 has been paid to the company, the shareholder has to make no further contribution to the company should it fail. As we have seen, the situation is very different for sole traders and partnerships who have unlimited liability for the debts of their businesses with the potential to lose both business and personal assets in a business failure.

General meetings

Sole traders and partners own their businesses and answer only to themselves. Sole traders and partners thus make major decisions about their organisations throughout the year as and when the need arises. Limited companies, on the other hand, are accountable to their shareholders. Every year each and every limited company must hold an annual general meeting (AGM) at which the shareholders come together to consider and vote on various significant resolutions affecting the company. When companies undertake other business transactions which require the agreement of shareholders at other times of the year, the directors will call an extraordinary general meeting (EGM). An EGM is any company meeting other than the annual general meeting. For example, the directors may call an EGM to ask shareholders to approve the takeover of another company. Shareholders have voting rights at the AGM and at EGMs. The size of these voting rights and the power of each shareholder depend upon the number of shares held. For each share held, a shareholder has one vote. The more shares that a shareholder owns, the more power that shareholder can exercise when voting on company resolutions.

Appointment of directors

One of the resolutions voted on at the AGM concerns the appointment of directors of the company. Limited companies, although answerable to their shareholders, are managed and run by directors appointed by the shareholders at the AGM. The directors are elected by the shareholders to run the company on their behalf. If shareholders are not happy with the performance of the current directors, they have the power to vote them out of office at the AGM and appoint different directors in their place. Directors are employees of limited companies placed in a position of trust by the shareholders. Ownership (by shareholders) and management (by directors) are thus separated, a situation that does not apply in the case of sole traders and partnerships. Of course, both directors and other employees can buy shares in their companies and thereby influence the direction and decisions of the companies which employ them. When sole traders and partnerships incorporate their businesses (transfer their business undertakings to limited companies set up for this purpose), the new companies issue shares to these former owners as payment for the assets transferred and to enable the original owners to retain control of their businesses.

Annual accounts

Because of this separation of share ownership and management, the directors of limited companies have a statutory obligation under the Companies Act 2006 to present annual accounts to the shareholders at the AGM. These accounts are a financial record of how the directors have managed the monies and other resources entrusted to them by the shareholders and how they have used that money and those resources to generate profits for shareholders during the past year. As we noted in Chapter 1 (Control, accounting and accountability), the directors present this account of their stewardship of the resources entrusted to them to help shareholders control the directors' actions and prevent them from exceeding their powers. All limited company accounts are filed at Companies House and are available for public consultation.

Auditors and annual accounts

As shareholders do not take part in the day-to-day running of the company, they do not know whether the accounts presented by the directors are a true and fair summary of the financial achievements during the year or not. Therefore, shareholders appoint independent auditors to check the annual report and accounts for inaccuracies, omissions and misrepresentations. These auditors then report to the shareholders on whether the annual report and accounts present a true and fair view of the company's profit or loss for the year and of the state of the company's affairs (the statement of financial position) at the year-end date. The audit report will also state whether the financial statements have been properly prepared in accordance with the relevant financial reporting standards and with the requirements of the Companies Act 2006. Shareholders are empowered by the Companies Act 2006 to choose the auditors they want to conduct the annual audit rather than the auditors that the directors would like to appoint.

Auditors of limited companies enjoy various protections against removal by the directors and this enables them to perform their audits efficiently and effectively without fear or favour to the shareholders' benefit. Not every company is required to have an audit. Those companies which must have an audit and those companies for which an audit is optional are specified in the Companies Act 2006. You will learn much more about these audit requirements and about auditing at a later stage in your studies.

Sole traders and partnerships prepare annual accounts, but these are used to determine any tax that is due on profits and to present to banks to support applications for loan and other borrowing facilities. There is no obligation upon sole traders or partnerships to publish their accounts publicly so that the financial affairs of sole traders and partnerships remain private and confidential. The annual accounts for sole traders and partnerships are not audited.

Formation documents

When limited companies are formed, they are registered with the Registrar of Companies. This registration comprises the name of the company and the names of the first directors (the names of the company and the directors can be changed at any time by the submission of the appropriate documentation to Companies House). In addition, two important documents are filed when a company is registered. The first is the Memorandum of Association. This document covers the limited company's objectives and its powers and governs the relationship of the company with the outside world. The second document is the Articles of Association, which covers the internal regulations of the company and governs the shareholders' relationships with each other.

WHY IS THIS RELEVANT TO ME?   Types of business organisation

To enable you as an accounting professional to:

* Appreciate the different types of business organisation that you will be dealing with during your professional career
* Understand how the different types of business organisation operating in the economy today are set up and run
* Compare and contrast the different types of business organisation you will be dealing with in your professional life

---

GO BACK OVER THIS AGAIN!   Do you feel confident that you can describe the different features of the various types of business organisations and distinguish between them? Go to the **online workbook** and have a go at Exercises 7.3 to make sure you can describe and distinguish between the different types of business organisation.

SUMMARY OF KEY CONCEPTS   Are you quite happy that you can describe the main features of each of the three different types of business organisations? Go to the **online workbook** to revise these main features with Summary of key concepts 7.1–7.3.

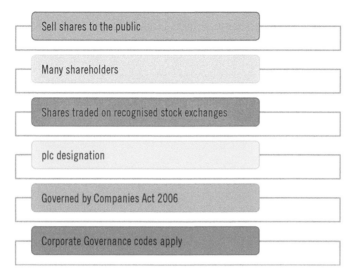

Figure 7.4 The characteristics of public limited companies (plcs)

Public limited and private limited companies

The Companies Act 2006 regulates all limited liability companies. However, there are two types of limited company covered in the Act: private limited companies and public limited companies. The distinctive characteristics of public limited companies are summarised in Figure 7.4. Private limited companies are prohibited from selling their shares to the public and usually have very few shareholders. Public limited companies can issue shares to the public and have many shareholders. The shares of public limited companies (but not those of limited companies which can only be traded privately) are traded on recognised stock exchanges such as those of London, New York, Paris, Hong Kong and Tokyo. Many of the businesses or websites you visit each day are run by public limited companies and these include your bank and the shops in which you buy your food. Private limited companies have the word limited or Ltd after their names while the names of public limited companies are followed by the letters plc. Look out for these company designations as you browse the web or go out into town.

Public and private limited companies are subject to exactly the same rules in the Companies Act 2006. Both types of limited company produce annual reports and accounts (these are also referred to by the term financial statements). Public limited companies are also subject to stock exchange rules and regulations. A more complex financial reporting regime applies to public limited companies in that they also have to comply with various corporate governance codes, which seek to improve their ethics and accountability. Chapter 10 provides a brief overview of the corporate governance code which applies to public limited companies.

WHY IS THIS RELEVANT TO ME?   Public and private limited companies

To enable you as an accounting professional to:

- Gain an awareness of the distinctive characteristics of the two types of limited company
- Appreciate the differences between public and private limited companies

GO BACK OVER THIS AGAIN!   Are you confident that you can distinguish between private and public limited companies? Go to the **online workbook** and have a go at Exercises 7.4 to make sure you understand the differences between private and public limited companies.

SUMMARY OF KEY CONCEPTS   Are you happy that you can describe the main features of private and public limited companies? Go to the **online workbook** to revise these main features with Summary of key concepts 7.4.

FINANCING BUSINESS

All businesses have to raise finance at the start of their lives and at regular intervals as they expand. Providers of finance to businesses require some form of reward for providing that finance. So what sort of finance is raised by different businesses and what are the payments made to each type of finance?

Capital introduced: sole traders and partnerships

We have already looked briefly at this method of financing for sole traders in Chapter 2 (The components of equity). When a sole trader or a partnership is set up, the owners pay money into the new venture. It will take a little time for trading income to begin to flow into the business so this start-up capital is needed to buy non-current assets with which to set up the operations of the business and to provide cash to ensure the continuity of trading in the early stages of the business's life.

As an example, look back to Chapter 3, Illustration 3.3. Julia paid £30,000 into her business bank account and then used this cash to pay the initial rent of £5,000 and to buy the cash register and the shelves and fittings for her shop for £11,000 on the same day. No trading had taken place at this point so Julia had made no cash profits from which to pay for these non-current assets. Without her initial payment into the business, Julia would not have had the cash with which to make these necessary investments to run her retail operation. Many businesses start up in the same way with the owners paying in cash to buy assets and meet initial expenses from their own resources.

Sole traders and partners do not charge their businesses interest on this capital introduced. Instead, they draw on this capital and the profits made by the business as their source of income from which to meet their personal expenses and to finance their lifestyles. Chapter 2 (The components of equity) noted that the term for these withdrawals is 'drawings', money taken out of the business by the owner(s) for their own personal use.

As sole traders and partners are considered to be an extension of their businesses, withdrawing money in this way from their businesses is perfectly acceptable. However, it is not possible for shareholders in limited companies to withdraw money from their companies in the same way as limited companies have a separate legal identity and are regarded as completely distinct from their owners.

Bank finance: all businesses

Banks provide short- and medium-term finance to businesses in the form of overdrafts and loans. In Chapter 2 we noted that such overdrafts and loans are described as borrowings under current and non-current liabilities in the statement of financial position. The cost of both these sources of finance is interest that the bank charges on the amounts borrowed.

Bank overdrafts have the following features (these features are summarised in Figure 7.5):

- Overdrafts are short-term finance.
- The overdraft amount varies each month depending on cash inflows and outflows during each month. The more cash received and the lower the amounts of cash paid out, the lower the overdraft will be and vice versa.

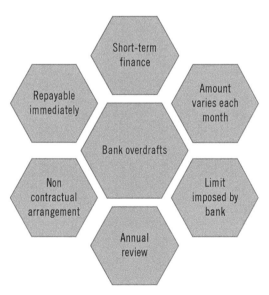

Figure 7.5 Features of bank overdrafts

- There is usually a limit on the amount of the overdraft allowed by the bank. When customers reach or exceed this overdraft limit, the bank is entitled to refuse any further credit on that account.

- Overdrafts are subject to an annual review by the bank to determine whether the overdraft limit should remain the same, increase or decrease.

- Overdrafts are not contractual arrangements and banks can ask for overdrafts to be repaid immediately.

Give me an example 7.1 provides a real life example of bank overdraft facilities offered by Lloyds Bank plc.

GIVE ME AN EXAMPLE 7.1   Bank overdrafts

Details of overdrafts offered by Lloyds Bank on 7 May 2017:

Business overdraft

- Make sure extra funds are there when you need them.

- Only pay interest on the funds you use.

- Apply for a limit that suits your business.

- In the event of movement in the Bank of England bank rate your interest rate will move immediately by the same amount without any prior notice to you.

Source: http://www.lloydsbank.com/business/retail-business/loans-and-financing/loans/business-overdraft.asp

---

Bank loans operate as follows (the features of bank loans are summarised in Figure 7.6):

- A fixed amount is borrowed for a fixed term, usually a period of 5–10 years.

- Repayments are made on a regular basis, either monthly or quarterly.

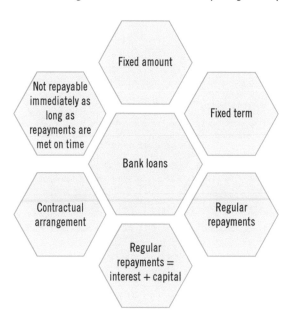

Figure 7.6 Features of bank loans

- Each monthly repayment consists of an interest element and a repayment of part of the sum originally borrowed.

- Loans are contractual arrangements. Banks can only demand immediate repayment of loans when the borrower has failed to meet a contractual repayment or a payment of interest by the due date.

How do bank loans work in practice? Give me an example 7.2 and Table 7.1 present the features of the different types of business loans offered by Lloyds Bank.

GIVE ME AN EXAMPLE 7.2   Bank loans

Table 7.1 Details of business loans offered by Lloyds Bank on 7 May 2017

Type of loan	Interest rate	Loan term	Loan amount	Key features
Base rate loan	Varies with Bank of England Bank Rate	1 to 25 years	£1,000+	✓ Rate fluctuates with Bank Rate ✓ No early repayment costs ✓ Borrow on a secured or unsecured basis ✓ Capital repayment holidays
Fixed rate loan	Fixed rate for full term of the loan	1 to 10 years	£1,000 – £50,000	✓ Fixed monthly repayments ✓ No early repayment costs ✓ Borrow on a secured or unsecured basis ✓ Capital repayment holidays
Commercial fixed rate loan	Can be fixed for periods from 1 year to the full term of the loan	1 to 25 years	£50,001 – £500,000	✓ Fixed monthly repayments ✓ Borrow on a secured or unsecured basis ✓ Break Costs will apply—these will be defined at the outset of your loan, giving you certainty around the costs involved should you decide to repay early during the fixed rate period. ✓ Capital repayment holidays

Source: http://www.lloydsbank.com/business/retail-business/loans-and-finance.asp

Notes to the above table: terms with which you may not be familiar

Bank of England Bank Rate: the Bank of England sets the interest rate (the base rate) it will pay to the commercial banks for the amounts of cash they deposit with the Bank of England. If the Bank lowers this base rate then interest rates charged by banks on loans to customers will fall. If the Bank raises this rate, then interest rates charged by banks on loans to customers will rise.

→

Secured or unsecured basis: when banks lend money to their customers, they want to be sure that they will receive the money back in the future. Banks can ask for security for loans taken out. Borrowers offer security in the form of assets such as land and buildings or other assets of the business: if the borrower is unable to repay the amounts borrowed, then the assets pledged as security to the bank will be taken by the bank and sold. The borrowings taken out are repaid from the sale proceeds from the sale of the assets. Where banks are confident that businesses will be able to repay what is borrowed, they will not request security. In these cases, the lending is said to be unsecured.

Capital repayment holidays: the amount borrowed is called the capital element of the loan. The capital element is distinct from the interest element of the loan. For example, if a borrower borrows £25,000 at an interest rate of 5 per cent, the capital amount of the loan is £25,000 and the annual interest on the loan is £25,000 × 5 per cent = £1,250. Each loan instalment repaid by a borrower consists of a repayment of part of the capital of the loan and a payment of interest. Should borrowers find that cash inflows are temporarily insufficient to repay both the capital and the interest elements in each instalment on a loan, then they can stop repaying the capital part of the instalments for a set period of time, just paying the interest element. This period is called a capital repayment holiday, a break from repaying the capital element of the loan. The outstanding capital balance of what is still owed does not fall, but it does not rise either. Once the capital repayment holiday finishes, then the borrower recommences payments of both the capital and the interest elements of the loan.

WHY IS THIS RELEVANT TO ME?　Bank finance

To enable you as an accounting professional to:

● Understand the difference between bank overdrafts and bank loans

● Appreciate the key features of overdraft and loan finance

GO BACK OVER THIS AGAIN!　Are you sure that you can distinguish between overdraft and loan finance? Go to the **online workbook** and have a go at Exercises 7.6 to make sure you do understand the differences.

SUMMARY OF KEY CONCEPTS　Are you confident that you can describe the main features of overdraft and loan finance? Go to the **online workbook** to revise these main features using Summary of key concepts 7.5.

Other types of long-term finance: public limited companies

Debenture loans/bonds/loan notes

Public limited companies can issue debentures, bonds or loan notes to the public. Debentures, bonds and loan notes are long-term loans with a fixed rate of interest and a fixed repayment date. Thus a plc might issue a £500 million loan note with an interest rate of 5.25 per cent and a repayment date of 31 January 2027. Lenders would then receive an interest payment of £26.25 million (£500m × 5.25 per cent) every year on the anniversary of the loan note's issue and full repayment of the £500 million plus any interest outstanding up to the date of repayment on 31 January 2027. An example of Corporate Bonds issued by a plc is presented in Give me an example 7.3.

Debentures, bonds and loan notes are traded on stock exchanges around the world so lenders can sell their holdings in these long-term loans without waiting for the repayment date.

GIVE ME AN EXAMPLE 7.3   Bonds

Next plc records the following corporate bond liabilities together with their associated interest rates and maturity dates in note 17 to the annual report and accounts for the financial year ended 27 January 2018.

Corporate bonds

	Balance sheet value	
	2018	2017
	£m	£m
Corporate bond 5.375% repayable 2021	328.4	329.5
Corporate bond 4.375% repayable 2026	280.1	284.0
Corporate bond 3.625% repayable 2028	300.0	300.0
	908.5	**913.5**

Source: http://www.nextplc.co.uk

7

WHY IS THIS RELEVANT TO ME?   Bond and debenture finance

To provide you as an accounting professional with:

- An awareness of bonds, loan notes and debentures as a means of raising finance for large companies
- A brief overview of the features of bonds and debentures

GO BACK OVER THIS AGAIN!   Are you convinced that you understand bonds, loan notes and debentures? Go to the **online workbook** and have a go at Exercises 7.7 to make sure you can describe these sources of finance.

SUMMARY OF KEY CONCEPTS   Do you think that you can describe the main features of bond, loan note and debenture financing? Go to the **online workbook** to revise these main features with Summary of key concepts 7.6.

Share capital: limited companies

All limited companies, whether public or private, issue share capital. Share capital is a source of indefinite long-term finance for a company. Shares subscribed by shareholders will be in issue for as long as the company exists. Share capital financing is not available to sole traders or partnerships unless they choose to transfer their operations to a limited company set up for this purpose. As well as issues of ordinary share capital, some companies also issue preference share capital.

Companies distribute dividends to their shareholders. Dividends are a share of the profit earned in a financial period (usually one year) paid out to the shareholders. Whereas interest on loans and overdrafts has to be paid no matter what the circumstances of the business are, companies do not have to distribute a dividend if the directors decide that it is not in the company's best interests to do so. For example, if the company were about to make a large investment in new non-current assets, it would make more sense for the company to hold onto its cash to make this investment rather than paying a dividend.

Before we consider dividends further and how these are calculated, let's look at the two types of share capital that companies issue.

Preference share capital

Preference shares are so called because holders of preference shares receive preferential treatment from the issuing company in the following ways:

- Preference shareholders must receive their dividends from the company before any distribution of profit is made to ordinary shareholders.
- Thus, if there are no profits left over for distribution after the preference dividends have been paid then the ordinary shareholders receive no dividend for that year.
- On the winding up/liquidation of a company, once all the claims of a company's creditors have been settled, any money left over and available to shareholders is repaid to preference shareholders before any payment is made to ordinary shareholders.

However, preference shareholders also suffer various restrictions as a result of this preferential treatment:

- The rate of dividend on preference shares is fixed. Thus, preference shareholders are not entitled to any further share of the profits available for distribution once their fixed rate of dividend has been paid.
- Preference shareholders have no right to vote in general meetings.

Preference shareholders' rights are restricted in the above ways as they take on a lower level of risk when compared to ordinary shareholders. Although the companies in which preference shareholders invest might still fail or not earn much profit, the fact that they are paid their dividends first and receive their money back in a liquidation before the ordinary shareholders means that they are taking less risk than ordinary shareholders who stand to lose everything. The advantages and limitations of preference shares are summarised in Figure 7. 7.

Ordinary share capital

Ordinary share capital is the name given to the most common form of share capital issued by companies. You will often see ordinary share capital referred to as equity share capital. Ordinary shareholders take on the highest risks when they buy shares in a company. Investors in ordinary shares might receive all of a company's profits as dividends (after the payment of any preference dividend) and see the value of their shares rise many times above what they originally paid for them or they could receive no dividends and nothing when the company goes into liquidation,

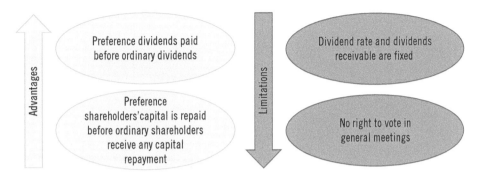

Figure 7.7 The characteristics of preference shares

losing all of their investment. All limited companies must issue ordinary share capital. Ordinary shares are the only shares that carry voting rights at company general meetings. The positive and negative aspects of ordinary shares are summarised in Figure 7.8.

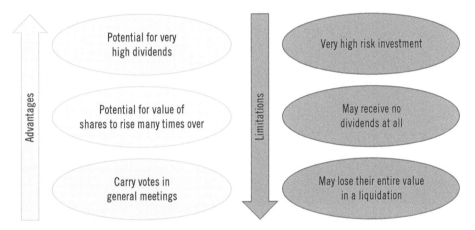

Figure 7.8 The characteristics of ordinary shares

WHY IS THIS RELEVANT TO ME?   Share capital: preference and ordinary shares

To enable you as an accounting professional to:

• Develop a clear awareness of the different types of share capital that companies issue

• Understand the characteristics of the two different types of share capital

---

GO BACK OVER THIS AGAIN!   Are you certain you understand how ordinary and preference shares differ? Go to the **online workbook** and have a go at Exercises 7.8 to make sure you can distinguish between these two types of share capital.

SUMMARY OF KEY CONCEPTS   Do you think that you could describe the main features of ordinary and preference shares? Go to the **online workbook** to revise these main features with Summary of key concepts 7.7.

Share capital: share issues at par value

Under the Companies Act 2006, every company can issue as many shares as it wishes. Share capital is increased simply by issuing more shares. Example 7.1 presents details of the par value of share capital.

EXAMPLE 7.1

Printers Limited has share capital made up of ordinary shares of £1 each and preference shares of 50 pence each. Printers can issue any number of shares it wishes. However, companies only issue shares as and when they need to raise funds rather than raising all the cash they can from shareholders immediately.

In Example 7.1, the ordinary shares have a par value of £1. The par value is the face value or nominal value of each share. Par values can be of any amount. As well as the ordinary shares with a par value of £1 each, Printers also has preference shares with a par value of 50 pence each. However, par values could be 1 pence or 12½ pence or 25 pence or any other amount that the founders of the company decide as indicated in Give me an example 7.4. The par value of a company's shares is stated in the Memorandum and Articles of Association.

7

At the start of a limited company's life, shares are issued at their par value. Thus, Printers' directors might decide to raise £20,000 on its first day to provide the company with sufficient capital to start operating. The directors decide to issue just ordinary shares. The ordinary shares have a par value of £1, so 20,000 £1 shares will need to be issued to raise the £20,000 required. Investors are said to subscribe for their shares and they pay cash to make this investment. After the share issue, the company will now have £20,000 cash in the bank and £20,000 in issued share capital. The double entry to record this issue of share capital will be debit cash £20,000 (increase the cash asset), credit ordinary share capital (increase the amount owed to the shareholders).

GIVE ME AN EXAMPLE 7.4   The par value of shares

As an example of par values of share capital, Balfour Beatty plc has ordinary shares with a par value of 50 pence each and preference shares with a par value of 1 penny each.

Source: *Balfour Beatty annual report and accounts 2017* www.balfourbeatty.com

---

MULTIPLE CHOICE QUESTIONS   Are you confident that you can calculate the sums raised from a share issue? Go to the **online workbook** and have a go at Multiple choice questions 7.1 to make sure you can calculate these amounts.

Share capital: shares issued at a premium

As companies grow, their shares increase in value. Therefore, when companies want to issue shares at a later stage of their lives, these new shares are issued at par value plus a premium to reflect this increase in value. Example 7.2 presents details of the issue of shares at a premium.

EXAMPLE 7.2

Printers' directors decide to issue a further 30,000 £1 ordinary shares after one year of trading, but they now set the issue price for these additional shares at £1.25. The issue price for each share is made up of the £1 par value and a 25 pence premium. How much cash will be raised and how will this be recorded in Printers' financial statements?

The cash raised is calculated by multiplying the 30,000 shares by the £1.25 issue price for each share. This gives total cash raised of 30,000 × £1.25 = £37,500. This £37,500 comprises £30,000 of ordinary share capital (the par value of £1 × 30,000 shares) and a share premium of £7,500 (30,000 shares issued × 25 pence). The £30,000 is credited to share capital and the £7,500 is credited to the share premium account in the statement of financial position with the whole £37,500 raised being debited to cash in the bank.

Example 7.2 tells us that the share premium is any amount raised from an issue of shares over and above the par value of the shares issued. Give me an example 7.5 presents an example of an issue of shares at a premium.

GIVE ME AN EXAMPLE 7.5   Shares issued at a premium to the par value

As an example of shares issued at a premium, note 21 in the Thrive Renewables 2015 annual report presents the following information: 'In February 2015, the company issued 724,921 new shares of £0.50 each at a premium of £1.78 each, raising new capital of £1.65 million, and in April 2015 the company issued 275,000 new shares of £0.50 each at a premium of £1.78 each, raising new capital of £627,000.'

Source: *Thrive Renewables annual report 2015* www. thriverenewables.co.uk

WHY IS THIS RELEVANT TO ME?   Share issues at par value and share issues at a premium

To enable you as an accounting professional to understand:

• How limited companies raise cash from share issues

• The financial effect of issuing shares at a premium

• The double entry required to record the cash raised through the issue of share capital in the accounting records

MULTIPLE CHOICE QUESTIONS   Could you calculate the sums raised from a share issue when shares are issued at a premium? Go to the **online workbook** and have a go at Multiple choice questions 7.2 to see if you can make these calculations correctly.

SUMMARY OF KEY CONCEPTS   Can you define share premium? Go to the **online workbook** to revise this definition with Summary of key concepts 7.8.

Share capital: bonus issues

As well as issuing shares for cash, limited companies also make what are called bonus issues of shares. Bonus issues are made when a company has a large surplus on its retained earnings on the statement of financial position. These retained earnings have not yet been distributed to shareholders as dividends and the company wants to keep these earnings within the business as share capital. This process is known as capitalising reserves, turning distributable retained earnings into new non-distributable share capital. No cash is raised in a bonus issue, but the number of shares in issue increases while the retained earnings reduce by a corresponding amount. Bonus issues are only made to existing ordinary shareholders and the amount capitalised as share capital is the par value of the shares issued.

A bonus issue is always expressed as a certain number of bonus shares for a certain number of shares already held by ordinary shareholders. Thus, a one-for-four bonus issue means that one new bonus share is issued to ordinary shareholders for every four shares they already hold. A two-for-five bonus issue means that two bonus shares are issued for every five shares currently held. Let's see how a bonus issue works with Example 7.3.

EXAMPLE 7.3

James plc currently has 12 million ordinary shares of £1 each in issue. The balance on retained earnings is currently £25 million. The directors propose a four-for-three bonus issue.

In this example, four bonus shares are issued for every three shares currently held. This means that 12m × 4 new shares ÷ 3 shares currently in issue = 16m new shares of £1 each are issued to ordinary shareholders. This transaction would be presented as shown in Illustration 7.1: £16 million is added (credited) to ordinary share capital and £16 million is deducted (debited) from retained earnings.

Illustration 7.1 James plc: bonus issue of four £1 shares for every three £1 shares already held by ordinary shareholders

	Before bonus issue	Debit £	Credit £	After bonus issue
Equity (credit balances)	£			£
Ordinary share capital	12,000,000		16,000,000	28,000,000
Retained earnings	25,000,000	16,000,000		9,000,000
	37,000,000			37,000,000

James plc now has 28 million ordinary £1 shares in issue compared to the original 12 million before the bonus issue. These newly issued bonus shares will receive dividends in the future just as the ordinary shares currently do. Issuing bonus shares is a good way of increasing the number of shares in issue and strengthening the fixed capital base of a company. Once the bonus shares have been issued the retained earnings balance falls and this limits the retained earnings that can be paid out in future as dividends.

Share capital: rights issues

From time to time, limited companies make new issues of shares to raise funds. However, companies cannot just issue new shares to anyone they want. The Companies Act 2006 prevents companies from issuing new shares to outside parties until those new shares have first been offered to current shareholders. Only when existing shareholders have turned down the opportunity to buy these new shares can the shares be offered to investors who are not currently shareholders of the company. These rights to subscribe for new issues of shares are known as pre-emption rights, the right to be offered first refusal on any new issue of shares.

Why does the Companies Act 2006 protect shareholders' rights in this way? Pre-emption rights prevent the dilution of existing shareholders' interests in a company. What this means and how pre-emption rights protect existing shareholders are illustrated in Example 7.4.

EXAMPLE 7.4

Joe and Bill each hold 50,000 ordinary shares in Painters Limited. Painters Limited has a total of 100,000 ordinary shares in issue, so Joe and Bill each own a 50 per cent interest in the company. The directors decide that Painters needs to issue another 100,000 shares. If the directors were able to offer the shares to external investors, then Joe's and Bill's interest in Painters would fall to 25 per cent each (50,000 shares ÷ (100,000 shares currently in issue + 100,000 new shares being issued)). They would thus suffer a 50 per cent reduction in their interest in the company as a result of new shareholders being brought in. Whereas before they each controlled 50 per cent of Painters, they now control only 25 per cent each as a result of this new issue of shares to new investors. The Companies Act 2006 thus requires the directors to offer the new shares to Joe and Bill first so that they can take up the new shares in proportion to their current holdings and each maintain their 50 per cent holding in the company. Only when Joe and Bill have declined the right to buy these new shares can the shares be offered to outside parties.

Rights issues: pricing

Rights issues are priced at a discount to the current market price to encourage shareholders to take up the issue. An example of a rights issue and how rights issues work is presented in Example 7.5.

EXAMPLE 7.5

If the current market value of one James plc £1 ordinary share is £3, then the directors will price the rights issue at, for example, £2.20 to encourage shareholders to take up their rights. £2.20 is an 80 pence discount to the current market price (£3.00 − £2.20). The number of shares will rise when the rights issue is complete. As you will know from studying economics, when supply increases, price goes down. Since there will be more James plc shares in issue after the rights issue the market price will fall. The discount to the current market price of the ordinary shares thus compensates James plc's shareholders for this anticipated fall in the market value of their shares.

Do note that the pricing of a rights issue at a discount to the market price is not the same as issuing shares at a discount. Issuing shares at a discount is illegal under the Companies Act 2006 and would involve, for example, selling shares with a par value of £1 for 99 pence or less. This is not allowed under company law.

How does a rights issue work? James plc's directors decide to make a rights issue of £1 ordinary shares, one for every four currently held. There are 28 million shares in issue after the bonus issue and the rights issue price is set at £2.20.

Your first task is to determine how many new shares will be issued. One new ordinary share is being issued for every four in issue, so this will give us 28,000,000 ÷ 4 = 7,000,000 new ordinary shares to issue.

How much money will this raise? Each share is being issued at £2.20, so an issue of seven million shares will raise 7,000,000 × £2.20 = £15,400,000.

You know from our earlier discussions (this chapter, Share capital: shares issued at a premium) that, with the par value of the shares being £1, there is a share premium to account for as well as the new addition to share capital. How much is this premium? Issuing £1 par value shares at £2.20 means that the premium on each share issued is £2.20 − £1.00 = £1.20. The total premium on the issue of seven million shares is then 7,000,000 × £1.20 = £8,400,000. Cash is thus debited with the £15,400,000 raised from the rights issue, ordinary share capital is credited with £7,000,000 and the share premium account is credited with £8,400,000. Give me an example 7.6 presents details of a rights issue recently undertaken by a listed company, Laird plc.

GIVE ME AN EXAMPLE 7.6   Rights issues of shares

On 28 February 2017, Laird plc, the electronics and technology group, announced a four-for-five rights issue of 217 million new shares at 85 pence per share. The company's shares were trading at 174.75 pence on the day before the rights issue was announced. The par value of each ordinary share is 28.125 pence, so the rights issue price of 85 pence per share was a large discount to the current market price but not a discount to the par value of the shares. The directors stated that the net proceeds from the rights issue of £175m would be used to reduce borrowings with the aim of strengthening the group's financial position and allowing continued investment in an operational improvement programme and in opportunities for growth in the future. Following the extraordinary general meeting on 16 March 2017 to approve the terms of the rights issue, the share price of Laird plc fell from 176.00 pence on 16 March to 142.50 pence on 17 March as the increase in the number of shares in issue resulted in a reduction in the share price.

Sources: http://www.laird-plc.com, http://www.google.co.uk/finance

---

WHY IS THIS RELEVANT TO ME?   Bonus and rights issues

To enable you as an accounting professional to understand:

- How bonus and rights issues work
- The financial effect of bonus and rights issues
- The double entry required to record share capital issued under bonus and rights issues in the accounting records

---

MULTIPLE CHOICE QUESTIONS   Are you convinced that you understand how bonus and rights issues work? Go to the **online workbook** and have a go at Multiple choice questions 7.3 to make sure you can calculate the entries to make to the relevant accounts for bonus and rights issues.

DIVIDENDS

We have already discussed the subject of dividends. It is now time to see how dividends for the year are calculated.

Dividends are distributions of profit to shareholders. They are not an expense of the distributing company in the way that wages, rent or electricity are expenses (Chapter 3, Expenses). Dividends are deducted directly from retained earnings in the statement of financial position and do not appear in the statement of profit or loss. The double entry to record a payment of a dividend is: debit retained earnings (retained earnings are reduced by the distribution to shareholders), credit the bank account (the cash asset is reduced by the payment out of the bank).

When a company decides to pay a dividend to the shareholders, a figure of pence per share is quoted. Dividends are always paid on the number of shares in issue. How does a dividend distribution work? Let's look at how the total dividend distribution is calculated through two examples, Example 7.6 and Example 7.7.

EXAMPLE 7.6

James plc declares a dividend of 12 pence per ordinary share. How much dividend will be paid out? There are 35 million shares in issue after the rights issue (Example 7.5). This means that holders of the 35 million £1 ordinary shares will receive 12 pence for each share that they hold. The total dividend payment will thus be 35,000,000 × £0.12 = £4,200,000. When this dividend is paid, cash at the bank will fall by £4,200,000 (credit the bank account) and retained earnings will be reduced by £4,200,000 (debit retained earnings).

EXAMPLE 7.7

When calculating preference dividends, the par value of the preference shares is simply multiplied by the dividend rate. Remember that preference dividends are paid at a fixed rate and preference shareholders receive nothing more than their contractually agreed preference dividend. James plc also has 10,000,000, 50 pence, 5 per cent preference shares in issue. This tells us that every 50 pence preference share receives a dividend of 2.5 pence (£0.50 × 5 per cent). The total preference dividend for the year will thus be £250,000 (10,000,000 shares × £0.025).

Public limited companies paying dividends usually make two distributions in each financial year. These are known as the interim dividend, paid part way through the financial year, and a final dividend based on the profits for the financial year.

DISTRIBUTABLE AND NON-DISTRIBUTABLE RESERVES

Dividends are paid from distributable reserves only. Ordinary share capital, preference share capital, share premium and revaluation reserves are all capital reserves and the funds in these capital reserves are not distributable to shareholders. To make a dividend distribution from any of these reserves would be illegal under the Companies Act 2006.

For our purposes, the only distributable reserve, the one that represents realised profits of the company, is retained earnings. Retained earnings are a revenue reserve and it is this reserve from which dividends can be paid. However, if a company has retained losses and a negative balance on retained earnings, no dividends, either ordinary or preference, can be paid. Only when a company has a positive balance showing that the company has made profits can a distribution be made from the retained earnings reserve.

WHY IS THIS RELEVANT TO ME?   Dividends

To enable you as an accounting professional to:

- Understand how dividends are calculated
- Distinguish between capital reserves and revenue reserves

MULTIPLE CHOICE QUESTIONS   Are you confident that you could calculate dividends correctly? Go to the **online workbook** and have a go at Multiple choice questions 7.4 to make sure you can calculate dividend distributions accurately.

CHAPTER SUMMARY

You should now have learnt that:

- Very small businesses organise themselves as sole traders or partnerships that take on unlimited liability for the debts of their businesses

- Larger businesses organise themselves as limited liability companies whose investors (shareholders) have no obligation to meet the debts of their company beyond their investment in their company's share capital

- Sole traders and partnerships raise money to finance their operations from their own capital resources, from the profits of their businesses, from bank loans and from bank overdrafts

- Limited liability companies raise money to finance their operations from the issue of ordinary and preference share capital and by borrowing from banks in the form of loans or overdrafts and by issuing bonds, loan notes and debentures

- The par value of a share is the face value or nominal value of that share

- A bonus issue involves the reduction of retained earnings and an increase in the issued share capital

- A rights issue is the issue of shares to shareholders at a discount to the current market price

- Dividends can only be distributed from retained earnings

QUICK REVISION   Test your knowledge with the online flashcards in Summary of key concepts and attempt the Multiple choice questions, all in the **online workbook**.

END-OF-CHAPTER QUESTIONS

Solutions to these questions can be found in the **online workbook**.

❯ DEVELOP YOUR UNDERSTANDING

❯Question 7.1

Which business format would be most suitable for the following businesses? Can you say why your chosen format would be most suited to each business?

- An oil exploration company
- A taxi driver
- A family run knitwear manufacturing business
- Two friends setting up a dance school

❯Question 7.2

An investor has £200,000 to invest and has to choose between three different investments:

- An investment in a £200,000 bond paying 5 per cent interest per annum
- An investment in a new issue of preference shares with a par value issue price of 50 pence paying an annual dividend of 3 pence per share
- An investment in a new issue of ordinary shares with a par value issue price of 25 pence paying an annual dividend of 2 pence per share.

How much will each investment return to the investor? Which investment would be preferable on the assumption that the investor wishes to maximise income from investing the £200,000?

❯Question 7.3

A printing company wishes to raise £3,000,000 to finance its expansion. It can do this in one of three ways: borrowing from the bank at an annual interest rate of 5 per cent, by issuing ordinary shares at their par value of 40 pence, which will require an annual dividend payment of 1.9 pence per share, or by issuing preference shares with a par value of 60 pence, which requires a fixed dividend of 3.15 pence per share. Which financing option will require the lowest cash outlay for the printing company?

❯❯ TAKE IT FURTHER

❯❯Question 7.4

Plants Limited runs a garden centre business selling garden plants and products to the public from its busy edge of town site. In the year to 31 October 2019, Plants Limited's issued share capital consists of 100,000 ordinary shares of 50 pence each and 100,000 preference shares of £1 each. The preference share dividend rate is 6 per cent. Preference dividends are payable on 31 October each year. An interim dividend of 10 pence per share was paid on the ordinary share capital on 15 May 2019 and the directors paid a final ordinary dividend of 20 pence per ordinary share on 15 October 2019.

Required

(a) Calculate the preference dividend that Plants Limited will pay for the year ended 31 October 2019.

(b) Calculate the total ordinary dividend for the year ended 31 October 2019.

(c) If retained earnings at 1 November 2018 were £45,000 and profit for the year to 31 October 2019 was £50,000, what is the balance on retained earnings after all the dividends for the year have been paid at 31 October 2019?

›› Question 7.5

Plants Limited is looking to expand its operations in the year to 31 October 2020, but needs to raise additional finance to do so. The company proposes raising £500,000 by the issue of 200,000 ordinary shares on 1 May 2020. Profits for the year to 31 October 2020 are expected to be £90,000. An interim ordinary dividend of 15 pence per share will be paid on 15 April 2020 and a final ordinary dividend of 25 pence per share will be paid on 15 October 2020.

Required

Using the information above, the information from Question 7.4 and the answer to Question 7.4:

(a) Calculate the amounts to be credited to ordinary share capital and share premium in the equity section of the statement of financial position in respect of the new issue of ordinary shares on 1 May 2020.

(b) Calculate the total dividends, both ordinary and preference, to be paid in the year to 31 October 2020.

(c) Calculate the expected balance on retained earnings at 31 October 2020 after dividends for the year have been paid.

›› Question 7.6

At 1 July 2019 Halyson plc had 500,000 ordinary shares of 25 pence each in issue together with 300,000 7½ per cent preference shares of £1 each. The balance on Halyson's retained earnings at 1 July 2019 is £5,200,000.

Halyson plc is proposing a bonus issue of seven new ordinary shares for every two ordinary shares currently held. Once this bonus issue is complete, a rights issue will be made of five new ordinary shares for every three ordinary shares held at a price of £0.95. These transactions will take place on 1 April 2020.

On 28 June 2020, Halyson plc will pay the preference dividend for the year and a total ordinary dividend for the year of 30 pence per share. The loss for the year to 30 June 2020 is expected to be £1,500,000.

Required

Calculate for Halyson plc:

(a) The number of bonus shares to be issued

(b) The par value of the bonus shares to be added to ordinary share capital

(c) The number of ordinary shares to be issued in the rights issue

(d) The amount to be credited to ordinary share capital and share premium as a result of the rights issue

(e) The preference dividend for the year to 30 June 2020

(f) The ordinary dividend for the year to 30 June 2020

(g) The balance on the ordinary share capital account at 30 June 2020

(h) The expected balance on retained earnings at 30 June 2020

7

8

RATIO ANALYSIS 1: PROFITABILITY, EFFICIENCY AND PERFORMANCE

LEARNING OUTCOMES

Once you have read this chapter and worked through the questions and examples in both this chapter and the online workbook, you should be able to:

- Understand the importance and advantages of using ratios to evaluate the profitability, efficiency, performance, liquidity and long-term financial stability of entities

- Understand how the financial statements and ratios interact in the interpretation of the profitability, efficiency, performance, liquidity and long-term financial stability of organisations

- Calculate profitability ratios for gross profit percentage, operating profit percentage, profit before tax percentage and profit after tax percentage

- Suggest economic reasons for the changes in profitability ratios year on year

- Calculate efficiency ratios for non-current asset turnover, revenue per employee and profit per employee
- Show how efficiency ratios help to explain changes in the profitability ratios
- Understand how increasing the revenue from each unit of fixed resource employed in the business will increase an entity's profits
- Calculate performance ratios for earnings per share, price/earnings ratio, dividends per share, dividend yield and dividend cover
- Explain what the performance ratios you have calculated mean from a shareholder's point of view
- Compare an entity's profitability, efficiency and performance ratios with the profitability, efficiency and performance ratios of other companies as a way of benchmarking an entity's financial outcomes

8

INTRODUCTION

In Chapters 2, 3 and 6 we looked at the three major accounting statements, how they are put together, how they integrate with each other and what they tell us individually about the profits and cash generated in each accounting period and the financial position of the entity at the end of each accounting period. However, the real skill in accounting lies not in an ability to produce these statements but in analysing and interpreting the information they contain. Such analysis and interpretation enable users to draw conclusions about how well an entity is performing and the strength of its financial position. Financial information as presented in the three major statements has to be analysed to determine the profitability of an entity, how efficiently its assets are being used, how well an organisation is performing to meet the expectations of its investors and how secure its future cash flows and financial stability are. These aspects are analysed under the headings of profitability, efficiency, performance, liquidity and long-term financial stability and we will consider each of these measures in turn in this and the next chapter.

When reading the business and financial pages, the importance of these indicators will readily become apparent as we see in Give me an example 8.1.

What these terms mean and how they are used in evaluating entities' profitability, efficiency, performance, liquidity and long-term financial stability will become clear as you work through this chapter and the next. To appreciate how common the above terms are and how relevant they continue to be in assessing companies' performance and financial position, quickly read through the Companies and Markets section in today's *Financial Times* and see how many of the above terms, among others, continue to appear.

> **GIVE ME AN EXAMPLE 8.1   A selection of terms linked to the analysis of companies' results and position**
>
> * Profitability
> * Earnings
> * Dividend cover
> * Dividend yield
> * Dividend per share
> * Earnings growth
> * Return on invested capital
> * Earnings per share
> * Profit margins
> * Revenue growth
> * Deleveraging
>
> * Operational efficiency
> * Market capitalisation
> * Free cash flow
> * Cost efficiency
> * Productivity
> * Price/earnings ratio
> * Rate of return
> * Creditworthiness
>
> Source: taken from a quick skim read of the *Financial Times* Companies and Markets section on 25 January 2017.

EVALUATING FINANCIAL STATEMENTS: RATIO ANALYSIS

How do users evaluate and assess financial statements? The technique most commonly used is ratio analysis. A ratio in its simplest form expresses the relationship between two different figures. The calculation of the same ratio over several different time periods enables comparisons to be made between those different time periods to determine whether that ratio is rising, falling or staying the same. In this way, the performance and position of entities can be evaluated by analysing the trends that emerge over time. Ratio analysis, however, is not just confined to financial information but can be applied to any sets of numbers where relationships can be established. Consider Example 8.1.

EXAMPLE 8.1

When grocery shopping you might be evaluating two different sizes of a particular product: one costs £1.50 for 100g and the other costs £4.00 for 250g: which one offers the better value? By calculating the per gram price, the ratio of cost for one unit of weight, you can determine that the 100g product costs 1.50 pence per gram, while the 250g product costs 1.60 pence per gram. Therefore, the smaller sized product offers better value. Bigger is not always cheaper!

GO BACK OVER THIS AGAIN!   Are you sure that you understand how ratios can be used to simplify the relationship between two figures to enable comparisons to be made? Go to the **online workbook** and look at Exercises 8.1 to see how ratios can be used in this way.

WHY IS RATIO ANALYSIS NEEDED?

Example 8.1 shows the value of ratios, expressing one figure in relation to another to highlight information critical to making an economic decision. However, why is ratio analysis needed in the interpretation and evaluation of financial statements? Again, a simple example will help to explain why ratios are such a useful tool in analysing financial performance and position. Consider the information presented in Example 8.2 and how this information is used to assess changes in profitability year on year.

EXAMPLE 8.2

A pottery company has sales of £110,376 in the year to 31 December 2018 and sales of £150,826 in the year to 31 December 2019. The company owners will see the year to 31 December 2019 as a great success in terms of the increase in sales achieved. Profit for the year to 31 December 2018 was £27,594 and £34,690 for the year to 31 December 2019. Again, you might say that the company has been successful in the most recent financial year as it has generated more profit than it did in the previous year. While it is true that profit has risen, the figures alone do not tell us whether the company is now more *profitable*. The figures for sales and profits have both increased, but is each sale in the year to 31 December 2019 generating as much, less or more profit as each sale in the year to 31 December 2018? A simple comparison, as shown in Table 8.1, of the profit to the sales in each year will tell us the answer to this question.

Table 8.1 Comparison of profit to sales in each year

	2019 Calculation	Ratio	2018 Calculation	Ratio
$\dfrac{\text{Profit}}{\text{Sales}} \times 100\%$	$\dfrac{£34,690}{£150,826} \times 100\%$	23%	$\dfrac{£27,594}{£110,376} \times 100\%$	25%

Calculating these two profitability ratios shows us that despite the rise in both sales and profits in 2019, each sale has generated less profit than sales in 2018. For every £1 of sales, 23 pence is profit in 2019 compared to 25 pence of profit per £1 of sales in 2018. Ratios thus provide a relative measure from which to determine simple relationships between the financial figures. Calculating the ratio for the two time periods has enabled us to highlight a variance in profitability that was not at all apparent from the raw figures as presented in the accounts.

8

GO BACK OVER THIS AGAIN!   Are you certain you could calculate ratios from a given set of data and draw valid conclusions? Go to the **online workbook** and have a go at Exercises 8.2 to check your understanding.

WHY IS THIS RELEVANT TO ME?   Why is ratio analysis needed?

As an accounting professional you will:

* Appreciate that larger numbers do not necessarily indicate greater success or an improvement in relative terms
* Understand how ratios can be used to determine changes relative to other figures
* Carry out ratio analysis on sets of financial statements in order to evaluate the profitability, performance and financial position of different entities

Now that we have this information showing reduced profitability in 2019 we can ask questions to determine why the pottery company's profitability has fallen this year. If the company had sold exactly the same goods at exactly the same prices to exactly the same customers in both years, then the profitability percentage, the pence of profit from each £1 of sales, should have been exactly the same. As the profitability percentage has fallen, financial statement users will want to know the reasons for the change and will ask questions with a view to identifying these reasons. Questions asked will focus on changes in the business and the economic climate with a view to explaining this fall. Examples of such questions (among others) might be as follows:

* Has the pottery business reduced selling prices to increase sales in an attempt to increase the company's share of the local pottery sales market?
* Has there been an increase in the price of clay used to make the pottery or has there been a rise in the potters' wages which the owner has chosen not to pass on to customers?
* Has the pottery business offered discounted prices to bulk buyers of its goods?
* Has a rival business opened in the area forcing selling prices down through increased competition?
* Is an economic recession forcing the owner to reduce prices to attract customers?

GO BACK OVER THIS AGAIN!   Are you sure that you understand how profitability would fall in the circumstances outlined in the questions above? Visit the **online workbook** Exercises 8.3 to see how profitability would fall as a result of the reasons suggested.

Ratios are thus a starting point in the interpretation and evaluation of financial information. Calculating the ratios gives us information about which relationships have changed. We can then seek out explanations for these changes to assist us in understanding the business and how it operates and then use this information in making decisions about the future prospects of the business.

8

WHY IS THIS RELEVANT TO ME?   Why is ratio analysis needed?

As an accounting professional you will:

- Calculate ratios for businesses and compare these ratios to ratios from earlier accounting periods
- Use ratios to evaluate the performance of different parts of an organisation
- Use ratios to determine aspects of a business in which improvements could be made
- Evaluate the effect of internal and external changes on a business and how these changes have affected the financial statement figures and the ratios derived from them

RATIOS, FIGURES OR BOTH?

Given that ratios are so useful in interpreting an organisation's results, should we just ignore the financial statement figures once we have calculated the ratios? While ratios are an excellent interpretative tool, it is important to realise that the interpretation of financial statements relies on both the figures presented in the statement of profit or loss, the statement of financial position and the statement of cash flows *and* the ratios derived from these figures. Just taking the figures or the ratios on their own would be insufficient to enable users to form a full understanding of what the financial statements are telling them about the profitability, performance, efficiency and liquidity of an entity. Thus, an evaluation of an entity should look at both the figures presented in the financial statements and the ratios derived from those numbers. To understand why both the figures and the ratios are used together, consider Examples 8.3 and 8.4.

EXAMPLE 8.3

An entity has a profitability percentage of 20 per cent compared to its competitor with a profitability percentage of 10 per cent. Logically, based on just this ratio, users will prefer the company with a profitability percentage of 20 per cent as this is higher. However, the entity with the 20 per cent profitability has a profit of £50,000 and sales of £250,000 while its competitor has a profit of £10,000,000 and sales of £100,000,000. Which is the preferable company now? Clearly the company with sales of £100 million and profit of £10 million will attract greater attention. This is a much larger company, probably very well established and with higher profits (if not higher profitability) from which to pay regular dividends to shareholders and with a longer, more stable and more firmly grounded trading record. Hence it is vital to look at the financial statement figures as well as the ratios when evaluating an organisation's financial performance and position.

EXAMPLE 8.4

A profit of £1 million sounds impressive. However, the £1 million figure has no context. If the profit of £1 million was generated from sales of £10 million, this would give a profitability percentage of 10 per cent (£1m/£10m × 100 per cent). Yet if the £1 million profit was generated from sales of £100 million this would give a profitability percentage of just 1 per cent (£1m/£100m × 100 per cent). Profitability of 10 per cent is definitely preferable to 1 per cent profitability. Hence, it is vital to look at the ratios as well as the financial statement figures when evaluating an organisation's financial performance and position.

Even more useful would be information comparing the profitability percentage achieved in prior years: if the entity generating 10 per cent profitability this year had achieved 20 per cent profitability in each of the previous five years, the 10 per cent profitability in the current year would be seen as a very poor performance, but might be understandable if those profits had been generated during a period of contraction in the economy. However, if the profitability percentage in the previous five years had been 5 per cent, then doubling the profitability percentage to 10 per cent would be seen as a very worthwhile achievement indeed.

WHY IS THIS RELEVANT TO ME?   Ratios, figures or both?

As an accounting professional you will appreciate:

- That the figures and the ratios based on them are both equally valuable in analysing and interpreting financial statements

- The interlinking nature of both ratios and figures in the analysis and interpretation of financial results

- The different perspectives that both ratios and financial statement figures bring to the analysis and interpretation of financial results

---

GO BACK OVER THIS AGAIN!   Do you understand how ratios and financial statement figures interact? Go to the **online workbook** and have a go at Exercises 8.4 to check your understanding.

THE ADVANTAGES OF RATIOS: SUMMARY

The preceding pages have presented a lot of arguments and ideas, so let's just pause for a moment to summarise how ratios and ratio analysis are advantageous in the evaluation of financial statements:

- Ratios are easy to calculate and to understand.

- Ratios highlight trends and variances by simplifying data into key indicators.

- Ratios help to express relationships between different figures in the financial statements.

- Calculating ratios across different time periods helps us to build up a picture of the trend in a particular indicator.

- Because ratios are a proportion calculated on a consistent basis across different time periods, this helps to overcome the problem of figures changing from year to year.

- Ratios, of course, are not the final answer: changes in ratios over different accounting periods will just indicate that we need to investigate why those ratios have changed and to rationalise the changes by reference to different economic conditions prevailing in each accounting period, different product mixes or the strategy the organisation is pursuing in relation to its goals.

• Ratios are thus not an end in themselves; they are an indicator of change or movement that prompts further questions and further action to correct unfavourable movements or to take further actions to maintain the positive trend.

REFER BACK   To illustrate the ratios discussed below and in the next chapter we will use the statement of financial position, statement of profit or loss and statement of cash flows for Bunns the Bakers presented in Chapters 2, 3 and 6. You should refer to Illustrations 2.1, 3.1 and 6.1 in these chapters or refer to the copies available in the **online workbook** as you work through the rest of this chapter and the next.

PROFITABILITY RATIOS

Now that we have considered the role of ratios in conjunction with the financial statement figures, it is time to look at the specific ratios used in analysing organisations' profitability. While we have already looked at a simple example of a profitability ratio earlier in this chapter (Example 8.2), we will now think about profitability ratios in much more depth and detail and consider the ratios presented in Figure 8.1.

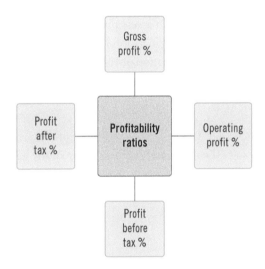

Figure 8.1 Profitability ratios

As we noted in Chapter 3 (Chapter 3, Introduction), profit is one of the most discussed numbers in any set of financial statements. However, to put profit into context, we have to know whether profits are higher or lower and how these profits compare with results from previous accounting periods. In money terms: is the profit of an organisation rising or falling? In relative terms: is the entity making more or less profit per pound of sales than in previous years? Profitability ratios compare the various profit figures shown in the statement of profit or loss to the revenue for the year in order to make this assessment.

Bunns the Bakers' statement of profit or loss (Illustration 8.1) shows the revenue and profit figures for the years ended 31 March 2019 and 31 March 2018.

Illustration 8.1 Bunns the Bakers: revenue and profit figures for the years ended 31 March 2019 and 31 March 2018

	2019	2018
	£000	£000
Revenue	10,078	9,575
Gross profit	5,543	4,979
Operating profit	895	767
Profit before tax	760	614
Profit for the year	547	442

Following the principle discussed earlier that we must consider ratios and the absolute figures together, we should first highlight the trends in the revenue and profits in Illustration 8.1 before we calculate any ratios. All the figures given for the revenue and the different profits for 2019 are higher than the revenue and profits in 2018. This looks good: in money terms, revenue and profits are rising. However, as we have already noted, these raw figures only tell us that Bunns the Bakers has made more profit on the back of higher revenue in the current year, but do not tell us whether the company is more *profitable*. To assess profitability, we need to compare the various profit figures to the sales made by the organisation to see whether more or less profit is being generated per £ of sales through the calculation of various ratios.

Gross profit percentage

As we saw in Chapter 3 (Chapter 3, Different categories of profit), gross profit is the profit left over after deducting from sales the direct costs of production of the goods sold or, in Julia's case, after deducting the costs of buying in goods for resale. This ratio is very useful when assessing how effectively the organisation is controlling its costs of production or costs of buying in goods for resale. This ratio is calculated as follows:

$$\text{Gross profit \%} = \frac{\text{Gross profit}}{\text{Revenue}} \times 100\%$$

Looking at Illustration 8.1, the company has made a gross profit in the year to 31 March 2019 of £5,543,000 from revenue of £10,078,000. This gives the organisation a gross profit percentage for 2019 of:

$$\frac{£5,543,000}{£10,078,000} \times 100\% = 55.00\%$$

Conventionally, ratios are calculated to two decimal places.

Have Bunns the Bakers achieved a higher ratio in 2019 compared with 2018? Let's calculate the gross profit ratio for 2018 to see whether 2019's gross profit percentage is higher or lower than 2018's. Gross profit in the statement of profit or loss (Illustration 8.1) for the year ended

31 March 2018 is £4,979,000 from revenue of £9,575,000, so this gives a gross profit percentage for 2018 of:

$$\frac{£4,979,000}{£9,575,000} \times 100\% = 52.00\%$$

> **WHY IS THIS RELEVANT TO ME?**   Gross profit percentage
>
> As an accounting professional you will:
> - Find information relevant to the gross profit percentage calculation in the financial statements
> - Know and apply the gross profit percentage calculation
> - Calculate your own gross profit percentage figures from any given statement of profit or loss

> **MULTIPLE CHOICE QUESTIONS**   Are you confident that you can calculate a gross profit percentage from a given set of financial information? Go to the **online workbook** and have a go at Multiple choice questions 8.1 to test out your ability to calculate this ratio.

Interpretation of the results

The increase in gross profit percentage is encouraging. Bunns the Bakers are making 55 pence of gross profit from each £1 of sales in 2019 compared to a gross profit of 52 pence from each £1 of sales in 2018. However, as we noted earlier, just calculating the ratios is not enough: in your role as an accounting professional, you will be expected to investigate in order to determine the reasons why ratios have changed when compared with the previous year. The way to do this is to consider and enquire into possible reasons for the changes or to rationalise these changes by reference to the economic factors affecting the organisation both locally and nationally.

Why might Bunns the Bakers be generating a higher gross profit percentage in the current year compared to the previous year? It is important to explain this change as it might be expected that each sale less the cost of sales will generate the same gross profit percentage every time.

There are two aspects to the gross profit of an organisation, the revenue and the cost of sales, so either or both of these figures might have been subject to certain changes to give a higher gross profit percentage. Therefore, possible reasons for the increase in 2019 might be as follows:

- An increase in selling prices that is higher than the rise in costs incurred in producing or buying in the goods for sale.
- A change in the types of sales made from lower profitability products such as bread to higher profitability goods such as pies, pastries and ready-made sandwiches.
- A fall in the price of input materials thereby lowering the cost of sales while maintaining selling prices at the same level.

- An increase in the productivity of the workforce, producing more goods per hour or selling more goods per shop than in the previous year.
- The company might have benefited from bulk discounts from suppliers: when goods are ordered in larger quantities, suppliers often give their customers a discount for placing larger orders. Bulk discounts received reduce the cost of raw materials in the production process thereby lowering the cost of sales and increasing the gross profit.

These are just some of the possible reasons for the change in the gross profit percentage and you can probably think of other perfectly valid reasons to explain this improvement. As an accounting professional you will be expected to calculate the ratios and then think about and offer reasons why ratios are changing in order to understand and explain the economic trends underlying the movements in these figures.

WHY IS THIS RELEVANT TO ME?   Interpretation of the results

As an accounting professional you should appreciate that:

- You will be expected to think about changes in ratios and present reasons why those ratios are changing
- Senior managers and other users of accounting information will want to know why the gross profit percentage is changing: they will not just accept the changes without any explanation
- Business leaders and other users of accounting information do not have to be told that ratios are changing, they want to know *why* they are changing so that action can be taken to extend favourable or to correct unfavourable movements

---

GO BACK OVER THIS AGAIN!   How certain are you that you could determine the causes of rises and falls in the gross profit percentage? Go to the **online workbook** and have a go at Exercises 8.5 to make sure you can distinguish between factors that will cause the gross profit percentage to rise and factors that will cause it to fall.

MULTIPLE CHOICE QUESTIONS   Are you confident that you could determine factors affecting the gross profit percentage? Go to the **online workbook** and have a go at Multiple choice questions 8.2 to test out your ability to determine these factors.

Other profitability ratios

As well as the gross profit figure, Illustration 8.1 gives statement of profit or loss figures for operating profit, profit before tax and profit for the year (= profit after tax). Profitability ratios can be calculated for these figures as shown in Table 8.2.

Using the figures for revenue and for profits in Illustration 8.1, we can calculate the other profitability percentages for Bunns the Bakers for the two years ending 31 March 2019 and 31 March 2018. These figures are shown in Table 8.3.

Table 8.2 Profitability ratios for operating profit, profit before tax and profit for the year

Ratio	Calculation	What does this ratio tell us?
Operating profit %	$\dfrac{\text{Operating profit}}{\text{Revenue}} \times 100\%$	Determines profitability on the basis of revenue less all operating costs, before taking into account the effects of finance income, finance expense and taxation
Profit before tax %	$\dfrac{\text{Profit before tax}}{\text{Revenue}} \times 100\%$	Bases the profitability calculation on profit before taxation to eliminate the distorting effect of changes in tax rates. The profit before tax percentage is the profitability of the entity after deducting all costs incurred and taking into account income earned from all sources, both trading and investment
Profit after tax %	$\dfrac{\text{Profit for the year}}{\text{Revenue}} \times 100\%$	Calculates profitability for the period after adding all income and deducting all expenses and charges for the period under review

8

Table 8.3 Other profitability percentages for Bunns the Bakers for the two years ending 31 March 2019 and 31 March 2018

	2019 Calculation	Ratio	2018 Calculation	Ratio
Operating profit %	$\dfrac{\pounds895,000}{\pounds10,078,000} \times 100\%$	8.88%	$\dfrac{\pounds767,000}{\pounds9,575,000} \times 100\%$	8.01%
Profit before tax %	$\dfrac{\pounds760,000}{\pounds10,078,000} \times 100\%$	7.54%	$\dfrac{\pounds614,000}{\pounds9,575,000} \times 100\%$	6.41%
Profit after tax %	$\dfrac{\pounds547,000}{\pounds10,078,000} \times 100\%$	5.43%	$\dfrac{\pounds442,000}{\pounds9,575,000} \times 100\%$	4.62%

These profitability ratios have risen, too, so it is quite clear that Bunns the Bakers is more profitable in 2019 than it was in 2018 as shown in Figure 8.2. The rise in gross profit is part of the explanation for the increase in the above ratios. There is now more gross profit from which to pay all the other operating and finance expenses and still leave a larger profit for the year. Cost control will also be a factor and we can investigate which costs are lower or higher than in the previous year and determine how these rises and falls have affected profits and profitability in the current year. However, we can also investigate the efficiency with which assets are being used within the business. The greater the efficiency and productivity of these assets, the higher the revenue and profits will be.

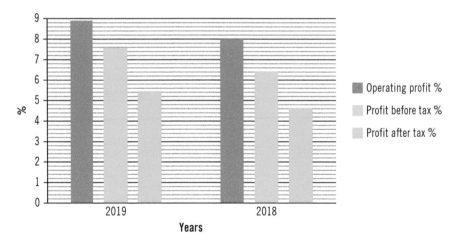

Figure 8.2 Bunns the Bakers' operating profit, profit before tax and profit after tax percentages

WHY IS THIS RELEVANT TO ME?   Profitability ratios

As an accounting professional you will:

- Understand how ratios relevant to assessing profitability are calculated
- Calculate those profitability ratios yourself
- Use the calculated profitability ratios as a foundation on which to build explanations for changes in the ratios in comparison to previous years

MULTIPLE CHOICE QUESTIONS   Think that you can calculate operating profit, profit before tax and profit after tax percentages? Go to the **online workbook** and have a go at Multiple choice questions 8.3 to test your ability to calculate these ratios.

SUMMARY OF KEY CONCEPTS   How well have you grasped the formulae for gross profit percentage, operating profit percentage, profit before tax percentage and profit after tax percentage? Go to the **online workbook** to take a look at Summary of key concepts 8.1–8.4 to reinforce your understanding.

EFFICIENCY RATIOS

Efficiency ratios consider how effectively and productively the resources of the organisation are being used to create both revenue and profit. An organisation's resources fall into two categories. First, non-current assets used in the production and sale of goods and services and, second, the employees engaged within the business as illustrated in Figure 8.3. Various ratios can be calculated to demonstrate how efficiently these resources are being used within an organisation and these ratios should also help to explain the improved profitability of Bunns the Bakers in the year to 31 March 2019.

Non-current asset turnover

This ratio compares the sales achieved by an organisation with the non-current assets in use in that organisation to determine how many £s of sales are produced by each £ of non-current

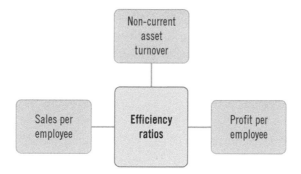

Figure 8.3 Efficiency ratios

assets. Ideally, this ratio will rise over time as non-current assets are used more efficiently to generate increased revenue.

This ratio is calculated as follows:

$$\text{Non-current asset turnover} = \frac{\text{Revenue}}{\text{Non-current assets}}$$

We have already seen that Bunns the Bakers has revenue of £10,078,000 for the year ended 31 March 2019 and revenue of £9,575,000 for the previous financial year. From the statement of financial position in Illustration 2.1, total non-current assets at 31 March 2019 and 31 March 2018 are £11,865,000 and £11,355,000 respectively. This gives the following figures for non-current asset turnover:

$$2019: \text{Non-current asset turnover:} \frac{£10,078,000}{£11,865,000} = £0.85$$

$$2018: \text{Non-current asset turnover:} \frac{£9,575,000}{£11,355,000} = £0.84$$

The figures show a slight improvement over the year. In 2018 each £1 of non-current assets generated revenue of 84 pence and in 2019 this has improved to 85 pence. Our conclusion from this ratio would be that non-current assets are being used more efficiently to generate revenue for the business as more revenue is being produced per £ of non-current assets.

However, a word of caution is needed at this point. As we saw in Chapter 2 (How are assets and liabilities valued?), users have to be careful when using information on assets employed within an organisation. The carrying amount at which assets are recorded in the statement of financial position may be increased by restating these assets to current values. Conversely, this amount may be too low because assets bought many years ago are still being used within the business. When such assets are still recorded at their original cost less any depreciation charged, these figures will now be seriously out of date and produce much less meaningful comparisons.

Similarly, when an organisation leases assets, a situation common in the retail industry as shops are often rented from landlords, these leased assets do not currently appear on the statement of financial position at all as the organisation does not control them. Therefore, retailers' non-current assets might be misleadingly low on account of the absence of these leased assets from their statements of financial position (this situation will change for financial statements for accounting periods commencing on or after 1 January 2019 due to the introduction of IFRS16

Leases, as you will learn in your later studies). Despite the potential shortcomings in this ratio, the non-current asset turnover figure does present users with relevant information on how effectively the organisation is using its long-term assets to generate revenue.

> **MULTIPLE CHOICE QUESTIONS**   Are you sure that you can calculate non-current asset turnover ratios? Go to the **online workbook** and have a go at Multiple choice questions 8.4 to test your ability to calculate this ratio.

Revenue and profit per employee

Unlike non-current assets, employees are not recognised in financial statements due to the very high level of measurement uncertainty associated with their valuation (Chapter 2, Assets). However, employees are a vital part of every organisation and how they perform during their working hours will determine how successful and how profitable organisations are. Increased productivity on the part of employees, generating more output or selling more goods during the hours worked each week, will have a significant impact upon both revenue and profitability. Employees are usually paid a fixed weekly wage, so the more they produce for that fixed weekly wage, the more profit entities will make. As an example of this, think about Bunns the Bakers' shop employees. They will be paid the same amount each week for selling 10 sandwiches or 400 sandwiches, but the latter sales figure will lead to much higher profits in each shop. Increasing sales while keeping input costs the same inevitably leads to higher profits. This principle holds where any cost is fixed: the more production or the more sales that can be generated from this fixed cost, the more profitable organisations will be.

> **NUMERICAL EXERCISES**   Are you convinced you understand how increasing output while keeping input costs the same can lead to higher profits? Visit the **online workbook** Numerical exercises 8.1 to reinforce your understanding of how this is true.

If employees are not given a monetary value within financial statements, how can we assess whether they have been more or less productive during each accounting period? In many jurisdictions, organisations must disclose the average number of employees during each financial reporting period in the annual report and financial statements. You may have to search for this information in the notes to the financial statements, but it will be there and you will be able to use this information to make meaningful comparisons of the revenue and profit per employee across different years. The higher the revenue and profit per employee, the more efficiently organisations are working to generate returns to satisfy the business's objectives of profit and revenue growth. Where these ratios are falling, management can look into the reasons for declining revenue and profit per employee. Are operations overstaffed and is there scope to reduce employee numbers to improve the efficiency, productivity and profitability of operations?

These measures of employee efficiency are calculated as follows. While operating profit per employee is calculated, you could just as easily calculate per employee figures for gross profit, profit before tax or profit after tax (= profit for the year). Whichever measure you use, you must be consistent in your calculation of the ratio so that you are comparing like with like across different accounting periods. Similarly, the measure calculated below is based on all employees, but the ratios could be calculated using just production employees or production plus retail employees or any other combination of employee numbers deemed suitable, provided that the calculation continues to be consistently applied.

$$\text{Revenue per employee} = \frac{\text{Total revenue}}{\text{Total number of employees}}$$

$$\text{Profit per employee} = \frac{\text{Operating profit}}{\text{Total number of employees}}$$

From the notes to Bunns the Bakers' accounts, it can be determined that the average number of employees in the year to 31 March 2019 was 120 and 112 in the year to 31 March 2018. Using these figures and the figures for revenue and operating profit in Illustration 8.1, the following efficiency ratios can be calculated:

$$\text{2019: Revenue per employee} = \frac{£10,078,000}{120} = £83,983$$

$$\text{2018: Revenue per employee} = \frac{£9,575,000}{112} = £85,491$$

$$\text{2019: Operating profit per employee} = \frac{£895,000}{120} = £7,458$$

$$\text{2018: Operating profit per employee} = \frac{£767,000}{112} = £6,848$$

While revenue per employee has fallen in 2019, operating profit per employee has risen by £610, a rise of 8.91 per cent (($£7,458 – £6,848$)/$£6,848 \times 100$ per cent). This increase suggests that costs have been well controlled this year and that the company's employees are working effectively to generate increased profit for the business. This increase in profit per employee might also go some way to explaining the increased profitability noted earlier in this chapter: more profit has been generated per unit of resource employed, possibly due to higher productivity, and, as a result, a higher profit and higher profitability percentages have been produced.

WHY IS THIS RELEVANT TO ME?   Efficiency ratios

To enable you as an accounting professional to:

• Understand ratios that are relevant to determining the effectiveness of asset utilisation

• Calculate and apply these ratios yourself

• Appreciate that the more revenue and profit that can be generated from a fixed cost resource, the more profitable and successful an organisation will be

MULTIPLE CHOICE QUESTIONS   Do you reckon you can calculate revenue and profit per employee ratios? Go to the **online workbook** and have a go at Multiple choice questions 8.5 to test your ability to calculate these ratios.

SUMMARY OF KEY CONCEPTS   Are you quite certain you can remember the formulae for non-current asset turnover, revenue per employee and profit per employee? Go to the **online workbook** to take a look at Summary of key concepts 8.5–8.7 to reinforce your understanding.

Sales and profit per unit of input resource

One further aspect of efficiency merits our attention at this point. It is common practice in the retail sector to measure sales and profits per square metre or square foot of selling space (where shops differ greatly in size from superstores down to small high street outlets) or per shop (where shop size does not vary significantly). When these figures rise year on year, then more has been produced from the same unit of resource: input resources have been used more effectively and efficiently to produce more sales and hence more profits. Let's see if Bunns the Bakers are producing more sales and profits from their resources by calculating asset utilisation ratios (Figure 8.4).

Bunns the Bakers had 19 shops all of similar size open to the public in the year to 31 March 2018. During the year to 31 March 2019 an additional shop was opened on 1 October 2018, exactly six months into the current year. During the year to 31 March 2019, then, Bunns the Bakers had 19 + (1 × 6/12) = 19.5 shops selling the company's goods and products. Dividing the figures for the number of shops into the revenue for each year will give us the following results for revenue per shop:

$$2019: \text{Revenue per shop: } \frac{£10,078,000}{19.5} = £516,821$$

$$2018: \text{Revenue per shop: } \frac{£9,575,000}{19} = £503,947$$

These figures tell us that Bunns the Bakers has achieved higher sales per shop and so is using the company's resources much more efficiently, squeezing more output from the same unit of

Figure 8.4 Asset utilisation ratios

resource. A similar calculation can be undertaken to find out whether more profit has been generated from the resources used. The focus of our attention here will be the operating profit per shop, the sales less all the operating costs of the business.

$$2019: \text{Operating profit per shop: } \frac{£895,000}{19.5} = £45,897$$

$$2018: \text{Operating profit per shop: } \frac{£767,000}{19} = £40,368$$

Again, just as in the case of the employees, the shops have generated higher profits per shop in 2019 compared to 2018. More revenue and more profit have been generated from the same resources and so the business is more profitable in comparison to the previous year.

GO BACK OVER THIS AGAIN!   Are you sure you understand how increasing income per unit of input resource leads to higher profits? Visit the **online workbook** and look at Exercises 8.6 to prove to yourself that this is true.

A real life example of increasing sales from the same inputs resulting in higher profits is presented in Give me an example 8.2. As can be seen, Ted Baker generated more sales from each unit of retail space, resulting in increased operating profit per unit of input resource.

GIVE ME AN EXAMPLE 8.2   Ted Baker's annual report and accounts for the 52 weeks to 28 January 2017 presents the following figures:

	52 weeks ended 28 January 2017	52 weeks ended 30 January 2016
Retail revenue	£328.4 million	£294.9 million
Operating profit	£67.0 million	£59.4 million
Average square footage of retail space	387,373 square feet	357,096 square feet

Retail revenue and operating profit have certainly increased, but is the retail space being used more efficiently and productively to generate higher revenue and operating profit from each unit of input resource? Using the figures presented, we can calculate the retail revenue per square foot of retail space. In the 52 weeks to 28 January 2017, the sales per square foot of retail space were £847.76 (£328,400,000 ÷ 387,373 square feet) while in the 52 weeks to 30 January 2016 sales generated per square foot of retail space were £825.83 (£294,900,000 ÷ 357,096 square feet). Thus more sales per unit of resource have been achieved in the 52 weeks to January 2017 when compared to the 52 weeks to January 2016. The available retail space has been used more effectively and efficiently to produce higher sales per unit of input resource. But has this greater efficiency resulted in higher profits from each square foot of retail space? Operating profit per square foot of retail space has risen from £166.34 in the 52 weeks to 30 January 2016 (£59,400,000 ÷ 357,096 square feet) to

£172.96 in the 52 weeks to 28 January 2017 (£67,000,000 ÷ 387,373 square feet) so higher sales per unit of input resource have resulted in higher profits as more sales and hence more profit have been squeezed out of each unit of selling space.

WHY IS THIS RELEVANT TO ME?   Sales and profit per unit of input resource

To enable you as an accounting professional to:

* Appreciate that increasing sales per unit of input resource is often the key to improving an organisation's profitability

* Devise suitable efficiency ratios to measure output per unit of input resource to see if this is rising, falling or staying the same

---

GO BACK OVER THIS AGAIN!   Can you identify ways in which to increase sales and profit per unit of input resource? Go to the **online workbook** and have a go at Exercises 8.7 to test your understanding of how this works.

PERFORMANCE RATIOS

These ratios, illustrated in Figure 8.5, are of particular interest to an entity's shareholders as they measure the returns to the owners of shares in the business. Shareholders invest money into the shares of a business with a view to earning dividends from the profits made by that business. The various ratios considered under this heading first compare the profits generated to the number of shares in issue and then think about the dividends paid out on each share. Comparisons of dividends to the market price of each share tell shareholders what their return is on that share. In this way they can assess whether they could earn more by investing their money in alternative investments, while comparing dividends paid with profits generated helps investors to decide how safe their future dividend income will be.

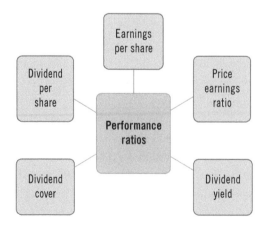

Figure 8.5 Performance ratios

Earnings per share (EPS)

The first performance ratio that shareholders consider is the earnings per share (this is frequently abbreviated to EPS). This figure is produced simply by dividing the profit for the year by the number of ordinary shares in issue. This figure represents the dividend that would result if all the profits for the period were paid out to ordinary shareholders as dividends. As we noted in Chapter 7, such a pay-out is most unlikely as the directors hold back some of the profits each year from which to finance future investment in the company.

EPS is calculated as follows:

$$\text{Earnings per share} = \frac{\text{Profit after taxation and after preference dividends}}{\text{Number of ordinary shares in issue}} \times 100 \text{ pence}$$

The profit after taxation is equivalent to the profit for the year. In situations in which an entity has preference shares in issue, any dividends paid on those preference shares will be paid out before any dividends are paid to ordinary shareholders. Therefore, this prior claim on the profits of an entity has to be deducted from profit for the year before the profits available for distribution to the ordinary shareholders can be determined. Note that EPS is always expressed in pence per share.

Looking at the figures for Bunns the Bakers, the profit after taxation (= profit for the year) for 2019 is £547,000 and £442,000 for 2018. The number of shares in issue can be observed in the statement of financial position. As shown in Illustration 2.1, Bunns the Bakers had 2,500,000 £1 shares in issue in the year to 31 March 2019, while in the previous year there were only 2,400,000 £1 ordinary shares. The increase in the number of shares indicates that additional shares have been issued during the year to 31 March 2019. The calculations for EPS for the two years under consideration are thus:

$$2019: \text{Earnings per share} = \frac{£547,000}{2,500,000} \times 100 \text{ p} = 21.88 \text{ pence}$$

$$2018: \text{Earnings per share} = \frac{£442,000}{2,400,000} \times 100 \text{ p} = 18.42 \text{ pence}$$

Bunns the Bakers has no preference shares in issue, so there are no preference dividends to deduct from the profit for the year before the EPS figures can be calculated. Therefore, the EPS calculation is simply based on the profit for the year divided by the number of ordinary shares in issue. Given the rise in EPS, shareholders will be pleased and the stock market will give the shares a higher valuation based on these increased returns.

MULTIPLE CHOICE QUESTIONS   Are you confident that you can calculate a figure for earnings per share? Go to the **online workbook** and have a go at Multiple choice questions 8.6 to test your ability to calculate this ratio.

EPS is a key figure in the evaluation of an entity's performance by the stock market and by stock brokers and traders. A review of the financial press will show you that where profits and thus EPS are expected to increase, the share price rises ahead of the announcement of earnings for the financial period under review. Similarly, where an entity's actual profits and EPS do not meet market expectations, share prices of that entity are marked down by the market. This reduction in the market price of the shares arises first from the fact that the results are a disappointment and second because the flows of cash to shareholders in the form of dividends from that entity are likely to be lower than expected. Ideally, the EPS figure should keep rising each year. Where this is the case, the share price will keep rising too and a rising share price is a source of happiness to shareholders as such rises indicate increasing wealth. In reality, EPS rise and fall in line with the economy: during periods when the economy surges, profits, and hence EPS, rise, but when the economy contracts and slows down, profits reduce, causing EPS and share prices to fall. Similarly, when companies' results and EPS are better than expected, share prices rise, but when they fall or are expected to fall, then the share price falls, too. Give me an example 8.3 provides two examples to illustrate these share price movements.

GIVE ME AN EXAMPLE 8.3   The effect of profits on share prices

The online fashion retailer Boohoo.com saw pre-tax profits for the year to 28 February 2017 rise 97 per cent to £30.9m. Over the same time period, revenue rose 51 per cent to £294.6m. The share price, which stood at 49.75 pence on 27 April 2016, rose almost 3.80 times to 188.75 pence over the course of the year to 26 April 2017.

Sources: *Financial Times*, 27 April 2017 and This is Money. co.uk http://www.thisismoney.co.uk/money/markets/article-4446616/Boohoo-s-profits-rise-97-year-amid-share-price-hike.html

At the close of business on 24 April 2017, Whitbread plc's shares stood at 4,307 pence. At the start of business on 25 April 2017, the share price had fallen 6.66 per cent to 4,020 pence as a result of slowing sales growth, profits that rose less strongly than expected and worries about reduced consumer spending. Profit before tax for the 52 weeks to 2 March 2017 was up 5.7 per cent to £515.4m against a market expectation of £554m. The share price fall occurred despite an increase in the final dividend of 6 per cent to 95.80 pence.

Source: *ShareCast News*, Whitbread warns of tough consumer outlook, 25 April 2017 http://sharecast.com/news/whitbread-warns-of-tough-consumer-outlook/25844885.html

---

WHY IS THIS RELEVANT TO ME?   Earnings per share

As an accounting professional you will be required to:

- Calculate the earnings per share ratio
- Be aware of the effects that profits or losses will have on the earnings per share of an entity
- Understand how the stock market values companies' shares on the basis of earnings per share

Price/earnings ratio (the P/E ratio)

The price/earnings ratio is linked to the EPS. This ratio divides the EPS into the current market price of that share. This gives a number that is an indicator of how many years of current period earnings are represented in the share price today. Alternatively, you can look at this ratio as the amount that a shareholder would be willing to pay today for every £1 of current earnings made by a company. A quick glance at the financial pages will show you that every listed company has a different P/E ratio (as shown in Give me an example 8.4), some higher and some lower than others. Typically, shares in companies with steady or rising profits have a higher P/E ratio as the earnings are perceived to be more secure and enduring than from other shares. On the other hand, shares in companies whose earnings are expected to be subject to lower or negative growth rates have lower P/E ratios as the earnings in these companies are expected to be much less secure and so P/E ratios for shares in these companies are lower. You might say that the P/E ratio is an indicator of the market's confidence in a particular company and its ability to maintain or grow its current earnings: the more likely it is that a company will continue to produce profits, earnings and dividends for shareholders, the higher the P/E ratio of that company will be.

GIVE ME AN EXAMPLE 8.4   Differing price/earnings ratios

A glance at the *Financial Times* Share Service for Friday 28 April 2017 shows the following information for three companies:

Company	P/E ratio
Debenhams	7.77
Next	9.82
Ted Baker	26.24

Source: *Financial Times* for Friday 28 April 2017

Ted Baker has a high P/E ratio, indicating that shareholders are willing to pay £26.24 for every £1 of today's earnings. Ted Baker markets itself as a global lifestyle brand that designs and sells clothing and fashion accessories to men and women who value something different. The company has very strong UK and international branding and more than doubled revenue and profits from 2012 to 2017. There is a very clear expansion strategy in place and the company's worldwide presence and strong products have encouraged investors to anticipate much higher profits, earnings per share and dividends in the future. The share price reflects these future expectations and investors' confidence that the directors' long-term strategic goals will be achieved.

Next plc conducts almost all of its business in the UK. The market is worried that the rising cost of living and the failure of the growth rate in wages to match inflation over the medium-term future will reduce sales of clothing and accessories at Next as consumers cut back on non-essential purchases. Next buys its products from overseas producers and pays for these products in US dollars. As the £:$ exchange rate has weakened since June 2016, Next will be paying higher prices for its products but will find it difficult to pass these price rises on to consumers in a highly competitive market, resulting in lower profits and cash inflows. In addition, there has been a trend away from spending on clothing to spending on experiences and services. Brokers expect profitability and cash flows to remain weak in non-food retail during 2017. All these factors contribute to an expectation of lower growth in sales, profitability and cash at Next which is reflected in the lower P/E ratio of 9.82.

Debenhams is a retailer of general merchandise. The company has suffered various problems in recent years, resulting in downgrades in profit expectations, and has lost sales and customers to other retailers and to online sellers owing to the undifferentiated nature of the products it sells. As a result, the P/E ratio of the company suggests that investors expect that the future performance of the business will deliver low returns to shareholders with little prospect of growth in profits and cash inflows.

The price/earnings ratio is calculated in the following way:

$$\text{Price/earnings ratio} = \frac{\text{Market value of one ordinary share}}{\text{Earnings per share}}$$

Share prices for Bunns the Bakers, when their results were released for the years ended 31 March 2019 and 31 March 2018, were 310.7 pence and 254.2 pence respectively. These prices and the EPS calculated above give P/E ratios as follows:

$$2019: \text{Price/earnings ratio} = \frac{310.7}{21.88} = 14.2$$

$$2018: \text{Price/earnings ratio} = \frac{254.2}{18.42} = 13.8$$

The share price has risen as the EPS have increased in 2019. Given the rise in EPS in the current financial year, the stock market would expect future earnings to be more secure (and that a higher dividend will be paid from higher earnings) and so the price/earnings ratio has also risen. Given the nature of Bunns the Bakers' products, investors would also expect customers to continue buying such products in the foreseeable future. Indeed, they might even buy additional treats to cheer themselves up during a difficult economic period. A higher level of confidence in the shares to continue producing an enduring earnings and dividend stream is thus being shown by the higher P/E ratio.

GO BACK OVER THIS AGAIN!   Are you sure you understand the relationship between price and earnings in the price/earnings ratio? Go to the **online workbook** and have a go at Exercises 8.8 to test your understanding of this relationship.

MULTIPLE CHOICE QUESTIONS   How quickly do you think you can calculate price/earnings ratios? Go to the **online workbook** and have a go at Multiple choice questions 8.7 to make sure you can calculate this figure.

Dividend per share (DPS)

This ratio is used by shareholders to determine how much dividend is being paid on each share. As in the case of EPS, the ideal situation for shareholders is for the dividends to keep rising each year. Such increases indicate confidence in the company's ability to continue generating rising profits into the future. In addition, higher dividends result in rising share prices as expectations of future dividend increases feed into the market's valuation of the shares. The DPS can be compared to the EPS to calculate the pay-out ratio, the percentage of the EPS that have been distributed as dividend to the shareholders over the year.

The DPS figure is worked out in almost exactly the same way as EPS, but the total dividends paid out are substituted for the profits after taxation and after preference dividends. This ratio is calculated as follows:

$$\text{Dividend per share} = \frac{\text{Total ordinary dividends}}{\text{Number of ordinary shares in issue}} \times 100 \text{ pence}$$

From the statement of cash flows in Illustration 6.1, we can see that the dividends paid out in the year to 31 March 2019 were £90,000 compared with £72,000 in the year to 31 March 2018. This gives DPS figures for the two years as follows:

$$\text{2019: Dividend per share} = \frac{£90,000}{2,500,000} \times 100 \text{ p} = 3.60 \text{ pence}$$

$$\text{2018: Dividend per share} = \frac{£72,000}{2,400,000} \times 100 \text{ p} = 3.00 \text{ pence}$$

Comparing these figures to the EPS for the two years gives a pay-out ratio (dividend per share as a percentage of earnings per share for the year) of:

$$\text{2019: Payout ratio} = \frac{3.60 \text{ pence}}{21.88 \text{ pence}} \times 100\% = 16.45\%$$

$$\text{2018: Payout ratio} = \frac{3.00 \text{ pence}}{18.42 \text{ pence}} \times 100\% = 16.29\%$$

DPS has risen and this represents a higher pay-out ratio as well. The company has thus paid out more DPS this year as a percentage of EPS, but has still retained a significant proportion of the earnings (over 83 per cent in both years under review) with a view to reinvesting these into the business to generate further expansion in the future and to increase both sales and profits.

Dividend yield

Shareholders invest in companies firstly to generate income in the form of dividends and secondly to increase their wealth through the capital appreciation (the increase in the market price of a share over the year) of their shares' value. These same shareholders could just as easily invest their cash in the safety of bank or building society accounts and earn interest on their deposits. Is the dividend and capital appreciation they are earning on their shares sufficient compensation for the risk they are taking by investing in the stock market?

The dividend earned by shareholders is compared with the market price of a share to give the dividend yield. This figure is calculated as follows:

$$\text{Dividend yield} = \frac{\text{Ordinary dividends per share}}{\text{Current market price of one ordinary share}} \times 100\%$$

For Bunns the Bakers, the dividend yield for the financial years ended 31 March 2019 and 31 March 2018 is as follows:

$$\text{2019: Dividend yield} = \frac{3.60 \text{ pence}}{310.7 \text{ pence}} \times 100\% = 1.16\%$$

$$\text{2018: Dividend yield} = \frac{3.00 \text{ pence}}{254.2 \text{ pence}} \times 100\% = 1.18\%$$

The dividend yield does not appear to be very high at present, though it compares well with the Bank of England base rate of 0.50 per cent. By investing in a building society account with a more favourable interest rate, shareholders could gain a much better monetary return of around 1.50 per cent to 2.00 per cent. However, using this building society interest rate as a benchmark would ignore the fact that the share price has risen from 254.2 pence a year ago to 310.7 pence today, a rise of 22.23 per cent ((310.7 − 254.2)/254.2 × 100 per cent). This capital appreciation, along with the dividends received, represent the total return to shareholders over the year. When looking at the dividend yield, it is important to remember that a low return does not necessarily indicate a poorly performing share. Both the capital appreciation in the share price and the dividend actually received have to be taken into account.

Dividend cover

This ratio measures how many times the current year ordinary dividend could be paid from the profit for the year. Dividend cover looks at the profit after taxation and after any preference dividends that have to be paid first. This ratio is a measure of the security of the dividend that has been paid: the higher the ratio, the more secure the dividend. A dividend cover of 1.0 would indicate that all the EPS were being paid out as dividends with no retention of profits within the entity to finance future expansion and development. Whereas a dividend cover of 3.0 would indicate that the current year dividend could be paid out three times and that two-thirds of the profit for the year is being retained within the business.

The dividend cover ratio is calculated in the following way:

$$\text{Dividend cover} = \frac{\text{Profit after tax and after preference dividends}}{\text{Total ordinary dividends}}$$

Looking at Bunns the Bakers, the dividend cover ratio for the two financial years that concern us is:

$$2019: \text{Dividend cover} = \frac{£547,000}{£90,000} = 6.08 \text{ times}$$

$$2018: \text{Dividend cover} = \frac{£442,000}{£72,000} = 6.14 \text{ times}$$

As Bunns the Bakers have no preference shares in issue, the relevant number to use in this calculation is the profit for the year as given in the statement of profit or loss. From the results of the above calculations, the ratio has fallen slightly, but a dividend cover of over six times is very safe indeed and shareholders can anticipate that their dividend will continue to be paid for the foreseeable future.

WHY IS THIS RELEVANT TO ME?   Performance ratios

As an accounting professional you will be required to:

• Understand ratios relevant to investors and the stock market

• Understand how these ratios are calculated

• Calculate these ratios yourself

• Comment meaningfully on the ratios you have calculated

Are you certain that you can distinguish between the five performance ratios? Go to the **online workbook** and have a go at Exercises 8.9 to test your understanding of which ratio does what.

Are you convinced that you can calculate dividend per share, pay-out, dividend yield and dividend cover ratios? Go to the **online workbook** and have a go at Multiple choice questions 8.8 to make sure you can calculate these figures.

Can you remember the formulae for earnings per share, price/earnings ratio, dividend per share, pay-out ratio, dividend yield and dividend cover? Go to the **online workbook** to take a look at Summary of key concepts 8.8–8.13 to reinforce your understanding.

Will Bunns The Bakers' shareholders be happy with the company's performance?

How have Bunns the Bakers performed this year? Shareholders will consider the following factors:

- EPS and DPS are both higher than in 2018.
- The increase in the P/E ratio indicates the market's expectation that the company will continue producing rising earnings and dividends for shareholders into the foreseeable future.
- While the dividend yield fell very slightly from 1.18 per cent to 1.16 per cent, the increase in the share price over the year will have more than compensated for this reduction.
- Taken together, the dividend yield and the increase in the share price have comfortably exceeded the returns on what are perceived to be safer investments (bank and building society deposit accounts).
- Shareholders will therefore be happy with the dividends paid and the increase in the market value of their shares.
- The dividend cover indicates that future dividends should be easily affordable from profits.
- The low dividend pay-out ratio indicates that the company is keeping plenty of profit back with which to finance future growth and expansion.
- While shareholders might want profits, earnings, dividends and share price to be even higher, they can be satisfied with the company's performance in the year ended 31 March 2019 when comparing this performance with the previous year.

WHY IS THIS RELEVANT TO ME?   Evaluation of performance ratios

As an accounting professional you will be expected to:

- Appreciate what factors shareholders and the stock market will take into account when assessing an entity's performance
- Be able to make an objective assessment of an entity's performance yourself

RETURN ON CAPITAL EMPLOYED

A common ratio that you will find in other books on accounting is the return on capital employed (abbreviated to ROCE). This ratio is calculated as follows:

$$\frac{\text{Profit before interest and tax}}{\text{Capital employed}} \times 100\%$$

Capital employed is defined as the equity of an entity plus the long-term borrowings. Looking at the statements of financial position of Bunns the Bakers at 31 March 2019 and 31 March 2018 (Illustration 2.1) equity totals up to £8,459,000 and £7,767,000 respectively. Long-term borrowings (included in non-current liabilities) at the two accounting dates are £2,700,000 and £3,000,000. Profit before interest and tax is equivalent to the operating profit line in Illustration 8.1 and this amounts to £895,000 for the year to 31 March 2019 and £767,000 for the year to 31 March 2018. This gives us the following figures for return on capital employed for the two years as follows:

$$2019: \text{ROCE} = \frac{£895,000}{(£8,459,000 + £2,700,000)} \times 100\% = 8.02\%$$

$$2018: \text{ROCE} = \frac{£767,000}{(£7,767,000 + £3,000,000)} \times 100\% = 7.12\%$$

What is this ratio trying to do? ROCE is used to compare the different profits of different companies that have different capital structures. As we saw in Chapter 7, some companies raise their finance solely through share capital while others rely on loans and still others use a mixture of both share and loan capital to finance their businesses. In this way, the operating profits generated by these different capital structures can be compared to determine which entities produce the highest returns from their capital structures. Investors can then determine which entities they will invest their money into to produce the highest returns. Return on capital employed is often used to compare returns available from companies with interest rates available from banks and building societies to decide whether it would be safer to invest in these much less risky investments rather than in a particular company.

However, the ROCE ratio suffers from a number of problems. We saw in Chapter 2 that not all the assets of an entity are reflected in organisations' statements of financial position. Similarly, the figures presented on the statement of financial position are not necessarily as up to date as they might be. The equity of an entity is made up of share capital that may have been issued many years ago along with retained earnings that have been accumulated over many different accounting periods. These figures would need to be adjusted for changes in the purchasing power of the pound to bring all the pounds tied up in equity up to current day values for this ratio to be meaningful. After all, the profit before interest and tax has been earned in the current year, but this is being compared to share capital and retained earnings from previous years when the value of each pound was very different from what it is today. As noted in Give me an example 8.5 dealing with Ryanair, this is tantamount to comparing apples and pears so that the comparison loses its validity.

It should be possible to restate all the share capital and retained earnings figures to current values (for example by multiplying the market value of each share by the total number of shares in issue) to produce a suitable figure for equity. However, this is a time-consuming exercise and users of accounts might prefer to look at the total shareholder return as represented by the dividend yield and the increase in the market value of shares over the year as the best indicator of the returns available from each company. Users are completely free to use the ROCE ratio as they see fit, but they must be fully aware of the severe limitations that this ratio presents and how these limitations will affect their perceptions of the returns available from each entity.

WHY IS THIS RELEVANT TO ME?   Return on capital employed

To enable you as an accounting professional to understand:

• The way in which return on capital employed is used by entities and individuals

• The limitations of the return on capital employed ratio

• That total shareholder return represents a more effective way in which to distinguish between different investment opportunities

THE IMPORTANCE OF CALCULATING AND PRESENTING RATIOS CONSISTENTLY

Emphasis has been placed throughout this chapter on the need to calculate and present ratios consistently year on year. Why is this consistency so important? Failure to calculate and present ratios consistently from year to year will mean that comparisons are distorted and figures misleading rather than being accurate portrayals of the financial position compared to previous accounting periods. The dangers of trying to compare information that is not consistently presented and the distortions that this gives rise to are illustrated in Give me an example 8.5.

WHY IS THIS RELEVANT TO ME?   The importance of calculating and presenting ratios consistently

As an accounting professional you will be expected to:

• Present unbiased reports with consistent data that is not misleading

• Present data that has been compiled and calculated consistently in order to produce fair and valid comparisons between different reporting periods

• Be aware of the dangers of not comparing like with like

HOW WELL ARE WE DOING? COMPARISONS WITH OTHER COMPANIES

So far we have just looked at the financial statements and ratios of Bunns the Bakers. The company seems to be moving in the right direction with increased profits and profitability, improved efficiency leading to rising revenue and shareholders who should be content with the returns they are receiving. However, we have looked only at internal information with no benchmark against which

8

Michael O'Leary's ability to spin a tale has reached a new level this week. Along with the gullibility of parts of the media in accepting it. Hook, line and sinker.

'Ryanair cuts Stansted winter capacity by 40 per cent,' claimed his press release. The assertion was patently rubbish. But it is almost universally already accepted as fact. On the most charitable assessment, he is planning to cut Stansted winter capacity by 14 per cent. The probability is that the year-on-year decline in Ryanair passenger numbers at Stansted will be much lower even than that. BAA, Stansted's owner, is forecasting a drop of 6–7 per cent.

To get to the claim of a drop of 40 per cent Mr O'Leary is comparing an apple with a pear. He is comparing the number of aircraft he is operating from Stansted, his biggest base, this summer (40) with the number he plans to deploy in the winter (24). But the airline industry is highly seasonal. Comparing Ryanair's summer capacity with its winter capacity at any airport is about as useful as saying 'ice-cream sales to fall by 40 per cent this winter' or 'temperature to fall by 40 per cent'. Shock horror.

Last winter Ryanair operated between 26 and 28 aircraft at Stansted. This year it is planning to operate 24, a decline of at most 14 per cent year on year and a long way from the claimed fall of 40 per cent. The decline will doubtless be even less in the number of flights operated year on year. Mr O'Leary chose to describe only the number of aircraft overnighting at Stansted. He gave no numbers for the volume of weekly flights that includes services operating in and out of Stansted from other Ryanair bases.

The summer/winter capacity comparison is about as silly as comparing profits/losses between different quarters of the year rather than year on year. Not even Ryanair has yet adopted that approach as a new accounting standard.

This week's spin was egregious even by Mr O'Leary's standards. A year ago, when he staged the same show over cutbacks at Stansted, at least he had the good grace to compare an apple with an apple. But the result was much less impressive.

to compare our company's results. Therefore, we cannot say how well Bunns the Bakers is doing in comparison with the market, whether it is doing better, worse or just as well as its peer companies.

To determine the company's relative success in comparison to other bakery sector companies, we need to compare Bunns the Bakers' figures and ratios with those of a competitor or a series of competitors. In this way, we can benchmark the financial performance of our company against a company in the same line of business to decide whether Bunns' ratios are in line with the sector or whether they are lower or higher. Ratios are a relative measure and, as such, they can be compared with other relative measures from other companies to highlight differences and trends. Such comparisons make ratios especially useful in understanding the profitability, efficiency, performance, liquidity and long-term financial stability of several organisations and in providing individual business entities with a target to aim for.

Ideally, when making inter-company comparisons of ratios and financial statement figures, we should only compare:

* similar businesses
* of similar size
* in a similar industry

- in a similar location
- over the same accounting period

in order to eliminate random variances arising from differences in activities, size, industry, geographical location and economic factors. All comparative data should be consistently prepared to avoid distortions and bias in the analysis. In addition, organisations can also compare:

- budgeted or planned performance data to see where the plan went well or went off course
- industry data and averages for the same accounting period

when making assessments of their own profitability, efficiency and performance.

WHY IS THIS RELEVANT TO ME?   How well are we doing? Comparisons with other companies

As an accounting professional it is important for you to:

- Appreciate that a full evaluation of an entity's profitability, efficiency and performance cannot be made just from looking at data generated from internal sources
- Understand how comparative data from outside an entity can be used to assess and evaluate that entity's profitability, efficiency and performance
- Source comparative data to make assessments of an entity's profitability, efficiency and performance

---

Undertaking comparisons

One company that is in the same industry as Bunns the Bakers is Greggs plc. Greggs is engaged in bakery retail throughout the United Kingdom and has 1,854 shops supplied by eleven regional bakeries (Greggs Annual Report for the 52 Weeks Ended 30 December 2017, page 12). To test your knowledge and your ability to calculate and interpret the ratios of another company, you will now need to turn to the **online workbook**, Numerical exercises 8.2, to undertake the analysis of the financial statements of Greggs plc and to compare Bunns the Bakers' 2018 results with this competitor company.

NUMERICAL EXERCISES   Do you think you can calculate profitability, efficiency and performance ratios for Greggs plc and interpret them in a meaningful way? Are you sure you can use the ratios you have calculated to draw conclusions about Bunns the Bakers' profitability, efficiency and performance in comparison to a competitor? Have a look at Numerical exercises 8.2 which presents extracts from the financial statements of Greggs plc and then have a go at the various exercises linked to the two companies in the **online workbook**.

APPENDIX: RATIOS CONSIDERED IN THIS CHAPTER

To assist your learning, the ratios we have considered in this chapter are summarised in Table 8.4.

8

Table 8.4 Calculations and descriptions for the profitability, efficiency and performance ratios covered in this chapter

	Calculation	What does this ratio tell us?
Profitability ratios		
Gross profit %	$\dfrac{\text{Gross profit}}{\text{Revenue}} \times 100\%$	Calculates profitability after deducting all the direct costs of goods sold from sales to determine how effectively an entity is controlling its costs of producing goods for sale or buying in goods for resale.
Operating profit %	$\dfrac{\text{Operating profit}}{\text{Revenue}} \times 100\%$	Determines profitability on the basis of revenue less all operating costs, before taking into account the effects of finance income, finance expense and taxation.
Profit before tax %	$\dfrac{\text{Profit before tax}}{\text{Revenue}} \times 100\%$	Bases the profitability calculation on profit before taxation to eliminate the distorting effect of changes in tax rates. The profit before tax percentage is the profitability of the entity after deducting all costs incurred and taking into account income earned from all sources, both trading and investment.
Profit after tax %	$\dfrac{\text{Profit for the year}}{\text{Revenue}} \times 100\%$	Calculates profitability for the period after adding all income and deducting all expenses and charges for the period under review.
Efficiency ratios		
Non-current asset turnover	$\dfrac{\text{Revenue}}{\text{Non-current assets}}$	Calculates the £s of sales from each £1 of non-current assets to determine how effectively and efficiently non-current assets are being used to generate revenue.
Revenue per employee	$\dfrac{\text{Revenue}}{\text{Total number of employees}}$	Determines how productively employees are working to generate sales for an entity: the higher the sales per employee figure, the higher the organisation's profitability will be.
Profit per employee	$\dfrac{\text{Operating profit}}{\text{Total number of employees}}$	Determines how much profit each employee generates during an accounting period. The higher the profit per employee, the more efficiently employees are working to fulfil the business's objectives of profit generation.

	Calculation	What does this ratio tell us?
Sales per unit of input resource	$$\frac{\text{Revenue}}{\text{Total units of input resource}}$$	Focuses on the productivity of each unit of resource employed in generating sales for the business.
Profit per unit of input resource	$$\frac{\text{Operating profit}}{\text{Total units of input resource}}$$	Indicates how efficiently each unit of resource is employed to generate profits for the organisation.
Performance ratios		
Earnings per share	$$\frac{\text{Profit after taxation and after preference dividends}}{\text{Number of ordinary shares in issue}} \times 100 \text{ pence}$$	Represents the profit in pence attributable to each ordinary share in issue for a given accounting period.
Price/Earnings ratio	$$\frac{\text{Market value of one ordinary share}}{\text{Earnings per share}}$$	Indicates the price an investor is willing to pay for £1 of earnings in a company today or the number of years of profit represented in the current share price.
Dividend per share	$$\frac{\text{Total ordinary dividends}}{\text{Number of ordinary shares in issue}} \times 100 \text{ pence}$$	The dividend paid out on each ordinary share in issue.
Dividend payout ratio	$$\frac{\text{Dividend per share}}{\text{Earnings per share}} \times 100\%$$	Determines the % of earnings per share paid out as dividends together with the % of earnings held back for future investment in the business.
Dividend yield	$$\frac{\text{Ordinary dividends per share}}{\text{Current market price of one ordinary share}} \times 100\%$$	Expresses the dividend paid out on each share for an accounting period as a % of the current share price.
Dividend cover	$$\frac{\text{Profit after tax and after preference dividends}}{\text{Total ordinary dividends}}$$	Assesses how many times the total dividend could be paid out of current year profits after deducting all prior claims on those profits.
Return on capital employed	$$\frac{\text{Profit before interest and tax}}{\text{Capital employed}} \times 100\%$$	Capital employed = equity + long term borrowings. This ratio is used to determine the profitability of a business to facilitate comparisons with the return on capital employed of other businesses which have different capital structures.

8

CHAPTER SUMMARY

You should now have learnt that:

- Financial statement figures are an absolute performance measure while ratios are a relative performance measure
- Financial statement figures and ratios interact in the interpretation of profitability, efficiency and performance
- Ratios are a very good way in which to understand the changing relationship between two figures
- Managers use ratios to understand and improve the operations of a business
- Profitability ratios are calculated by dividing revenue into gross profit, operating profit, profit before tax and profit after tax
- Ratios are just a starting point in identifying the reasons for changes in financial statement figures year on year
- Efficiency ratios comprise of non-current asset turnover, revenue per employee and profit per employee
- Efficiency ratios can be used to understand changes in profitability
- Increasing the revenue from each unit of fixed resource employed in the business will increase an entity's profits
- Performance ratios are calculated for earnings per share, dividends per share, dividend yield and dividend cover
- The price/earnings ratio compares the current price of a share with the earnings per share
- Performance ratios are used by shareholders to assess how well an organisation has performed over an accounting period
- Assessments of an entity's profitability, efficiency and performance should never take place in a vacuum but should be compared with measures from other companies in the same industry to provide a better understanding of how an entity's results compare to those of peer companies in the market

QUICK REVISION   Test your knowledge with the online flashcards in Summary of key concepts and attempt the Multiple choice questions, all in the **online workbook**.

8

END-OF-CHAPTER QUESTIONS

Solutions to these questions can be found in the **online workbook**.

❯ DEVELOP YOUR UNDERSTANDING

❯Question 8.1

Cuddles Limited produces teddy bears. The statements of profit or loss for the years ended 30 April 2019 and 30 April 2018 are presented below.

	2019 £000	2018 £000
Revenue	34,650	29,360
Cost of sales	15,939	14,093
Gross profit	18,711	15,267
Distribution and selling costs	5,355	4,550
Administration expenses	3,654	3,083
Operating profit	9,702	7,634
Finance income	150	75
Finance expense	750	650
Profit before tax	9,102	7,059
Income tax	2,182	1,694
Profit for the year	**6,920**	**5,365**

Other information for the two years 30 April 2019 and 30 April 2018:

	2019	2018
Total dividends paid for the year	£4,400,000	£3,700,000
Number of shares in issue during the year	20,000,000	18,500,000
Number of employees during the year	275	250
Non-current assets at the financial year end	£21,655,000	£18,820,000

Cuddles Limited had no preference shares in issue in either of the two years ended 30 April 2019 and 30 April 2018.

For Cuddles Limited calculate the following ratios for the years ended 30 April 2019 and 30 April 2018 (all calculations should be made to two decimal places):

* Gross profit percentage
* Operating profit percentage
* Profit before tax percentage

- Profit after tax percentage
- Non-current asset turnover
- Revenue per employee
- Operating profit per employee
- Earnings per share
- Dividends per share
- Dividend pay-out ratio
- Dividend cover

> Question 8.2

The following information has been extracted from the financial statements of DD Limited for the years ended 30 June 2019 and 30 June 2018:

	2019	2018
Profit for the year	£8,622,350	£7,241,330
Number of ordinary shares in issue during the year	37,192,500	36,197,500
Number of preference shares in issue during the year	22,000,000	20,000,000
Ordinary dividend for the year	3,347,325	2,895,800

Further information for the two years 30 June 2019 and 30 June 2018:

- The preference shares have a par value of 50 pence each and a dividend rate of 4 per cent.
- Market values of one ordinary share:

30 June 2017	220 pence
30 June 2018	260 pence
30 June 2019	325 pence

For DD plc calculate the following ratios for the years ended 30 June 2019 and 30 June 2018:
- Earnings per share
- Dividends per share
- Dividend pay-out ratio
- Dividend cover
- Dividend yield
- Growth in the share price over the course of each year

You should make all your calculations to two decimal places.

>> TAKE IT FURTHER

>> Question 8.3

The following are extracts from the income statements (= statements of profit or loss), statements of financial position and notes to the financial statements for Bovis Homes Group plc (years ended 31 December 2017 and 31 December 2016, https://www.bovishomesgroup.co.uk/investors/reports-and-presentations), Persimmon plc (years ended 31 December 2017 and 31 December 2016, https://www.persimmonhomes.com/corporate/investors/results-presentations-and-financial-reports) and Crest Nicholson plc (years ended 31 October 2017 and 31 October 2016, https://www.crestnicholson.com/investor-relations/reports-results-and-presentations). All three companies build residential housing in the UK.

	Bovis Homes Group plc		Persimmon plc		Crest Nicholson plc	
	2017	2016	2017	2016	2017	2016
	£m	£m	£m	£m	£m	£m
Revenue	1,028.2	1,054.8	3,422.3	3,136.8	1,043.2	997.0
Cost of sales	843.6	845.8	2,350.6	2,265.4	768.3	731.2
Gross profit	184.6	209.0	1,071.7	871.4	274.9	265.8
Operating profit	121.2	160.0	955.1	770.5	211.6	203.8
Profit before tax	114.0	154.7	966.1	774.8	207.0	195.0
Profit for the year	91.3	120.8	786.9	625.3	168.6	156.8
Non-current assets	15.7	57.6	542.1	482.9	110.0	118.7
Dividends paid (total)	63.8	60.4	416.6	338.3	84.3	70.3

	2017	2016	2017	2016	2017	2016
	Number	Number	Number	Number	Number	Number
Employees: average during the year	1,297	1,186	4,535	4,526	905	849
Shares in issue (million)	134.661	134.522	308.856	308.498	255.760	254.364
Houses sold in the year	3,645	3,977	16,043	15,171	2,935	2,870

None of the three companies had any preference shares in issue in either of the accounting periods shown above.

Required
For the three companies for both 2017 and 2016 calculate:

- Gross profit percentage
- Operating profit percentage
- Profit before tax percentage
- Profit after tax percentage
- Non-current asset turnover
- Revenue per employee
- Operating profit per employee
- Earnings per share
- Dividends per share
- Dividend pay-out ratio
- Dividend cover

Make your calculations to two decimal places other than for revenue per employee and operating profit per employee, which should be made to the nearest whole £.

>> Question 8.4

Using the ratios you have calculated in Question 8.3 for the three companies:

* Suggest reasons for the changes in profitability over the two years for all three companies. To assist you with your analysis you should consult the annual reports and accounts of the companies at the websites given at the start of Question 8.3 to see what factors have affected the profitability of each company this year.

* Evaluate the performance of the three companies from the point of view of the shareholders.

>> Question 8.5

From the financial press or Internet, track the share price of the three companies in Question 8.3 for one week and calculate the average share price for each company.

Using your average share price, the earnings per share and the dividends per share from the answers to Question 8.3, calculate:

* Dividend yield
* Price/earnings ratio.

Using a share price tracker on the Internet, look back to the same week you have chosen a year ago and track the share price for that week. Average the share price for that week a year ago and then calculate the percentage increase in the share price over the past year. Which of the three companies has produced the best total return over the year?

RATIO ANALYSIS 2: LIQUIDITY, WORKING CAPITAL AND LONG-TERM FINANCIAL STABILITY

9

LEARNING OUTCOMES

Once you have read this chapter and worked through the questions and examples in both this chapter and the online workbook, you should be able to:

- Understand what is meant by the term 'liquidity'

- Appreciate that the length of the cash flow cycle varies for different types of business

- Calculate the current ratio and the quick ratio and explain what each of these ratios tells you about the short-term liquidity of an organisation

- Understand the shortcomings of current and quick ratios in the assessment of entities' short-term liquidity

- Define the term working capital and state its components

- Calculate ratios for inventory days, receivables days and payables days and discuss what these ratios tell you about the short-term liquidity of an entity

- Calculate the cash conversion cycle and explain what this means for a particular entity

- Show how organisations manage to meet their liabilities as they fall due from year-end cash and from future cash inflows from sales despite having current and quick ratios that fall well below the expected norms

- Calculate the gearing ratio, debt ratio and interest cover and explain what these ratios tell us about the long-term solvency and financial stability of an organisation

INTRODUCTION

The previous chapter considered profitability, efficiency and performance ratios in the interpretation and evaluation of the financial results of each accounting period's trading and operations. These ratios concentrated on the statement of profit or loss as the source of data on which to build these ratios and the evaluations based upon them. Chapter 6 discussed the importance of cash flows and how cash flows and their timing are the key to the survival of any entity. The cash flows of an organisation are extremely important in your evaluation of the liquidity of that organisation and you should quickly go over the lessons of Chapter 6 again before reading further in this chapter. This is to ensure that you fully appreciate the importance of cash flow information in the assessment of an entity's financial position and its financial stability.

This chapter will look at liquidity ratios and the related analysis provided by working capital ratios. Liquidity ratios and working capital ratio assessments are built upon the information contained in the statement of financial position. In addition, we will consider how an entity's capital structure contributes to an assessment of that entity's long-term financial stability. We saw in Chapter 7 that businesses issue shares and take on borrowings with which to finance their activities: the proportions in which share capital and borrowed funds finance an entity have a bearing on the ability of that entity to continue operating when economic conditions become less favourable. We will look at the key ratios in the assessment of entities' capital structures as well as evaluating organisations' ability to survive with high levels of borrowings.

The International Accounting Standards Board recognises the critical importance of information on an organisation's liquidity, solvency, cash flow generating capacity and its ability to raise additional funds to finance operations:

> Information about the nature and amounts of a reporting entity's economic resources and claims can help users to identify the reporting entity's financial strengths and weaknesses. That information can help users to assess the reporting entity's liquidity and solvency, its needs for additional financing and how successful it is likely to be in obtaining that financing…Information about priorities and payment requirements of existing claims helps users to predict how future cash flows will be distributed among those with a claim against the reporting entity.
>
> Source: IASB *Conceptual Framework for Financial Reporting*, paragraph 1.13

Analysis of these aspects is critical to any assessment of an entity's short- and long-term survival prospects. It is these aspects and the analysis of this information that will form the main subject of this chapter.

REFER BACK   To illustrate the ratios discussed later we will use the statement of financial position, statement of profit or loss and statement of cash flows for Bunns the Bakers presented in Chapters 2, 3 and 6. You should refer back to Illustrations 2.1, 3.1 and 6.1 in these chapters or look up the copies available in the **online workbook** as you work through this chapter.

LIQUIDITY AND THE CASH FLOW CYCLE

Liquidity refers to the ability of an entity to raise cash to pay off its liabilities as they become due for payment. Any company that is unable to generate this cash with which to meet its debts will be unable to survive and will file for bankruptcy; in this situation, an administrator is appointed to sell the company's assets and the cash raised from these asset sales is used to pay at least some of what is owed to the company's creditors. Insolvent companies have more liabilities than assets, so it is unlikely that the liabilities of such companies will be repaid in full as shown in Give me an example 9.1.

GIVE ME AN EXAMPLE 9.1   Insolvent companies failing to repay all their debts

Plymouth Argyle have moved a step closer to coming out of administration after creditors voted in favour of a deal to reduce the club's debt. Plymouth's proposed Company Voluntary Arrangement had offered creditors less than a penny in every pound owed…The League One outfit entered administration in March [2011] with debts of over £17m, divided between more than 240 unsecured creditors. By voting in favour of the CVA, the club's unsecured creditors stand to lose the vast majority of their money as just 0.77 pence of every pound owed will be returned.

Amongst the big losers are Plymouth City Council, who will get back just over £2,000 from the £285,000 due. Inscapes, the company who laid Argyle's brand new pitch last summer, will be handed £2,695 of the £350,000 worth of payments still outstanding.

Source: Reprinted with permission from BBC Sport: www.bbc.co.uk/sport/0/football/13313804

How do business entities generate cash from their operations? Some businesses sell their goods for cash so they immediately have money with which to pay suppliers and other parties (such as employees or banks) what they are owed. Other entities sell goods to customers on credit, allowing their customers time in which to pay. In this case, organisations will have to wait for payment, but the cash will be expected to flow in eventually to meet the demands of creditors as they become due. What effect do these two different approaches to selling goods have on the length of the cash flow cycle? The cash flow cycle for retailers and manufacturers is illustrated in Figures 9.1 and 9.2.

Figure 9.1 The cash flow cycle for retailers

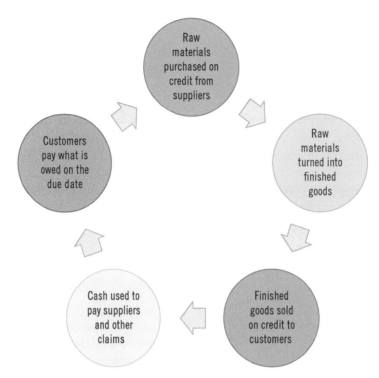

Figure 9.2 The cash flow cycle for manufacturers

Figure 9.1 shows that the retailing cash flow cycle is very short: goods are purchased on credit from suppliers, sold on for cash and are then paid for. Figure 9.2 shows that the manufacturing cycle is much longer. Raw materials bought on credit from suppliers first have to be converted into finished goods inventory. These finished goods are then sold to customers, but they demand time in which to pay. In the meantime, suppliers will be demanding payment and will most likely have to be paid before customers have settled what is owed. A store of cash will thus have to be retained within the business to meet the demands of suppliers and of other claims upon the business while waiting for customers to pay what is owed. There are thus many delays in the manufacturing cash flow cycle, first in producing the goods and then in waiting for the cash from customers. We shall consider the effect these different business cycles have on our assessment of a business's liquidity when we look at working capital management. However, you should appreciate at this early stage how the cash flow cycle operates and how it is vital for entities to have cash available to meet liabilities as they fall due.

WHY IS THIS RELEVANT TO ME?   Liquidity and the cash flow cycle

To enable you as an accounting professional to:

• Appreciate that different businesses have different cash flow cycles

• Evaluate the speed at which different types of business generate cash from their operations with which to pay their debts

• Understand that the faster an entity converts its sales into cash, the more liquid that business is

---

GO BACK OVER THIS AGAIN!   Are you quite sure you understand how vital the cash flow cycle is to businesses? Go to the **online workbook** and look at Exercises 9.1 to enable you to appreciate the need to ensure cash inflows from which to pay liabilities as they fall due.

LIQUIDITY RATIOS

Have a look at Bunns the Bakers' current assets (Illustration 2.1): these are made up of inventory, trade and other receivables and cash. Now look at the current liabilities, which show the current portion of long-term liabilities, that part of borrowings that is due for repayment within one year, trade and other payables (the amounts due to suppliers and for other liabilities such as rent, business rates and electricity among others) and current tax liabilities. Along with the cash and cash equivalents already available, the other current assets are used to generate cash from sales of inventory and receipts from receivables to pay off the current liabilities. Short-term assets are thus used to meet short-term liabilities: this is the liquidity, the availability of cash in the near future, referred to in the IASB's Conceptual Framework for Financial Reporting cited earlier (this chapter, Introduction). How is the ability of short-term assets to meet short-term liabilities assessed? Not surprisingly, the first step in this assessment will be through the calculation of ratios.

Current ratio

The first ratio that we will look at compares current assets to current liabilities in an attempt to determine whether an organisation has sufficient short-term assets from which to meet short-term liabilities. This ratio is called the current ratio and is calculated as follows:

$$\text{Current ratio} = \frac{\text{Current assets}}{\text{Current liabilities}}$$

This figure is expressed as a ratio and tells us how many £s of current assets there are for each £ of current liabilities. Calculating the current ratio for Bunns the Bakers at 31 March 2019 and 31 March 2018 gives us the following results:

$$2019: \text{Current ratio:} \frac{£334,000}{£840,000} = 0.40:1$$

$$2018: \text{Current ratio:} \frac{£319,000}{£707,000} = 0.45:1$$

What do these ratios mean? At 31 March 2019, Bunns the Bakers has 40 pence of current assets for each £1 of current liabilities, while at 31 March 2018 the company had 45 pence of current assets for each £1 of current liabilities. This might not sound very good as the company does not seem to have much in the way of current assets with which to meet liabilities as they fall due.

However, remember that the statement of financial position is just a snapshot of the financial position at one day in the year: the position will change tomorrow and the next day and the day after that as goods are produced, sales are made, cash flows in and liabilities are paid. The current ratio also ignores the timing of the receipt of cash and of the payment of liabilities.

How quickly is cash received by the business? If this is immediately at the point of sale then the entity will have a very positive cash inflow from which to meet its liabilities. If cash is received from trade receivables some time after the sales were made then a much more careful management of cash inflows and outflows will be required. The current ratio's logic assumes that all the liabilities will be due for payment on the day following the statement of financial position date; this is highly unlikely and we will investigate the likely payment pattern for liabilities later on in this chapter to show that, contrary to appearances, Bunns the Bakers is a very liquid, cash generative business indeed (this chapter, Current liabilities: the timing of payments).

WHY IS THIS RELEVANT TO ME?   Current ratio

To enable you as an accounting professional to:

- Understand what the current ratio represents and how it is used in the assessment of short-term liquidity
- Calculate current ratios for organisations
- Appreciate the shortcomings of the current ratio as a key measure in short-term liquidity assessment

---

GO BACK OVER THIS AGAIN!   Do you really understand what the current ratio is trying to do and what factors you have to take into account when using it? Go to the **online workbook** and have a go at Exercises 9.2 to check your understanding.

MULTIPLE CHOICE QUESTIONS   Are you convinced that you can calculate a current ratio from a given set of financial information? Go to the **online workbook** and have a go at Multiple choice questions 9.1 to test out your ability to calculate this ratio.

Quick (acid test) ratio

This ratio is a modification of the current ratio and ignores inventory in its assessment of an entity's ability to pay its short-term liabilities. Why is inventory taken out of the calculation? There is always a chance that inventory produced by an organisation will not be sold quickly, so that this inventory cannot be counted as convertible into cash in the near future. Therefore, the quick (acid test) ratio only takes account of current assets that are cash or that are readily realisable in cash: trade receivables are readily convertible into cash as the entity has a contractual right to receive the money due for sales already made to customers. The quick (acid test) ratio is calculated as follows:

$$\text{Quick (acid test) ratio} = \frac{(\text{Current assets} - \text{Inventory})}{\text{Current liabilities}}$$

Using Bunns the Bakers' statement of financial position at 31 March 2019 and 31 March 2018 the following quick ratios can be calculated:

$$\text{2019: Quick ratio: } \frac{(£334,000 - £60,000)}{£840,000} = 0.33{:}1$$

$$2018: \text{Quick ratio:} \frac{(£319,000 - £55,000)}{£707,000} = 0.37:1$$

These ratios are inevitably lower than the current ratios calculated earlier as inventory is taken out of the current assets with no corresponding decrease in current liabilities. Again, this paints a very gloomy picture of Bunns the Bakers' short-term liquidity as the company only has 33 pence of readily realisable current assets per £1 of current liabilities at 31 March 2019, a figure that has fallen from 37 pence per £1 of current liabilities at 31 March 2018.

How realistic is the assumption that inventory will not sell quickly? It all depends upon the particular activity in which an entity is engaged. A moment's thought should convince you that the quick ratio is completely irrelevant to any assessment of Bunns the Bakers' short-term liquidity. The company sells freshly baked goods from their shops in towns. People usually get up too late to make their own sandwiches or snacks to take to work (or are too lazy to do so!) and will go out at lunch time to buy the company's products, which will sell quickly rather than being stockpiled for several weeks or months before they are sold. Therefore, what is produced today is sold today and cash is received immediately from cash paying customers at the till. Even if there are sandwiches, pies and pastries left towards the end of the day, shop staff will discount the prices in order to tempt customers to buy up the left over inventory so only very small amounts of the goods produced will be wasted.

The quick ratio may be much more relevant in a manufacturing situation. The swift pace of change in markets and products means that any advance production might result in such goods becoming obsolete or out of fashion so that entities are unable to sell them to recover the costs of producing or buying them. As a result of this risk, many companies today only produce to order rather than manufacturing goods in the hope that they will sell. Such an approach removes the risk of goods becoming obsolete and the losses that disposal of such goods will incur as, first, discounts are given on the original selling price and then goods have to be scrapped as interest in them finally runs out. It is particularly important only to produce goods to order in the high-tech sector; new developments are taking place every few minutes so that products are being improved all the time and earlier models quickly become outdated. As a result, high-tech goods such as laptops, tablets, mobile phones and other electronic devices are produced as orders come in to avoid the losses that would arise if several months' advance sales of such goods were produced all at once.

Consider Give me an example 9.2, which shows a sudden fall in demand resulting in obsolete goods that have to be discounted to entice customers to buy them.

Where entities are subject to this kind of unpredictable pattern of demand that can suddenly be turned off or interrupted by, for example, an economic downturn, a change in consumer tastes or technological developments, your evaluation of liquidity will be much more cautious. If an organisation does not enjoy steady demand for its products then that organisation is at much higher risk of suffering liquidity problems and you would expect that entity to maintain much higher current and quick ratios as well as operating a very sophisticated forecasting system to stop production of its goods at the first sign of a decline in demand. In Bunns the Bakers' case, office workers will keep visiting their outlets at lunch time and shoppers will drop in throughout the day as they seek out the company's value for money products, so declines in demand will not be a problem for this organisation.

9

S Africa faces reality after World Cup party

Global Insight: Richard Lapper in Johannesburg

Just ten days ago, Mary Muthui was doing a roaring trade in football scarves, beanie hats and vuvuzelas at her stall in the Rosebank Mall crafts centre in Johannesburg. But yesterday—less than two weeks after the end of South Africa's much acclaimed World Cup—the 28-year-old trader was struggling to unload anything at all and was offering the controversial plastic horn for a quarter of the R120 ($16, €12, £10) that football fans were paying last month. 'It's very, very slow,' she said. 'I have sold less than 50 vuvuzelas since the final.' [Note: The 2010 World Cup final was held in Johannesburg on 11 July 2010]

WHY IS THIS RELEVANT TO ME?   Quick ratio

As an accounting professional you must:

- Understand what the quick ratio represents and how it is used in the assessment of short-term liquidity
- Understand the situations in which inventory obsolescence is a risk and those in which it is not
- Calculate quick ratios for organisations
- Appreciate the situations in which the quick ratio is applicable and not applicable in an assessment of short-term liquidity

GO BACK OVER THIS AGAIN!   How well have you grasped what the quick ratio is trying to do and what factors you have to take into account when using it? Go to the **online workbook** and have a go at Exercises 9.3 to check your understanding.

SUMMARY OF KEY CONCEPTS   Can you remember the formulae for current and quick ratios? Go to the **online workbook** to take a look at Summary of key concepts 9.1 and 9.2 to reinforce your understanding.

MULTIPLE CHOICE QUESTIONS   Are you confident that you can calculate a quick ratio from a given set of financial information? Go to the **online workbook** and have a go at Multiple choice questions 9.2 to test out your ability to calculate this ratio.

Current and quick ratios: the traditional view

Convention has it that a business entity needs a current ratio of 2:1, £2 of current assets for every £1 of current liabilities, and a quick ratio of 1:1, £1 of trade receivables and cash for every £1 of current liabilities, in order to be able to survive financially. On a conventional reading of the figures for Bunns the Bakers, then, the assessment would be that the company is heading into bankruptcy. Bunns the Bakers has nowhere near current and quick ratios of 2:1 and 1:1, so the question must be asked how the company manages to survive quite happily on much lower ratios than convention dictates.

WORKING CAPITAL

A much more effective way in which to assess liquidity is to look at the working capital cycle, the time it takes for an entity to turn raw materials into goods for sale, sell these goods, collect the cash and then pay suppliers for goods and raw materials supplied. The length of this working capital cycle is determined through the use of the three working capital ratios presented in Figure 9.3. We looked at the cash flow cycle at the start of this chapter for both retailers and manufacturers, but it is now time to look in more detail at the components of working capital and how to use these as a guide to the liquidity and cash flow generating capability of an organisation.

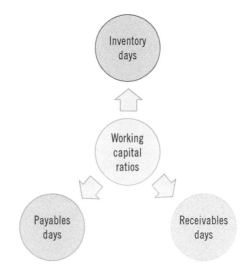

Figure 9.3 The three working capital ratios

First, though, what is working capital? The basic definition of working capital is as follows:

Working capital = current assets − current liabilities

Working capital thus comprises:

- Inventories of raw materials for use in production, of finished goods ready for sale or of goods purchased for resale to customers.
- Trade receivables from customers of the business who have been provided with a credit facility by the entity.
- Cash in the bank or in hand that is held to meet day-to-day needs.
- Trade payables of the business which require settlement on a daily basis. For the purposes of the working capital calculation, amounts due to lenders and money due to settle tax liabilities are ignored as these (as we shall see in this chapter, Current liabilities: the timing of payments) do not require payment on a day-to-day basis, being settled on a monthly or three-monthly basis.

WORKING CAPITAL RATIOS

In order to evaluate the efficiency of working capital management, the ratios in Table 9.1 are used.

Table 9.1 Working capital ratios, how they are calculated and what they tell users

Ratio	Calculation	What does this ratio tell us?
Inventory days (also known as stock days)	$\dfrac{\text{Inventory}}{\text{Cost of sales}} \times 365$	• This ratio measures the average stockholding period, how long an entity holds goods in inventory before they are sold • The more quickly inventory turns over the better, as inventory is turned into sales (and hence into cash) much more quickly while obsolete inventories and the risk of deterioration (and hence loss of future cash inflows from the sale of this inventory) are minimised • However, when calculating their optimum level of inventory holding, businesses should consider future demand (no inventory, no sale), any anticipated future shortages or price rises, discounts available for buying in bulk, storage, insurance and any other costs involved in holding inventory
Receivables days (also known as debtor days)	$\dfrac{\text{Trade receivables}}{\text{Credit sales}^1} \times 365$	• This ratio indicates the average credit period taken by customers, the length of time it takes for credit customers to pay what they owe • Evaluates the efficiency of the credit control system and the speed with which credit sales are turned into cash • Where this ratio is increasing, steps can be taken to speed up payments (e.g. by offering early settlement discounts) to minimise the funds tied up in receivables: it is better to have cash in our bank account than in our customers' bank account
Payables days (also known as creditor days)	$\dfrac{\text{Trade payables}}{\text{Cost of sales}^2} \times 365$	• This ratio measures how quickly the business is paying off its purchases made on credit • Ideally, the receivables days and payables days should be equal: as cash is received, it is used to pay off liabilities • Paying trade payables before trade receivables have paid usually has a negative impact upon cash flow: see the profit ≠ cash example for Start Up in Example 6.1 in Chapter 6

[1]Strictly this ratio should use only credit sales in the calculation of receivables days: sales made for cash have already been settled and thus no cash is outstanding from these transactions. Therefore, cash sales should be omitted in the determination of receivables days, the number of days of credit allowed to credit customers. However, in practice, companies do not disclose separate figures for their cash sales and their credit sales, so it is normal just to use total sales in this calculation.

[2]Again, while trade payables should be compared to purchases of goods on credit, entities do not publish details of their credit purchases, so cost of sales is used to approximate the cost of purchases. In reality, cost of sales may include the wages and salaries of production operatives in the manufacturing part of a business, which should not strictly be classified as purchases on credit, but the cost of sales is a useful substitute for the credit purchases of a business.

As long as you are consistent in your calculations (as noted in Chapter 8, The importance of calculating and presenting ratios consistently), the relationships and ratios produced should provide a suitable like-for-like basis on which to assess the working capital strengths or weaknesses of a business.

Are you certain you can distinguish between the three working capital ratios? Go to the **online workbook** and have a go at Exercises 9.4 to make sure you can make these distinctions.

The working capital ratios for Bunns the Bakers are as follows:

2019: Inventory days: $\dfrac{£60,000}{£4,535,000} \times 365 = 4.83$ days

2018: Inventory days: $\dfrac{£55,000}{£4,596,000} \times 365 = 4.37$ days

Trade and other receivables for Bunns the Bakers at 31 March 2019 and 31 March 2018 from the statement of financial position are £62,000 and £75,000 respectively. By looking at the notes to the financial statements we can determine that the actual trade receivables, as distinct from other receivables and prepayments, are £25,000 at 31 March 2019 and £35,000 at 31 March 2018. This will give us the following receivables days for the two accounting periods:

2019: Receivables days: $\dfrac{£25,000}{£10,078,000} \times 365 = 0.90$ days

2018: Receivables days: $\dfrac{£35,000}{£9,575,000} \times 365 = 1.33$ days

This ratio is very low, but, as most sales will be made for an immediate cash payment from customers in the shops, this is not at all surprising. As we noted in Chapter 2 (Current assets), credit sales will be limited to a small number of credit customers such as supermarkets.

The rest of the sales will be made for cash to customers as they come into the shops and make their purchases, so a very low receivables days ratio would be expected in such a situation.

Trade and other payables for Bunns the Bakers at 31 March 2019 and 31 March 2018 from the statement of financial position are £390,000 and £281,000 respectively. By looking at the notes to the financial statements we can determine that the actual trade payables, as distinct from other payables, are £300,000 at 31 March 2019 and £220,000 at 31 March 2018. This will give us the following payables days for the two accounting periods:

2019: Payables days: $\dfrac{£300,000}{£4,535,000} \times 365 = 24.15$ days

2018: Payables days: $\dfrac{£220,000}{£4,596,000} \times 365 = 17.47$ days

> **WHY IS THIS RELEVANT TO ME?**   Working capital ratios
>
> As an accounting professional you will be expected to:
> * Understand what working capital ratios are and what they represent
> * Be able to calculate working capital ratios for organisations
> * Use working capital ratios to assess the efficiency of working capital management in entities

SUMMARY OF KEY CONCEPTS   Do you think you can remember the formulae for the three working capital ratios? Go to the **online workbook** to take a look at Summary of key concepts 9.3–9.5 to reinforce your understanding.

MULTIPLE CHOICE QUESTIONS   Are you certain you can calculate working capital ratios from a given set of financial information? Go to the **online workbook** and have a go at Multiple choice questions 9.3 to test out your ability to calculate these ratios.

What do these figures tell us? First, that, in 2019, inventories are sold within 4.8 days, a very slight increase on the 4.4 days it took to sell inventory in 2018. Much of Bunns the Bakers' inventory will comprise raw materials ready for use in the production of bread, pies, pastries and other bakery goods. Finished goods themselves will probably represent only one day's production as goods are produced fresh and ready for delivery and sale the next day. Certain other inventories, such as soft drinks, which have a longer sell-by date, can be kept in storage for several weeks or months before they are out of date, but most of the company's raw materials will be delivered on a daily basis and turned into finished goods for sale on the same or the next day.

This is a very low inventory days ratio and indicates that stocks are turned into sales very quickly indeed. As most of these sales are for cash, the receivables days are also very low. However, trade payables are settled every 24 days in the year to 31 March 2019 (an increase on the previous year) so Bunns the Bakers is holding on to the cash received from customers before they pay this cash out to their suppliers. Money is received at the point of sale, but the company holds on to the cash until the time to pay their suppliers comes around.

The cash conversion cycle

The ratios shown in Figure 9.3 enable us to calculate the cash conversion cycle (sometimes referred to as the operating cycle or working capital cycle). The cash conversion cycle tells us how quickly inventory is turned into trade receivables and how quickly trade receivables are turned into cash with which to pay trade payables (Figure 9. 4). The shorter this cycle, the better the working capital is being managed and the more readily cash is available with which to meet liabilities. Conversely, the longer this process, the higher the investment required in working capital and the higher the emergency sources of cash will need to be (for example, financing by an agreed short-term overdraft from the bank) to pay liabilities as they fall due.

The cash conversion cycle is calculated in the following way:

Inventory days + receivables days − payables days

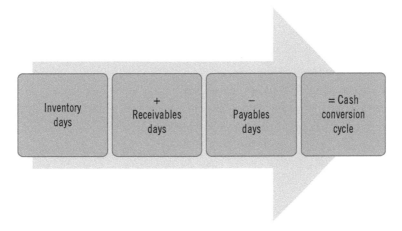

Figure 9.4 The cash conversion cycle

For Bunns the Bakers, the cash conversion cycle for the two years under consideration is as follows:

2019: Cash conversion cycle: 4.83 inventory days + 0.90 receivables days − 24.15 payables days
= −18.42 days

2018: Cash conversion cycle: 4.37 inventory days + 1.33 receivables days − 17.47 payables days
= −11.77 days

The figures above and Figure 9. 5 show that the cash conversion cycle figures for both years are negative. This means that Bunns the Bakers are converting their sales into cash well before they have to pay their suppliers. The negative cash conversion cycles also mean that the company is

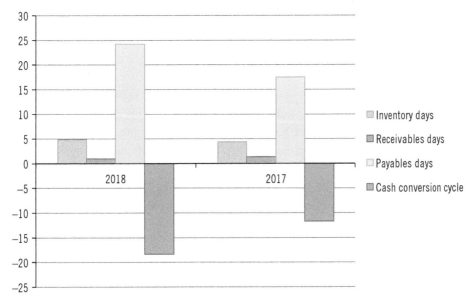

Figure 9.5 Bunns the Bakers' working capital ratios and cash conversion cycle

holding onto this cash for several days before it is paid out and this will enable the company to use this cash to generate additional finance income (interest receivable) on their surplus bank deposits. This additional interest may not amount to much in total in the statement of profit or loss, but it is an important extra source of income for the company and this spare cash is being used effectively to generate additional profits for the shareholders. From Bunns the Bakers' point of view, the increase in the cash conversion cycle this year means that they are taking an extra 6.65 days (18.42 days – 11.77 days) in which to pay their suppliers, indicating that they are holding onto their cash for longer. By using the credit facilities provided by their suppliers, Bunns the Bakers do not have to rely on a short-term bank overdraft to finance their working capital: this finance is in effect being provided by the company's suppliers.

WHY IS THIS RELEVANT TO ME?   Working capital ratios and the cash conversion cycle

To equip you as an accounting professional with the ability to:

● Calculate additional ratios with which to evaluate short-term liquidity

● Calculate the length of the cash conversion cycle

● Interpret the results of the working capital ratio and the cash conversion cycle calculations

● Appreciate how working capital ratios and the cash conversion cycle help to supplement the current and quick ratios in liquidity analysis

---

GO BACK OVER THIS AGAIN!   Are you quite sure that you understand what the cash conversion cycle is telling you? Go to the **online workbook** and have a go at Exercises 9.5 to check your understanding.

MULTIPLE CHOICE QUESTIONS   How easily can you calculate the cash conversion cycle from a given set of financial information? Go to the **online workbook** and have a go at Multiple choice questions 9.4 to test out your ability to undertake the required calculations.

WHY IS WORKING CAPITAL SO IMPORTANT?

Organisations need short-term finance to enable them to buy raw materials with which to produce goods to sell to customers. As indicated in Figure 9.2, a firm's suppliers cannot wait for payment until the raw materials have been turned into finished goods, sold on credit and then paid for by that firm's customers. Such a period would be too lengthy and the supplier might well have gone bankrupt while waiting for payment. Therefore, manufacturers and their suppliers rely on short-term credit provided by banks in the form of overdrafts. These overdrafts are used to finance the purchase of materials and the payment of wages to workers to tide them over the short-term lack of funds that arises when waiting for products to be manufactured and sold and for customers to pay. Such short-term working capital allows organisations to build up momentum with this short-term finance being paid back when projects are up and running and cash inflows from customers are financing cash outflows to suppliers.

The importance of working capital is illustrated in Give me an example 9.3.

GIVE ME AN EXAMPLE 9.3   **German companies scramble to adjust to suddenly overfilled order book**

Industrialists do not usually complain when their business is thriving. But after several months in which orders have been more than double the level [of] a year before, Ulrich Reifenhäuser, owner of the eponymous German plastics machinery maker, says he is longing for growth rates to ease.

'I really hope that this will start to level off and that growth rates will come down again. I am hoping for a more moderate growth rate,' says the managing director of Reifenhäuser group, an engineering company employing 1,200 staff and based between Cologne and Bonn.

Mr Reifenhäuser is not alone. Orders in Germany's key export driven sectors such as machinery, cars and chemical goods are pouring in at such a speed that many companies are struggling to cope with the sudden demand boom.

Significant parts of the country's plants are running at full speed again, driven by a fast rise in demand from China and the US in particular. Some companies are already expanding capacity and many are rehiring contract workers.

'We are approaching a normal capacity utilisation in our sector,' said Manfred Wittenstein, president of VDMA, the German engineering association...

But the upbeat mood in the sector is still damped by fears that the upswing could be blown off course by a lack of finance, as some companies struggle to obtain the large amounts of working capital that are suddenly needed to finance the new orders.

'There are more and more signs that banks refrain from giving loans to small companies,' Mr Wittenstein warns.

Research by Demica, a UK based working capital solutions provider, shows that 78 per cent of German companies are faced with difficulties in obtaining traditional bank credit. Some 59 per cent say they will be left with insufficient working capital to take advantage of the economic upswing.

'The credit crunch has come back to the fore in the past six weeks,' Mr Reifenhäuser says. 'Some of our customers are not able to receive project finance.'

Mr Heitmann of Lanxess says a full recovery of the financial system is crucial for a sustained economic upturn. 'The sooner we tidy up the financial system and get back to financial stability the faster we will reach pre-crisis levels,' he says.

Source: Daniel Schäfer, 2010, *German companies see order books overfill,* the Financial Times, 4 July. Used under licence from the Financial Times. All Rights Reserved.

WHY IS THIS RELEVANT TO ME?   Why is working capital so important?

To enable you as an accounting professional to appreciate that:

- Entities need short-term finance with which to finance growth and to start up new projects
- Short-term finance has to come either from cash saved within the entity or from outside sources such as bank overdrafts
- The required short-term finance is not always readily available from outside sources

CURRENT LIABILITIES: THE TIMING OF PAYMENTS

Our calculations in the Current ratio section earlier showed that at 31 March 2019 Bunns the Bakers has only 40 pence of current assets for each £1 of current liabilities. At that point we also noted that the current and quick ratios take no account of when liabilities are actually due for payment and make the assumption that all liabilities might call in the money owed to them at the statement of financial position date. Let us now think about how much of Bunns the Bakers' current liabilities might actually be due for payment on the day after the statement of financial position date so that we can assess how liquid the company really is and how easily it can afford to pay its debts from the current assets it already owns.

Bunns the Bakers' statement of financial position shows the following current liabilities at 31 March 2019:

	£000
Current portion of long-term borrowings	300
Trade and other payables	390
Current tax liabilities	150
	840

At 31 March 2019, Bunns the Bakers has £212,000 of cash with which to meet these current liabilities. This does not appear to be a good position to be in, as current liabilities exceed the cash available with which to pay them. However, by thinking about when these liabilities will actually fall due we will be able to see that the company can meet its liabilities very easily from the cash it has at the year end together with all the cash generated from sales in the days and weeks after the year end.

First, let us think about when the current portion of long-term borrowings will be payable. When an entity borrows money from a bank under a formal loan agreement, the entity and the bank sign a contract. This contract governs the loan terms, the terms of repayment and the interest that is payable on the loan. As long as the borrower does not breach the terms of the contract (e.g. by failing to pay either any interest due or a loan instalment by the agreed date), then the bank cannot demand its money back immediately and has to wait for the borrower to meet each repayment as it becomes due. The £300,000 due at 31 March 2019 probably represents 12 monthly payments of £25,000 each so that the most that could be due on 1 April 2019 would be £25,000. The other monthly repayments would be due one month after this, two months after this and so on. This is a very pessimistic assumption: most loan instalments are payable at the end of the month rather than at the beginning, giving the company up to 30 days to save up for the next payment. But for now we will assume that loan repayments are due on the first day of each month so that £25,000 is repayable on 1 April 2019.

While bank loans are covered by contracts in this way, bank overdrafts are not. Should the entity you are evaluating have an overdraft with its bank, do remember that overdrafts are repayable on demand so that all of the overdraft should be added in to the calculation of immediate liquidity on the day after the statement of financial position date.

Turning now to what is owed to suppliers, we saw earlier that trade payables amount to £300,000 and that this represents 24.15 days of purchases. We noted that suppliers of raw materials will deliver to the company each day so that the ingredients going into the bread, sandwiches, pies and pastries are always fresh. Therefore, the total amount due to trade payables on 1 April 2019 would be £300,000/24.15 = £12,422, with £12,422 due on 2 April, £12,422 on 3 April and so on. In reality, these amounts will not be spread so evenly, but the £12,422 is a useful average to work with, based on the payables days we calculated earlier. The other payables of £90,000 (£390,000 − £300,000 trade payables) will probably be payable to a variety of different creditors at different times over the next two to three months. However, as we are cautious accountants, let us assume that one-quarter of this amount is due tomorrow, which represents £90,000/4 = £22,500 payable immediately.

Tax liabilities for limited liability companies in the UK are payable in quarterly instalments three months, six months, nine months and 12 months after the statement of financial position date, so the earliest that any of the £150,000 tax is due would be 30 June 2019, three months after 31 March 2019. Therefore, none of the tax liabilities will be due on 1 April 2019.

Summarising our results below tells us that we have only a fraction of the total current liabilities at 31 March 2019 to pay on 1 April 2019. The figures below may be seriously overestimated as the long-term borrowings are probably repayable at the end of April 2019 rather than at the beginning of the month and it is unlikely that 25 per cent of the other payables is actually due one day after the year end:

	£
Current portion of long-term borrowings	25,000
Trade payables	12,422
Other payables	22,500
Current tax liabilities	—
Total payable on 1 April 2019	59,922
Cash available at 31 March 2019	212,000
Surplus cash available on 1 April 2019 (£212,000 − £59,922)	152,078

Thus, when it comes to determining how liquid a company is and how easily it can meet its current liabilities when they fall due, timing is critical. In addition, we should not forget that cash will be coming into the business on 1 April 2019 as sales are made at the tills. How much will this be? Given that annual sales are £10,078,000 and that there are, say, 300 trading days a year, this would give daily sales of £33,593. As this cash will come into the business on every trading day of the year, there is always going to be plenty of cash available from which to meet debts as they become payable. Therefore, the current and quick ratio, while giving a good idea of how many £s of current assets are available to meet each £ of liabilities, should not be used as the final indicator of how easily a company can meet its liabilities as they fall due. You must think about the timing of receipts and payments of cash and the way in which an entity manages its cash inflows and outflows to make a full evaluation of an entity's short-term liquidity.

To illustrate the truth of this approach, just think about your own situation for a moment. If we all drew up our own personal statement of financial position at the end of each calendar year and included everything that we had to pay for the next 12 months and compared this to what cash we had available at the start of the year, we would all be in despair. However, we know that all our liabilities for the next 12 months are not due immediately on 1 January and that we have monthly inflows of cash from our salaries that will gradually pay what we owe throughout the year. Cash outflows are matched by cash inflows and, with a bit of luck, we will be able to save some cash towards a holiday or towards some other treat for ourselves. We do not worry that we do not have enough cash now to pay off everything that is due in the next 12 months and neither do businesses.

WHY IS THIS RELEVANT TO ME?   The timing of payments and the shortcomings of the current and quick ratios

To enable you as an accounting professional to:

- Appreciate that an entity's current liabilities will never all be due for payment at the same time unless that entity is in liquidation
- Calculate the amounts due for payment on the day after the statement of financial position date as part of your assessment of an entity's liquidity
- Forecast monthly cash outgoings for the next year to determine whether entities can meet those monthly outgoings from current trading
- Appreciate how timing of payments analysis helps to overcome the shortcomings of the current and quick ratios in liquidity analysis

---

GO BACK OVER THIS AGAIN!   Are you sure you understand how the timing of payments is critical to an assessment of short-term liquidity? Go to the **online workbook** and look at Exercises 9.6 to enable you to appreciate that not all liabilities are due immediately and that the assumptions of the current and quick ratios are invalid when assessing an entity's ability to meet its short-term liabilities.

CAPITAL STRUCTURE RATIOS: LONG-TERM SOLVENCY AND FINANCIAL STABILITY ASSESSMENT

Working capital, cash conversion cycle and current and quick ratios measure short-term liquidity and the ability of entities to pay their debts on a short-term (within the next 12 months), day-to-day basis. But just as there are ratios with which to measure short-term liquidity, there are also ratios to determine long-term solvency and financial stability (Figure 9.6). As we saw in Chapter 7, companies have a choice of financing models through which to raise the capital required to finance their operations for the long term. They can either raise the necessary funds through an issue of share capital or they can raise the money from borrowings from the bank or the money markets. Many companies combine both share capital and borrowings in their long-term financing. The combination of the two will have implications for our assessment of how easily entities will be able to repay those borrowings while still servicing that long-term capital from profits either through the distribution of dividends to shareholders or the payment of interest on borrowings. This is the solvency, the availability of cash in the longer term, referred to in the IASB's Conceptual Framework quoted earlier in this chapter.

When assessing long-term solvency and financial stability, the ratios in Table 9.2 are used.

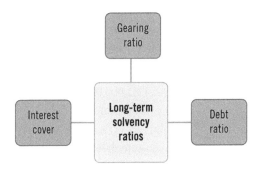

Figure 9.6 Long-term solvency and financial stability ratios

Table 9.2 Long-term solvency and financial stability ratios, how they are calculated and what they tell users

Ratio	What does this ratio tell us?
$\text{Gearing ratio} = \dfrac{\text{Long and short-term borrowings}}{\text{Equity}} \times 100\%$	• The gearing percentage is often seen as a measure of risk: companies with higher borrowings are supposedly more risky than those with lower borrowings
$\text{Debt ratio} = \dfrac{\text{Total liabilities}}{\text{Total assets}}$	• This ratio measures the £s of liabilities per £1 of total assets • The lower the ratio, the more secure the entity
$\text{Interest cover} = \dfrac{\text{Profit before interest and tax}}{\text{Interest}}$	• Assesses how many times interest payable on borrowings is covered by operating profits (in the same way that dividend cover measures how many times the ordinary dividend is covered by profit for the year) • The higher the figure, the better, as a high figure indicates an ability to continue meeting interest payments from profits in the future

WHY IS THIS RELEVANT TO ME?   Capital structure ratios: long-term solvency and financial stability assessment

As an accounting professional you will be expected to:

• Understand what gearing, debt and interest cover ratios are telling you about an entity's long-term solvency and financial stability

• Calculate gearing, debt and interest cover ratios for organisations

• Evaluate the results of gearing, debt and interest cover ratio calculations to produce an assessment of an entity's long-term solvency and financial stability position

Gearing ratio

Looking at the statement of financial position for Bunns the Bakers (Illustration 2.1), the company has borrowings of £300,000 in current liabilities and borrowings of £2,700,000 in non-current liabilities, giving a total borrowings figure of £3,000,000 at 31 March 2019. At 31 March 2018, the figures are £300,000 and £3,000,000 giving total borrowings of £3,300,000. Equity in the statement of financial position in Illustration 2.1 is £8,459,000 at 31 March 2019 and £7,767,000 at 31 March 2018. Using these figures we can calculate gearing percentages as follows:

$$2019: \text{Gearing \%}: \frac{£3,000,000}{£8,459,000} \times 100\% = 35.47\%$$

$$2018: \text{Gearing \%}: \frac{£3,300,000}{£7,767,000} \times 100\% = 42.49\%$$

Gearing has fallen this year as borrowings represent a lower proportion of equity than in previous years. This fall is partly due to the repayment of £300,000 during the year to 31 March 2019 and partly due to the increase in equity as a result of the issue of new share capital and the profits retained for the current year. The statement of cash flows (Illustration 6.1) shows us that the company has repaid £300,000 of its borrowings over each of the past two years, so this debt seems to be very manageable. The percentage of borrowings to equity is low and, given the consistency of the trade in which Bunns the Bakers are engaged and the constant demand that their products enjoy, it would be perfectly logical to draw the conclusion that the company's long-term financing strategy is very stable and poses no solvency risk to the organisation.

MULTIPLE CHOICE QUESTIONS   How easily do you think you can calculate gearing from a given set of financial information? Go to the **online workbook** and have a go at Multiple choice questions 9.5 to test out your ability to calculate this ratio.

Debt ratio

Total assets and total liabilities just have to be read off the relevant lines of the statement of financial position (Illustration 2.1). The company has total assets of £12,199,000 at 31 March 2019 and total assets of £11,674,000 at 31 March 2018. Similarly, total liabilities at 31 March 2019 amount to £3,740,000 and £3,907,000 at 31 March 2018. Comparing the total liabilities with the total assets gives us the following results:

$$2019: \text{Debt ratio}: \frac{£3,740,000}{£12,199,000} = 0.31:1$$

$$2018: \text{Debt ratio}: \frac{£3,907,000}{£11,674,000} = 0.33:1$$

Bunns the Bakers has 31 pence of total liabilities for every £1 of total assets at 31 March 2019 compared to 33 pence of total liabilities for every £1 of total assets at 31 March 2018. This is not a high figure and it would be reasonable to conclude that the company is highly solvent and financially stable.

MULTIPLE CHOICE QUESTIONS Are you quite confident that you can calculate the debt ratio from a given set of financial information? Go to the **online workbook** and have a go at Multiple choice questions 9.6 to test out your ability to calculate this figure.

Interest cover

The gearing percentages and debt ratios are not high, but how easily can the company meet its interest obligations? To determine the interest cover, we will need to turn to the statement of profit or loss in Illustration 3.1. This statement tells us that the finance expense (= interest payable) for the years to 31 March 2019 and 31 March 2018 was £150,000 and £165,000 respectively. This expense now needs matching to the operating profit (the profit before interest and tax) of £895,000 and £767,000 for the two years that concern us.

$$2019: \text{Interest cover}: \frac{£895,000}{£150,000} = 5.97 \text{ times}$$

$$2018: \text{Interest cover}: \frac{£767,000}{£165,000} = 4.65 \text{ times}$$

Increased profits and reduced finance expense in 2019 mean that this ratio has improved greatly this year. Given that interest is covered nearly six times by the operating profit, we can conclude that Bunns the Bakers is a very secure company indeed, with low gearing, low total liabilities to total assets and with a very strong interest cover ratio that indicates that the company will be able to keep servicing its long-term borrowings into the foreseeable future.

SUMMARY OF KEY CONCEPTS Can you remember the formulae for the three long-term solvency and financial stability ratios? Go to the **online workbook** to take a look at Summary of key concepts 9.6–9.8 to reinforce your understanding.

MULTIPLE CHOICE QUESTIONS Are you completely confident that you can calculate interest cover from a given set of financial information? Go to the **online workbook** and have a go at Multiple choice questions 9.7 to test out your ability to calculate this ratio.

WHEN ARE BORROWINGS RISKY?

How much borrowing is too much? The answer to this question is, 'it all depends'. Provided that an organisation has sufficiently strong cash inflows from operations and can afford to keep paying the interest as well as saving money towards repayment of borrowings, then that organisation will be able to borrow as much as it likes. Profitability, remember, is not enough: we saw in Chapter 6 that, without the associated inflows of cash from operations, profit means nothing. Many profitable companies have gone out of business because they were unable to generate the necessary cash flows from which to repay borrowings they had taken on.

Let's illustrate these issues with Give me an example 9.4 and 9.5.

What lessons can we draw from Give me an example 9.4 and 9.5? First, as with the current and quick ratios, you should never jump to conclusions based on isolated figures. An apparently

At the end of January 2018, Next plc had borrowings of £1,088.5 million and equity of £482.6 million. The gearing ratio based on these figures is 225.55% (£1,088.5m/£482.6m × 100%). Looked at in isolation, this figure would suggest that Next plc has seriously over-borrowed and is in imminent danger of collapse. And yet, the company is still trading and lenders are falling over themselves to lend the company money: of the total borrowings of £1,088.5 million, £135.0 million was lent to the company on an unsecured basis during the 52 weeks ended on 27 January 2018. Clearly, lenders would not continue to provide this amount of funding unless they had cast iron confidence in Next's ability to repay this debt. Therefore, several additional factors must be taken into consideration before we can draw a conclusion on the long-term solvency position of Next plc.

Affordability

Is this debt affordable? Next plc had an operating profit of £759.9 million and interest payable of £35.0 million for the 52 weeks ended 27 January 2018, giving interest cover of 21.71 times (£759.9m/£35.0m). This level of interest is thus very affordable and sales and profits would have to collapse to very low levels before the interest on the borrowings could not be covered by profits from operations.

Repayment dates

When are the borrowings repayable? Of the total borrowings, only the bank overdraft of £45 million and the unsecured loans of £135 million are due for repayment in the next 12 months. The remainder of the borrowings is made up of bonds, of which £328.4 million is due in 2021, £280.1 million is repayable in 2026 and £300.0 million is due for repayment in 2028, so the company has plenty of time in which to save up the necessary cash to meet these repayment dates. The interest rates on the three bonds are fixed at 5.375 per cent, 4.375 per cent and 3.625 per cent respectively, so the company will not suffer higher interest charges if there were to be a sudden increase in bank base rates.

Operating cash inflows

How easily can this debt be repaid? Cash inflows from operations amounted to £721.2 million for the financial year ended 27 January 2018. With annual cash inflows this strong, there is little doubt that the company has the operating cash inflows to meet these liabilities when they become due.

In reality, the group's bankers will probably offer the company new loans with which to repay their existing loans when they are due for payment, fixing the interest rates on these new loans for a further five to 10 years. Much public company borrowing is rolled over in this way: borrowings are not actually repaid, they are just swapped for new borrowings at rates of interest fixed at a suitable level given the prevailing market rate of interest at the time the new borrowings are taken out.

Consistency of product demand

As a clothing retailer appealing to the 16–35 age group, Next has a consistency of demand for its goods ensuring a steady stream of profits and cash flows for the foreseeable future. There is nothing risky in its business and nothing to suggest that its products will suddenly go out of fashion. This would not be the case for a mobile phone manufacturer, for example, whose products might suddenly become obsolete if a revolutionary new technology were to be introduced to the market by a competitor.

Source: *Next 2018 report and accounts* www.next.co.uk

9

GIVE ME AN EXAMPLE 9.5   The dangers of borrowing too much

The private equity firm Terra Firma bought EMI plc in 2007 for £4.2 billion. Despite turning the ailing music business round and generating much improved profitability, with operating profit rising to nearly £300 million, by late 2010 it was clear that Terra Firma had paid far too much for EMI. Interest on the borrowings used to fund the acquisition could not be met from the improved operating cash inflows, resulting in Citigroup, Terra Firma's lender, taking control of EMI in February 2011. Organisations that do not keep within their borrowing capacity will not survive, so it is important for entities to borrow only as much as they can afford to service through interest payments and to repay when the debt becomes due. Contrast Terra Firma's situation with that of Next, whose interest cover of 21.71 times and operating cash inflows of £721.2 million from which to meet annual interest payments of around £35 million indicate that their borrowings are highly affordable.

Source: *Guardian* news 5 February 2010; *Financial Times* news 14 February 2010

---

unhealthy gearing ratio turns out to be perfectly sound when all the facts are taken into consideration. When evaluating long-term solvency and financial stability, you should look at:

- The interest cover to determine how affordable the borrowings are: does the business generate sufficiently high profits from which to meet interest payments?
- The dates on which repayments are to be made: the more distant the repayment date, the higher the chance the business has of meeting repayment by that date.
- The strength of the operating cash inflows from the statement of cash flows: high operating cash inflows indicate that there will be sufficient cash on hand both to repay borrowings when they become due for payment and to pay the annual interest payable on those borrowings.
- The consistency of demand for a company's products: the more consistent the demand, the less likely the company will be to face financial difficulties in the future and be unable to meet its liabilities when they become due. You should also think about the likelihood of new products from different firms replacing the current market leader's products: the more likely this is, the riskier the business will be and the higher the possibility that they could eventually default on their borrowings.

WHY IS THIS RELEVANT TO ME?   When are borrowings risky?

To enable you as an accounting professional to:

- Appreciate that apparently high levels of borrowings do not always indicate potential problems for an organisation in meeting repayments when these become due
- Evaluate the affordability of long-term borrowings and the ability of entities to repay those borrowings from current resources and cash inflows
- Consider the consistency of demand for a business's products and the impact that replacement products would have on a business's long-term solvency and financial stability

NUMERICAL EXERCISES   Do you think you can calculate long- and short-term solvency and financial stability ratios, working capital ratios and evaluate the cash conversion cycle and timing of payments for a real company? Can you interpret these ratios in a meaningful way? Have a look at Numerical exercises 9.1 dealing with the financial statements of Greggs plc and then have a go at the various exercises linked to this example in the **online workbook**.

APPENDIX: RATIOS CONSIDERED IN THIS CHAPTER

To assist your learning, the ratios we have considered in this chapter are summarised in Table 9.3.

Table 9.3 Calculations and descriptions for the liquidity, working capital and long-term financial stability ratios discussed in this chapter

	Calculation	What does this ratio tell us?
Liquidity ratios		
Current ratio	$\dfrac{\text{Current assets}}{\text{Current liabilities}}$	The current ratio presents the £s of current assets per £1 of current liabilities. The ratio shows us whether an organisation has sufficient short-term assets with which to meet short-term liabilities immediately.
Quick (acid test) ratio	$\dfrac{(\text{Current assets} - \text{inventory})}{\text{Current liabilities}}$	This ratio removes inventory from current assets and then compares the resulting figure with current liabilities. Inventory is removed from current assets on the assumption that it is not readily convertible into cash in the near future. The quick ratio compares current assets that are cash or that are readily realisable in cash (trade receivables) with current liabilities in an attempt to determine whether an entity is able to cover immediately its short-term commitments from readily realisable current assets.
Working capital ratios		
Inventory days	$\dfrac{\text{Inventory}}{\text{Cost of sales}} \times 365$	This ratio measures the average stockholding period, how long an entity holds goods in inventory before they are sold. The shorter the inventory holding period the better, as inventory is turned into sales (and hence into cash) much more quickly while obsolete inventories and the risk of deterioration (and hence loss of future cash inflows from the sale of this inventory) are minimised.

→

	Calculation	What does this ratio tell us?
Receivables days	$\dfrac{\text{Trade receivables}}{\text{Credit sales}} \times 365$	This ratio indicates the average credit period taken by credit customers. This is the length of time it takes for credit customers to pay what they owe.
Payables days	$\dfrac{\text{Trade receivables}}{\text{Cost of sales}} \times 365$	This ratio measures how quickly the business is paying off its suppliers for purchases made on credit. Ideally, the receivables days and payables days should be equal: as cash is received, it is used to pay off liabilities.
Cash conversion cycle	Inventory days + receivables days – payables days	The cash conversion cycle tells us how quickly inventory is turned into trade receivables and how quickly trade receivables are turned into cash with which to pay trade payables. The shorter this cycle, the better the working capital is being managed and the more readily cash is available with which to meet liabilities as they fall due.
Long-term solvency (financial stability) ratios		
Gearing %	$\dfrac{\text{Long and short-term borrowings}}{\text{Equity}} \times 100\%$	The gearing percentage compares all borrowings to the equity of an entity. This ratio is often seen as a measure of risk: companies with higher borrowings are supposedly more risky than those with lower borrowings.
Debt ratio	$\dfrac{\text{Total liabilities}}{\text{Total assets}}$	This ratio measures the £s of liabilities per £1 of total assets. The lower the debt ratio, the more secure the entity.
Interest cover	$\dfrac{\text{Profit before interest and tax}}{\text{Interest (finance expense)}}$	Assesses how many times interest payable on borrowings is covered by operating profits to determine the affordability of monies borrowed. The higher the figure, the better, as a high figure indicates an ability to continue meeting interest payments from profits in the future.

9

CHAPTER SUMMARY

You should now have learnt that:

- An entity's liquidity depends upon how quickly goods purchased and traded are turned into cash

- Current and quick ratios express the relationship between current assets and current liabilities at an arbitrary point in time, the statement of financial position date

- Current and quick ratios make the misleading and unrealistic assumption that creditors will demand the payment of all monies owed on the day immediately following the accounting period end

- Careful working capital management is vital to an organisation's short-term liquidity

- Working capital ratios are used to determine the speed of an entity's cash conversion cycle

- A full appreciation of the short-term liquidity of an organisation must be based upon an assessment of the timing of cash receipts and cash payments

- Long-term solvency and financial stability depends upon an entity's ability to repay interest and borrowings from operating cash flows

QUICK REVISION   Test your knowledge with the online flashcards in Summary of key concepts and attempt the Multiple choice questions, all in the **online workbook**.

END-OF-CHAPTER QUESTIONS

Solutions to these questions can be found in the **online workbook**.

❯ DEVELOP YOUR UNDERSTANDING

❯ Question 9.1

Samoco plc operates a chain of in town grocery convenience stores and edge of town supermarkets across the UK. The company is expanding rapidly and is adding new stores every year. Below are the statements of profit or loss for the company for the years ended 31 May 2019 and 31 May 2018 together with statements of financial position at those dates.

Samoco plc: Statements of profit or loss for the years ended 31 May 2019 and 31 May 2018

	2019 £m	2018 £m
Revenue	13,663	12,249
Cost of sales	12,570	11,330
Gross profit	1,093	919
Distribution and selling costs	121	108
Administration expenses	240	225
Operating profit	732	586

→

	2019 £m	2018 £m
Finance income	20	15
Finance expense	104	84
Profit before tax	648	517
Income tax	162	129
Profit for the year	**486**	**388**

Samoco plc: statements of financial position at 31 May 2019 and 31 May 2018

	2019 £m	2018 £m
ASSETS		
Non-current assets		
Property, plant and equipment	**6,040**	**5,150**
Current assets		
Inventories	485	500
Other receivables	45	40
Cash and cash equivalents	122	99
	652	639
Total assets	**6,692**	**5,789**
LIABILITIES		
Current liabilities		
Current portion of long-term borrowings	240	216
Trade payables	830	790
Other payables	150	140
Dividends	200	180
Current tax	170	150
	1,590	1,476
Non-current liabilities		
Long-term borrowings	2,230	2,024
Pension liabilities	756	524
	2,986	2,548
Total liabilities	**4,576**	**4,024**
Net assets	**2,116**	**1,765**
EQUITY		
Called up share capital	110	100
Share premium	145	140
Retained earnings	1,861	1,525
Total equity	**2,116**	**1,765**

9

Notes to the financial statements:

- Samoco plc's sales are made on an entirely cash basis, with no credit being allowed to customers at its convenience stores and supermarkets. Therefore, at 31 May 2019 and 31 May 2018 there were no monies owed by trade receivables.

- Finance expense is made up entirely of interest payable on the long-term borrowings.

- Samoco plc's long-term borrowings are repayable by equal annual instalments over the next 10 years.

Required

(a) Using the financial statements for Samoco plc calculate for both years:

- Current ratio

- Quick ratio

- Inventory days

- Payables days

- The cash conversion cycle

- Gearing %

- Debt ratio

- Interest cover

(b) Using the ratios you have calculated and the financial statements above, evaluate the liquidity, working capital and long-term solvency and financial stability of Samoco plc at 31 May 2019.

> **Question 9.2**

A colleague who has just started studying accounting on her business degree has read in another book that companies without current ratios of 2:1 and quick (acid test) ratios of 1:1 will find it difficult to meet their current liabilities as they fall due. She has just noticed your current and quick ratio calculations for Samoco plc in Question 9.1 and has concluded that the company is about to collapse. Using the information in Question 9.1, ratios that you have already calculated and details of when liabilities can be assumed to be due for payment presented below, calculate the maximum amount of the current liabilities of Samoco plc that could be due for repayment on the day after the statement of financial position date (1 June 2019 and 1 June 2018). Draw up arguments to put to your colleague to show her that a simple reliance on current and quick ratios as an indicator of short-term liquidity fails to address all the relevant issues.

For the purposes of this exercise you should assume that current liabilities are due for payment as follows:

- Bank loans: repayable in 12 monthly instalments

- Trade payables: repayable according to your payables days calculations in Question 9.1

- Current tax: due in four instalments: three months, six months, nine months and 12 months after the statement of financial position date

- Other payables: assume that 20 per cent of this figure is payable immediately

- Dividends: due for payment in August 2019 and August 2018

You can assume that there are 360 days during the financial year on which Samoco plc's shops are open and trading.

>> TAKE IT FURTHER

>> Question 9.3

Listed below is information relating to four companies:

- Ted Baker is a global lifestyle brand that operates through three main distribution channels: retail (including e-commerce), wholesale and licensing (including territorial and product licences). The company offers a wide range of fashion and lifestyle collections.

- Nichols is a producer of still and carbonated soft drinks.

- The Weir Group is an engineering company which focuses mainly on the production and maintenance of pumps and valves for use in the mining, oil and gas industries.

- National Express is a leading public transport operator with bus, coach and rail services in the UK, Continental Europe, North Africa, North America and the Middle East.

	Ted Baker	Nichols	Weir Group	National Express
Year ended	27/01/2018	31/12/2017	31/12/2017	31/12/2017
Income statement	£m	£m	£m	£m
(= statement of profit or loss)				
Revenue	591.7	132.8	2,355.9	2,321.2
Cost of sales	230.9	72.2	1,619.2	1,405.1
Operating profit	70.7	28.7	223.1	197.9
Finance expense	3.3	—	38.2	44.6

	Ted Baker	Nichols	Weir Group	National Express
Year end date	27/01/2018	31/12/2017	31/12/2017	31/12/2017
Statement of financial position	£m	£m	£m	£m
Total assets	449.2	127.4	3,593.5	3,451.5
Total liabilities	225.1	28.1	2,122.4	2,285.1
Current assets				
Inventory	187.2	4.8	586.8	24.9
Trade receivables	42.7	31.3	492.9	238.8
Other receivables	22.8	3.4	179.2	134.4
Cash and cash equivalents	16.7	36.1	284.6	314.3
Current assets (total)	**269.4**	**75.6**	**1,543.5**	**712.4**
Bank overdrafts	76.0	—	0.1	—
Bank loans	5.5	—	388.3	167.4
Trade payables	36.3	6.8	341.7	258.5
Other current liabilities	59.0	16.8	383.6	500.8
Current liabilities (total)	**176.8**	**23.6**	**1,113.7**	**926.7**
Total equity	224.1	99.3	1,471.1	1,166.4
Total borrowings	128.5	—	1,127.8	1,225.4

9

Using the financial information, calculate for all four companies:

- Current ratio
- Quick ratio
- Inventory days
- Receivables days
- Payables days
- The cash conversion cycle
- Gearing percentage
- Debt ratio
- Interest cover

≫ Question 9.4

Given the activities of each company, comment on how you would expect each company to generate its cash inflows together with an assessment of the liquidity, solvency and long-term financial stability of each company. Your answers should address the following issues, among others:

- The current and quick ratios of the four companies.
- The cash conversion cycles of the four companies.
- Why do the inventory, receivables and payables days vary so much in the four companies?
- The gearing levels in the four companies and whether these are manageable.

9

CORPORATE GOVERNANCE AND SUSTAINABILITY

10

LEARNING OUTCOMES

Once you have read this chapter and worked through the questions and examples in both this chapter and the online workbook, you should be able to:

- Understand the control problems that arise within limited liability companies as a result of shareholders appointing directors to run the companies in which they invest

- Describe how the agency problem arises whenever a task is delegated to another party

- Define what is meant by the term corporate governance

- Describe the roles and responsibilities of the various participants in the corporate governance process

- Outline how corporate governance is used to monitor and control directors' actions and decisions to focus on the long term success of a business

- Describe how the Corporate Governance Code and other regulations work together to assure the integrity of the financial reporting process

- Appreciate that the modern corporation has responsibilities beyond just generating a profit for shareholders

- Describe corporate social responsibility reporting and what it involves

- Define the term sustainability

- Appreciate that the modern business entity is expected to present more than just financial information about its operations and activities
- Discuss how information about a range of performance measures beyond mere financial measures is beneficial to an organisation and its long-term survival

10

INTRODUCTION

Directors are appointed by shareholders to run companies on their behalf (Chapter 1, Control, accounting and accountability) (Figure 10.1). Shareholders firstly want to know that the resources entrusted to the directors are being used effectively and efficiently to generate profits and dividends. As shareholders are not involved in the day-to-day running of the company, their only source of financial information about their company is the annual report and accounts. The annual report and accounts are prepared by the directors. Shareholders thus have an information asymmetry problem: the directors know all about the company but shareholders know only what they are told (Figure 10.1). As a result of this information asymmetry, various other questions arise for shareholders. How can they be sure that what the directors are telling them in the annual financial statements is a fair representation of what has actually happened during the past 12 months? Are the directors hiding anything? Do the annual financial statements tell them everything they need to know for decision making purposes? Apart from the financial results, how can shareholders be sure that the directors are running the business honestly, ethically and in accordance with the law? Is their company a good corporate citizen or are the directors engaging in illegal or morally suspect behaviour? What controls are there on the directors to make sure that they always take the right decisions and always act in the best interests of the shareholders?

These questions also arise as a result of the agency problem. In these situations, someone (the agent) is entrusted to undertake a task by someone else (the principal). In the case of limited companies, the shareholders are the principals who appoint the directors as their agents (Figure 10.1).

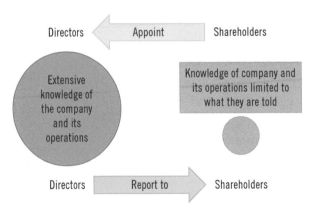

Figure 10.1 Information asymmetry between directors and shareholders

In an ideal world, the aims and objectives of the shareholders and of the directors would be exactly the same. However, the agency problem means that agents will always act in their own best interests and not in those of their principals. Directors will therefore seek to maximise the short-term profits of the company and thereby their own remuneration rather than taking decisions now that will generate long-term benefits for the shareholders. This is not a problem in small companies in which shareholders and directors are the same persons. But in listed companies (public limited companies, plcs), directors do not remain in their posts for lengthy periods of time, so, by the time today's investments pay off in say 5 or 10 years' time, the directors may no longer be employed by the company and so they will gain no benefit from considering the long-term interests of shareholders at the expense of their own short-term advantage.

Happily, help is at hand. The Companies Act 2006 together with Corporate Governance as enshrined in the Corporate Governance Code provides rules and guidance on many aspects of organisational management with a view to ensuring that entities are fully under control, that directors are not exceeding their powers and that business entities are run for the long-term benefit of stakeholders and not just to satisfy the short-term interests of directors. This chapter will consider in outline how these legal and governance rules work in order to limit shareholders' concerns over the running of their companies.

WHY IS THIS RELEVANT TO ME?   The information asymmetry and agency problems

To enable you as an accounting professional to understand:

- What is meant by the terms agency problem and information asymmetry
- The control problems that arise when shareholders delegate the running of companies to directors
- The causes of the problems that may arise from information asymmetry and the agency problem

---

GO BACK OVER THIS AGAIN!   Do you fully appreciate the control problems that arise in limited liability companies as a result of the agency problem and information asymmetry? Go to the **online workbook** and have a go at Exercises 10.1 to check your understanding.

CORPORATE GOVERNANCE: A BRIEF HISTORY

Following a series of financial scandals and corporate collapses in the late 1980s and early 1990s which had undermined the credibility of reported financial information and eroded trust in business, the Financial Reporting Council, the London Stock Exchange and the accountancy profession established the Committee on the Financial Aspects of Corporate Governance with Sir Adrian Cadbury as its chair. The aim of the committee was to consider the ways in which investor confidence in the honesty and accountability of listed companies should be restored. The Committee's report in 1992 was named after its chair and is always known as the Cadbury Report. All the proposals in the Cadbury Report were built on existing good practice, but the report gave them much more formal recognition and established the basis on which all publicly listed and public interest companies would henceforth be governed.

CORPORATE GOVERNANCE: A DEFINITION

What is meant by the term corporate governance? Section 2.5 of the Cadbury Report provides the following definition:

> Corporate governance is the system by which companies are directed and controlled. Boards of directors are responsible for the governance of their companies. The shareholders' role in governance is to appoint the directors and the auditors and to satisfy themselves that an appropriate governance structure is in place. The responsibilities of the board include setting the company's strategic aims, providing the leadership to put them into effect, supervising the management of the business and reporting to shareholders on their stewardship. The board's actions are subject to laws, regulations and the shareholders in general meeting.

The original report produced by the Cadbury Committee has been updated over the intervening years to embrace additional aspects in Corporate Governance. However, the main features are clear from the above quotation. The current Corporate Governance Code is built up of the main principles, supporting principles and code provisions. The aim of the Corporate Governance Code is to ensure that shareholders and boards of directors interact and work together to ensure that their company is effectively directed and controlled. Before we consider how the Code shows how effective direction and control can be achieved, let's look at the different parties who play a role in the corporate governance process.

SUMMARY OF KEY CONCEPTS   Can you remember the definition of corporate governance? Go to the **online workbook** to revise this definition with summary of key concepts 10.1.

CORPORATE GOVERNANCE: THE PARTIES INVOLVED

Figure 10.2 sets out the key participants in the corporate governance process. These participants and their corporate governance roles and responsibilities will each be considered in turn. Once these roles and responsibilities are clear, we can then determine how the interaction of the various parties aims to ensure that publicly listed and public interest companies are effectively directed and controlled in order to address the concerns that shareholders have.

The board of directors: executive and non-executive directors

All companies have a board of directors who are responsible for running the company. The board of directors is made up of two categories of director: executive and non-executive. Both executive and non-executive directors are elected by the shareholders. The executive directors are responsible for the day-to-day running and management of the company, implementing policies and dealing with all the operational issues that arise on a daily basis. Executive directors are employees of the company and are remunerated on the basis of their employment contracts with the company.

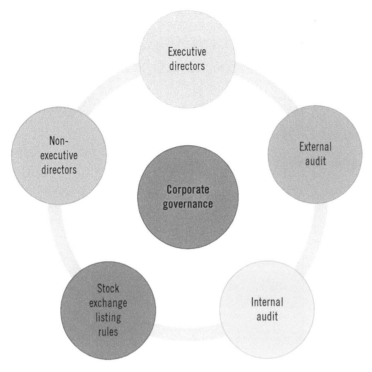

Figure 10.2 The key parties involved in the Corporate Governance process

Non-executive directors, on the other hand, do not perform any executive management functions. They are thus not involved in any day-to-day running of the business. Despite being members of the board of directors, non-executive directors are not employees of the company but charge fees for their services rather than receiving a salary.

Non-executive directors attend monthly board meetings and also set up and run various board committees. These board committees are composed of non-executive directors only and they fulfil critical functions in relation to financial reporting (the audit committee), directors' remuneration and the nomination of new board members. Figure 10.3 summarises the roles and responsibilities of both the executive and the non-executive directors.

10

WHY IS THIS RELEVANT TO ME?   Board of directors: executive and non-executive directors

To enable you as an accounting professional to understand:

- The different roles of the executive and non-executive directors in the running of listed and public interest companies
- That executive directors are excluded from the financial reporting (audit), directors' remuneration and nomination committees

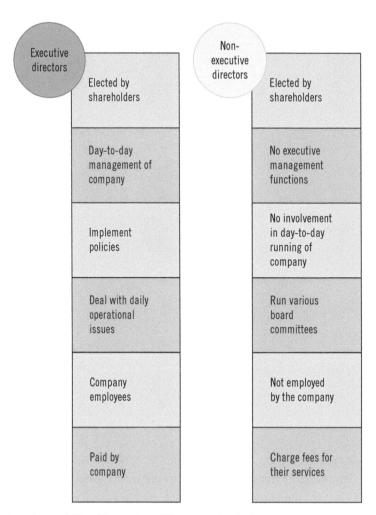

Figure 10.3 The roles and responsibilities of the executive and the non-executive directors

---

SUMMARY OF KEY CONCEPTS   Are you certain you can describe the different duties and roles of executive and non-executive directors? Go to the **online workbook** to check your recollection with summary of key concepts 10.2.

GO BACK OVER THIS AGAIN!   Are you confident that you can distinguish between the roles of the executive and non-executive directors? Go to the **online workbook** and have a go at Exercises 10.2 to check your ability in this area.

External audit

The directors prepare the financial statements for their company on an annual basis. As we noted earlier (this chapter, Introduction: the information asymmetry and agency problems) accounting results for the year might not reflect all the relevant facts and figures. Alternatively, because directors control the financial reporting process and content, the annual report and accounts might be presented in a more favourable way than is warranted in order to secure greater financial rewards and continued employment for the directors. Therefore, shareholders require reasonable assurance that the figures in the annual report and accounts present a true and fair view of the results for the year together with all the relevant disclosures and details required by both the Companies Act 2006 and by the financial reporting standards issued by the International Accounting Standards Board.

In order to gain this assurance, shareholders (not directors) appoint auditors annually at the annual general meeting. Auditors are qualified accountants who are completely independent of the company they are auditing. They review the financial statements presented by the directors, undertake testing of balances and transactions on a sample basis in order to verify that the financial statements present a true and fair view of the financial position of the company at the year end and of the profit or loss and the cash flows for the year. In addition, auditors use their expert knowledge and experience to ensure that all the disclosures required by the Companies Act 2006 and by International Financial Reporting Standards have been made in full and that no material information is omitted. All audit procedures are carried out in accordance with International Standards on Auditing (ISAs) issued by the International Auditing and Assurance Standards Board (IAASB).

Auditors report directly to shareholders without any interference from the directors in order to safeguard the independence of their report and their findings. The audit report comments on the financial statements prepared by the directors (note that the auditors do not prepare the financial statements—this is a common misunderstanding of the auditors' role). Where the financial statements do not make all the relevant disclosures or where directors have obstructed the auditors in the performance of their duties, then the auditors can inform the shareholders of their concerns in their report or in person at the annual general meeting.

The auditors' work and their reports enable users of financial statements to place a high degree of confidence in the audited financial information and in the audit reports attached to them. The auditor and the audit process also facilitate the workings of the capital markets which require assurance on the truth and fairness of financial information as a basis for the buying and selling of shares. Audited information is also used as a reliable basis for both investment in and lending to limited liability companies.

10

WHY IS THIS RELEVANT TO ME?   External audit

To provide you with:

- A brief overview of the role of external auditors in the financial reporting regime
- A foundation for your later studies in auditing

SUMMARY OF KEY CONCEPTS   Do you think you can describe the roles and responsibilities of external audit? Go to the **online workbook** to check your abilities in this area with summary of key concepts 10.3.

GO BACK OVER THIS AGAIN!   Are you certain you understand the role and activities of external auditors? Go to the **online workbook** and have a go at Exercises 10.3 to check your understanding.

Internal audit

The internal audit function on the other hand is set up by the board of directors. As the name indicates, internal audit activities are undertaken by individuals working within the organisation. Whereas external audit is narrowly focused on the truth and fairness of the annual financial report and accounts and their compliance with the relevant legislation and international financial reporting standards, internal audit is given a very much wider ranging remit. While external audit aims to verify past results, internal audit is focused on not just past but also current operations as well as being forward looking and proactive. Internal audit concentrates attention upon the entire range of organisational operations involving an assessment of the effectiveness of the risk management, control and governance procedures alongside an evaluation of the integrity and accuracy of the reporting and internal control systems. Internal audit reports provide evaluations of every aspect of a business's activity with a view to improving and enhancing those activities to further the business's objectives and to help it achieve its aims. The aim of internal audit is always to add value to an organisation and its activities.

In the same way as external audit, internal audit, despite being staffed by employees of the business, aims to provide independent reports of its findings. This independence is enhanced by reporting not to the executive directors (who might be criticised by internal audit or seek to limit the internal auditors' range of activities) but to the independent non-executive directors on the audit committee. Internal auditors are not involved in the day-to-day operations of a business (you cannot be independent when you are evaluating your own work) but stand back from daily operational activities to present an objective overview of operations and activities, their effectiveness and their compliance with the legal and ethical obligations of the entity. This organisational independence from management enables unrestricted evaluation of management activities and personnel. Figure 10.4 presents a comparison of internal and external audit.

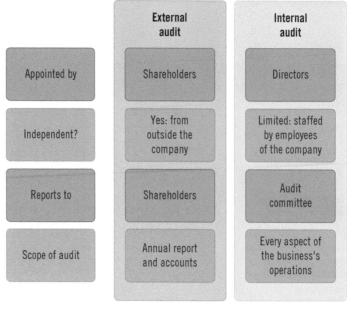

	External audit	Internal audit
Appointed by	Shareholders	Directors
Independent?	Yes: from outside the company	Limited: staffed by employees of the company
Reports to	Shareholders	Audit committee
Scope of audit	Annual report and accounts	Every aspect of the business's operations

Figure 10.4 A comparison of external and internal audit

Directors have a responsibility to ensure that organisational operations and activities are fully under control and that assets are adequately safeguarded (for example, how easily could cash be stolen from a business?). To fulfil these responsibilities, the board of directors will set up an internal control system which puts in place checks and balances whose aim is both to prevent fraud and errors occurring and to result in their discovery if they do. Internal audit will assess and evaluate these internal control systems to determine their effectiveness and their ability to prevent the theft of assets and the occurrence of errors. In addition, a rigorous review of the internal controls will enable internal auditors to assess the reliability of information used in the financial and management reporting systems as well as evaluating an organisation's full compliance with laws and regulations.

WHY IS THIS RELEVANT TO ME?   Internal audit

To enable you as an accounting professional to appreciate:

* The extensive and wide ranging role of internal auditors within organisations
* The differences in the roles and responsibilities of both internal and external auditors
* How internal auditors continually monitor management and operations in shareholders' best interests

SUMMARY OF KEY CONCEPTS   Are you sure that you can describe the roles and responsibilities of internal audit? Go to the **online workbook** to check your abilities in this area with Summary of key concepts 10.4.

GO BACK OVER THIS AGAIN!   Are you confident that you understand what internal auditors do? Go to the **online workbook** and have a go at Exercises 10.4 to check your understanding.

GO BACK OVER THIS AGAIN!   Are you able to distinguish between the roles and responsibilities of internal and external auditors? Go to the **online workbook** and have a go at Exercises 10.5 to check your abilities in this area.

10

Stock exchange rules

Public limited companies can apply to have their shares listed on a recognised stock exchange. All companies accepted and listing their shares on the London Stock Exchange must ensure that they comply with the mandatory listing rules. The aim of these listing rules is to protect investors and to uphold the highest standards of conduct in those companies listing their shares. The listing rules guarantee the efficiency and regulation of the stock market, providing, in the same way as auditors do for company financial statements, a high degree of confidence in the operations and integrity of the market. One of the listing rules requires that all companies listing on the Stock Exchange should abide by the Corporate Governance Code. The rules dictate that listed companies provide a statement in their annual report and accounts stating how the principles in the Corporate Governance Code have been applied. Confirmation of compliance with the Code's provisions is also required. In situations where listed companies have not complied with the Code's principles, they must provide an explanation of their non-compliance. This regime is referred to as 'comply or explain'. This oversight by the Stock Exchange provides an additional safeguard for investors. Compliance with the listing rules ensures that boards of directors study the Code to make sure that they do comply. Studying the Code in this way will help the directors to determine whether their company is complying or not. Where they are not complying, they can take steps to make sure that their procedures and operations are in full compliance.

WHY IS THIS RELEVANT TO ME?   Stock exchange rules

To enable you as an accounting professional to appreciate:

● The role of the stock exchange rules and oversight in corporate governance

● The disclosures companies have to make in their annual reports and accounts to certify compliance with the stock exchange rules

---

SUMMARY OF KEY CONCEPTS   Are you quite sure you understand the role of the stock exchange rules in corporate governance? Go to the **online workbook** to check your understanding with summary of key concepts 10.5.

ADDRESSING SHAREHOLDER CONCERNS

Now that the participants in the corporate governance process are clear, we can consider the ways in which these participants and the Corporate Governance Code itself work together to meet shareholders' concerns. These concerns fall under various headings, so we shall consider each issue in turn under a separate heading.

Long-term success v. short-term profits

Firstly, let's consider how the Corporate Governance Code addresses the issue of whether the directors' focus should be on long-term success or short-term profits. Shareholders invest for the long term, whereas directors aim to achieve the highest short-term profits possible in order to maximise their remuneration. These opposing aims pull in opposite directions as shown in Figure 10.5.

Figure 10.5 The opposing aims of directors and shareholders

Given this tension between the two opposing interests, shareholders will want reassurance that it is their long-term interests that are at the centre of directors' decision making. Both the Companies Act 2006 and the Corporate Governance Code recognise this conflict and give shareholders' interests priority. The Companies Act 2006 and the Corporate Governance Code together emphasise that it is the long-term success of the company that counts. Section 172(1) of the Companies Act 2006 imposes a duty on directors to promote the success of the company and requires directors to consider the likely consequences of any decision in the long term. This long-term focus is given further emphasis in the Corporate Governance Code which stresses as a main principle that '[e]very company should be headed by an effective board which is collectively responsible for the *long-term success* of the company' (Corporate Governance Code, Section A Leadership, emphasis added). This aim of long-term success is a recurring theme in the Corporate Governance Code, with this objective being stated once in the preface (paragraph 4) and twice in the introductory section on Governance and the Code (paragraphs 1 and 4).

Company decision making

Directors should work together as a board, to make decisions as a body not as individuals. However, shareholders will worry that the board of directors might not be acting in the best interests of the business, might be taking unnecessary risks or might include directors who are acting on their own initiative without consulting the other directors about the decisions they are taking. Section A of the Corporate Governance Code deals with the leadership of a company and states the main principle that 'every company should be headed by an effective board which is *collectively* responsible for the long-term success of the company' (emphasis added). The board is thus required to work as a unit and to take decisions together rather than individual directors making decisions without consulting the board as a whole. How does this work in practice? Give me an example 10.1 presents Ted Baker's statement relating to board operations in the company's Corporate Governance report. This example illustrates the directors' collective responsibility for decision making exercised by the board working together as a complete unit as a means of preventing risky individual actions in key strategic and operational decisions.

GIVE ME AN EXAMPLE 10.1   Collective decision making by the board

'BOARD OPERATION

The Board meets regularly throughout the year. It considers, with the support of the Board Committees and the Executive Committee, all issues relating to the strategy, direction and future development of the Group. The Board has a schedule of matters reserved to it for decision that is regularly updated. These include decisions on the Group's strategy, financial budgets, major capital expenditure and transactions, appointment of territorial and product licence partners, store openings, dividend policy, Group bonus and risk profile. The requirement for Board approval on these matters is understood and communicated widely throughout the Group.'

Ted Baker Annual report and accounts 2017/2018

Source: http://www.tedbakerplc.com

As well as collective responsibility for decisions, the Code emphasises that a clear division of responsibilities should exist within the board of directors. The executive directors are responsible for running the business on a day-to-day basis while the non-executive directors' role is to run the board and its associated committees. Section A of the Code sets out the main principle that '[t]here should be a clear division of responsibilities at the head of the company between the running of the board and the executive responsibility for the running of the company's business. No one individual should have unfettered powers of decision' (Section A Leadership, Supporting principles) so that every board member participates in the decision making process as illustrated by the wording presented in Give me an example 10.1. In order to ensure that there is a clear division of duties, the Code requires that 'the roles of chairperson and chief executive should not be exercised by the same individual' (Section A, Leadership, Code provision 2.1). This clear division of duties ensures that no one person has unrestricted decision-making responsibility. In situations in which one individual makes all the decisions, then risks are increased as opposing views and counsels are ignored and there is no restraining hand to rein in dominant personalities. Splitting the leadership of the company and requiring key decisions to be taken by the board of directors as a whole will reassure shareholders that the direction of the business is fully under control and extreme or excessively risky actions are being avoided.

This all sounds like a very good control mechanism on the executive directors but what is to prevent the executive directors simply overwhelming the non-executive directors through sheer force of numbers and forcing their policies through? This problem is addressed in a supporting principle to Section B of the Code which requires that each company board should comprise of a suitable combination of executive and non-executive directors. Code provision B1.2 takes this further and dictates that half the board, excluding the chair (who should always be a non-executive director), should be made up of non-executive directors. This provision thus aims to ensure that the non-executive directors cannot be dominated by the executive directors to enable effective enforcement of corporate governance in each and every company. Give me an example 10.2 presents an example of how this works in practice.

GIVE ME AN EXAMPLE 10.2   *Non-executive and executive director numbers*

The board of Ted Baker plc is made up of 2 executive directors, one non-executive chair and 3 non-executive directors. The three non-executive directors have lengthy experience in e-commerce, digital transformation and brand marketing, banking and international retail and are all considered to be independent. Through this structure, the board has a balance of skills, experience and independence in combination with the executive directors' knowledge and experience in both the fashion industry and finance. The number of non-executive directors comfortably exceeds the number of the executive directors so that the non-executive directors can fulfil their oversight and advisory roles effectively.

Source: *Ted Baker Annual report and accounts 2017/2018*, http://www.tedbakerplc.com

WHY IS THIS RELEVANT TO ME?   Company decision making

To enable you as an accounting professional to appreciate that:

- The executive directors run the business on a day-to-day basis
- The non-executive directors run the board and its associated committees
- The Corporate Governance Code requires that no one individual should have unfettered powers of decision making and control
- All board members both executive and non-executive participate in the decision making process
- The chair and chief executive roles are exercised by different individuals

GO BACK OVER THIS AGAIN!   Are you sure you understand the roles of the various parties in the decision-making process in companies? Go to the **online workbook** and have a go at Exercises 10.6 to check your appreciation of the Corporate Governance Code requirements in this area.

Board effectiveness

As we have seen, the Corporate Governance Code requires companies to be headed by an effective board. But how is this effectiveness achieved and what steps should directors be taking to ensure that they are effective? Directors should avoid complacency and just following the same approaches as in the past. They should question and test the strategy and direction of the company to make sure that the strategy adopted by the company is the most effective means of achieving the company's long-term goals. There should be procedures in place to ensure that directors are fulfilling their roles and responsibilities effectively and they should actively question their own effectiveness and review what they have achieved to determine what they might have done better. What does the Corporate Governance Code have to say about these aspects of board effectiveness?

Section B of the Code deals with effectiveness and states the main principle that '[t]he board and its committees should have the appropriate balance of skills, experience, independence and knowledge of the company to enable them to discharge their respective duties and responsibilities effectively'. The other main principles outlined in Section B are presented in Figure 10.6. These are the factors essential in promoting the effectiveness of the board and of the individual board members. To be effective, directors must have sufficient time in which to fulfil their duties, they need induction on starting in their roles and they should update their skills and knowledge on a regular basis. Timely information is essential to enable them to fulfil their roles together with periodic assessment of their performance by their fellow directors and feedback on whether they are meeting the requirements of the role. Shareholders are also involved in the assessment process as they are given a regular say on their directors' performance through the opportunity to re-elect the directors or to reject their re-appointment. A continuous flow of new blood onto boards to replace those retiring and to reinforce and strengthen the directors as a body is also required. Diversity on the board will encourage a

10

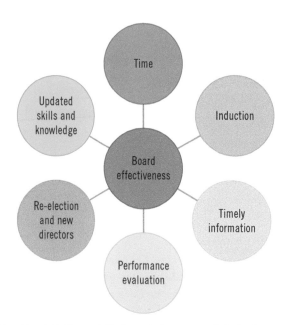

Figure 10.6 The main principles of board effectiveness in the Corporate Governance Code Section B

range of opinions and ideas to be put forward and a board with a suitable balance of skills will enable the shareholders to be confident that all the different aspects of controlling and directing the company are covered.

Non-executive directors have considerable knowledge, skills and experience gained in running other businesses as they are recruited from other publicly listed companies or other senior positions. This prior experience brings valuable insights and knowledge to boards of directors to ensure that these boards are effective in directing and controlling their companies. The non-executive directors provide an advisory and oversight function on the board. In this role, a main principle in Section A of the Code states that they should constructively challenge the executive directors and help to develop proposals on strategy. The non-executive directors' role is to take an independent, broad overview of the business and its progress to ensure that it is moving in the right direction and adopting the correct strategies through which to achieve its aims. As they are not employees of the company, non-executive directors are able to adopt a much more objective overview of the business which executive directors, due to their close involvement in the day-to-day affairs of the company, cannot take.

As a further control on the executive directors, the non-executive directors are required to meet as a body (without the executive directors being present) to discuss the company's affairs and to appraise the performance of the executive directors in meeting the objectives of the business. One of the main principles in Section B of the Code requires the board to 'undertake a formal and rigorous annual evaluation of its own performance and that of its committees and individual directors'. Appraisal of this kind ensures that directors are fulfilling their responsibilities effectively and acts as a timely corrective to any shortcomings in this respect.

To enable you as an accounting professional to understand:

- The steps boards of directors will take to ensure they fulfil their roles effectively
- That non-executive directors provide an oversight function on boards
- How board effectiveness is assessed

GO BACK OVER THIS AGAIN!   Are you confident you can say how boards ensure they are effective? Go to the **online workbook** and have a go at Exercises 10.7 to check your understanding.

Ensuring the integrity of financial statements

One of the most important duties of the board of directors is to prepare and present the annual financial statements. As we have seen earlier in this chapter, the shareholders' main concern relates to the completeness of the annual report and financial statements and whether they present a true and fair view of the profits, cash flows and financial position of the company in compliance with the reporting requirements of both the Companies Act 2006 and International Financial Reporting Standards.

What provisions are there in the Corporate Governance Code to ensure that the information presented in the annual report and financial statements shows a true and fair view of profits, cash flows and the statement of financial position and that all the information presented is complete and unbiased?

As the financial statements are audited by independent auditors from outside the company, the auditor's report already adds credibility to the financial information presented (this chapter, External audit). However, there is a risk that the directors may bully the auditor into accepting a reduction in the disclosures made or to agree to accounting treatments that are biased, reflecting the concerns of the directors rather than the true and fair view required by the Companies Act 2006. What guiding principles does the Corporate Governance Code provide with a view to preventing such misleading financial statements?

The Corporate Governance Code (Section C) requires that 'the board should present a fair, balanced and understandable assessment of the company's position and prospects'. This duty is imposed on the board as a whole, so all the members of the board of directors, both executive and non-executive, have to read, review and consider the financial statements to ensure that they adhere to these requirements. Further safeguards are added in the Code's supporting principles. As noted earlier (this chapter, The board of directors: executive and non-executive directors), the audit committee is made up of non-executive directors. There should be at least three independent non-executive directors on the audit committee, at least one of whom should have recent, relevant financial experience (Corporate Governance Code, Code Provision 3.1). This recent relevant financial experience will enable the audit committee to assess whether the report and

10

financial statements present a fair, balanced and understandable assessment of the company's position and prospects as mandated by the Corporate Governance Code. This supporting principle also requires the audit committee members to have competence relevant to the sector in which the company operates. This competence gives the audit committee a benchmark against which to evaluate the report and financial statements of an organisation and will enable the audit committee members to see potential gaps or potentially misleading information due to their in-depth sector knowledge and experience.

Code Provisions 3.2 and 3.4 also emphasise the audit committee's role in meeting the requirements of the code with respect to the financial statements. The audit committee's main role and responsibilities set out in written terms of reference should include:

- 'To monitor the integrity of the financial statements of the company and any formal announcements relating to the company's financial performance, reviewing significant financial reporting judgements contained in them (3.2).

- Where requested by the board, the audit committee should provide advice on whether the annual report and accounts, taken as a whole, is fair, balanced and understandable and provides the information necessary for shareholders to assess the company's position and performance, business model and strategy (3.4).'

As well as reviewing the final report and financial statements to ensure that they meet the requirements of the code, the audit committee is also charged with various duties that relate to ensuring the integrity of the financial records upon which the report and accounts are based. Thus Section 3.2 of the supporting principles also requires the audit committee to review the company's internal financial controls and internal control and risk management systems. Alongside this duty, the audit committee is tasked with monitoring and reviewing the effectiveness of the company's internal audit function and assessing the effectiveness and independence of the external auditors. The audit committee makes recommendations on the appointment and reappointment of the external auditor for the shareholders' consideration. Where the external auditor's independence appears to have been compromised, the audit committee can recommend the removal of the external auditor to the shareholders.

In addition to overseeing the external audit process, the audit committee and the external auditors meet on a regular basis to discuss the financial statements and any issues arising. These meetings between the members of the audit committee and the external auditors help to maintain auditor independence and the integrity of the external audit process: there are no executive directors on the audit committee who might pressure the external auditors in the ways suggested earlier, so the external auditors are free to express their opinions on the financial statements and any shortcomings they have identified. As the audit committee members are non-executive directors with a purely oversight role and whose fees are not affected by the financial results, there is no incentive for the audit committee members to pressurise the external auditors into accepting less than complete or misleading disclosures. Give me an example 10.3 provides extracts from the audit committee report of Ted Baker plc to illustrate the issues we have been considering in this section to show you how these provisions of the Code work in practice.

'AUDIT COMMITTEE REPORT

Dear Shareholder,

The role of the Audit Committee is to monitor the integrity of the Group's financial statements and reporting responsibilities and to maintain its internal control and compliance procedures.

This year, the Audit Committee met four times. In its meetings it focused on the Group's risk management, internal controls, tax, and external risk factors ...

This Audit Committee Report has been prepared in accordance with the Code and includes:

- a description of the significant issues that the Audit Committee considered in relation to the financial statements, and how these issues were addressed;
- an explanation of how the Audit Committee

has assessed the effectiveness of the external audit process and the approach taken to the reappointment of the external auditor, and information on the length of tenure of the current audit firm and when a tender was last conducted; and

- an explanation of how the Group's auditors' objectivity and independence are safeguarded when providing non-audit services.

Meetings with senior management, internal audit and the external auditor, together with the regular circulation and review of board papers and financial information, have enabled the Audit Committee to discharge its duties and responsibilities effectively.'

Ted Baker Annual report and accounts 2017/2018
Source: http://www.tedbakerplc.com

WHY IS THIS RELEVANT TO ME?   Ensuring the integrity of the financial statements

To enable you as an accounting professional to understand:

- How the Corporate Governance Code requires the board of directors as a whole to present a fair, balanced and understandable assessment of the company's position and prospects
- The ways in which the audit committee monitors the integrity of the financial statements
- That the audit committee is responsible for monitoring and reviewing the internal control and risk management systems of a company
- That the audit committee monitors the performance of the internal and external auditors
- The way in which the audit committee helps to maintain the independence and integrity of the external audit process

GO BACK OVER THIS AGAIN!   Do you think you understand how the integrity of the financial statements is assured? Go to the **online workbook** and have a go at Exercises 10.8 to check your understanding.

Directors' remuneration

As the directors run the company, what is to stop them deciding their own remuneration and paying themselves excessive amounts at the shareholders' expense? What restraints are there on the directors to prevent them abusing their position in this way?

The main principles stated in Section D of the Corporate Governance Code require that 'executive directors' remuneration should be designed to promote the long-term success of the company. Performance-related elements should be transparent, stretching and rigorously applied. There should be a formal and transparent procedure for developing policy on executive remuneration and for fixing the remuneration packages of individual directors. No director should be involved in deciding his or her own remuneration.' As a result of these clear principles, directors are unable to set their own remuneration. The remuneration of the executive directors is decided by the remuneration committee which is staffed entirely by non-executive directors. As the non-executive directors are responsible for evaluating the executive directors' performance (this chapter, Board effectiveness), they are in a very good position to determine the executive directors' remuneration. In this way, the Corporate Governance Code seeks to ensure that directors' remuneration is not excessive for the levels of profits and performance achieved.

Shareholder communications

The final shareholder concern relates to communications from their directors and how effective these are. Section E of the Corporate Governance Code presents the main principles in this area: 'There should be a dialogue with shareholders based on the mutual understanding of objectives. The board as a whole has responsibility for ensuring that a satisfactory dialogue with shareholders takes place. The board should use general meetings to communicate with investors and to encourage their participation.' Communications take place through the annual report and accounts and through the annual general meeting. Other communication opportunities are afforded to shareholders by the directors as illustrated in Give me an example 10.4.

10

GIVE ME AN EXAMPLE 10.4 *Shareholder communications*

'COMMUNICATION WITH SHAREHOLDERS

The Group attaches considerable importance to the effectiveness of its communication with its shareholders. The full report and accounts are sent to all shareholders and further copies are distributed to others with potential interest in the Group's performance.

Led by the Chief Executive, the Chief Operating Officer and the Finance Director, the Group seeks to build on a mutual understanding of objectives between the Company and its institutional shareholders by making general presentations after the interim and preliminary results; meeting shareholders and potential investors to discuss long-term issues and gathering feedback; and communicating regularly throughout the year via its investor relations programme. All shareholders have access to these presentations, as well as to the Annual Report and Accounts and to other information about the Company, through the investor relations website at www.tedbakerplc.com. Shareholders may also attend the Company's Annual General Meeting at which they have the opportunity to ask questions.

Non-Executive Directors are kept informed of the views of shareholders by the Executive Directors and are provided with independent feedback from investor meetings.'

Ted Baker Annual report and accounts 2017/2018
Source: http://www.tedbakerplc.com

Communications with shareholders thus take place on a regular basis to keep them informed of developments and other matters affecting them as shareholders. There is no attempt to keep matters hidden from the shareholders.

CORPORATE SOCIAL RESPONSIBILITY REPORTING

So far in this chapter, the main focus of corporate governance has been upon the directors of the company and their relationship with the shareholders. However, there are other stakeholders to consider together with a wider reporting and operational role for entities. Our discussions in Chapter 1 (The users of accounting information) reviewed the interests and information needs of other parties such as employees, customers, suppliers, the government and the general public. Should companies and businesses also be taking these other parties into account both in their operations and in their annual reports? Do companies have any reporting responsibilities beyond informing shareholders of profits generated and dividends paid?

The US economist, Milton Friedman, famously took a very strong line against businesses adopting any other approach than that of generating profit. Writing in *The New York Times Magazine* (September 13, 1970), Friedman quoted the following lines from his 1962 book Capitalism and Freedom:

> There is one and only one social responsibility of business—to use its resources and engage in activities designed to increase its profits so long as it stays within the rules of the game, which is to say, engages in open and free competition without deception or fraud.

On this view of a business, companies only exist to make a profit for shareholders and directors' sole responsibility is towards those shareholders. This view ignores entirely the effect that businesses and the products they produce have on the natural environment, on consumers, on communities and on other interested parties. As long as a profit is being made and made legally, nothing else is seen to matter. By extension, this argument proposes that directors should only report financial data and ignore any other performance measures and indicators.

By the 1960s, however, commentators and business people had begun to challenge the view that business had no other responsibilities beyond the mere generation of profit. Stakeholder theory presents the idea that directors and managers should balance the interests of all stakeholders (those with a stake or interest in a business) and not favour one group of interests over another. Employee welfare and development and a concern for the local environment and the people living within it were suggested as other measures that entities should consider when planning operations, designing new products and reporting on performance. This corporate social responsibility reporting approach is illustrated in Figure 10.7.

In the UK, this corporate social responsibility approach has also received attention in the Companies Act 2006. Section 172 of the Act sets out directors' duties in detail (emphasis added):

10

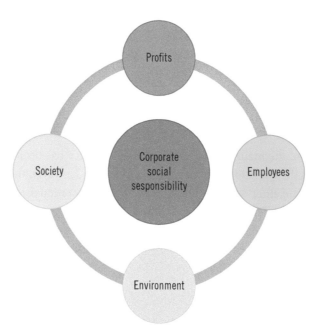

Figure 10.7 The corporate social responsibility reporting model for companies

Duty to promote the success of the company

Section 172 (1) A director of a company must act in the way he considers, in good faith, would be most likely to promote the success of the company for the benefit of its members as a whole, and in doing so have regard (amongst other matters) to—

(a) The likely consequences of any decision in the long term,

(b) The interests of the company's employees,

(c) The need to foster the company's business relationships with suppliers, customers and others,

(d) The impact of the company's operations on the community and the environment,

(e) The desirability of the company maintaining a reputation for high standards of business conduct, and

(f) The need to act fairly as between members of the company.

Notably, as indicated by the highlighted sections, directors are not just required to promote the success of the company for the benefit of shareholders (members) but for the benefit of other stakeholders and society as a whole as well. We saw in Chapter 1 (Users of accounting information) that there are various other user groups of financial accounting information besides shareholders, lenders and other creditors and it is the additional interests of these groups that the Companies Act 2006 requires directors to take into account.

This requirement to consider other interested parties as well as shareholders now extends to presenting information in the strategic report presented to shareholders. Section 414C of the Companies Act 2006 states that the following information should be presented by companies quoted on a stock exchange:

i.   environmental matters (including the impact of the company's business on the environment),

ii. the company's employees, and

iii. social, community and human rights issues,

including information about any policies of the company in relation to those matters and the effectiveness of those policies.

WHY IS THIS RELEVANT TO ME?   Corporate social responsibility reporting

To enable you as an accounting professional to appreciate:

- That the current view is that annual reports should report information relevant to a wider range of stakeholders than just shareholders
- The directors' duties as set out in company legislation
- The wide ranging duties that directors must fulfil in promoting the success of the company
- That directors should consider a wider range of interests than just those of shareholders

---

SUMMARY OF KEY CONCEPTS   Can you recall all the requirements of the directors' duty to promote the success of the company? Go to the **online workbook** to revise these requirements with Summary of key concepts 10.6.

10

The rationale for corporate social responsibility reporting

Why have business organisations bought into the corporate social responsibility debate? Why have they chosen, voluntarily, to consider and report to a wider set of stakeholders on aspects of their operations which do not immediately generate additional profit for their shareholders?

Business organisations exist only to serve society, so society is the ultimate shareholder in every business. Therefore, society's concerns and interests should be awarded the same level of attention and importance as those of investors. Business does not operate independently of society and its expectations, therefore companies should be accountable not just to shareholders but also to society as a whole. This accountability would extend to the products produced and sold by a business and the resources entrusted to it. Employees should be treated with due consideration and enabled to fulfil their potential within the organisations they work for. Customers should not be harmed by the products they buy while suppliers should be treated fairly and not pressured to reduce their selling prices to enable buying organisations to profit at their expense. The public at large should expect organisations to avoid polluting the air, land and water sources and that all waste products from processes and operations are handled safely to protect individuals and the wider environment from harm.

Today's consumers want reassurance that the products they buy are sourced and produced ethically without causing harm either to the environment or to those individuals producing those products. Shareholders also want to be confident that the profits made by their companies are not generated from exploiting workers or the environment. Companies are eager to protect their reputations as reputational damage is difficult and time consuming to repair and can adversely affect sales and profits. Looking after the workforce, ensuring that suppliers are paid on time, looking into supply chains to check for unethical or environmentally unfriendly practices are all part of the risk management that organisations undertake to protect their reputation and shareholders' investment. Disclosing information on these aspects of company performance helps the public and other interested parties to assess the social responsibility of businesses and assists in enhancing each organisation's reputation for fair dealing and adherence to ethical principles. Customers like to buy goods and services from organisations which share their values, so considering other aspects of performance and reporting on these helps both to present entities in a positive light and to boost revenue and profits. Such actions also help to build the reputation of the business and show that it is caring for the long-term interests of all its stakeholders, not just the short-term interests of the directors and shareholders.

WHY IS THIS RELEVANT TO ME?   The rationale for corporate social responsibility

To enable you as an accounting professional to appreciate:

● That companies are accountable to society as a whole not just to investors

● That there are sound business advantages to adopting socially responsible policies

● That the reputation of a company is a valuable asset which requires protection from damage

---

GO BACK OVER THIS AGAIN!   Are you sure that you appreciate the reasons why companies adopt and report socially responsible attitudes and activities? Go to the **online workbook** and have a go at Exercises 10.9 to check your understanding.

SUSTAINABILITY AND ENVIRONMENTAL REPORTING

The ultimate long-term strategy for every business is to make its activities sustainable. What does this mean? *Our Common Future* (the Brundtland report) presented by the World Council on Environment and Development in 1987 defines sustainable development as that which 'meets the needs of the present without compromising the ability of future generations to meet their own needs'. This vision requires that all demands placed upon the natural environment by people and business organisations be met without reducing the capacity of the environment to provide for future generations. Businesses are therefore expected to concern themselves with issues such as climate change and energy use and to pay proper attention to the effects of their operations on the natural environment.

Unilever is one company that has been developing and reporting its sustainability strategy over many years. Give me an example 10.5 presents Unilever's strategy for sustainable business which forms part of the group's sustainable living plan.

GIVE ME AN EXAMPLE 10.5   Unilever's strategy for sustainable business

'We are living in a world where temperatures are rising, water shortages are more frequent, food supplies are increasingly scarce and the gap between rich and poor increasing. Populations are growing fast, making basic hygiene and sanitation even more of a challenge. At Unilever we can see how people the world over are already affected by these changes. And the changes will pose new challenges for us too, as commodity costs fluctuate, markets become unstable and raw materials harder to source.

We believe that business must be part of the solution. But to be so, business will have to change; there is not "business as usual anymore". Sustainable, equitable growth is the only acceptable business model. Our vision is to grow our business, whilst reducing our environmental footprint and increasing our positive social impact.

In 2010 we launched the Unilever Sustainable Living Plan, which is our blueprint for sustainable business. We will achieve our vision through our Plan, which is helping us to decouple our growth from our environmental impact while increasing our positive social impact, driving profitable growth for our brands, saving costs and fueling innovation.'

Source: https://www.unilever.com/sustainable-living/the-sustainable-living-plan/our-strategy/

10

Unilever is just one example of many businesses that have adopted sustainability and corporate social responsibility as part of their long-term strategy. Any annual report that you look at will provide details on these sustainability and CSR strategies together with statistics relating to what has been achieved over the past year and how improvements have been made. Have a look at Ted Baker's Sustainability report on pages 28–30 of the 2017/2018 Annual report and accounts, available at http://www.tedbakerplc.com/~/media/Files/T/Ted-Baker/results-and-reports/report/2018/ted-baker-annual-report-2017-2018.pdf.

The rationale for adopting and reporting a sustainability strategy

As we have seen in this chapter, businesses must consider the long term not just the short term. A sustainability strategy represents the ultimate focus on the long term with the aim of ensuring the business's survival into the indefinite future. This approach accords well with shareholders' long-term investment horizon (this chapter, Long-term success v. short-term profits). However, there are many other benefits that a sustainability strategy brings. Give me an example 10.6 presents just four of the benefits generated by or expected from Unilever's adoption of its sustainable living plan.

> **GIVE ME AN EXAMPLE 10.6   Benefits of Unilever's sustainable living plan**
>
> Since the adoption of its sustainable living plan, Unilever has generated the following benefits:
>
> - An annual return of 13 per cent on its shares over 10 years compared to an annual return of 5 per cent on the FTSE100 (Unilever is a constituent company of the FTSE100), a return over 10 years of 220 per cent v. a return of 66 per cent for the FTSE100 as a whole.
> - A reduction in the water usage in its factories resulting in a saving of €50m in supply chain costs since 2008.
>
> - A reduction of 40 per cent per tonne of production in CO_2 emissions from energy used in the group's factories by 2020, a figure at or below 2008 levels despite significantly higher production volumes.
> - 60 per cent of raw materials were sourced from renewable sources by 2015.
>
> Sources: https://www.unilever.com/sustainable-living/ and https://www.ft.com/content/1f2ea6dc-fe66-11e6-8d8e-a5e3738f9ae4

As is evident from Give me an example 10.6 Unilever's strategic focus on sustainability has also generated considerable benefits for shareholders in line with Friedman's insistence on profit generation as the only social responsibility of business. Positive news generates headlines for businesses together with favourable market reactions to both products and share prices. In these ways, adopting a sustainability strategy produces benefits for both shareholders and the environment and demonstrates that what is good for the environment also turns out to be good for shareholders and investors.

Companies are also recognising their wider duty of care to the public and the planet and their obligation to look after the natural resources entrusted to them. All stakeholders have an interest in the wellbeing of the planet. As a result of this interest, a stewardship report that focuses on the environment and on how natural resources have been managed and preserved is required by all these stakeholders alongside the financial results. Where damage has been caused to land, air or water, stakeholders will expect directors to report on the steps that have been taken to repair this damage and to prevent further damage in the future.

Environmental and sustainability reporting will assist companies in managing the risks that arise from any business activity. Actively seeking to avoid polluting natural resources will reduce the impact of economic penalties against organisations. The Deepwater Horizon oil spill in 2010 is estimated to have cost BP $61.6 billion (https://www.ft.com/content/ff2d8bcc-49e9-11e6-8d68-72e9211e86ab) and resulted in a fall in the share price which has not yet been recovered over the intervening eight years. Sound risk management policies are also applied by the capital markets: any potential investment which appears too risky will not attract funding or will be required to pay a higher rate of interest to compensate for the increased risk attached to the project. Based on this principle, capital markets take into account not just ordinary business risks but also environmental risks and the environmental policies of companies seeking inward investment. Companies with more effective environmental risk management policies will attract funding at lower interest rates as the risks are lower. Ethical investment funds will withhold investment from companies which do not adopt a suitably responsible approach to the environment while socially responsible investors will avoid companies that fail to do the right thing. Again, this twin pronged approach benefits shareholders in reducing costs and increasing profits.

Sustainability information presented is relevant in that it assists consumers and investors in making rational economic decisions. The disclosure of such details indicates a fully transparent approach to reporting and shows the organisation as having nothing to hide. Such disclosure is also part of good corporate governance which dictates that all entities should report on all of their activities and their total impact. Competitive advantage may be another benefit of sustainability reporting as consumers favour organisations adopting a responsible approach to the use of natural resources and the environment over those with a less responsible approach.

WHY IS THIS RELEVANT TO ME?   Sustainability and environmental reporting

To enable you as an accounting professional to understand:

- How a sustainability approach enables businesses to promote their long-term success

- The commercial, finance, financial and reputational advantages gained by organisations promoting and reporting a sustainable and environmentally conscious approach in their businesses

---

GO BACK OVER THIS AGAIN!   Are you confident that you appreciate the reasons why companies adopt sustainability and environmentally responsible approaches in their businesses? Go to the **online workbook** and have a go at Exercises 10.10 to check your understanding.

10

CHAPTER SUMMARY

You should now have learnt that:

- Agency and information asymmetry problems arise when shareholders appoint directors to run companies on their behalf

- Shareholders need to be assured that directors are acting in the shareholders' best long-term interests and not in their own short-term interests

- Corporate governance is the system by which companies are directed and controlled

- Effective corporate governance involves executive directors, non-executive directors, external auditors, internal audit, the stock exchange listing rules and shareholders

- Executive directors run the company, non-executive directors run the board

- Non-executive directors make up the membership of the audit committee, the nominations committee and the remuneration committee

- External auditors report on the truth and fairness of the annual financial statements and their compliance with legislation and international financial reporting standards

- Internal audit undertakes investigations and reports on every aspect of a company's operations, internal control, strategy and corporate governance

- The Corporate Governance Code and the Companies Act 2006 require directors to promote the long-term success of their company

- Effective corporate governance requires that no one individual should have unfettered power and that all directors should run the business together as a body

- At least half of the directors on each board of directors should be independent non-executive directors

- Boards of directors and shareholders evaluate each director's performance

- The audit committee monitors the integrity of the annual report and accounts, receives reports from internal audit, monitors and evaluates internal control and oversees the external audit process and the external auditor

- Companies have a wider duty than just making profit for the shareholders

- Business organisations serve society and so are accountable to society as a whole

- Adopting socially responsible, environmentally friendly and sustainable business practices helps to generate long-term success for businesses through commercial, financing, reputational and risk minimisation advantages

QUICK REVISION   Test your knowledge with the online flashcards in Summary of key concepts and attempt the Multiple choice questions, all in the **online workbook**.

10

END-OF-CHAPTER QUESTIONS

Solutions to these questions can be found in the **online workbook**

❯ DEVELOP YOUR UNDERSTANDING

❯ Question 10.1

Explain the rationale behind the requirements of the Corporate Governance Code.

❯ Question 10.2

Explain the rationale behind Corporate Social Responsibility reporting.

❯ Question 10.3

Why is sustainability such an important issue for businesses today?

≫ TAKE IT FURTHER

≫ Question 10.4

The aim of the Corporate Governance Code is control. Discuss.

≫ Question 10.5

The only responsibility of business is to generate a profit. Discuss.

≫ Question 10.6

The proper function of accounting is the measurement of profits and cash flows and the presentation of assets and liabilities. Discuss.

10

ANNOTATED STATEMENTS

Illustration 2.1: Bunns the Bakers plc: annotated statement of financial position at 31 March 2019

	2019 £000	2018 £000
ASSETS		
Non-current assets		
Intangible assets	50	55
Property, plant and equipment	11,750	11,241
Investments	65	59
	11,865	11,355
Current assets		
Inventories	60	55
Trade and other receivables	62	75
Cash and cash equivalents	212	189
	334	319
Total assets	12,199	11,674
LIABILITIES		
Current liabilities		
Current portion of long-term borrowings	300	300
Trade and other payables	390	281
Current tax liabilities	150	126
	840	707
Non-current liabilities		
Long-term borrowings	2,700	3,000
Long-term provisions	200	200
	2,900	3,200
Total liabilities	3,740	3,907
Net assets	8,459	7,767
EQUITY		
Called up share capital	2,500	2,400
Share premium	1,315	1,180
Retained earnings	4,644	4,187
Total equity	8,459	7,767

Annotations:

Present economic resources controlled by the entity as a result of past events. An economic resource is a right that has the potential to produce economic benefits. Assets must be quantifiable in monetary terms in such a way that they are faithfully represented in the statement of financial position.

Intangible assets have no material substance and include intellectual property rights, patents, licences and trademarks.

Assets with material substance including land and buildings, vehicles, machinery, fittings and equipment.

Inventories comprise of raw materials for use in the production process and of finished goods for sale and goods bought in for resale.

Money due from customers for goods supplied on credit terms and other money due from other parties external to the business.

Present obligations of the entity to transfer economic resources as a result of past events. Liabilities must be quantifiable in monetary terms in such a way that they are faithfully represented in the statement of financial position.

Amounts owed to suppliers for goods provided on credit and other money due to other parties external to the business.

Liabilities the entity must meet that are due for payment more than 12 months after the statement of financial position date.

The number of shares in issue multiplied by the par (face) value of each share.

Profits earned by the business in earlier accounting periods not yet distributed as dividends to the shareholders.

Amounts received on the issue of share capital over and above the par (face) value of each share.

Assets not purchased for resale in the normal course of business. Non-current assets are held for long-term use within the business to produce goods or services.

Holdings of shares and loans in other companies

Short-term assets whose economic benefits will be used up by the entity within the next 12 months. Current assets change constantly during the trading cycle as inventory is turned into goods for sale and then into cash and new inventories are bought in and turned into more goods for sale and into more cash in an ever repeating cycle.

Cash held within the business and in bank current and short-term deposit accounts.

Short-term liabilities that will be paid within the next 12 months. As with current assets, current liabilities are constantly changing as liabilities paid are replaced by new liabilities incurred.

Bank overdrafts and loan instalments due within the next 12 months.

Tax payable to local taxation authorities on the profits made by the business during the past 12 months.

Long-term liabilities due to be paid by the business more than 12 months after the statement of financial position date.

Loan instalments that are due more than 12 months after the statement of financial position date.

The residual interest in the assets of the entity after deducting all of its liabilities. Remember that assets – liabilities = equity.

Illustration 3.1: Bunns the Bakers plc: statement of profit or loss for the years ended 31 March 2019 and 31 March 2018

	2019	2018
	£000	£000
Revenue	10,078	9,575
Cost of sales	(4,535)	(4,596)
Gross profit	**5,543**	**4,979**
Distribution and selling costs	(3,398)	(3,057)
Administration expenses	(1,250)	(1,155)
Operating profit	895	767
Finance income	15	12
Finance expense	(150)	(165)
Profit before tax	760	614
Income tax	(213)	(172)
Profit for the year	**547**	**442**

Note: income and profit figures are shown without brackets while items of expenditure are shown in brackets. This is to help you understand which items are subtracted and which items are added to determine the result (profit or loss) for the year.

Revenue, cost of sales, gross profit, distribution and selling costs, administration expenses and operating profit all form the trading part of the statement of profit or loss

Sales income earned in an accounting period. Revenue represents sales made in the ordinary course of business, in this case from selling bakery and related goods.

Gross profit = Revenue − Cost of sales

The costs of selling and distributing goods such as advertising, transporting bakery goods from the main bakery to the shops, costs of running the shops and shop wages.

Operating profit = Gross profit − Distribution and selling costs − Administration expenses

Interest received and receivable on surplus cash deposited with the company's bank.

The direct costs of making the sales included in Revenue. These could be the costs of making bakery goods (including ingredients and bakers' wages) or the direct costs of buying in related products for resale.

All the costs of running the trading operation that do not fall under any other heading including legal expenses, audit, accountancy and directors' salaries. All these costs are essential in running the business but they cannot be allocated to the costs of making and producing or distributing and selling the goods sold.

Finance income and finance expense form the financing part of the statement of profit or loss.

The tax charged on the profit for the year. For UK companies, this tax is called Corporation Tax.

Interest paid and payable on borrowings used in financing the business's operations.

Profit before tax = operating profit + finance income − finance expense

Profit for the year (also called profit after tax) = profit before tax − income tax

Cash generated from operations reconciles the operating profit for the year to the cash generated from operating activities in the year by adjusting for certain non-cash transactions in the statement of profit or loss and changes in working capital.

Depreciation and amortisation of non-current assets are not cash flows but an accounting adjustment to reflect the economic benefits of non-current assets used up in each accounting period. The cash outflow associated with non-current assets is the actual cash paid to acquire them.

Cash generated from day to day trading activities from which to finance day-to-day operations. Surplus cash can be used for expansion and investment.

Taxation arises on profits from operations so taxation paid is deducted from cash flows from operating activities.

Cash invested in new long-term capacity from which to generate new income by expanding and improving the business.

Cash received from the sale or scrapping of non-current assets.

Cash raised from or paid to long-term providers of finance.

Cash raised from the issue of new share capital.

Capital element of long-term borrowings repaid in the year to the providers of long-term debt finance from operating cash inflows.

Cash and cash equivalents on the statement of financial position at the end of last year.

Illustration 6.1: Bunns the Bakers plc: statement of cash flows for the years ended 31 March 2019 and 31 March 2018

Cash generated from operations	2019	2018
	£000	£000
Operating profit for the year	895	767
(Increase)/decrease in inventories	(5)	8
Decrease in trade and other receivables	13	9
Increase/(decrease) in trade and other payables	109	(15)
Amortisation of intangible non-current assets	5	7
Depreciation of property, plant and equipment	394	362
(Profit)/loss on disposal of property, plant and equipment	(3)	4
Cash from operating activities	1,408	1,142
Taxation paid	(189)	(154)
Net cash inflow from operating activities	1,219	988
Cash flows from investing activities		
Acquisition of property, plant and equipment	(910)	(600)
Acquisition of investments	(6)	(11)
Proceeds from sale of property, plant and equipment	10	47
Interest received	15	12
Net cash outflow from investing activities	(891)	(552)
Cash flows from financing activities		
Proceeds from the issue of ordinary share capital	235	148
Dividends paid	(90)	(72)
Repayment of current portion of long term borrowings	(300)	(300)
Interest paid	(150)	(165)
Net cash outflow from financing activities	(305)	(389)
Net increase in cash and cash equivalents	23	47
Cash and cash equivalents at the start of the year	189	142
Cash and cash equivalents at the end of the year	212	189

Note: cash inflows (money coming in) are shown without brackets while cash outflows (money going out) are shown in brackets. Work through the above statement of cash flows, adding the figures without brackets and deducting the figures in brackets to help you understand how the cash inflows and outflows add up to the subtotals given.

Cash and cash equivalents at the end of the current year on the statement of financial position.

= operating profit in the statement of profit or loss (= profit after tax + income tax + finance expense − finance income).

(Increase)/decrease in inventories, (increase)/decrease in trade and other receivables and increase/(decrease) in trade payables represent the cash effects of movements in working capital over the course of the accounting year.

Profits and losses on the disposal of property, plant and equipment are the difference between sale proceeds and carrying amount and are thus not a cash flow. The cash flow associated with disposals of property, plant and equipment are the actual cash receipts from the sale of the assets.

Cash inflows and outflows from long term investing.

Investment of surplus cash from which to generate interest or dividend income to boost profits.

Interest received from investing surplus cash in current or non-current asset investments.

Dividends paid to shareholders as a return on their investment in the company.

Interest paid on long- and short-term borrowings as a return to lenders for providing debt finance to the company.

Net increase in cash and cash equivalents = net cash inflow from operating activities (£1,219) − net cash outflow from investing activities (£891) − net cash outflow from financing activities (£305) = £23.

TERMINOLOGY CONVERTER

Terms used in this book	Equivalent term or terms
Allowance for receivables	Provision for doubtful debts
Capital	Equity
Capital and reserves	Equity
Carrying amount	Net book value
Cash conversion cycle	Operating cycle, working capital cycle
Equity	Capital, capital and reserves
Finance expense	Interest payable
Finance income	Interest receivable
Inventory	Stock
Inventory days	Stock days
Irrecoverable debts	Bad debts
Nominal ledger	General ledger
Payables	Creditors
Payables days	Creditor days
Purchase day book	Purchases listing
Purchase returns day book	Purchase returns listing
Receivables	Debtors
Receivables days	Debtor days
Revenue	Turnover, sales
Sales day book	Sales listing
Sales returns day book	Sales returns listing
Statement of financial position	Balance sheet
Statement of profit or loss	Income statement, statement of financial performance, profit and loss account

SEARCHING FOR THE ANSWERS?

You'll find complete, clearly-explained solutions to all the end-of-chapter questions in the student resources section of the **online resources** that accompany this book:

 www.oup.com/uk/scott_financial-student-resources/

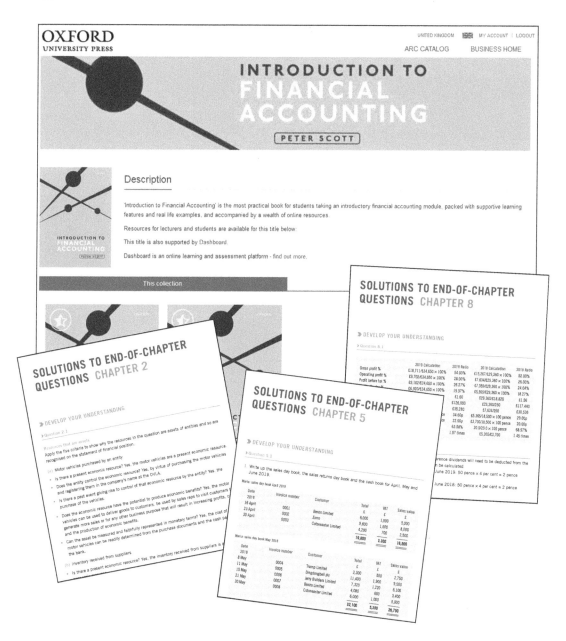

GLOSSARY

Accountability Managers provide an account of how they have managed resources placed in their care. In this way, those appointing managers can assess how well their managers have looked after the resources entrusted to them.

Accounting The summarising of numerical data relating to past events and presenting this data as information to managers and other interested parties as a basis for both decision-making and control purposes.

Accounting equation Assets – liabilities = equity or assets = liabilities + equity. As equity includes the difference between income and expenditure, the equation can be expanded to assets + expenses = liabilities + equity + income.

Accruals Expenses incurred during an accounting period but not paid for until after the accounting period end are still recognised as a liability in the statement of financial position and as an expense in the statement of profit or loss.

Accruals basis of accounting All income and expenditure are recognised in the accounting period in which they occurred rather than in the accounting period in which cash is received or paid.

Acid test ratio See Quick ratio.

Agency problem This problem arises in situations in which one person (the agent) is appointed to undertake a task by the principal. Agency theory says that the agent will always act in their own best interests, not in the best interests of the principal.

AGM Annual general meeting.

Allowance for receivables The allowance for receivables is calculated as a percentage of trade receivables after deducting known irrecoverable debts. This allowance is an application of the prudence concept, assuming that not all trade receivables will pay what is owed. Also referred to as the provision for doubtful debts.

Annual general meeting A meeting held every year by limited liability companies at which shareholders consider and vote on various significant resolutions affecting the company.

Articles of Association A document that covers the internal regulations of a company and governs the shareholders' relationships with each other.

Assets Defined by the IASB as 'a present economic resource controlled by the entity as a result of past events.'

Balance sheet Another term for the statement of financial position.

Bond A long-term loan to an organisation with a fixed rate of interest and a fixed repayment date.

Bonus issues An issue of shares to shareholders from retained earnings. A bonus issue does not raise any cash.

Books of prime entry The first point at which a transaction is recorded in the accounting system. Books of prime entry are the sales day book, the sales returns day book, the purchase day book, the purchase returns day book, the cash book, the petty cash book and the payroll.

Business entity Any organisation involved in business. Businesses may be sole traders, companies with limited liability or partnerships.

Business entity convention The business is completely separate from its owners. Only business transactions are included in the business's financial statements.

Cadbury Report The name by which the report of the Committee on the Financial Aspects of Corporate Governance published in 1991 is most commonly known.

Capital account The equity part of the statement of financial position for sole traders. The capital account is the sum of the opening capital balance plus the profit for the year (minus a loss for the year) minus any drawings made by the sole trader during the year.

Carrying amount Cost or fair value of a non-current asset—the accumulated depreciation on that non-current asset. Net book value is an equivalent term that you might also come across to describe the result of deducting accumulated depreciation from the cost or fair value of a non-current asset.

Cash book A book of prime entry that records cash receipts and cash payments.

Cash conversion cycle Inventory days + receivables days – payables days. Also known as the working capital cycle or the operating cycle.

Cash flow cycle The time it takes a business to convert inventory into a sale and to collect cash either at the point of sale or from trade receivables with which to pay trade payables.

Cash flows from financing activities One of the three sections in the statement of cash flows. This section represents the cash raised from the issue of share capital and loans and the cash spent in repaying borrowings and paying interest and dividends.

Cash flows from investing activities One of the three sections in the statement of cash flows. This section represents the cash spent on buying new non-current assets, the cash received from selling surplus non-current assets and the cash received from interest and dividends on investments made.

Cash flows from operating activities One of the three sections in the statement of cash flows. This section represents the cash generated from sales less the cash spent in both generating those sales and in running the organisation.

Comparability An enhancing qualitative characteristic of financial information. Information should be comparable over time. The usefulness of information is enhanced if it can be compared with similar information about other entities for the same reporting period and with similar information about the same entity for other reporting periods. Comparability does not mean consistency, although consistency of presentation and measurement of the same items in the same way from year to year will help to achieve comparability. Similarly, comparability does not mean uniformity of presentation.

Compensating error These arise when two or more errors cancel each other out.

Complete reversal of entries Transactions are posted to the correct accounts, but the debit and credit entries are reversed. Amounts debited and credited to the accounts to correct complete reversal of entry errors must be twice the original amount of the transaction, firstly to reverse the incorrect entry and then to add what should have been debited or credited originally.

Consistency The presentation or measurement of the same piece of accounting information on the same basis each year.

Corporate governance The system by which companies are directed and controlled.

Corporate social responsibility Social and environmental considerations are integrated into the management of the operations of an organisation. May be abbreviated to CSR.

Cost of sales The direct costs attributable to the sale of particular goods or services.

Creditor days See Payables days.

Creditors Persons to whom entities owe money. See also Payables.

Credits A term used in double-entry bookkeeping. Credits represent liabilities, capital and income as well as reductions in assets and expenses.

Current assets Short-term assets that will be used up in the business within one year. Examples include inventory, trade receivables, prepayments and cash.

Current liabilities Short-term liabilities due for payment within one year of the year-end date. Examples include trade payables, taxation and accruals.

Current ratio Current assets divided by current liabilities. Used in the assessment of an entity's short-term liquidity. This ratio should be used with caution in the evaluation of an entity's liquidity.

Debenture A long-term loan to an organisation with a fixed rate of interest and a fixed repayment date.

Debits A term used in double-entry bookkeeping. Debits represent assets and expenses as well as reductions in liabilities, capital and income.

Debt ratio Total liabilities divided by total assets. An indicator of how reliant an entity is upon external parties to fund its assets.

Debtors Persons who owe money to an entity. See also Trade receivables.

Debtor days See Receivables days.

Depreciation The allocation of the cost of a non-current asset to the accounting periods benefiting from that non-current asset's use within a business. Depreciation is *not* a way of reflecting the market value of assets in financial statements and it does not represent a loss in value.

Direct method An approach to preparing the statement of cash flows that involves disclosing the gross cash receipts from sales and the gross cash payments to suppliers.

Directors Persons appointed by the shareholders at the annual general meeting to run a limited company on their behalf.

Discounts allowed An allowance given to trade receivables to encourage early payment of amounts owed. A sales invoice presents two prices: the price after taking the discount into account and the price if the discount is not taken up. Sales are initially recorded at the discounted price. Discounts allowed not taken up by customers are added to the value of sales.

Discounts received Suppliers reward their customers with discounts for early payment or bulk purchases. Discounts received are a source of income in the statement of profit or loss, a deduction from cost of sales and a deduction from trade payables.

Distributable reserves Retained earnings available for distribution to shareholders as a dividend.

Distribution The distribution of retained profits to shareholders as a dividend. A distribution is not an expense of a company but a deduction from retained earnings.

Dividend A distribution of profits to shareholders.

Dividend cover A comparison of the total dividend for an accounting period to the profit after taxation. This ratio is used to assess the expected continuity of dividend payments. The higher the ratio, the more likely the dividend payment will continue into the future.

Dividend per share The total dividend for a period divided by the number of ordinary shares in issue multiplied by 100 to give a figure of dividend per share in pence.

Dividend yield The dividend per share as a percentage of the current share price.

Double entry An accounting methodology which recognises that every transaction has two effects on the figures in the financial statements.

DPS See Dividend per share.

Drawings Amounts taken out of a business by a sole trader for personal rather than business use. Drawings are in effect a repayment of the amounts owed by the business to the owner. Drawings are not an expense but a deduction from capital. Drawings are not permitted in limited liability companies.

Dual aspect The recognition that each accounting transaction has a double effect on the amounts stated in the financial statements.

Duality principle Each transaction has an equal and opposite effect on two or more accounts.

Earnings per share The profit after taxation and after preference dividends divided by the number of ordinary shares in issue multiplied by 100 to give a figure of earnings per share in pence.

Economic resource A right that has the potential to produce economic benefits.

Efficiency ratios Measures of non-current asset turnover and revenue and profit per employee to determine how well an organisation has used its resources to generate profits.

EGM Extraordinary general meeting.

EPS See Earnings per share.

Equity The capital of an entity on its statement of financial position. Equity is, in theory, the amount the owners of the business would receive if all the business assets and liabilities were sold and settled at the amounts stated in the statement of financial position.

Equity share capital This is an equivalent term for ordinary share capital.

Error of commission A transaction is posted to the correct type of account (income, expense, asset, liability or capital) but the wrong account is debited or credited.

Error of omission A transaction is completely missed out of the double-entry record.

Error of original entry The correct accounts are debited and credited to the double-entry record, but the wrong amount is recorded.

Error of principle A transaction is posted to the wrong type of account.

Exceptional income Income and expenditure that arise from transactions that are not in the ordinary course of business.

Expenses Defined by the IASB as 'decreases in assets, or increases in liabilities, that result in decreases in equity, other than those relating to distributions to holders of equity claims'.

Extraordinary general meeting A meeting called by the directors of a limited company to request the approval of shareholders for certain business transactions. An extraordinary general meeting is any meeting of the shareholders as a body other than the annual general meeting.

Fair value The amount at which an asset could be sold or a liability settled in the open market.

Faithful representation A fundamental qualitative characteristic of financial information. Financial information must not only represent relevant economic phenomena (transactions and events), but it must also faithfully represent the phenomena that it purports to represent. Perfectly faithful representation of economic phenomena in words and numbers requires that the information presented must have three characteristics: it must be complete, neutral and free from error.

Financial accounting The reporting of past information to parties external to the organisation.

Gearing ratio Long- and short-term borrowings divided by the total statement of financial position equity figure ×

100%. A measure designed to help financial statement users assess whether an entity has borrowed too much money. The gearing ratio should be used in conjunction with the interest cover ratio in making this assessment.

General ledger See Nominal ledger.

Going concern A business that has sufficient demand for its products and sufficient sources of finance to enable it to continue operating for the foreseeable future.

Gross pay The contractually agreed rate of pay × the hours worked before any deductions for income tax (PAYE) or national insurance (NIC).

Gross profit Sales less the direct costs of making those sales.

Gross profit percentage The gross profit of an organisation divided by the sales figure × 100%.

Historic cost The original cost of an asset or liability at the time it was purchased or incurred.

IAASB International Auditing and Assurance Standards Board.

IAS International Accounting Standard.

IASB International Accounting Standards Board.

IFRS International Financial Reporting Standard.

Income Defined by the IASB as 'increases in assets, or decreases in liabilities, that result in increases in equity, other than those relating to contributions from holders of equity claims'.

Income statement An equivalent term for the statement of profit or loss.

Indirect method An approach to preparing the statement of cash flows that ignores total inflows and outflows of cash from operations. Instead, the operating profit for a period is adjusted for increases or decreases in inventory, trade receivables, prepayments, payables and accruals and for the effect of non-cash items such as depreciation and profits and losses on disposal of non-current assets in order to determine the cash flows from operations.

Information asymmetry This arises in situations in which one party knows much more about a subject than another as a result of a principal delegating a task to an agent.

Insolvency The inability of an entity to repay all that it owes to its creditors.

Interest cover Trading profit divided by finance cost (interest payable). This ratio shows how many times interest payable on borrowings is covered by operating profit. The higher the ratio, the more likely entities will be able to continue paying the interest on their borrowings.

Inventory A stock of goods held by a business.

Inventory days Inventory divided by cost of sales × 365 days. This ratio measures the average stockholding period, the length of time an entity holds goods as stock before they are sold.

Irrecoverable debts Trade receivables from which cash will not be collected. Irrecoverable debts are an expense in the statement of profit or loss, not a deduction from sales. Also known as bad debts.

ISA International Standard on Auditing.

Liabilities Defined by the IASB as 'a present obligation of the entity to transfer an economic resource as a result of past events'.

Liquidity The ability of entities to meet payments to their creditors as they become due.

Loan notes A long-term loan to an organisation with a fixed rate of interest and a fixed repayment date.

Management accounting Cost and management accounting is concerned with reporting accounting and cost information to users within an organisation to assist those internal users in making decisions and managing the business.

Materiality The IASB Framework defines materiality thus: 'Information is material if omitting it or misstating it could influence decisions that … users … make on the basis of financial information about a specific reporting entity. In other words, materiality is an entity-specific aspect of relevance based on the nature or magnitude, or both, of the items to which the information relates in the context of an individual entity's financial report.'

Memorandum of Association This document covers a limited company's objectives and its powers and governs the relationship of the company with the outside world.

Money measurement The measurement of financial results in money terms.

National insurance Both employees and employers make national insurance contributions. For employees, this is a deduction from their salary and determines employees' entitlement to certain state benefits. For employers, national insurance contributions are levied on the value of each employee's gross pay. Often abbreviated to NIC.

Net profit The surplus that remains once all the expenses have been deducted from total income.

NIC See National insurance.

Nominal ledger Also known as the general ledger. The nominal ledger is an alphabetical listing of all the double-entry accounts of an entity.

Non-current asset turnover Revenue is divided by non-current assets to determine how many £s of sales are generated from each £ of non-current assets.

Non-current assets Assets held within the business long term for use in the production of goods and services. Non-current assets are retained within the business for periods of more than one year and are not acquired with the intention of reselling them immediately or in the near future.

Non-current liabilities Liabilities due for payment more than 12 months from the statement of financial position date.

Operating cycle Another term for the cash conversion cycle or working capital cycle. See Cash conversion cycle.

Operating profit The profit that remains after all the costs of trading, direct (cost of sales) and indirect (distribution and selling costs and administration expenses), have been deducted from sales revenue.

Operating profit percentage Determines profitability on the basis of revenue less all operating costs before taking into account the effects of finance income, finance expense and taxation.

Ordinary share capital The most common form of share capital issued by companies conferring on holders the right to receive all of a company's profits as dividends and to vote at company meetings.

Par value The face value or nominal value of a share.

Payables days Trade payables divided by cost of sales × 365 days. This ratio measures the average period taken to pay outstanding liabilities to trade suppliers.

PAYE Pay as you earn. This is a deduction from gross pay to reflect the income tax due on each payment of wages or salary to an employee.

Performance ratios Ratios of particular interest to an entity's shareholders as they measure the returns to the owners of the business.

Periodicity The preparation of financial statements for a set period of time, usually one year.

Petty cash book A record of cash received from the bank and cash expenditure on small items such as stamps, office refreshments and cleaning. Petty cash is used to pay expenses to suppliers who do not offer credit terms to businesses.

Pre-emption rights The rights of existing shareholders to subscribe to new issues of share capital before those shares can be offered to non-shareholders.

Preference share capital Preference shares receive a fixed rate of dividend that is paid before the ordinary shareholders receive any dividend. Preference share capital is returned to preference shareholders before any amounts are returned to ordinary shareholders on the winding up of a company. However, preference shareholders have no right to vote in company general meetings.

Prepayments Amounts paid in advance for goods and services to be provided in the future. These amounts are recognised as prepayments at the statement of financial position date and as a deduction from current period expenses.

Price/earnings ratio The current market price of a share divided by the latest earnings per share figure. The ratio provides an indication of how long it would take for that share to pay back its owner in earnings if the share were purchased today and earnings remained the same for the foreseeable future.

Profit The surplus remaining after all expenses are deducted from total income.

Profit after tax The profit that remains once all the expenses and charges have been deducted from sales revenue and any other income for the accounting period added on.

Profit after tax percentage Profit for the year (= profit after tax) divided by revenue × 100%.

Profit and loss account Another term for the statement of profit or loss.

Profit before tax Sales − cost of sales − distribution and selling costs − administration expenses + finance income − finance expense.

Profit before tax percentage Profit before tax divided by revenue × 100%.

Profit for the year Profit after tax.

Profit per employee Calculated by dividing the number of employees during an accounting period into the operating profit for the period.

Profitability An assessment of the profits made during an accounting period by comparing current period profits and profitability percentages to those of previous periods.

Prudence The process of exercising caution in the production of financial statements in the expectation of less favourable outcomes. Prudence is only exercised under conditions of uncertainty.

Purchase day book A listing of all purchase invoices by date, supplier, internal invoice number, gross amount, VAT and net amount. The net amount of each purchase invoice is categorised into different types of expenditure ready for posting to the nominal ledger accounts.

Purchase ledger A record of invoices and credit notes received from and cash paid to each trade payable. The purchase ledger is a record outside the double-entry system but the total of all individual purchase ledger balances should be equal to the closing balance on the trade payables control account.

Purchase listing This is an equivalent term for the purchase day book.

Purchase returns The cancellation of a purchase by returning goods to suppliers. The accounting effect of purchase returns is to reduce expenses in the statement of profit or loss and trade payables in the statement of financial position.

Purchase returns day book A listing of all credit notes (negative purchases) received from suppliers by date, supplier, internal credit note number, gross amount, VAT and net amount. The net amount of each credit note is categorised into different types of expenditure ready for posting to the nominal ledger accounts.

Purchase returns listing This is an equivalent term for the purchase returns day book.

Quick ratio Also known as the acid test ratio. The quick ratio compares current assets that are readily convertible into cash with current liabilities as a measure of an entity's short-term ability to pay what it owes over the next 12 months. This ratio should be used with caution in the evaluation of an entity's liquidity.

Ratio(s) The expression of the relationship(s) between two different figures.

Realisation Profits should not be anticipated until they have been earned through a sale.

Receivables Amounts of money owed to an entity by parties outside the organisation.

Receivables days Trade receivables divided by sales × 365 days. This ratio measures the average period taken to collect outstanding debts from credit customers.

Reducing balance A method of allocating depreciation on non-current assets to accounting periods benefiting from their use. This method uses a fixed percentage of cost in the first year of an asset's life and then applies the same percentage to the carrying amount of assets in accounting periods subsequent to year 1. The reducing balance method allocates a smaller charge for depreciation to each successive accounting period benefiting from a non-current asset's use. Residual value is ignored when calculating reducing balance depreciation.

Relevance A fundamental qualitative characteristic of financial information. To be relevant, information must be capable of making a difference in the decisions made by users. Relevant information may be predictive and assist users in making predictions about the future or it may be confirmatory by assisting users to assess the accuracy of past predictions. Relevant information can be both predictive and confirmatory.

Residual value The amount which the original purchaser of a non-current asset thinks that the asset could be sold for when the time comes to dispose of it.

Return on capital employed Operating profit (profit before interest and tax) divided by the equity of an entity plus any long-term borrowings × 100%.

Revenue Sales of goods and services made by an entity in the ordinary (everyday) course of business.

Revenue per employee Calculated by dividing the revenue for an accounting period by the number of employees employed during that accounting period.

Rights issues An issue of shares to existing shareholders at a discount to the current market price. This is not the issue of shares at a discount, which would be illegal under the Companies Act 2006.

ROCE See Return on capital employed.

Sales = revenue.

Sales day book A listing of all sales invoices by date, customer, invoice number, gross amount, VAT and net amount. The net amount of each sales invoice may be categorised into different types of sales ready for posting to the nominal ledger accounts.

Sales ledger A record of invoices and credit notes sent to and cash received from each trade receivable. The sales ledger is a record outside the double-entry system but the total of all individual sales ledger balances should be equal to the closing balance on the trade receivables control account.

Sales listing = sales day book.

Sales returns The cancellation of a sale by a customer returning goods. The accounting effect of sales returns is to reduce sales in the statement of profit or loss and trade receivables in the statement of financial position.

Sales returns day book A listing of all credit notes (negative sales) by date, customer, invoice number, gross amount, VAT and net amount. The net amount of each credit note may be categorised into different types of sales ready for posting to the nominal ledger accounts.

Share capital A source of very long-term financing for limited companies. All limited companies must issue share capital that will remain in issue for as long as the company exists.

Share premium The amount subscribed for shares in a limited company over and above the par value of each share.

Shareholders Owners of share capital in limited companies. Shareholders may be either ordinary shareholders or preference shareholders.

Stakeholder theory The theory that a business's moral and ethical values should be applied in the management of organisations for the benefit of all stakeholders rather than just for the benefit of shareholders.

Statement of cash flows A summary of the cash inflows and outflows of an entity for a given period of time.

Statement of financial position A summary of the assets, liabilities and equity of an entity at a particular point in time.

Statement of profit or loss A statement of income and expenditure for a particular period of time. Also referred to as the income statement or the profit and loss account. The statement of profit or loss also forms part of the statement of financial performance presented by entities.

Stewardship The process of looking after resources entrusted to a person.

Stock A different term for inventory.

Stock days See Inventory days.

Straight line A method of allocating the cost of non-current assets to the accounting periods benefiting from their use. The straight line method allocates the same charge for depreciation to each accounting period benefiting from a non-current asset's use within a business.

Sustainability The long-term objective of business entities, aiming to remain in operational existence for the indefinite future.

T account Used in double entry to record and accumulate transactions. Each T account has a debit (left hand) and credit (right hand) side. The balance on each T account at the end of each accounting period is carried forward as an asset, liability or equity or written off to the statement of profit or loss as an expense or income.

Timeliness An enhancing qualitative characteristic of financial information. The decision usefulness of information is enhanced if it is available to users in time for it to be capable of influencing their decisions. While the decision usefulness of information generally declines with time, information that can still be used in identifying trends continues to be timely in the future.

Trade payables control account A summary account adding the opening credit balance of trade payables to the purchase day book totals for the accounting period and deducting the purchase returns day book totals, cash paid and discounts received in order to arrive at the closing trade payables balance at the end of the accounting period. The balance on the trade payables control account should be the same as the total of all the individual supplier balances on the purchase ledger.

Trade receivables Amounts owed to an entity by customers for goods and services supplied on credit.

Trade receivables control account A summary account adding the opening debit balance of trade receivables to the sales day book totals for the accounting period and deducting the sales returns day book totals, cash received and irrecoverable debts in order to arrive at the closing trade receivables balance at the end of the accounting period. The balance on the trade receivables control account should be the same as the total of all the individual customer balances on the sales ledger.

Trial balance A listing of all the debit and credit balances on the nominal ledger. The total debit balances should be equal to the total credit balances. If they are not then an error in the double-entry process has occurred.

Turnover The term used in financial statements in the UK to describe sales or revenue.

Understandability An enhancing qualitative characteristic of financial information. Understandability should not be confused with simplicity. Financial statements that excluded complex information just because it was difficult to understand would not result in relevant information that was faithfully presented. Reports that excluded such information would be incomplete and would thus mislead users. Readers of financial reports are assumed to have a reasonable knowledge of business and economic activities in order to make sense of what they are presented with but when they are unable to understand the information presented, then the IASB recommends using an adviser. To help users understand information presented, that information should be classified, characterised and presented clearly.

Unsecured Loans for which no assets of an entity have been pledged in the event that the entity fails to repay the amounts borrowed.

Verifiability An enhancing qualitative characteristic of financial information that enhances the usefulness of information that is relevant and faithfully represented. Verifiability provides users with assurance that information is faithfully presented and reports the economic phenomena it purports to represent. To ensure verifiability, it should be possible to prove the information presented is accurate in all major respects. The accuracy of information should be capable of verification by observation or recalculation.

Working capital Current assets less current liabilities.

Working capital cycle See Cash conversion cycle. This is another term for the cash conversion cycle which is also known as the operating cycle.

INDEX

Note: Tables and figures are indicated by an italic *t* and *f* following the page number.